PR 1.3 2017

D0905049

East Meadow Public Library
1886 Front Street, East Meadow, NY 11554
(516) 794-2570
www.eastmeadow.info

ALSO BY KIM PHILLIPS-FEIN

Invisible Hands: The Businessmen's
Crusade Against the New Deal

FEAR CITY

WELCOME TO
FEAR CITY

A Survival Guide for Visitors to the City of New York

FEAR CITY

NEW YORK'S FISCAL CRISIS AND THE
RISE OF AUSTERITY POLITICS

KIM PHILLIPS-FEIN

Metropolitan Books

Henry Holt and Company   New York

Metropolitan Books
Henry Holt and Company
Publishers since 1866
175 Fifth Avenue
New York, New York 10010
www.henryholt.com

Metropolitan Books® and m® are registered trademarks of
Macmillan Publishing Group, LLC.

Copyright © 2017 by Kim Phillips-Fein
All rights reserved.
Distributed in Canada by Raincoast Book Distribution Limited

Lines from "The Photograph of the Unmade Bed" copyright © 2016 by the Adrienne Rich
Literary Trust. Copyright © 1971 by W. W. Norton & Company, Inc., from *Collected Poems:
1950–2012* by Adrienne Rich. Used by permission of W. W. Norton & Company, Inc.

Library of Congress Cataloging-in-Publication data

Names: Phillips-Fein, Kim, author.
Title: Fear city : New York's fiscal crisis and the rise of austerity politics /
    Kimberly Phillips-Fein.
Description: First Edition. | New York : Metropolitan Books, 2017. | Includes
    bibliographical references and index.
Identifiers: LCCN 2016033559| ISBN 9780805095258 (hardback) |
    ISBN 9780805095265 (electronic book)
Subjects: LCSH: Financial crises—New York (State)—New York—History—
    20th century. | Fiscal policy—New York (State)—New York—History—20th century. |
    New York (State)—New York—Economic conditions—20th century. | BISAC:
    HISTORY / United States / State & Local / Middle Atlantic (DC, DE, MD, NJ, NY, PA). |
    HISTORY / United States / 20th Century.
Classification: LCC HB3722 .P497 2017 | DDC 330.9747/1043—dc23
LC record available at https://lccn.loc.gov/2016033559

Our books may be purchased in bulk for promotional, educational, or business use. Please
contact your local bookseller or the Macmillan Corporate and Premium Sales Department at
(800) 221-7945, extension 5442, or by e-mail at MacmillanSpecialMarkets@macmillan.com.

First Edition 2017

Designed by Kelly S. Too

Printed in the United States of America

1 3 5 7 9 10 8 6 4 2

For my parents,
Charlotte Phillips and Oliver Fein,
and for Clara, Jonah,
and Greg

Did mere indifference blister
these panes, eat these walls,
shrivel and scrub these trees—
mere indifference?

Adrienne Rich,
"The Photograph of the Unmade Bed" (1969)

CONTENTS

PART III: LEGACIES

FEAR CITY

Introduction

On October 30, 1975, the *New York Daily News* printed the most famous headline in its history: "Ford to City: Drop Dead."

The previous day, President Gerald Ford had delivered a speech at the National Press Club in Washington on the looming bankruptcy of New York City. Once inconceivable, such a collapse fit with the climate of the time. American politics in the autumn of 1975 had taken on the qualities of a grotesque. Saigon had fallen just a few months before Ford's speech. The memory of President Nixon's resignation in the midst of the Watergate scandal was still fresh. Oil shocks in 1973 had made it clear that the United States could not control supplies of the black gold on which its economy depended, and rapid inflation throughout 1974 and 1975 transformed each paycheck into a game of chance. Across the country, people had been boycotting meat and sugar to protest exorbitant prices. Massive corporate bankruptcies, near-bankruptcies, and financial collapses shook familiar business icons: the Penn Central railroad in 1970, the defense giant Lockheed in 1971, and the Long Island–based Franklin National Bank, the twentieth largest in the country, in 1974.

The prospect of New York City's collapse seemed a further terrifying lurch. The leading men at the city's biggest banks—including First

National City Bank (the forerunner of Citibank), Morgan Guaranty, and Chase Manhattan—had spoken out in favor of federal aid for New York. Executives from around the country had traveled to Washington to testify that if the city went under, the fragile national economy might topple as well. Cold Warriors warned that the city's bankruptcy would bolster the Soviet Union. Lawmakers in Washington, Albany, and New York City itself eagerly awaited any hint that Ford might lend his support to a bailout deal. How would it look—what would it mean—for New York City, the country's largest metropolis, the home of Wall Street, the heart of American finance, to wind up in bankruptcy court?

But President Ford and his closest advisers—a circle that included his chief of staff, Donald Rumsfeld, and the chairman of his Council of Economic Advisers, Alan Greenspan—strongly opposed federal help for New York. They were convinced that the city had brought its problems on itself through heedless, profligate spending. Bankruptcy was thus a just punishment for its sins, a necessary lesson in how the city should change to move forward. And as far as the national economy was concerned, Ford and his circle believed that the banks, the businessmen, and the city were scaremongering, that the economic impact of the city's financial collapse would easily be contained—that the market had already factored it in. Accordingly, Ford promised to veto the bills that were circulating through Congress to provide emergency aid to New York. Instead, he supported reforms to existing bankruptcy regulations that would make it easier for the city to file. The meaning was clear: New York could go bankrupt, and the federal government would do nothing to help.

For the president, as for much of the nation, New York City stood for urban liberalism, an example of the central role that government might play in addressing problems of poverty, racism, and economic distribution. At the National Press Club, Ford challenged New York's network of municipal hospitals and its free public university as lavish, unnecessary extravagances. The federal government should not give a penny in bailout funds that allowed New Yorkers to continue these indulgences, he said. Why should other Americans "support advantages in New York that they have not been able to afford for their own communities?"

The harsh lesson was intended not only for New York. Ford believed that the United States had to face a new reality: the country—indeed, the world—had entered an era of slowed economic growth, an age of austerity, in which it was no longer possible for the government to pay for many social services to which the American people had grown accustomed. The citizens' basic attitude toward government had to be transformed. Americans needed a revived philosophy of individual initiative centered on fiscal responsibility and limited spending. In the last few minutes of his talk, Ford scolded the nation : "If we go on spending more than we have, providing more benefits and more services than we can pay for, then a day of reckoning will come to Washington and the whole country just as it has to New York City." And "when that day of reckoning comes, who will bail out the United States of America?"[1]

On that note, the president departed for California. He was embarking on a fundraising trip for his 1976 presidential campaign on the home turf of his main rival on the right: the former governor of the state, Ronald Reagan.

Even before Ford's speech, there were many in New York who felt that they had been abandoned. A few months earlier, in the spring of 1975, a woman named Lyn Smith wrote a letter to her senator, the liberal Republican Jacob Javits. Smith described the housing conditions in a South Bronx neighborhood near her home. The city, it seemed to her, had stopped making any effort to demolish burned-out buildings, despite their dangers. "When a house burns down they don't destroy the frame, they leave it standing—you never know when it's going to fall. A little boy I know or knew named Ralfy lives in the South Bronx he was playing in one of the broken down houses and he fell through the floor he's dead now but if that building had been torn down he wouldn't be dead." Smith's tone—flat, apathetic, resigned, quietly bearing witness but hardly even launching a protest—is perhaps the most haunting aspect of her missive. "I don't know why I wrote this letter you'll probably never read."[2]

For a woman like Lyn Smith, austerity meant not only budget cuts but a political mood of bleak hopelessness. The fiscal crisis involved discarding a set of social hopes, a vision of what the city could be. For Ford

and those around him, the New York City fiscal crisis was a story of the
bankruptcy—economic and moral alike—of liberal politics. It proved
that using government to combat social ills would end in collapse. It
provided a spectacular repudiation of the Great Society, the War on
Poverty, even the New Deal. But for ordinary people, the fiscal crisis
meant something different: it marked a change in what it meant to be a
New Yorker and a citizen. We are still living with the consequences of
this transformation today.

Forty years after the fiscal crisis, the 1970s remain a touchstone of
New York City politics, the nightmare era to which no one wants to
return. The classic cinema of the 1970s and 1980s memorialized these
years of disinvestment and blight in films such as *Taxi Driver*, *The
Panic in Needle Park*, *The Taking of Pelham One Two Three*, and *Fort
Apache, The Bronx*, which portrayed New York as a sea of filth and
despair, an urban cesspool. The decade is widely remembered as a
time of crime, violence, lawlessness, disorder, graffiti-covered subways,
inflation, unemployment, and budgets completely out of control—an era
of social breakdown, economic malaise, and political collapse.[3] The
politics of the country more generally are recalled with a similar sense
of failure: this is the decade when the old American dream fell apart,
when unemployment and inflation replaced the steady prosperity of the
postwar years, and the international supremacy of the United States
ceased to be something to take for granted. As Christopher Lasch wrote
in the opening pages of his 1979 bestseller, *The Culture of Narcissism*,
"Those who recently dreamed of world power now despair of governing
the city of New York."[4]

The common wisdom about the crisis holds that its primary cause
was the flagrant irresponsibility of politicians such as John Lindsay,
the idealistic mayor in the late 1960s who saw fighting poverty as a top
priority for city government, and, even more, his successor Abraham
Beame, who submitted to political pressures that endangered the city's
solvency. Lindsay threw money at entrenched social problems without
regard for budget realities; Beame was unable to resist the newly power-

ful public sector unions. The result of their foolish overspending was that the city soon found itself with debts that it had no reasonable way of ever paying back.[5]

At the same time, paradoxically, the crisis is sometimes noted as a great triumph for New York: the moment when the city repudiated an older tradition of irresponsible altruism. Everyone—labor, business, the banks, ordinary citizens—is thought to have accepted the need for austerity and chipped in. Many of those who led New York through the valley of the shadow of default remember it as a time of solidarity, an era when the common people were willing to do what it took to rescue the city from its shame. As Felix Rohatyn, the Lazard Frères investment banker who helped to broker the deals that ultimately kept the city out of bankruptcy, later wrote, "The people of the city were willing to make real sacrifices as long as they believed that those sacrifices were relatively fairly distributed, that there was an end in sight and that the result would be a better city, a better environment, and a better life."[6]

This book takes a different view. Here, the budget comes to life as the place where opposing visions of the city's future were contested, fought out, and finally decided. For much of the twentieth century, New York City did have an unusually expansive and generous local welfare state, the result of generations of organizing by labor unions, reform groups, and working-class and poor people. The institutions they built were hardly extravagant or unnecessary. New York's public sector—which made the city, in the words of historian Joshua Freeman, something like an island of social democracy in the midst of postwar America—helped to create much of what was most distinctive in the city: its democratic sensibilities, its working-class ethos, its common public life. The fiscal crisis permanently altered these ideas and this vision. Contemporaries were stunned by the swiftness of the cuts to social services, enacted at a time of intense need. And in addition to the pain caused by the contraction of the public sector, the experience of the fiscal crisis seemed to delegitimize an entire way of thinking about cities and what they might do for the people who live in them.

But just as the city's pre-crisis spending should not be treated as wasteful and irrelevant, its financial difficulties should not be reduced to a parable of municipal irresponsibility or a story about how local governments tend to succumb to the insatiable demands of pressure groups. The dynamics of the crisis created a sense that New York City's problems were entirely its own fault, which made it harder to see where the power really lay: at the level of the state and the federal government, which had created the policies that led to the unraveling of the city. It was federal subsidies for homeownership and federal investment in highways, for instance, which encouraged middle-class residents to move from New York to the surrounding suburbs, depriving the city of income tax revenue even though it remained the economic motor of the tristate area. And it was federal policies that made it easy for manufacturing companies that had once formed the city's economic base—such as the celebrated garment industry—to move away in search of cheaper labor, first to the southern United States and then overseas. Nor did New York create the racial fears and hostilities that led middle-class white people to flee to the suburbs as the city drew in more African Americans, as well as Latinos and other immigrants. America's political system failed to adequately confront such challenges, just as it failed to confront the urban poverty that was the result of capital flight and deindustrialization.

The city's politicians tried to skirt these problems in myriad different ways, but in the city budget they proved impossible to avoid forever. The city turned to debt in an effort to sidestep an open debate over whether it could continue to make good on its efforts to carve out a distinctive set of social rights. While the city's financial problems were real enough, its elected leaders' evasion of these political arguments—the attempt to use debt to settle problems that were at heart political—was the deeper failure. New York expanded its borrowing at a time when public debt was growing across the country, when bankers were enthusiastically marketing and buying its bonds and notes. Although they would later excoriate the city for its irresponsibility, these financiers played a central role in encouraging its indebtedness when it suited their purposes to do so.[7]

Finally, it is important to recognize that many of the New Yorkers most affected by the budget cuts did not meet the crisis with a spirit of equanimity and sacrifice. To remember it this way is an act of forgetting, for the retrenchment brought into the open fierce disagreements over the city's future. It is certainly true that people in the economic and political elite quickly reached consensus that sharp budget cuts and the restructuring of the city government were the only way back to fiscal health. Beyond the inner circles of power, though, there was far more resistance to the transformation of New York. Rather than accept a shrunken version of their city, ordinary New Yorkers loudly protested the contraction of the public sphere. When they were faced with the withdrawal of services that had become tantamount to rights, many people asserted their demands all the more forcefully, as long as they were able to do so.

They were driven to do so because they intuited that New York would emerge from the crisis a changed metropolis. The people who would come to have the deciding vote would be those who belonged to the moneyed elite: the ones who could decide whether or not to invest in New York, who had the access to private capital on which, it was suddenly clear, the city relied. The 1970s crisis was a crucial point on the way to a new New York, helping transform the city into the highly stratified metropolis it is today—a city of apartments bought as investment properties for the wealthy of the world even as almost 60,000 New Yorkers live in home-less shelters, a city that's among the most unequal in a nation that has itself become radically more hierarchical than it was during the post-war era. Today, many people describe this transformation as "progress," seeing the shining contemporary city as a vanquishing of the dismal past. This book, though, suggests that in the process, New York lost as much as it gained. The struggle over whom the city government would serve, and on what terms, echoes the deepening conflict over the future of the United States as a whole.

Crises are disorienting events, revealing that long-accepted facts differ from a new reality. New York's fiscal crisis, in addition, also threw sharply different perceptions of the city—indeed, of the world—into conflict with each other. For the bankers who rebelled against the city's old fis-cal practices, it became the chance to assert a modern, technocratic, and market-oriented ethos, rejecting New York's long tradition of a robust public sector aimed at supporting the working classes. For the residents who saw their firehouses threatened with closure, their children's teachers laid off, and their roads going unpaved, the crisis marked a power grab by financiers who wanted to recast New York as a white-collar professional city. For the men who were catapulted by the events of the crisis into positions of unusual decision-making power (and the few women who joined them), the fiscal crisis was a nerve-racking but exciting time of late nights, early breakfasts, and meetings around the clock, an urgent struggle to save the city from bankruptcy against all odds. For lifelong New York politicians, it was a bewildering shift in priorities and expectations, a time when they were blamed for bankrupting the city by trying to protect services and jobs, the very things they formerly had been lauded for providing.[8]

Race and class were at once omnipresent and invisible in the fiscal crisis. The crisis saw a group of almost universally white elites remake life in a city that was becoming increasingly black and brown. The collapse of the postwar social compact in New York happened at the very moment when it was losing its white middle-class population, when more and more of those using city services were low-income minorities. Many of the elites at the time blamed those impoverished African Americans and Latinos (and the public sector workers who served them) for New York's financial problems. And yet the crisis provided a way to change the politics of the city in profound ways without ever talking about race or class explicitly. The threat of bankruptcy elided policy choices, making it appear as though there were simply no alternatives— as though the transformations were brought about not by anyone's decisions, but by the abstractions of fiscal rectitude and financial necessity.[9]

The story of this sea change in political rhetoric is not only one of New York City, or even of urban politics.[10] Some left-leaning scholars have described the 1975 crisis as the dawning of a new conservative age.[11] In a certain sense it was: the spectacular failure of the New York City government crystallized the antigovernment ethos that was gaining momentum nationally during the 1970s. But at the same time, the crisis was also the product of the postwar liberal era, and it transformed liberalism as much as it galvanized the right. After all, the people who brought austerity to New York City were not free-market zealots or right-wing political leaders. Many of them were self-identified liberals who believed government had a legitimate role to play in the economy. Yet these people also became ardent promoters of the idea that New York had to make deep budget cuts, drive a hard bargain with its unions, streamline services, improve efficiency, and reinvent its government. They continued to see themselves as committed to a liberal agenda, but what this meant had undergone a profound change.

The transformations in the city's politics mirrored those taking place within the national Democratic Party, where longtime liberals were re-evaluating their old commitments and priorities as the long postwar economic boom drew to a close. Like liberals at the local level, national Democrats became far more ambivalent in their support for labor unions, for civil rights, for an activist government. The story of the fiscal crisis reminds us that the move to the right in American politics of recent years should not be seen only in terms of the rise of the conservative movement, but also as a story of the remaking of liberalism, a shifting of the common ground of American politics for people on both sides of the aisle.[12]

Today, fiscal crises are back in the headlines. A wave of municipal bankruptcies followed the financial panic of 2008, culminating in the collapse of Detroit in the summer of 2013. Greece is still on the verge of collapse, its society imploding as its government strips away social benefits despite a 2015 voter referendum rejecting austerity. Puerto Rico has already defaulted on some of its nearly $70 billion debt. And in late summer of 2016 its finances were placed under the management of an unelected fiscal control board charged with slashing government spending.

The politics of inevitability that defined New York in the 1970s have been at work in all these cases as well. Just as happened in New York, the long-standing tensions that create fiscal crises seem to vanish from consideration in the heat and drama of the moment. Modern politicians and economists employ a moralistic rhetoric of responsibility and belt-tightening just as they did in 1975, but they do so with far more confidence than at that earlier moment, thanks to the intervening forty years of antigovernment politics. As a city, or a nation, struggles to avoid default, the debate becomes framed in the narrowest possible terms: Which programs to cut? Which taxes to levy? How to balance the budget most quickly? How to satisfy the lenders and the banks, whose presence is under normal conditions invisible, but who become the main actors in the fiscal drama the moment their money seems in danger?

Nonetheless, today as in the 1970s, austerity remains a political choice. The forces that make it seem the only option obscure the underlying reasons why cities become poor, why wealthy metropolises come to have governments starved for funds. Beneath the narrow debates about how debts can be repaid reverberate larger, as yet unresolved questions about what kind of society we want to have, about who will pay for certain kinds of social provisions and whether we will have them at all. At the end of the day, these are inescapably political questions, not accounting ones.

In the contemporary crises, from Detroit to Greece to Puerto Rico, there has been a sense that events are at once completely shocking and entirely anticipated. That is how it was in New York City in 1975 as well. At first no one could believe that the city could actually go bankrupt. And yet once its finances began to unravel, failure appeared almost to have been foreordained. Both the crisis and the government responses to it suddenly seemed almost inevitable. To question that inevitability is the project of this book.

PART I

ORIGINS

1. Warnings

When the West Side Highway first opened in 1930, it seemed to promise a glorious "new era of speed in motor transportation," in the words of the Manhattan borough president. In a city of subways, the wide, elevated road opened up new possibilities for car transportation. Rising on steel archways above the busy streets of the meatpacking district, it appeared sure to last forever.[1]

By the early 1970s, though, the highway's asphalt had been worn down by the vast traffic of the postwar years. The surface had eroded under the tons of salt dumped on it each winter; cars and trucks bumped over the uneven metal plates the city had used to patch the gaping spaces. The skeletal supports that held up the elevated portions of the highway were rusting, damaged by decades of rain and melting snow. Mayor John Lindsay planned a major repair for the deteriorating structure, and construction began in the autumn of 1973. As the city's commissioner of highways put it, "You can't just fill cavities on this highway. You have to put in new teeth."[2]

The work had barely started when the disaster the city feared came to pass. In December 1973, the highway simply buckled under the weight of a repair truck carrying asphalt at the intersection of

Little West 12th and Gansevoort Streets in the West Village. A tremendous hole ripped open in the road, the broken pieces on either side
sloping down in a sharp diagonal to the street below. The driver of the
truck managed to leap out as his vehicle plunged to the ground, taking
with it a four-door sedan that had been driving along behind.[3] Miracu-
lously, neither driver was badly hurt. But the downtown stretch of
the highway had to be closed to traffic immediately. The city shut
down the highway uptown as well, closing it from 72nd to 79th Streets
for repairs slated to take at least a year.[4]

The sudden closure of the West Side Highway irritated commuters
and city residents who found their streets clogged by rerouted traffic.
But for some, the quiet highway became a respite. Upper West Side
children played on the empty tree-lined road, exulting in the freakish
expanse of open space.[5] The highway became a path for cyclists long
before bike lanes were marked around the city. Novelist Frederic Morton described the eerie peace of the "splendid promenade" where he
would go for moonlit strolls on winter evenings, enjoying the cracked
road as though it were a Roman ruin and watching the cats frisk among
the broken stones.[6] A young downtown artist, Terence Sellers, wrote in
her journal about glimpsing the "enormous towers of the World Trade
Center" looming from the deserted highway, the second of the newly
built pair emerging into view "as if one was not enough."[7] But while
the closed highway might have been splendid, it was hardly safe. In the
summer of 1974, a fourteen-year-old boy fell to his death at the corner
of Little West 12th and Gansevoort, tumbling through the forty-by-
fifty-foot hole that had been left gaping when the truck ripped through
the pavement nine months earlier.[8]

In the early 1970s, the entire city was a bit like the West Side Highway. The promises and the visions of an earlier era had come up against
their limits. Everyone knew that things might collapse. And though
no one was willing to talk too openly about the possibility of failure,
the problems of the city were common knowledge, unmistakable and
impossible to hide. There was perhaps something appealing about this
disrepair, a certain freedom in the unkempt metropolis. Yet there was
also real danger. And there was no rescue in sight, nothing that would

come in to close the holes, to fix what had been broken, to save the people who lived in the city that was slowly falling apart.

When a person goes bankrupt, there's always the last punishing expense: the extra medical bill or tuition payment, the final credit card charge, the mortgage interest rate that ticks up at just the wrong moment. But this is never the full story. The tragedy has its climax, but its origins lie deep in the past—the lost job, the student debt, the divorce, the illness, the long-hoped-for raise that never materialized. For a city, it's the same. There's the short version of events, and then there's the one that goes back.

The collapse of New York in the 1970s stunned the nation because for so long, the city had embodied a kind of government and society whose success seemed unassailable. During the decades that followed World War II, New York represented the fullest realization of the confident liberalism that dominated American politics. Throughout the 1950s and 1960s, people who visited New York from other parts of the country, whether from small rural towns or from cities such as Chicago, Los Angeles, and San Francisco, found much to wonder at. They marveled not only at the familiar postcard attractions—the Statue of Liberty, the Empire State Building, the magnificent skyline—but also at the way that New Yorkers lived.

New York City had been at the forefront of social reform ever since the early twentieth century. Progressive reformers had pressed for housing market regulations to ensure that apartments for poor people were not dangerous firetraps. Labor organizers had won laws protecting workers on the job after the Triangle Shirtwaist Factory fire of 1911. In the early 1930s, following the onset of the Great Depression, the city government had been plagued by fiscal problems; it was saved from default by bankers who extended a loan and demanded service cuts. But these cuts were rolled back within a few years, when Mayor Fiorello La Guardia was able to win funding from Franklin Delano Roosevelt—the former New York State governor occupying the White House—for a vast array of public works and social programs.[9]

As a result, during the postwar period New York provided a

remarkable range of services to its citizens, through an extensive public sector hard to imagine today.[10] At its peak, the city ran a network of twenty-four municipal hospitals, along with dozens of neighborhood primary care and pediatric clinics. Its health department even conducted original research into matters of public health. Over the decades, the city built numerous parks and playgrounds, elementary and secondary schools, public housing, swimming pools, college campuses, piers, highways, bridges, and airports. In the 1960s, it opened day care centers for low-income mothers and treatment clinics to help drug addicts. Its sprawling library system included public research libraries that rivaled many private university collections.

Physically, too, the city was opened up to everyone by the far-reaching system of inexpensive public transportation. In 1950, the subway fare was just 10 cents a ride (equivalent to less than a dollar today); a bus ride was 7 cents. The Metropolitan Museum of Art and the Museum of Natural History had no charge for entry, not even a recommended amount. The city ran three radio stations and two public television stations, and the City Center of Music and Drama offered bargain tickets on theater, opera, symphony, and ballet—high culture at low prices.[11] New York also controlled its Board of Education, which was a separate entity in many other cities, and it took on responsibilities (such as running the court system and a network of college campuses) that elsewhere were the province of county or even state governments.

Before New York became the decrepit city of the early 1970s, in other words, it had been the capital not only of high finance and Wall Street, but also of a certain robust strain of democratic politics: a demonstration of citizenship bound up with social as well as political rights. The most visible, obvious examples of public investment—the subways, the parks, the city university—were impossible to overlook. But there were also countless other ways that the city government made itself felt in the lives of New Yorkers, less monumental but no less vital.

Greenpoint-Williamsburg, a neighborhood at the northern edge of Brooklyn abutting the East River, is today the epicenter of the Brooklyn renaissance: an enclave of hipsters, artisanal food, craft beers, locally made chocolate, cool bars, and luxury apartment buildings built to take full advantage of the riverfront views. This transformation into a garden of consumer pleasures would have shocked the people who lived there in the middle years of the twentieth century. Back then, the area was packed with immigrants from southern and eastern Europe and their descendants, and filled with the factories where they labored.[12] It was a working-class part of the city: 95 percent of the residents of North Brooklyn (a region that included Greenpoint-Williamsburg as well as Bushwick, Bedford-Stuyvesant, and Crown Heights) earned incomes under $5,000 per year in 1955, the equivalent of about $44,000 per year today.[13]

Life for the people who lived in the wood-frame houses dotting the half-industrial area was never easy. But even in the poorest neighborhoods, the city government provided substantial assistance in ways both large and small. Greenpoint Hospital, a municipal health center, cared for neighborhood residents; the Greater New York Health Council offered workshops on nutrition; an old police station on Stagg Street had been transformed into a city youth center. In the summers, a child growing up in North Brooklyn in the 1950s could participate in a special chorus program run by the Board of Education, or swim at the public McCarren Pool, or attend marionette plays presented by the Parks Department in McCarren Park.[14] In the winters, the park was home to a city Christmas tree.[15]

A similar scene played out in Morrisania and Mott Haven, two South Bronx neighborhoods largely populated by poor black and Latino families. By the 1970s they had become prime examples of urban despair, and even during the postwar years they were already experiencing white flight and disinvestment. The construction of the Cross-Bronx Expressway in 1955 further hurt the communities, displacing residents and destroying housing stock.[16] Yet despite their many problems, during the 1950s these neighborhoods too benefited from the expansive activism of the city government. A family worried about the polio virus that spread through the city in a "mild epidemic" in 1955, for example, could get immunizations through a city-run program at the neighborhood child health center, which brought the new Salk vaccine to more than 170,000 children.[17] Crooked teeth might have been treated at the orthodontic clinic that the Morrisania City Hospital opened in 1950.[18] Indeed, the local public hospitals were so heavily used in the 1940s and 1950s that the city expanded its programs to provide medical care to people at their homes.[19]

In Morrisania, the Forest Houses public housing project, built during the 1950s, offered space for 1,350 families, and sought from the outset to create an integrated neighborhood bringing together blacks, whites, and Latinos.[20] A few blocks away, Morris High School boasted a new gym and cafeteria constructed by the city. Annual talent shows there pulsed with rhythm and blues—a kind of training ground for performers who might go on to such neighborhood institutions as Club 846, where Thelonious Monk and Charlie Parker were regulars in the 1940s and 1950s, and the Tropicana Club, a Latin music club where stars like Tito Puente often came to play.[21]

When the children of the South Bronx and Greenpoint-Williamsburg grew older, they might, if they were strong enough students, go to college at one of the city's public campuses and earn a bachelor's degree without paying tuition. In the 1950s and 1960s, the four-year schools were joined by two-year community colleges. No other city in the country ran a network of municipal colleges of this scope. And in addition to the university system, the city operated a continuing education program through which people who had never been to high school or even elementary school could earn equivalency degrees, attending daytime or evening classes held in community centers and other locations.[22]

This heavy investment in libraries, hospitals, subways, buses, health clinics, museums, theater, education, and art had a great deal to do with the political economy of New York in the postwar years. The city then was industrial: at the end of World War II, 41 percent of its workforce was employed in blue-collar jobs, including 28 percent in manufacturing. But in contrast to the steel towns of Pennsylvania or the South Side of Chicago, New York was not dominated by a single massive employer. Its factories were small shops rather than gargantuan assembly lines employing thousands of people, of the kind found at River Rouge near Detroit. Its industries were diverse and specialized, many serving a local or regional rather than a national market. Blue-collar jobs outnumbered white-collar ones, the frenetic activity of the port was as important a part of downtown as Wall Street, and the trade in physical commodities was as critical as the exchange of financial instruments. New York was a city of making, lifting, and transporting, and to many it seemed clear that the people who did this work were those for whom the city should run.[23]

The city's politics reflected its economic structure. The working class was socially visible and politically strong; its unions were a recognized force, an accepted part of the life of the city as a whole. A quarter to a third of the city's workers were in unions: they represented everyone from dental technicians to machinists, commercial artists to barbers, movie publicists to people who serviced vending machines.[24] The industrial nature of the city also meant that there was a clear economic rationale to the investment in public goods. The subways got workers to their jobs, the clinics kept them healthy, and the libraries and universities offered skills training and an avenue for upward mobility and the purchasing power that went with it. The city's small manufacturers— many of whom had much in common socially with the people who worked in their plants—benefited from all these services themselves. Even when the business owners objected to taxes, the small scale and dispersion of their companies made it difficult for them to influence the city's politics as much as the working classes did.

To be sure, there was always some strain underneath the surface of the postwar city, with its institutions criticized from both left and right. Civil rights activists fiercely denounced the myriad ways that city government failed people of color; as they pointed out, the city was a far easier place to live in for the predominantly white middle classes than for the racially diverse poor.[25] The elites, meanwhile, were often skeptical of the "social democratic" bent of the city and its deep investments in the public sector. Heads of national corporations, financial executives on Wall Street, real estate developers whose main priority was finding ways to boost property prices—many of the powerful longed to create a different kind of New York City. They imagined it remade as a gleaming white-collar consumers' paradise of corporate headquarters and rising real estate values. They viewed the garment and electrical manufacturers of downtown as a waste of valuable space, eyesores that tarnished the potential of the city. Ever since the 1920s, these leaders had described their ambition to zone away industry, expand parkland to raise land values, and build highways that could allow "decentralization" of the city's economy—that is, moving factories to the suburbs.[26] Sometimes, they warned that the hospitals, libraries, schools, and social workers placed an unsustainable weight on city budgets.

Still, despite such tensions, in the mid-twentieth century New York appeared prosperous, powerful, and successful. Its politics were at the left edge of urban liberalism, demonstrating that it was possible to run a city government that did far more for its citizens than most American cities ever dreamed of accomplishing.

Significantly, the political vision that New York's public institutions expressed was not limited to the city alone. It was part of the liberal politics that had emerged in the 1930s and that seemed in certain respects to dominate the United States during the postwar years: a society that saw promoting working-class consumption as an important way to generate overall prosperity, and an activist government that was willing to intervene to improve the quality of life for ordinary people. The difference was that New York pushed this vision much further than other parts of the country, and did so in ways that were deeply linked to the big-city environment. For much of the country, the "New Deal order" had become intertwined with the rise of suburbia and the flight from cities. New York was a reminder that there was also an urban version of this political and social sensibility, one that emphasized common spaces and public investment more than the private greenswards of lawns and country clubs. The city almost seemed to proclaim a right to happiness and pleasure, even for people insignificant in terms of wealth and power. That was the promise implicit in the ordinary, everyday monuments of the local health clinics, the free museums, the affordable transportation: a right to belong to the city and to have the city belong to you.[27]

———

By the early 1970s, this confident and prosperous city seemed frayed almost beyond recognition.

New York's once-beautiful parks were dirty and deteriorating. Its glorious research library was deep in the red. The public hospitals were dilapidated, their emergency rooms overcrowded and their equipment out of date. The city university was struggling to meet demand. Fires had started to tear through the once stable neighborhoods of the South Bronx.

The economy that had supported the expansive social sector of the postwar years was falling apart. The small manufacturers that had once populated downtown Manhattan and the outer boroughs were slowly departing the city, seeking cheaper land and a more tractable, nonunion workforce in the suburbs, the South, and overseas. Shipping companies moved to New Jersey, pulled by new transportation technologies that required a port deeper than New York's harbor, and pushed along by real estate developers eager to rezone Lower Manhattan so it could be developed without the behemoth of the port and the grime of industry.[28] By 1966, fewer than half the manufacturing jobs in the New York metropolitan region were in the city itself. This loss of jobs was most pronounced in those industries where employment had once been strongest, such as apparel and garment production, electrical manufacturing, and printing and publishing.

For more than a century, New York had been able to assimilate millions of immigrants in its insatiable demand for human labor, but increasingly the jobs that earlier generations had held were no longer there. When the national economy went into recession in the early 1970s, the loss of jobs turned into a flood: between the late 1960s and the mid-1970s, half a million jobs disappeared from the city. Job loss and the attendant deepening poverty (especially severe for black and Latino New Yorkers) meant that more and more people were in need of city services. The number of people in the city receiving some form of public assistance rose from 322,921 in 1960 to a high of 1,255,721 in 1972—approximately one out of every eight New Yorkers.[29]

At the same time, New York, like many other cities in the Northeast and Midwest, was increasingly affected by federal policies that encouraged middle-class people to leave the cities. They were drawn to suburbia by tax incentives that favored homeownership, by the construction of new highways that made it easier to commute to work, and by social expectations that celebrated racially homogenous, family-oriented communities of prosperous homeowners. They were also driven out of cities by racial fears, anxious about the slightest hint that black or Latino people might be moving into their communities. As one Queens retiree told the *New York Times* in 1964, "I would be the first to move out if a Negro family moved into this neighborhood. Property devaluates as soon as a Negro moves into an area."[30] In 1940, less than 7 percent of New Yorkers were nonwhite; by 1970, more than one-fifth of the city's population was black and 16 percent was Latino. Almost a quarter of the city's white population would move out during the 1970s—a decade when New York's overall population fell by more than 800,000, even as its Latino population increased by 17 percent and the black population grew slightly. The city also became older and poorer: the portion of its population over 65 rose from 8 to 12 percent between 1950 and 1970, while the portion with incomes lower than the national median climbed from 36 to 49 percent.[31]

The problems that New York confronted were not unique, but the scope of the city's public sector brought them to the fore. As New York's economy declined, its local welfare state became the subject of rising conflict. How was the city to pay for social services as incomes that might sustain income taxes fell, as sales that might generate sales taxes dropped, as property values that might produce property taxes declined? How was it to cope with social needs that were increasing as the economy worsened, when the economic downturn made it hard even to meet the regular level of demand? Such questions were not simply economic but political, a challenge to the city's public institutions. Racial politics played a role as well: as services became increasingly used by African American and Latino residents, many Italians, Poles, Jews, and other working-class white people in the city began to resent that their tax dollars were being used to benefit people they viewed as unworthy and inferior. An editorial by the chairman of one Brooklyn neighborhood group summed up this barely disguised racial hostility, complaining that "for years, we have witnessed the appeasement of nonproductive and counter-productive 'leeches' at the expense of New York's middle class work force."[32]

Meanwhile, as small manufacturers departed, the city's business elite was itself in a state of transformation. Corporate executives, financial industry managers, and real estate developers did not have a large workforce benefiting from the generous public sector, as the old industrial employers once had. These businesspeople disliked the expansive social sector, which seemed to them unnecessary, and they feared that taxes would have to keep being raised to pay for more services for poor people. They wanted lower taxes for themselves, and to use tax incentives to attract and retain business—not to pay for day care, health care, or more spaces in the city university system.

Responding to these competing demands—from business elites on the one hand and poor New Yorkers on the other—was extremely difficult, and only became more so as the city's expenditures rose dramatically, from about $2.5 billion a year in the early 1960s to over $10 billion a year by the early 1970s. What did the money buy? The largest area of growth in the budget was in human services: welfare, health care, education, and family support. The amount spent on welfare increased fivefold, health care spending quadrupled, the amount spent on family support services tripled, and the amount for education more than doubled.[33] There were some new programs as well, including a graduate school for the City University of New York, initiatives to help address the rising problem of drug abuse, and manpower training for the unemployed. But most of the new expenses—nine out of every ten dollars—reflected increased spending on programs the city had been operating already.[34]

Because of the heated rhetoric around public sector unions that would follow the onset of the crisis, it is important to note that salaries of the city's labor force were unexceptional. Although public workers did see their wages climb during the 1960s, they were not paid much more than their counterparts in other cities, taking the cost of living into account. Workers in comparable jobs were paid more in Detroit, Chicago, Washington, and Los Angeles (although pensions were better in New York).[35] More notable was how many people the city government employed: over 414,000 by 1970, an increase of 55 percent over 1960. Out of every hundred people with jobs in New York City, eleven were employed by the city itself.[36] In a way, New York made up for the loss of industrial jobs over the 1960s by becoming the employer of last resort, so that by the early 1970s, local government employed more than seven times as many people as the largest private employer, New York Bell Telephone Company.[37]

To a significant extent, this expansion of New York's spending on public employees and the services they administered was made possible by federal and state funding linked to the mid-1960s "War on Poverty." Federal grants rose from a mere 6 percent of the city's budget in 1964–65 to nearly 17 percent by 1970–71. State grants rose as well, though less dramatically—climbing from 19 percent in 1964–65 to 26 percent in 1970–71.[38] By the end of the 1960s, more than 40 percent of the city's revenues came from higher levels of government.[39]

Here, too, New York was not unique. For a few short years in the mid-1960s, cities, states, and the federal government had an unusual relationship. In the aftermath of African American protests and uprisings in Harlem, in Watts, Los Angeles, and throughout the Jim Crow states, liberals had come to believe both that the federal government had a moral obligation to provide aid and that by doing so it might stave off further social upheaval. As a result, Washington carried out the kind of progressive taxation of incomes that was hard for cities to accomplish on their own, then shared part of these revenues. City officials might have imagined that the federal commitment to coping with economic disparities that were the legacy of racial inequality marked a lasting change in social policy—that it meant new revenues would continue to flow far into the future.

But that was not the case. The problem with relying on federal money to pay for a larger city government became evident after Richard Nixon was elected in 1968. Nixon shifted social spending to prioritize fighting crime. He made it clear that the era of the Great Society was over: the federal government would no longer increase its grants to cities to mitigate the problems of urban poverty. He promised to end what he deemed the "era of permissiveness," arguing that too much federal largesse had left the American people "soft" and "spoiled."[41] He also began to change the terms of some federal spending, so that instead of specifically targeting antipoverty efforts, the money was distributed to state governments as general-purpose block grants.

Over the first half of the 1970s, substantial aid to the city did still come in from Albany and Washington: federal grants accounted for roughly 20 percent of the city's annual budget, and state grants covered a bit less than 25 percent. But the War on Poverty period, when rapidly rising aid (especially federal aid) made possible the growth of social services, had come to a close.[42] And while programs with federal funding augmented the city's efforts to aid its poorest residents—both Medicaid and welfare were paid for through a combination of federal, state, and local money—they also placed heavy new demands on locally generated revenues. In New York State, localities were made responsible for a full quarter of the spending on these programs, a much higher proportion than elsewhere in the country. Of all the states and territories participating in federal welfare programs, forty-three paid all the costs of doing so without requiring any contribution from the localities, and none of those that did pass along costs required cities to contribute as much as New York.[43]

Nor could the city easily keep expanding its revenue base to compensate for shortfalls in the amount it received from the state or federal government. Despite New York's size and power, many aspects of its budget were beyond its control. According to the state constitution, passed in the nineteenth century and last amended in 1938, New York City had to win approval from the state legislature to levy taxes—not an easy task, since the legislature was often Republican-dominated and generally skeptical of New York's social generosity. The state constitution also limited the annual amount the city could raise in taxes to cover its operating expenses: in a given year, the city could not levy

property taxes worth more than 2.5 percent of the five-year average of
the total assessed value of its real estate.[44] The city also faced a constitutional limit on its ability to borrow: its total debt could not go above
10 percent of that five-year average.[45] Other factors, too, restricted the
city's ability to tax. Even if it could tax incomes at rates radically higher
than other municipalities, for instance, there was little point in doing
so—people would move outside the city limits, thus evading the taxes
altogether.

On top of all that, New York's various efforts to attract and retain
business also cut into its budget. In the 1970s, the city helped subsidize
an expensive renovation of Yankee Stadium even as the neighborhoods
around it burned. It offered many tax breaks for office towers (such as
the World Trade Center) and for middle-income housing developments.
It granted "hardship" tax reductions to such companies as the New York
Stock Exchange and Con Edison, as well as to Rockefeller Center.[46] Such
subsidies to business groups and real estate interests further diminished
the amount that could be raised from local revenues.

Aid from federal and state governments had helped the city to expand
its welfare state during the 1960s, at a time of rising anger and unrest
among poor black and Hispanic New Yorkers. But at the same time it
postponed the growing conflict between those who wanted to see the
city's social programs become still more inclusive and those who
wanted to shrink them. By the early 1970s, the limits of outside funding were becoming clear, setting the stage for the fight over what kind of
city New York would become.

The blows hammering New York seemed to be felt throughout the
country and around the world, as the hierarchies and faiths that had
ordered the postwar era were coming undone. Only a decade earlier, the
United States had seemed to extend a promise of ever-greater prosperity, mobility, and security to its citizens, a promise that their material
conditions would constantly improve as time went on. This had never
been fully realized, of course; the progress left out many, from women
to African Americans to poor people untouched by the economic growth
of the postwar years. But the promise existed nonetheless. By the mid-

1970s, though, it had been broken. The anticipated future of prosperity and confidence could be counted on no longer.

So it was in New York. The old expectations had started to give way. The simplest aspects of the city's physical infrastructure—its roads and highways—could no longer be relied on. At any moment, they might buckle, leaving nothing but a steep descent into empty air below.

2. The Gap

The proliferation of public services in the 1960s and their increasing insufficiency in the 1970s affected the daily lives of millions of New Yorkers. But at the same time, a parallel drama was playing out in City Hall, where government officials were struggling to halt the city's downward slide. Several mayors in a row took on the challenge, which was expressed in purest form in a single document: the city budget.

All budgets tell stories about the future. They are ways of describing how money will be raised and what it will be used to accomplish, always written before the money is actually in hand. This is true on a large scale with municipal budgets and government budgets more generally: they outline a society's dreams and its constraints. As time goes on, the dreams may or may not come to be realized, and the constraints may or may not turn out to be absolute.

From the outside, the formal process of creating New York City's budget seemed quite orderly. The city's fiscal year ran from July 1 to June 30, and the mayor was required by law to submit a balanced budget for the forthcoming year to the City Council and the Board of Estimate by April 15. (The voting members of the Board of Estimate included the five borough presidents, the comptroller, the president of the City

Council, and the mayor himself.) This budget was an imposing document, running to more than a thousand pages. But for all its apparent precision, it contained any number of speculations rather than facts. The mayor had to guess how much money would come from Albany and Washington. There was no predicting expenses for unexpected emergencies, from blizzards to riots. Unions might demand more money than anticipated in their contracts. Taxpayers were supposed to pay their taxes—but what if they were delinquent?

The mayor and his staff could try to divine how militant the unions were, how much support there might be for the city in the state capital, what pull New York congressmen would have in Washington. But there were no guarantees ahead of time, which made even the final version of the mayor's budget proposal closer to educated guesswork than a hard-and-fast plan. As the scholar Charles Brecher wrote in 1974, New York City's budget was far from an "immutable document." Making the budget was a political process, one that articulated the city's hopes as much as its reality.[1]

Those hopes and that reality began to diverge sharply over the 1960s and early 1970s, as each of New York's mayors confronted the same basic fiscal dilemma. As jobs disappeared, as middle-class people fled to the suburbs, as poverty deepened in the city, New York was spending more than it was earning in revenues. No matter how hard the city tried to avoid this imbalance, the gap kept coming back.

There were three possible courses of action for New York. The city could try to come up with more income, by lobbying Albany for the right to levy heavier taxes or seeking to win more money from the state and federal governments. It could try to contain costs, by making cutbacks in services or driving a harder bargain with its labor unions. Or the city could borrow money, thereby closing the gap for the moment, and hope that the political situation would change and economic conditions improve.

Faced with this choice, New York's mayors in the 1960s and 1970s decided to borrow. One after another, they mobilized financial mechanisms to displace the conflicts the city confronted in the present onto the future.

———

Robert F. Wagner Jr., the man who governed New York from 1954 to 1965, was the first mayor of the postwar years to seriously confront the budget gap. For him, the city's worsening fiscal problems posed a profound threat to the liberal causes to which he had devoted his life.

Wagner was the son of the famed U.S. Senator who represented New York State during the 1930s and whose name adorns the Wagner Act, the law granting workers the right to organize unions and undertake collective bargaining. The chain-smoking mayor was literally raised in the city's liberal establishment—when he was a child, growing up in the German immigrant neighborhood of Yorkville on the Upper East Side, his entertainment involved hanging around the poker games his father hosted at their home for the leading politicians of New York State. When he became mayor in 1954, winning election six months after his father died, he governed in keeping with the New Deal politics the senior Wagner had helped to define. Known for his careful, deliberate, and understated political style (his favorite response to a social problem was to establish a commission to study it), he made New York one of the first municipalities in the country to extend collective bargaining rights to public sector workers, in what became known as the "Little Wagner Act." He appointed black and Latino officials to city positions that had long been the province of whites only; bucked anti-Communists (including Robert Moses) to help left-leaning theater director Joseph Papp bring free Shakespeare to Central Park; and built new projects all over the city that embodied the connection between government and the citizenry—parks, playgrounds, libraries, public housing, and more than three hundred new public schools. Wagner's efforts were rewarded: he was elected to a mayoral second term by a margin of more than 900,000 votes, and then won a third (at that time, the mayoralty had no term limits) despite breaking with the Tammany political machine that had helped power him to victory in the previous years.[2]

It would have been a glorious political career, were it not for the tensions worsening in the city by the end of Wagner's tenure. As activists took inspiration from the civil rights movement sweeping the South, protests and political agitation in the city began to grow. In the late 1950s and early 1960s, African American and Latino parents started pressuring the city to end the de facto segregation of its public schools and improve conditions for students of color, who were often taught by the least experienced teachers in the most dilapidated schools in the city. The campaign culminated in a massive one-day boycott in February 1964, involving more than 460,000 schoolchildren.[3] Then, in the summer of 1964, an off-duty police officer shot and killed a fifteen-year-old African American boy in Harlem, triggering a week of protests and uprisings in black neighborhoods throughout the city. The events demonstrated widespread anger at the city's enduring racial inequalities.[4] The public sector that Wagner and the postwar liberals had worked so hard to build appeared incapable of fully delivering on its promises to black and Latino people in New York. And it was becoming increasingly overstressed.

Starting in January 1965, the *New York Herald-Tribune* published a devastating series of articles describing the "city in crisis," cataloging a myriad of social ills for which the Wagner administration seemed to have no solution. "Poverty is everywhere," read the first piece. More than 70,000 young people were out of work and out of school. Eighty thousand manufacturing jobs had left the city since 1960. The number of people on welfare in New York was greater than the entire population of Alaska. Black Southerners who had come to New York seeking a better life found themselves trapped in ghettos, while Puerto Rican immigrants were living in even more desperate straits. The hospitals were "supposed to be the best in the world, but most patients and many doctors know better." Crime was on the rise: there were 636 homicides in 1964, compared to 390 in 1961.[5] Even traffic jams seemed out of control. "New York, Greatest City in the World—and Everything Is Wrong with It," read the headline introducing the multipart exposé.[6]

Wagner's response was to find some way for city government to redouble its efforts, to become more energetic still. On the national level, the spring of 1965 was a high-water point for liberalism. Congress was debating the Voting Rights Act, which would overturn black disenfranchisement in the South, and legislation that would create Medicare and

Medicaid—the first major expansion of the welfare state since World War II. Wagner was eager to place New York at the forefront of the social changes sweeping through the nation. He proposed the largest budget in the city's history: $3.875 billion (the equivalent of $28.5 billion today). The money would go to hire more police officers, to employ more teachers to help address the inequities in the public schools, and to pay for the growing welfare rolls—an average of 4,500 more people being added to them each month.[7] Wagner argued that this new spending was particularly necessary to deal with racial inequality in the city: the Harlem riots and the school boycotts had made it clear that black New Yorkers were being treated as second-class citizens. In a special meeting before the city's Board of Estimate, he spoke of the growing "plight of that major sector of our population" that had for so long been denied "equal access to, and opportunity for, significant participation in the benefits of urban living."[8]

But how would the city come up with the revenue to pay for the increased spending? To obtain the needed funds, Wagner proposed to "borrow now, repay later."[9] Specifically, he wanted to borrow $255 million to cover the gap between the expenses laid out in the new budget and the revenues available. Usually, taking on debt was reserved for the capital budget, for expensive improvements in infrastructure—roads, transit, and the like. But Wagner wanted to borrow in order to finance the operating expenses of the city, openly admitting that New York needed more money to get through a single year than it expected to receive in taxes and transfer payments from the state and federal governments.

How would this debt be repaid? The mayor offered a plan that barely hung together: he proposed to raise taxes on real estate beyond the limit imposed by the state constitution—which, as mentioned above, only allowed the city to collect 2.5 percent of the total assessed value of its taxable property per year to cover operating expenses. Wagner wanted to increase this to 3 percent. To do that, it would first be necessary to amend the constitution, which required a vote by the citizens of the entire state as well as passage by the state legislature. No one knew whether New York State voters would endorse this constitutional change. If they didn't, the city would be left holding the bag on more than a quarter billion dollars.

Despite the obvious difficulties, Mayor Wagner insisted that his proposal was better than lobbying Albany for a new income tax in the city or for a payroll tax to be split between employers and employees. Either one of those, he argued, would damage the city's already fragile economy. He cited an old fiscal axiom: "A good loan is better than a bad tax." To those who suggested that taking on such debt was problematic in and of itself, he responded that borrowing was far better than curtailing the services that were needed to lessen the burden of poverty in New York: "I do not propose to permit our fiscal problems to set the limits of our commitments to meet the essential needs of the people of this city."[10]

Surprisingly, Wagner's plan met with approval from the Board of Estimate, the City Council, and the state legislature, which endorsed his proposal to begin action to amend New York's constitution. His budget, complete with the $255 million debt, was authorized. Finalizing the change to the constitution, though, would require a second vote from the legislature, as well as a statewide voter referendum. The city's business establishment was harshly critical of the prospect. The Citizens Budget Commission, a watchdog group, warned that "fiscally the city is being run into the ground and there is a total lack of will to face the consequences of past errors."[11] Real estate magnates, including Harry B. Helmsley and Norman Tishman, joined with other city businessmen (such as the president of Macy's) to form the City Tax Council, an organization devoted to campaigning against the increase in real estate taxes that Wagner envisioned.[12] The *New York Times* pronounced the budget "reckless." It denounced the mayor for the "dangerous, unreal 'balancing' of the city budget," and the "gamble that in November of next year voters will step forward and volunteer to tax themselves more heavily to rescue the city from self-invited bankruptcy."[13]

Shortly after, Wagner decided that he did not want to be in office when the bills came due. Although the assumption early in 1965 had been that he would run for a fourth term, that summer he announced that he would not seek reelection after all.

————

John Vliet Lindsay, the six-foot-four "matinee-idol mayor" who succeeded Wagner in 1966, seemed to embody a new future for the city: a
leader for the postindustrial town to come, hinting at a break with
New York's working-class past.[14] He had grown up in prosperous
circumstances—Riverside Drive and Park Avenue, with a summer home
in Cold Spring Harbor—and had been educated at the finest elite institutions: the Buckley School in the city as a young child, St. Paul's in New
Hampshire for prep school, then the inevitable Ivy League for college
(in Lindsay's case, Yale). Driven by a zeal for public service, he graduated early to enlist in the Navy and went to law school with an eye
toward politics. Before winning the mayoral election, he had served in
Congress as a representative for the Upper East Side.

Lindsay entered political life as an unorthodox, liberal Republican
(he supported medical insurance for the elderly and wanted to create a
federal department of urban affairs) at a time when progressive Republicanism was still viable within the GOP. He seemed to represent a break
from the old-style liberalism embodied by Wagner. Lindsay was never
dependent on the city's Democratic political machines. The city's labor
unions did not view him as an ally, as was made clear in the first week
of his administration, when the transit workers went on an eleven-day
strike that brought wintry New York to a halt. The New York Times
adored him—its endorsement proclaimed that "Mr. Lindsay brings
youth, intelligence and energy to the formidable job of overseeing the
affairs of a great city in danger of decline"—but the paper was wary
about whether he would be able to rise to the challenges ahead.[15]

Lindsay was driven by a patrician sense of obligation to the city. One
of his first acts as mayor was to cut his own salary by $5,000 (equal to
over $36,000 today), and he even offered to pay for a paint job for Gracie
Mansion out of his own pocket. (The officials at the Parks Department,
responsible for the mansion, declined.)[16] He insisted that city government could and should be on the front line of the struggle for social
justice. For the politically intense young men and women who joined
the Lindsay administration, the mood seemed akin to that of John F.

Kennedy's Camelot in the early 1960s, or even of the "brain trust" of Franklin Delano Roosevelt during the New Deal. They felt they were pioneering new policies to cope with urban inequality and the poverty that Michael Harrington had famously chronicled in *The Other America*, published in 1962.

They certainly had plenty to do: the city's economy only worsened over the Lindsay years. Manufacturing jobs kept leaving New York, and they were not replaced by new service-sector ones at the same rate. (Even when they were, the service-sector jobs generally did not pay as well, which had an impact on city revenues: for each one that replaced a manufacturing job, the city lost about $1,000 in annual income taxes.)[17] Lindsay's first term saw strong economic growth in the city, but when the national economy ceased growing in the late 1960s, so did New York's. Unemployment began to tick upward, hitting 5.8 percent in 1972, the highest level since 1961.[18] Crime, too, kept relentlessly climbing: the number of homicides rose from 653 in 1966 to 1,043 in 1969 and 1,680 in 1973, Lindsay's last year in office. Heroin use was rising throughout the city, and small parks and squares that had formerly been neighborhood gathering points instead filled with drug users and addicts, becoming known as "needle parks."

As the city's social and economic problems grew, so did political organizing among the city's poor. New York under Lindsay was a politically intense place, a swirl of radical mobilizations. In Harlem, East Harlem, and the South Bronx, the Black Panthers and the Young Lords—a Puerto Rican organization modeled on the Panthers—criticized inequities in city services, arguing that black and Latino New Yorkers received substandard care at the city's hospitals, couldn't get their garbage picked up by city sanitation trucks, and were shut out of the best schools in the city university system. (In the mid-1960s, the city's high school population was 38 percent minority, but only 10 percent of students in the City University system were black and 3 percent Puerto Rican.)[19] Welfare rights organizers educated women about their right to receive cash assistance and food stamps, and activists staged protests at welfare centers, demanding grants to pay for such necessities as beds, dust mops, telephones, and clothes for their kids to wear to school. In the summer of 1970, the Young Lords, working with radical doctors, organized a sit-in at Lincoln Hospital in the South Bronx in order to call public attention to the "dirt and grime and general dilapidation of the building," which made it, as one internal hospital report admitted, "a completely inappropriate place to care for the sick."[20]

Even the city's jails became a contested space. Only one month after the protests at Lincoln, hundreds of prisoners awaiting trial at the Manhattan House of Detention (widely known as "the Tombs") rioted for hours, taking over four floors of the jail, setting fire to furniture and bedding, knocking out the bulletproof glass windows, and holding three guards hostage. Meanwhile, on the fringes of the city's politics, radical groups such as the Weather Underground set off bombs at banks, corporate headquarters, and government buildings, protesting the continued U.S. participation in the Vietnam War.[21]

Lindsay tried to cope with the surge of radicalism by expressing sympathy, even solidarity, with the protesters, at times in ways that could not help but exacerbate the tensions he sought to soothe. When one angry voter asked why "all the taxes came out of white pockets only to be spent in the black neighborhoods," he replied that "we have three hundred years of neglect to pay for."[22] He posted subway advertisements exhorting white New Yorkers to "Give a Damn" about the conditions of the ghetto. He walked the streets of Harlem the night in April 1968 when Martin Luther King Jr. was assassinated. Against the opposition of the leadership of the police union, he created a Civilian Complaint Review Board to deal with charges of police brutality. He sought to decentralize the school system so that African American and Latino parents could have more say over their children's education. And he dramatically increased spending on social welfare programs. By the end of Lindsay's first four years in office, the city's spending on social services and welfare had doubled— outstripping the spending on public schools, once the city's largest budget item. Health and hospital spending had risen by more than 50 percent. The mayor opened a new agency to treat drug addicts, and helped expand city funding for day care centers serving low-income children.[23]

But even as Lindsay sought to use the city government to ameliorate the problems of urban poverty, he ran into the deepening hostility of a different constituency: New York's business elite, who wanted him to cut spending on social welfare and redirect the city's efforts to helping the business class. There were fears of a "corporate exodus" from the city: in 1962, 77 of the 250 largest corporations in the United States were based in New York, but by the end of the decade 19 of them had moved out—most to suburbs just beyond the city limits. Increasingly concerned about the direction of the city, business leaders also began to organize. In 1965, fourteen business executives dismayed by the direction of the city started the Economic Development Council, which sought, in the words of its leader, retired General Foods chairman Clarence Francis, to foster "the concern and involvement of the business community" in New York politics.[24] Taxes were among their main concerns—both because of the real economic burden they represented and because of what they symbolized about the city and the "climate" it provided for business. As the president of the New York Stock Exchange wrote in one letter to Francis, "What troubles me as a New York-based business-man is the fact that New York's potential as a business center isn't being fully realized. We have the people, the capital resources, the tradition of business service, the know-how and the proper geography. But one overriding problem—the deterioration of the climate for business, especially in the realm of taxes—undermines the effectiveness of these many favorable elements."[25] A few years after the creation of the EDC, major real estate developers and landlords—people whose wealth was inextricably linked to the city, and who had no option to pick up and move out—formed another organization, the Association for a Better New York, to press for policies that would encourage companies to stay put—as one early press release put it, "to keep New York City as the prime corporate headquarters in the world and to improve economic and cultural life in the city."[26]

The mobilization of New York's business class posed a particular problem for Lindsay. For all his concern about the social problems of the city, he shared with these executives a vision of what New York City might become in the postindustrial era: a city whose economy was dominated by white-collar professionals and the business services they provided to corporate headquarters, a city in which real estate development and the financial industry would take on increasingly important roles. To that end, Lindsay pursued economic redevelopment strategies that focused on moving manufacturing from Midtown, SoHo, and Lower Manhattan to the outer boroughs, so that the city center could become a haven of white-collar work, tourism, and entertainment— "Fun City," as he called it. He set up early-warning programs for businesses seeking to relocate away from New York so he could court them with alluring tax incentives. He sought ways to bring the private sector into the provision of public goods—for example, by raising private money to restore parks that had fallen into disrepair, and by joining struggling municipal hospitals to New York's private academic health centers. He also spent millions of dollars on consulting contracts with the RAND Corporation, which advised ways to save money by restructuring the city's municipal services.[27]

In later years, Lindsay would be criticized from the right as the quintessential urban hypocrite—a "limousine liberal," in the unforgettable phrase of one of his political challengers—whose political fantasies and moralizing attitudes outstripped any sense of what might be realistic. In truth, it is more accurate to see him as foreshadowing a new kind of urban liberalism, shaped by the forces of the War on Poverty era but also far more open to market ideology and a strong role for the private sector in city politics. He was poised between an older industrial New York, with its long-standing social welfare traditions, and a new white-collar city that had no such allegiances. These conflicting priorities became ever more difficult to reconcile—in the budget as everywhere else.

Lindsay did not pursue Wagner's idea of amending the state constitution so that the city could raise more in property taxes to cover its annual expenses; the voter referendum on the amendment never took place. Instead, when preparing the budget for 1966–67, Lindsay proposed that Albany grant the city the power to levy a host of new taxes: most notably, a tax on personal incomes, business incomes, and commuter incomes. He also sought to raise taxes on the financial sector, asking for an increase in the stock transfer tax (which levied a small fee each time a stock traded hands) and for the right to expand the business income tax to banks, which had historically been exempt. His administration even promised to revisit the property tax exemptions that kept almost a third of the taxable property in the city off the rolls.[28] These new taxes would fund city government "sparely, but expansively," Lindsay said: his budget included hundreds of millions of dollars for libraries, parks, hospitals, community colleges, and antipoverty programs. "The budget is large, but the needs of the city are great," he declared in his budget message.[29]

The entire program met with stiff resistance from business groups in the city, which had been alerted by Wagner's borrowing to the need to pay more attention to the tax policies and spending habits of the city government. The Economic Development Council came out against Lindsay's proposals, objecting in particular to the personal income tax.[30] The leaders of the Morgan Guaranty Trust Company described the plans as unfair to business in general, to banks in particular, and to Morgan most of all.[31] The New York Stock Exchange threatened to leave the city altogether if the stock transfer tax went through, relocating to Connecticut or perhaps even California. G. Keith Funston, the NYSE president, embarked on an extensive lobbying campaign, meeting with city and state politicians to make the case against the tax. He barraged local newspapers with letters, and when the *Times* ran an editorial criticizing the exchange for its threat to depart the city, he wrote a lengthy personal letter to the publisher, A. O. Sulzberger, saying that this was no blackmail attempt: the NYSE really was prepared to leave for a better business climate if it had to.[32] The Lindsay administration tried to mollify the NYSE, with little success. "The fiscal and political pressures on the City Administration are so great we can look for no tax relief whatsoever from the City of New York," wrote NYSE representatives after a series of meetings with city officials. Welfare and cheap transit were higher priorities than tax cuts for business, they wrote. Given this, the Board of Governors should proceed "with all deliberate speed" to relocate the NYSE beyond the city limits.[33]

Despite these objections and threats, the state legislature supported most of Lindsay's program, passing into law the very taxes that Wagner had sought to avoid. In addition to the stock transfer tax hike it permitted an income tax, a revised business income tax, and a tax on commuter incomes (although this last one was much smaller than what Lindsay had requested). Growth in real estate values permitted more money to be raised through property taxes without changing the constitution.[34] At the same time, the city was the beneficiary of the wave of money coming from Washington and Albany to fund such programs as Aid to Families with Dependent Children (AFDC) and Medicaid. Over the course of Lindsay's first term, from 1965 to 1969, revenues from these other levels of government ballooned.

With all this new money flowing in, and the economy improving in the late 1960s, Lindsay was able to balance the budget during his first term in office and even to retire the debt that Wagner had incurred.[35] The delicate balance gave way, however, during his second term as mayor. New York was hit hard by the onset of a recession that began in 1969. As people lost their jobs, the city's revenues from income taxes and sales taxes were threatened. Property tax delinquencies were starting to rise, too, as landlords abandoned their buildings, in the worst cases even turning to arson to burn them down. More people needed city services as the ranks of the unemployed swelled. And with Richard Nixon in the White House, the surge of new funding from Washington was beginning to slow. Albany, too, was increasingly wary about transferring more money to New York City: the loss of manufacturing firms affected the entire state, from Buffalo to Rochester to Albany to the small industrial towns of the Hudson River Valley, and Governor Nelson Rockefeller wanted to be able to use the resources of the state to woo companies rather than pay for social services in New York City. Suddenly, Lindsay had to confront the same fiscal problem that had snared Wagner: the growing gap between the money he wanted to spend and the revenues that were coming into the city coffers.

The budget drama in the early 1970s was at once wrenching and repetitive. Every year, Lindsay would proclaim that the city's budget was reaching a "crisis" point. With great fanfare, he would issue dire public warnings that without more money the city would have to make all kinds of horrible cuts: fielding 14,000 fewer cops, canceling the fresh-

man class at the City University at New York, eliminating the Staten
Island Ferry. He presented multiple versions of the budget, showing how
much he would have to cut depending on how much aid the city received
from the state or from the federal government. He went to Albany to ask
for permission to levy a tax on advertising that targeted the New York
market, as well as new sales taxes on everything from haircuts and beauty
parlor treatments to cheap restaurant meals (which became known as the
"hot-dog tax"). Over Lindsay's two terms in office the city raised income
taxes multiple times, while property taxes climbed, and business taxes
were extended to cover a variety of small businesses and partnerships.
Overall, New York's taxes became much higher than in other municipalities. But none of it was enough. The gap remained.

Occasionally, Lindsay tried to address the city's underlying structural problems. Its revenue system—constrained by the constitutional
restrictions on property taxes, the large amount of untaxed property in
the city, and the city's dependence on Albany—simply did not allow it
to raise the money it needed to carry out the ambitious range of social
programs it had promised New Yorkers. Lindsay sought to win changes
in the state constitution that would enable "home rule," permitting the
city to set its own taxes without having to get permission from Albany,
and for a revision that would allow it to tax real estate more aggressively.[36] A state constitutional convention called in 1967 refused all
these proposals. In 1969, Lindsay proposed a new plan whereby Albany
would send a higher proportion of the state income tax to cities and
localities—essentially, redistributing wealth by using the state's greater
power to tax incomes.[37] Albany ignored the suggestion. The mayor even
argued that the state or the federal government should take over the
total cost of welfare and Medicaid, a proposal that would have made a
tremendous difference in the city's finances but which, needless to say,
met with little interest in either Albany or Washington.

These efforts failing, Lindsay made the same choice that Wagner had
years before, except that he did not announce it in his budget message
with the same fanfare. Hoping against hope that a windfall would eventually come from the state or the federal government, the city began to make
up the difference between expenses and revenues by borrowing money.

Especially striking was New York's increased use of short-term debt instruments known as tax-anticipation notes, revenue-anticipation notes, and bond-anticipation notes (or TANs, RANs, and BANs). These forms of debt were very different from the long-term "general obligation" bonds used to finance capital improvements. Those infrastructure upgrades had a long lifespan, so it made sense that payment for them would be spread out over multiple years as well; general obligation bonds took ten, twenty, or even forty years to mature, meaning that investors had to wait that long before presenting the bond for repayment with interest. The anticipation notes, on the other hand, usually matured about a year after they were issued, so they immediately created pressure on the next budget. Their issuance did not require any voter oversight or approval. Their collateral was anticipated revenue: taxes that had not yet been collected, transfer payments from the state or federal government that had not yet come in, and proceeds from a sale of long-term bonds that had not yet gone through. When Lindsay came into office, the total volume of TANs, RANs, and BANs stood at $433 million. By 1973—his last year in office—it had more than quadrupled, to over $2.1 billion, out of a budget of nearly $10 billion.[38]

The city said that these anticipation notes simply helped to smooth out the inevitable delays in public finance. The notes, it explained, enabled New York to meet its payroll while waiting for money to arrive from the state or federal governments or for assessed taxes to be collected. When those funds arrived, they would be available to pay off the short-term debt.

But in fact, the city was regularly overestimating the amount it would receive from the federal or state government. In 1972–73 and 1973–74, for example, the money that arrived from Washington was tens of millions of dollars less than the city had forecast.[39] When the expected funds did not arrive, the budget office did not revise the budget accordingly. Instead, it assumed that the missing money would still be arriving at some future point, and in fact used those anticipated funds as collateral for new debt.[40] As a result, the total amount of short-term debt was steadily increasing, and interest on that debt was eating up a rising proportion of the city's expenses.[41]

The city was also beginning to pay for current expenses out of its capital budget—diverting money that should have gone to pay for infrastructure maintenance and improvement (major one-time expenses) to the recurring costs of the city's daily life. In 1964–65, the year before Lindsay's term began, the city covered a small volume of expense budget items this way, on the order of $7 million. By 1973–74, though, the city was spending more than $250 million of its capital budget on annual expenses.[42] The Department of Social Services, for example, received more than $14 million from the capital budget. The vocational schools run by the Board of Education received $114 million—as though the city's children were a kind of infrastructure, even though the costs related to running schools were very different from the pipes, roads, and streetlamps that capital funds were intended to purchase.[43]

The city got ample help in running up these debts. New York State—which was eager to control its own costs—facilitated New York City's borrowing, granting the city the leeway to spend more of its capital budget on expense items (which otherwise would have violated the state constitution) instead of allowing new taxing powers or providing more generous state aid. The state legislature also repeatedly amended the law to permit the city to use RANs and BANs more aggressively—for example, to issue RANs not just for revenues that would be collected later that same year but for those expected to arrive in the following year as well, and to issue them without specifying the precise revenue streams that were being anticipated.[44] The banks, for their part, were happy to keep on lending money to New York and to help the city sell its notes to smaller banks and individual investors around the country. The major bond rating agencies, Moody's and Standard & Poor's, actually upgraded the city's bonds in 1972 and 1973, giving them an A rating instead of the Baa rating they had held since 1965.[45] After all, New York seemed to have an "amazing resiliency to withstand budget difficulties," a spokesman for Standard & Poor's said when explaining why his agency had revised its judgment of the city's debt.[46]

There was little federal oversight or regulation of municipal bonds, and New York was not legally required to provide financial information to investors or the general public. The city did not abide by what are known as "generally accepted accounting principles," which would have made it impossible to record expected revenues as though they were in hand while at the same time only noting expenditures once they were actually paid. New York was not alone here: a lack of clear information and deviation from standard accounting procedures were far from unusual in municipal budget offices at the time.[47] The result, though, was that New York could go from one year to the next without anyone being entirely clear about how much money it was actually spending, and how deeply in debt it really was—about $8.5 billion by the time that Lindsay left office, up from $4.4 billion at the end of the Wagner years, with most of that increase coming during Lindsay's second term.[48]

Over time, this aggressive use of debt meant postponing more than just taxes: it meant delaying conflict, putting off political fights about New York City's welfare state. As unemployment rose, as the city's public institutions strained at what was being demanded of them and came up short of funds, as advocates for the poor and those for the business class both insisted on their conception of the city, Lindsay turned to debt to evade open struggles about its priorities, and about the limits, disappointments, and failures of the postwar liberal regime.

Come what might, by the early 1970s Lindsay's eye was on political horizons beyond the city's limits. In 1972, he toyed with the idea of a presidential bid. Saying that he could no longer belong to the party of Goldwater and Nixon, he dropped his old affiliation with the Republicans and became a Democrat. He bombed out in the presidential primaries, though, and quickly withdrew from the race. But once he had seen the possibility of a larger political arena, it was impossible to reconcile himself to his old job. Soon, Lindsay announced that he would not seek another term as mayor of New York.

The man who would take Lindsay's place in City Hall in the election of 1973 was his comptroller, Abraham Beame. And if there was anyone who should have known and understood the problems the city was up against, it was he.

Beame was the opposite of the patrician Lindsay in almost every way: physically, ideologically, and temperamentally. Sixty-seven years old when he was elected, Beame was so short—only five feet two inches tall—that sometimes an aide would place an attaché case under his chair so he could stand on it when he rose to speak.[49] (Beame liked to joke that his height was an advantage when it came to dodging brickbats.) The first Jewish mayor of New York City, he had grown up in poverty on the Lower East Side, instead of the fancy addresses of the Lindsay family. He had attended City College, not the Ivy League. He was a product of the clubhouse and the city's political machines.

Beame was committed to the principles of order, loyalty, responsibility, and attention to detail—not to Lindsay's idea that the city government should help resolve inequities and racial injustices of centuries past. He wanted to solve the city's problems, certainly, but to do so without causing too much upheaval along the way. He subscribed to no grand causes, believed in no special mission, did not think he was bound to right any particular set of wrongs. Politics for him was no crusade for justice. What Beame did trust in above all else, what he believed in more than anything, was New York itself: its power, its wealth, its abundance, and its glory. It was inconceivable to him that this glorious metropolis could ever fail.

Beame's first term as comptroller had been under Wagner. He had been the only person on the Board of Estimate to vote against Wagner's borrowing, and under both Wagner and Lindsay he had railed against the policy of taking on debt. He had warned repeatedly that the "day of reckoning" would someday arrive. Once he actually became mayor, though, Beame found himself confronted by the same budget gap that had bedeviled his predecessors. And at that point, utterly uncertain about how to cope with the pressures the city faced, Beame too turned to borrowing to paper over the gap, attempting as best he could to make the budget tell the story he wanted it to tell.

It was Wagner who first ventured to put New York City significantly in debt. It was Lindsay who had made debt a perennial feature of the city's budgeting. But it was Beame who would become the central player—the villain or the scapegoat, depending on one's point of view—in the financial collapse of New York.

3. The Neighborhood Bookkeeper

Abraham Beame held the formal ceremony of his mayoral swearing-in on the morning of January 1, 1974, in his $375-a-month rental apartment in Belle Harbor, Queens. A judge who had been a friend for fifty-two years did the honors. Only Beame's family and a few news reporters were invited to attend.[1] At the public inauguration that followed, the newspapers noted the distinct absence of soaring rhetoric. In his speech, Beame promised to be a "matchmaker" joining the people of New York to their city, to usher in a "rebirth of faith and confidence in our city government."[2]

The man who would oversee the near-bankruptcy of New York had grown up in the immigrant Jewish community of the Lower East Side, a world that had mostly disappeared by the time he became the city's highest elected official. His parents, Philip and Esther Birnbaum, had met in a small town in Russia. His father was a political radical, a socialist, as Beame later remembered, who "fought against oppression" under the rule of the czar and the Cossacks. Learning that he was under surveillance, Philip fled to America before the czar's police could haul him off to prison, taking his two older sons with him. He would eventually change his last name to the Americanized "Beame." His pregnant wife went to London to have their baby, and then followed Philip, arriving at Ellis Island in 1906 with the three-month-old infant Abraham.[3]

Beame's childhood was difficult. His mother died when he was only six years old, and the family moved from one narrow railroad apartment on the Lower East Side to another, relocating so often that Beame would later joke that his father—who worked as a paper cutter in a factory making index cards and stationery—must never have paid the rent. The quarters were cramped: as a nine-year-old, Beame lived in a tiny tenement apartment on Essex Street with his father, his two older brothers, and a family friend.[4] The bathrooms were in the hallways; heat came from coal stoves. At one point, when money ran out to keep him at home, Beame was sent to live with an aunt.[5]

But if the living space was limited, the political imagination of the Lower East Side at the turn of the century was vast. The neighborhood was awash in political ideas—anarchism, socialism, and trade unionism—even for that majority of people whose energies were focused primarily on the day-to-day business of trying to get by. Irving Howe, in his classic study of the immigrant Lower East Side, hypothesized that its political intensity was driven by the absence of secure traditions and long-standing communal ties that might offer people a refuge from the harshness of their material lives. The neighborhood was also deeply shaken by the Triangle Shirtwaist fire of 1911, which killed 146 young garment factory workers. The apartment where the Beames would reside in 1916 was just down the block from the home of two of the victims, a pair of brothers aged nineteen and twenty-one.[6]

Socialism was the answer for many on the Lower East Side, promising a system at once both practical and utopian. In this moment, before the 1917 Bolshevik Revolution divided the world, socialism could encompass everything from the creation of health and safety codes for tenements and garment factories, municipal ownership of utilities, and trade unionism to revolutionary transformation and the radical remaking of the entire social order.[7] And when Beame's father arrived in his new country, he did not abandon his revolutionary politics as he did his name. Like so many on the Lower East Side, he remained an active and committed agitator, for whom politics was far more important than

religion. Political zeal transformed daily experiences, holding the keys
to a better life and a different world. The leading paper of the Yiddish
Lower East Side was the *Jewish Daily Forward*; its building at 175 East
Broadway, with a façade decorated with the heads of Karl Marx and
Friedrich Engels, was where all the Socialist politicians of the day came
to speak. Later in life, Beame remembered going as a child with his father
to hear the great Eugene V. Debs, who ran for president on the Socialist
ticket in 1912, speak at the *Forward* building: "You listen as a kid, and so
much stays with you."[8]

What did stay with him? Despite his nostalgia for the crowds at the
Forward building, young Abraham Beame himself was never a radical
like his father. He preferred scrapping in the streets to politics; as a
young boy, he was known as "Spunky" for his reluctance to quit a fight.
But he soon left the tough world of street games behind, choosing instead
to spend time at the neighborhood's settlement houses—charitable institutions run by wealthier New Yorkers who were outsiders in the Jewish
neighborhood. (As a young girl, Eleanor Roosevelt had volunteered
in one of them for two years.) For Beame, they held out the promise of
respectability absent from the world of the streets, their competitions
taking place in a far more genteel atmosphere. At the University Settlement, Beame played basketball and participated in recitation contests
for which he'd memorize poems such as Rudyard Kipling's "Gunga Din."
Once, after winning, he journeyed out to Newark to recite it for broadcast on the radio. (The University Settlement was also the place where, as
a teenager playing checkers, he met Mary Ingerman, who would become
his wife; they would have two children by the time Beame was thirty.)

The diversions of basketball and poetry were only occasional, though.
Mostly, Beame worked. As a child, he earned money by knocking on the
doors of neighbors who were too poor to own a timepiece to wake them
up for work. Starting at age thirteen, he labored at the paper factory
with his father from 4 p.m. until midnight. (He saved money by roller-
skating to and from school rather than taking public transportation.)
Despite this heavy workload, he was a legendary student, passing his
bookkeeping exams and the New York State Regents exams with perfect scores—the only one to do so in his class. As one classmate later

remembered, "This business of memorizing and doing his homework was an absolute fetish with this little guy."[9]

Beame got a free education at City College—from which he graduated cum laude—and went on to teach high school in Queens, while also earning his CPA and starting his own accountancy firm. His ambitions never focused on material acquisition for its own sake; he was obsessed with calculating figures and organizing money more than possessing it.

For an ambitious young man not particularly interested in business yet longing to make his way in the world, membership in a political club seemed a good path to upward mobility. Beame became active in Democratic Party politics early in the 1930s. His club of choice was the famous Madison Democratic Club in Brooklyn, one of the borough's oldest, having been founded in the early twentieth century by the Irish "Brooklyn Boss" John McCooey. Like the other Democratic clubs in the city, the Madison Club sought to secure the party vote by providing the working-class people in its district with material aid—some food, a letter, a favor—in return for loyalty at the polls.

Although the Madison Club began in Irish neighborhoods, McCooey helped to organize offshoots of the club in different ethnic enclaves throughout Brooklyn. The clubs were hierarchical. Each captain was responsible for a particular territory, charged with making sure the club boss knew who might need a job, a turkey at Christmas or kosher food at Passover, a bit of extra coal for warmth—and for turning out the voters on election day. The club bosses, in turn, reported back to McCooey; legend had it that he sometimes spoke with as many as two hundred people a day. He resented the telephone because it lessened the need for face-to-face contact so integral to the operation of the machine.[10]

McCooey died in the early 1930s, right around the time when Beame became active in the club, but the ethos of personal loyalty and clubhouse solidarity endured. This remained true even when the power of the city's political machines began to decline in the postwar years. Irwin Steingut, the club's new Jewish boss, ran the organization during the decade and a half when Beame served as a neighborhood captain. Years later, Beame would recall how impressed he had been to see the lines of people that Steingut had waiting to talk to him.[11]

The connections Beame had forged through the Madison Club were largely responsible for his first positions in city politics. Because of his expertise in accounting, the budget was a logical place for him to begin. He served as assistant director of the budget under Mayor William O'Dwyer in 1946, and then became budget director for Mayor Vincent Impellitteri in 1952, a position he would hold for nearly a decade. In 1961, he won his first election for comptroller. The *Times* had endorsed him for the position, calling him "probably the best informed man on city government and its fiscal affairs, inside or outside the Wagner administration."[12]

When Wagner withdrew from the mayoral race in 1965, Beame entered it. He framed his decision to campaign in the language of fiscal responsibility: "I owe this city a debt."[13] Beame won the Democratic nomination easily, but in the general election he faced not only the Republican Lindsay, but also the freewheeling founder of the *National Review*, Conservative Party candidate William F. Buckley Jr. As historian Vincent Cannato has argued, in contrast to this flashy pair, each a scene-stealer in his own right, Beame seemed a relic of old-fashioned working-class politics, a dull, insipid machine pol who still—the horror!—spoke with a New York accent. When Beame tried to celebrate his public education, Buckley—like Lindsay, a Yale man—sneered that it was indeed "obvious" that Beame's degree came from City College. President Johnson was slow to endorse, and newly elected New York Senator Robert F. Kennedy was also unenthusiastic about campaigning for Beame: as one journalist put it, the senator regarded Beame as an "embarrassing, losing candidate, who did not have any grasp of the larger issues." (Beame, for his part, never liked sharing the podium with Kennedy, fearing that most people in the audience really had come to hear the dashing young leader.) Beame's lack of passion and charisma almost came to seem a problem to Lindsay's campaign managers, who wanted to paint Beame as an oppressive machine boss and Lindsay as the passionate reformer. As one adviser put it, "Beame is so small and earnest. How are we ever going to incite people to rise up against their friendly neighborhood bookkeeper?"[14]

Lindsay won that race, and the next election. But by 1973, Beame was betting that after eight years of the limousine liberal, New Yorkers would prefer the neighborhood bookkeeper. He ran again, and campaigned against the idealism of the Lindsay years, presenting himself as the pragmatic candidate grounded in the nitty-gritty minutiae of the city's balance sheets. The *Times* endorsed his opponent, Representative Herman Badillo (the first Puerto Rican congressman, who spoke for the South Bronx), writing that Beame lacked "the special qualities of imagination and innovation that the Mayor of this city ought to have."[15] No matter, said Beame: Who needed those? The city government was first and foremost a "$10-billion corporation. Would you pick someone with no experience to manage it?" Lindsay might have had grand plans and dreams for the city, but Beame knew how to run a budget. As he put it, "A Mayor who doesn't know where the money is coming from or where it is going, who has to rely on other people to tell him, can't ever be his own man."[16] His campaign slogan was, "If you don't know the buck, you don't know the job."

Beame's tentative efforts on the campaign trail in 1973 at laying out a credible new agenda for the city came across as humble and decidedly uninspiring. Mostly, he wanted to keep things as they were, to change New York "from the inside out, without turning it upside down."[17] Lindsay had always kept one eye on the national stage. Not Beame. Other than the occasional winter jaunt to Florida, he had hardly even traveled outside of the city. New York was the beginning and the end of his horizons. He went to the Catskills to talk to vacationing constituents, and on the advice of Howard Rubenstein, an old Brooklyn friend who was making a name for himself in public relations, he gave press conferences in all the outer boroughs. (Rubenstein would scout out dramatic backdrops for Beame's appearances that would look good on television— neighborhoods in decline, piles of brick, anything that would help convey the sense that the city needed repair.)[18] Beame promised not to raise the subway fare, pledged his allegiance to free tuition at the city university, and argued that good health care "should not be considered a privilege or a commodity."[19] He was obsessed with details—the parking spot of the campaign bus, the placement of a sign.[20] Perhaps he had no vision. But it worked: Beame trounced Badillo and conservative

Democrat Mario Biaggi in the primary, and then defeated Republican State Senator John Marchi (who represented Staten Island) with 60 percent of the vote in the general election.

Once he was in City Hall, Beame wasted no time in starting to forge a new set of political friendships, trying to replicate the dense world of interconnected loyalties that made up the Democratic machine. When he received a letter of congratulations from Democratic senator Henry ("Scoop") Jackson of Washington, Beame replied immediately. "The tasks of running New York are tremendous," he wrote, "and I will need the help of everyone in the Senate and in the House who has a warm spot in their hearts for the great City of New York. Rest assured, I will call on you for that help in the future."[21]

Soon enough, he certainly would.

Nineteen seventy-four was not an easy year to become the mayor of New York City. The city's decay and violence were growing worse. On New Year's Eve 1973—the night before Beame was sworn in—thirteen people died in homicides, mostly in its poorer neighborhoods. It seemed clear that there might be some link between the conditions people lived in and the spate of deaths. "This neighborhood is so terrible," one police detective said of Morrisania. "We have burned-out buildings, vacant lots. . . . I lived here for a few months once, and I got to understand how people feel. You really feel like blowing your landlord's head off when you don't have any heat or hot water."[22] The city's dereliction even caught the imagination of psychics; one, quoted in a book of apocalyptic *Predictions for 1974*, forecast that New York City would declare bankruptcy.[23]

The bleakness of the city echoed that of the nation as a whole. The economic growth that had powered the United States and Western Europe through the 1950s and 1960s came to a halt; the recession that began in late 1973 was the most severe since the end of World War II. And while people were losing their jobs, rapid inflation ate away at their savings and their purchasing power. The old sure-fire Keynesian policy prescription—use government spending to boost a flagging economy!—no longer appeared viable: economists feared it would only spur even more inflation. Indeed, it seemed possible that the glorious history of economic expansion had reached a permanent end. The year before Beame won the mayoral election, the Club of Rome—an international organization of scientists, economists, and policymakers—had published a special report titled *The Limits to Growth*, arguing that the earth could not sustain much more population growth and that economic contraction was the way of the future. And the energy shortage that began in the fall of 1973, when the oil-producing nations of the Middle East boycotted the United States following its support for Israel in the Yom Kippur War, seemed to demonstrate the fragility of the American economy and its ultimate dependence on distant and potentially hostile regions of the world.

The reverberations of these national crises were directly felt in New York. Spiking energy prices, for example, affected the cost of everything from streetlamps to subways; it looked like Beame would have to break his campaign promise of no transit fare hikes. The mood in the city was dreary and pessimistic. In surveys, businessmen said that they anticipated lower profits and more bankruptcies in the coming year.[24] One out of three New Yorkers reported that they had "no confidence" that the police would come if they called for help.[25] "Let's face it," one unemployed ironworker and Vietnam veteran told journalist Pete Hamill, "the Depression is in the air."[26] Speaking before an audience of Staten Island Democrats, Beame said that his first two months in office had been the longest of his life. "Between the fare problem, the budget problem and the Federal energy crisis, it seems like much more than 60 days."[27]

To be sure, there were a few signs of life and possibility in the city, mostly in the cultural realm. A new club, CBGB's, opened on a deserted stretch of the Bowery, for instance, hosting Richard Hell, Patti Smith, Blondie, the Ramones, and other musicians from the emerging punk and alternative music scene.[28] On the other end of town, in the West Bronx, a young Jamaican immigrant who would become known as DJ Kool Herc had started to throw parties in the recreation room of his apartment complex, intending them to be a refuge from the gang conflicts that plagued the neighborhoods. In later years, the Herc dance-fests would become renowned for giving birth to hip-hop.[29] The subways of the city, meanwhile, were becoming canvas for graffiti artists, ranging from Taki 183 (who tagged his name and street number on subways and walls all over the city) to muralists whose work flared across whole cars and even entire trains. Graffiti was both celebrated and reviled from the moment of its birth: the Lindsay administration had spent $10 million a year trying to wash the subway cars clean, even as the *Village Voice* described graffiti as "the first genuine teenage street culture since the fifties" and City College organized art exhibits highlighting the originality of the murals.[30]

Even these stirrings of creativity and resilience, though, were closely linked to—indeed, were made possible by—the poverty of the city. The artists and musicians who clustered in the cheap apartments of Alphabet City and the Lower East Side mocked the commercialization of art, adopting an aesthetic that flaunted the absence of money. "No wave" art, music, and film were defined by their low production budgets; they relied on urban disinvestment, sustained by the low rents of lofts, warehouses, apartments that no one else wanted. In downtown lofts that had once housed small manufacturers, artists decorated makeshift theaters with old furniture, abandoned commercial signs, tossed-out tinsel, crutches, and children's toys to perform works that were half confession, half provocation.[31]

Abandonment and neglect helped open up spaces for artistic life, but for the most part their manifestations were prosaic and grim. Near Avenues B and C, drug dealers set up "shooting galleries" in empty lots, where they sold needles and heroin (for the shockingly low price of two to three dollars a bag) to users who would hide in the vacant buildings to get high.[32] In SoHo, residents of the newly up-and-coming artists' neighborhood argued over whether to allow methadone clinics, and protested the opening of dance clubs they thought likely to become centers of drug activity.[33] In the South Bronx, residents of Hunts Point said that junkies languished in the streets of the neighborhood late at night: "You have to walk down the street with a stick."[34] Inverting the stereotypical New York complaints about how there were too many Puerto

Rican immigrants in the city, the governor of Puerto Rico went so far as to blame reverse migration from the Bronx for problems on his island.[35]

The atmosphere of decline helped to stoke fears about crime. In 1974 there were 1,554 people killed in homicides, only a slight decline over the previous year, while rapes (4,054), robberies (77,940), assaults (41,068), and burglaries (158,321) were all up.[36] Crime statistics are notoriously slippery, subject to political considerations and changes in reporting, but the trend was clear. During the first weeks of Mayor Beame's term, newspapers were filled with reports of horrific crimes: a seven-year-old girl raped on the way home from a candy store, a young woman killed with an ax. Meanwhile, the boilermakers who worked for the Board of Education went out on strike in the middle of January, forcing frigid schools to shut down. And throughout all this, the city was continuing to lose jobs at least as rapidly as it had lost them in the previous few years, if not more so. In February 1974 it had 22,000 fewer jobs than a year before, and by April the gap was 38,000.[37] By the end of 1974, the city's unemployment rate stood at 7 percent.[38]

As mayor, Beame surrounded himself with advisers who were familiar with the longtime workings of the city, people who would be unlikely to call for new directions. This was his trusted inner circle, his real group of confidants. They were very different from the graduates of elite schools who had populated the Lindsay administration. Nor were they from the world of business, for the most part. Beame's thirty-seven-year-old son Bernard, known as Buddy, was his main campaign strategist. The mayor also received counsel from his Brooklyn friend, Howard Rubenstein, who remembered going to the beach out in Queens with Beame when he was still comptroller and seeing that the pockets of Beame's bathing suit were filled with notes in tiny handwriting on the budget. ("What if you go for a swim?" he wondered.)[39]

Beame's closest associate after his election, First Deputy Mayor James Cavanagh, had come up through the ranks of city government. Like Beame, Cavanagh was born poor, growing up in the Navy Yard section of downtown Brooklyn in a working-class Irish neighborhood. He had started working for the city in 1938, when La Guardia was mayor, and except for a stint in the army during World War II he had never stopped. He did not hold a college degree. Known for his white hair and unkempt suits, the affable Cavanagh liked to say that it wasn't "too bad" to move from being a clerk all the way up to first deputy mayor.[40] When Beame wanted to appoint the city's first black deputy mayor, he turned to the Harlem machine and selected David Dinkins. (When tax problems surfaced that kept Dinkins from being able to take the job, Beame selected American Airlines executive Paul Gibson Jr., also African American, instead.)

None of these were people likely to respond in a forceful or imaginative way to the myriad crises facing New York, any more than Beame was himself. "A circumspect and cautious man, Mr. Beame rarely tells anyone what he is up to," wrote *New York Times* reporter Maurice Carroll in a piece on Beame's first ninety days in office. "There is about the Beame team's operation at City Hall an air of persistent activity but there is very little urgency."[41] Perhaps his most daring act in his first few months as mayor was to walk the streets of his childhood neighborhood on the Lower East Side during the evening hours, in an effort to persuade New Yorkers that their city remained safe no matter what the rising crime rate might indicate.[42]

Beame's unwillingness to shake things up extended to the realm in which he was assumed to wield the most expertise: the city's finances. Like Wagner and Lindsay, Beame had no new ideas on how to handle the city's budget gap. Instead, he quickly resorted to the same method of dealing with it that they had used before him: debt.

Given how vigorously Beame had criticized the city for excessive borrowing when he was comptroller, this might seem surprising. But although Beame knew the city was in trouble, he had great difficulty believing that its problems could worsen as they did. The multifarious confusions in the city's accounting strategies made it easy even for people who should have known better to avoid reckoning with just how bad things really were. Besides, there was no other obvious solution. In the spring of 1974, as Beame prepared his first budget, he announced that the city had inherited from Lindsay a shortfall of nearly $1.5 billion per year. It was a gap, he said in one news conference, that "you need a magician" to close. The costs of running the city, he noted, were projected to grow by 16 percent per year, while revenues were only increasing at a rate of 2 percent. It seemed "an insuperable problem."[43]

To meet the legal requirement of balancing the budget, Beame proposed raising the sales tax, passing new real estate taxes, and assessing a fee on auto owners in the city. He asked for the power to increase the stock-transfer tax (Albany denied this, instead backing a higher tax on horse-race betting). He also suggested pushing some budget items off to the following fiscal year, to give the appearance of saving $75 or $80 million.[44] And his budget featured an unprecedented quantity of capital funds going toward annual expenses: a total of $564 million, more than twice the amount from the previous fiscal year.[45]

All of this maneuvering still left the city half a billion dollars in the red, so Beame also proposed to borrow $520 million. When he presented his package to the City Council, one councilmember asked what the plan might be the next year. "I wish I knew the answer," the mayor replied.[46]

Beame's $520 million was added to a debt load that was already growing extremely rapidly. By 1974, the city's overall debt burden (not just the gap between revenues and spending in that year's budget, but the total amount it owed its creditors) was in the ballpark of $10 billion—$1.5 billion more than it had been a year earlier, and $6 billion more than when Wagner left office in 1965.[47] The cost of servicing the city's debt was rising accordingly: 15 percent of the city's total budget for 1974–75 was devoted to payments on old debt, making that the third-largest item in the budget, almost twice the amount devoted to firefighters and police combined.

To keep making payments on its existing loans, the city had to borrow hundreds of millions of dollars afresh each month.[48] Each new round of borrowing added to the total debt servicing costs; each meant paying more down the line. The volume of New York City debt was so great that it risked overwhelming the national bond market—by the spring of Beame's first term, New York's bonds and notes accounted for nearly 28 percent of all the tax-exempt bonded debt in the country, up from historic levels around 18 percent.[49] And the situation in the budget office had grown so chaotic that it was difficult to know what the city's real fiscal needs were, or just how much it was relying on debt to make ends meet.

Beame seemed aware that the city's enormous debt might make it difficult to borrow more. In the spring of 1974 New York embarked upon an explicit advertising campaign for its bonds, the first in its history. It produced an elegant booklet on "Ten Good Reasons for Investing in the Tax-Exempt Bonds of the City of New York," which Chase Manhattan Bank then circulated to interested customers. The pamphlet made special mention of Beame's fiscal prudence, and pointed out that "during its entire history, since before the Revolutionary War, New York City has paid bond principal and interest without a single default."[50] Despite these assurances, though, interest rates for the city were rising, a sign that investors were starting to view New York as a riskier bet.[51]

What did Beame and his associates think they were doing? They probably believed that the city's situation was bound to change before too much longer, and that the city would be able to win more aid from the federal government. Beame was already meeting with Congressman Wilbur Mills, chairman of the House Ways and Means Committee, to talk about it. The mayor argued that the city paid Washington far more in income taxes than it received in support from the federal government (he quoted figures of $14.5 billion versus $2 billion).[52] Surely New York would be able to lay claim to more money if the situation grew serious enough. And in the meantime, the city could always keep borrowing.

There seemed to be no other choice. As Melvin Lechner, Beame's budget director, wrote in one memo to the mayor in September 1974, every solution to the fiscal problems of the city would only cause new problems. Higher taxes would drive people out; layoffs would add to unemployment; cutting services was politically impossible. The conclusion seemed to be that it was better to do nothing at all and hope that the creditors would not do anything either.[53] The major banks that had long handled the financing of New York were still happy to sell the city's notes and bonds to the rest of the country. As long as they were doing that, there was no reason to be too concerned. After all, the city was still the largest in the country, the home of Wall Street, a center of cultural and economic might. How could its government be nearly broke?

This position was plausible enough as long as everyone played along. But in 1974—as old orders globally continued to collapse—nothing seemed sacrosanct any longer, including the standing of New York City. In the middle of the summer, Fitch Investors Service, a bond-rating agency, downgraded the city's debt from A to BB (medium grade) for debt maturing before 1980 and to BBB (fair) for debt maturing thereafter. "It is true that the City has never defaulted on timely payment of debt service when due," the report read. "It is also true that the City has never faced the financial problems with which it is now confronted."[54] The neighborhood bookkeeper soon would find that he no longer knew the buck.

4. Sounding the Alarm

As spring turned to summer in Beame's first year in office, his decision to borrow began to face sharp criticism within the city government. The loudest critic was the city's comptroller, a fiercely ambitious thirty-seven-year-old named Harrison Jay Goldin. Goldin, a native of the Bronx, had little in common with Beame. He had not worked his way up through the city machines, instead attending elite schools—Princeton for college, Yale for law school—followed by a stint in the Justice Department under Robert F. Kennedy. Conflict between mayors and comptrollers is more or less inevitable, as the job of the comptroller is to monitor the city's spending. Beame himself, as comptroller, had been a thorn in the side of mayors Wagner and Lindsay. But the tension between Goldin and Beame was far more intense. Beame was certain that the younger man with the fancy degrees was determined to replace him in City Hall, and was on a campaign to do whatever he could to humiliate the mayor. Every warning from Goldin seemed a challenge to Beame's integrity, his competence, and his very right to occupy office.

Beame's anxieties seemed to be confirmed when Goldin, acting on a campaign pledge, hired three accounting firms to do independent audits of the city's finances. The reports came out in July. What they revealed was a level of chaos that ran entirely counter to Beame's public image of rectitude and stability. It turned out that the comptroller's office—Beame's former bailiwick—was swamped in paper, caught between a computerized system and back-of-the-envelope calculations. There were various discrepancies between the city's books and the funds that it actually had in the bank. And security was practically nonexistent. Rubber stamps bearing the signature of the comptroller lay around, easy to steal; one auditor swiped a stamp just to prove the point. Unnumbered checks sat in unlocked bureau drawers. Bearer bonds, essentially cash equivalents, were stacked in vaults that were left unguarded. One Monday in early August, Lower Manhattan was transfixed by the sight of thirteen red Wells Fargo trucks in a row, driving the bonds to a bank where they could be kept safely. (Goldin had passed a sleepless weekend before the move, wondering if there would be a heist on his watch: the problem with the bond storage had been reported in the newspapers, and he feared that thieves would see it as an invitation to steal.)[1]

Nothing could have made Beame angrier than these public revelations about the disorganization in the comptroller's office. It was all the worse because when the newspapers first reported the audits, Beame had been confined to his sickbed on doctor's orders with a bout of summer bronchitis—hardly a position of strength. When he finally emerged, pale and wheezing, to respond to Goldin's allegations, he spared no words in denouncing the "shabby" tactics of his young comptroller: "I will let no one assail my ability or my credibility by manipulating the falling chips to create a distorted picture of the events."[2]

As for Goldin, he had no interest in keeping quiet, no desire to maintain the city's discreet traditions. Later on, he would suggest that Beame always blamed the city's unraveling on him—the up-and-comer who was driven by ambition, who simply did not know to leave well enough alone. But the truth was that Goldin himself was growing panicked because of what he was hearing from some of the young men he had hired as consultants—especially Steve Clifford.

Steve Clifford was not the kind of person one might have expected to be advising the city government. Although he had impeccable educational credentials (including a degree from Harvard Business School) and had worked for the finance department during the Lindsay years, in the early 1970s he had retreated from regular work, dropping out and becoming a hippie. For a while, his major focus was making Plexiglas furniture with an artist friend. He wasn't exactly a political ideologue, or even very involved in political circles, but the young people in his milieu simply took the corruption of the establishment as a matter of faith. He grew his hair long and wore dashikis and blue jeans every day, whatever the weather.[3]

He still did some government consulting, though, to pay the bills. One 1973 job he took on for the Commission on Charter Reform involved writing a report on the function and purpose of the comptroller's office in New York City politics. Clifford concluded that the comptroller's job was hopelessly conflicted and outmoded. The problem was that it was a political job held by an elected official, which forced the comptroller to pander for votes instead of acting as the voice of financial responsibility. "What is the comptroller's primary role?" Clifford asked. "Accountant? Auditor? Budget maker? Budget administrator? Financial manager? Judge? Policy maker? Ultimately, as an elected official, he is primarily the politician, concerned with preserving and expanding his political power base, serving a city-wide constituency, getting reelected or running for a higher office." In the report, Clifford described the many ways a comptroller could put a good spin on the financial situation: moving operating expenses to the capital budgets, lowering the estimates for welfare caseloads, exaggerating the city's revenues. And such maneuvers could lead (and were in fact leading) to permanent problems: once the city hired employees, their jobs were protected by union contracts and public sentiment that made them hard to eliminate, even if the city's revenues could not actually cover those salaries.[4]

Despite this critique of the very role of the comptroller, Clifford got a job in Goldin's office to study and manage the city's cash flow operations and set up a cash management system. Soon, Clifford was a fixture at meetings under Goldin: they wouldn't start until he showed up in his dashiki, a cigarette hanging from his lips. "Where's your hippie?" Beame would ask if Clifford was running late.[5]

Clifford shared a cubbyhole of an office with Jonathan Weiner, another young man in his early thirties, who served as a special adviser to the controller. Weiner had served in the Lindsay administration, and loved the idea that urban government could craft innovative social policies addressing the problems of structural racism and inequality. But like Clifford, he was concerned about the finances of the city, especially the staggering rise in the amount of short-term debt. In May 1974, after Beame had announced his budget proposal, Weiner wrote a memo to Goldin criticizing the "outrageous gimmickry" that appeared to be part of the Beame plan and urging Goldin to "responsibly dissociate" himself from Beame's use of various "one-shot items" and "phony savings and revenues" to balance the budget. "Beame is storing up a lot of trouble for himself," Weiner noted. "What in fact will be done next year? Borrow again?"[6] Later in the year, Weiner wrote another memo, arguing that the city was borrowing so heavily that it would soon have to sharply raise real estate taxes, creating the specter of "a vicious spiral of higher tax rates chasing a diminishing tax base."[7]

Weiner and Clifford talked endlessly about the city's difficulties, almost scoffing at the errors of the Beame administration. The underlying problem was clear enough: the city was failing to generate the money it needed to cover its expenses and was borrowing to sustain itself. But what Clifford and Weiner focused on was less how the city had gotten itself into trouble than the variety of mechanisms it was using to cover up its situation. They noted, for example, that once the city submitted a bill to the federal or state government (such as for Medicaid), it would mark the entire billed amount as revenue, as though the money had already arrived. There was no procedure for correcting the accounts later.[8] Should Washington decline to give the city the full amount, the city would not recognize the difference as a loss—instead, it left the missing money on the books as though it would eventually arrive.[9] Clifford and Weiner also observed that the city was issuing tax-anticipation notes backed by property taxes it might never be able to collect because of rising property tax delinquencies and landlord abandonment. And they pointed out all the garden-variety budget tricks the city used to disguise its financial condition, such as pushing end-of-year expenses to the following financial year. All in all, New York was constantly over-estimating its revenues and underestimating its obligations.

In October 1974, Clifford wrote a memo to Goldin laying out all the problematic practices he and Weiner had discussed. "These practices produce a supposedly balanced budget, at least at the start of the year. Unfortunately, they do not generate any cash," he wrote. "By allowing the City to increase expenses without an immediate increase in taxa-tion, these practices encourage the City to over-commit itself and dis-regard the future consequences." The rationale for the budget gimmicks was that they would get the city through another year, and then a more sympathetic governor, president, or Congress would "bail us out." But it seemed unlikely to Clifford that congressional representatives would increase taxes in order to cover the salaries of city firemen who were actually earning more than their constituents. "I see no alternative to the City's fiscal problem other than a painful recognition that we are seriously over committed, and furthermore, that postponing the day of reckoning through unsound accounting and budgeting will only aggra-vate the problem."[10]

Clifford was hardly an ideal messenger: to most, he seemed a thirty-three-year-old kid with shaggy hair and an irreverent attitude. His memos dripped with sarcasm and contempt for the people in the city's administration—particularly Mayor Beame—who, as far as Clifford was concerned, had led the city into the quagmire, most of the time without even really realizing that they were doing so. The problem, he believed, was not really malfeasance but incompetence; the city's lead-ers were not lying to other people as much as they were lying to them-selves. But Goldin found it impossible to ignore what Clifford and Weiner were saying. After all, he had suddenly found himself in the unenviable position of being legally responsible for the accounts of a city that, far from being the most powerful and prosperous one in America, seemed to be borrowing immense amounts of money that it had no way of ever paying off. By the end of the year, Goldin asked Weiner to pre-pare a memorandum on New York City's brush with bankruptcy dur-ing the Great Depression.[11]

Meanwhile, Clifford began to talk to his friends in other parts of the city government, warning them about the city's problems.[12] To him, the financial practices of the city seemed sufficiently troubling that it was necessary to sound the alarm about what was going on. Otherwise, the comptroller would eventually be held responsible. The idea that releasing and publicizing the fiscal problems of the city could itself lead to a fiscal crisis did not seem to bother to him—rather, the core issue was that the city was refusing to face fiscal reality.

At the end of November he took his campaign still further, writing a memo addressed to an old friend from his days at the Commission on Charter Reform, liberal Republican State Senator Roy Goodman. It was titled, simply, "The Fiscal Crisis." Clifford detailed the city's deficit, and argued that it would be worse still the following year. Even if the city sharply raised real estate taxes, it would again confront a budget gap of more than a billion dollars. Clifford gave examples of the extreme measures that the city would have to undertake to bring the budget into order: eliminating the police force while also doubling the personal income tax rate, or closing the school system while also raising corporate income taxes. Given the impossibility (and the undesirability) of such options, the city would more likely resort to more gimmicks and more borrowing, until the "day of reckoning" arrived when bankers would "refuse to finance city short term debt unless they also appoint the Budget Director and Deputy Comptroller."

The lesson, Clifford concluded, was clear: "The city is fucked."[13]

What was so frightening about the situation the city faced? What was the worst that could happen?

The scenario feared by Clifford, Goldin, and Weiner was that New York might have to default on its debt (in other words, stop making debt payments when they came due) and perhaps declare bankruptcy. Over the months ahead, the specters of default and bankruptcy would haunt city discussions, used to justify all kinds of choices and actions that otherwise would have seemed out of the question. But although "bankruptcy" colloquially connotes being completely wiped out, in a legal sense bankruptcy simply gives a debtor time and space to create a plan for paying back some portion of a debt that he or she otherwise could not repay at all. Often, bankruptcy just involves exchanging short-term debt for debt that can be paid back over a longer time period. Why, then, was the prospect of New York's bankruptcy so alarming to so many people—something that had to be avoided at all costs, no matter what it meant for the city?

For Beame and other city officials, default and bankruptcy represented the ultimate embarrassment, a blow to their power and New York's prestige. First, there was a tremendous amount of uncertainty about how exactly a bankruptcy would proceed. The federal laws governing bankruptcy for cities had been devised with municipalities far smaller than New York in mind, and they were hardly adequate to cope with the problems of a giant metropolis. Then, should the legal situation somehow be worked out and the city be able to go into bankruptcy court, the elected officials of New York would have to turn their power over to a judge, who would make the final decisions about cutting services and costs and renegotiating contracts. How the city would run while its affairs were sorted out and its finances restructured was anyone's guess. Moreover, a bankruptcy could result in the city being unable to borrow any more money for years, constraining its budget even further and making it impossible to fund long-term infrastructure projects during that time. Beame and the other officials had no desire to relinquish their authority to judges and creditors, and to be known forevermore as the politicians who had allowed New York to collapse.

Various interest groups within the city also had their own reasons to be afraid of bankruptcy. For the banks that had long marketed the city's debt, and for the investors who owned it, default and bankruptcy meant the potential for large financial losses. Even though the city had a legal obligation to repay its debts, in bankruptcy this would be balanced against its need to continue to provide basic public services. Unlike a bankrupt company, which can be liquidated and have its assets sold to repay its debts, a bankrupt city would continue to exist, and in bankruptcy proceedings its responsibilities to the citizenry might be judged more important than its obligations to creditors. For the city's unions, meanwhile, bankruptcy would mean the certainty of salary cuts or job losses—to be determined by a judge and not by elected officials. It also meant that the contracts the unions had negotiated with the city might be deemed void, regarded as having a lower priority than the city's obligations to the people who had bought its bonds. Moreover, as the crisis unfolded, the unions themselves had begun to purchase hundreds of millions of dollars of the city's debt with their members' pension funds, giving the labor movement its own financial interest in keeping the city solvent.

Finally, New York City's bankruptcy would pose a range of problems for the country as a whole. It was clear that a bankruptcy of this magnitude and of a city of New York's importance would not simply be a local issue. Some people worried that the city's collapse would hurt those national banks that had invested heavily in city bonds and thus might destabilize the country's financial system, which was already reeling from the recession. No one knew exactly which banks were heavily exposed or how widespread the impact of a reduction in the value of the city's bonds was likely to be. A default by New York would also have an impact on credit markets around the country, making it far more difficult for other cities and states to borrow even in routine ways, since it would make investors wary about public debt more generally. Perhaps most of all, the financial collapse of New York would be the ultimate symbol of American economic decline, a demonstration to the whole world that the United States was no longer the preeminent nation it had been over the postwar years.

Over time, the fear of bankruptcy took on a life of its own. The idea that the city might actually use a bankruptcy to work out a deal to preserve services never had any real purchase in city politics. And there was no way for New Yorkers to weigh in on whether the sacrifices that they would be asked to make to avoid bankruptcy were worthwhile. On the contrary, it was assumed from the outset that bankruptcy was not a viable alternative, that anything would be preferable, and that the city should make any arrangement necessary in order to prevent default. That sense of desperation enabled a small group of people at the top of the city to win the power to make those choices. And ultimately, that group came to consist largely of people who had not been elected at all, and whose interests were very different from those of the New Yorkers who would be most affected by the cuts.

As the fall of 1974 wore on, the anxieties at the comptroller's office were beginning to spread through the rest of the city, most of all into the financial community. Interest rates for the city's new debts were climbing rapidly. At the beginning of November, the *New York Times* ran an editorial warning that "this city is sliding into bankruptcy with alarming speed."[14] At the end of November, after getting his memo from Steve Clifford, State Senator Roy Goodman held a press conference on the city's budget deficit, though he said nothing about his source in the comptroller's office. "The city is a sick patient with a rapidly spreading form of financial cancer," Goodman told the newspapers. "The City must perform radical surgery now and the State and Federal governments must provide massive monetary blood transfusions to restore sound fiscal condition."[15]

Faced with these warnings of metastasizing debt, Beame did something that none of his predecessors had been willing to countenance: he proposed budget cuts and layoffs of city workers. (Behind the scenes, the mayor also asked the unions' pension funds to purchase increased amounts of city bonds for their portfolios—which would, he said, provide the city with a badly needed infusion of cash while also demonstrating the "confidence" the unions held in its fiscal condition.)[16] In late November, Beame announced the largest city layoffs since the Great Depression, saying he would dismiss 1,000 "provisional" employees—ones who had not yet taken the civil service exams—and 510 members of the civil service.[17] Only a few weeks later he reported that the layoffs would total 3,725 city workers, including 400 police officers and 150 firefighters. His reluctance was evident from the outset. "I don't like to do this," he said in his December press conference in the Blue Room in City Hall, his soft voice quavering as he fought back tears. "I'd be the last one in the world to do this. I came up through the civil service. I know what it's like to get a job you worked for, you came up for. I don't want to hurt anybody."[18]

Even before the cuts were officially announced, people began to hold protests in the plaza in front of City Hall. Schoolchildren and parents pushing baby carriages came to demonstrate against plans to close fire stations near their schools. ("Keep our firemen here so we don't disappear," read one slogan on a sign carried by children from Our Lady Queen of Angels School in East Harlem.) The firefighters' union president denounced the planned cuts as "complete insanity" from the standpoint of public health.[19] "CAN YOU PLEASE HELP? Mayor Beame has put our lives in jeopardy," wrote one Bronx woman to her state senator, objecting to "reckless" cuts to the fire department.[20]

Other proposed budget cuts also aroused anger. The $18.9 million in cuts planned for the municipal university system brought out two thousand protesters—students and faculty from the various campuses. They ringed City Hall, blocking traffic and demonstrating under the bare trees in the park. "We want a whole education," read one sign.[21] Over the next months, Beame's mailbox would fill with angry complaints from city residents. One businessman warned that "without sufficient police protection this city will become a jungle."[22] Another correspondent predicted that anyone with the resources to flee New York would do so, leaving the city destitute. "Someday not too far off in the future, someone will make a study on how NEW YORK CITY became a GHOST CITY. He will find that it became that way because the Middle Class residents that lived there had been chased away . . . by having to pay taxes, and little by little being deprived of all public services."[23]

Beame himself felt it was a tragedy to lay off so many civil servants. Their salaries were modest; their only real reward was job security. Still, he offered no political defense of the local welfare state—no set of arguments about why it mattered, how it preserved economic mobility in the city, why it might be important as New York struggled with the transition to a service economy. All he had was a deep nostalgia for the city he had grown up in, rich with public services, and a sense of personal identification with the people who had worked for the city throughout their lives. That would prove a flimsy basis for defending a social order that seemed increasingly under siege.

———

New York State's government also did not favor the city politically, though it had formerly been committed to supporting its borrowing regime. Indeed, Republican governor Nelson Rockefeller, during his fourteen years in Albany, had presided over a massive expansion of public debt at the state level, mirroring the debt binge taking place in the city. But despite Rockefeller's image as a liberal Republican, his politics had in fact moved to the right in his last term. This went beyond his signing into law stringent minimum sentences for people convicted of drug-related crimes, beyond his decision to send in National Guardsmen to retake Attica Correctional Facility after a 1971 prisoner uprising there. Rockefeller's economic politics were also becoming more conservative, as he grew ever more concerned about the "business climate" of New York State, and worried that its higher levels of taxes were a factor in driving industry out altogether.[24]

In December 1973, Rockefeller resigned as governor to explore a run for the presidency, leaving New York State in the hands of his lieutenant governor, Malcolm Wilson. Rockefeller became Gerald Ford's vice president in 1974, and that November, the state elected a new leader: Democrat Hugh Carey, an Irish Catholic who had spent seven terms in the House of Representatives for a white working-class Brooklyn district that stretched from his native Park Slope to Bay Ridge.[25] Carey's election was a surprise. Not only had New York State voted Republican for years, but the new governor's personality was hardly that of an outgoing politician: he was moody, enigmatic, brooding, and unpredictable, given to occasional flights of paranoia and holding grudges. Still, the fall of 1974 was a good time to be a Democrat. Once Carey captured the hard-fought Democratic primary, he was able to ride the wave of post-Watergate hostility to Republicans, beating Wilson with 57 percent of the vote. The victory immediately catapulted Carey to the forefront of the national Democratic party, fueling rumors that he might be a good vice-presidential candidate in 1976, or even perhaps a presidential prospect.

The *New York Times* described Carey as an old-fashioned liberal, whose "bread-and-butter, New Deal, pro-labor liberalism" resembled that of John F. Kennedy, Hubert Humphrey, and Robert Wagner. "He is more likely to be concerned about the minimum wage and revenue sharing than amnesty or abortion," the paper opined. "On fiscal matters, he obviously leans to the traditional Democratic tax philosophy of soak the rich and big business."[26] But as would soon become obvious, Carey was eager to break from the past.

Nineteen seventy-five did not begin auspiciously in New York City. On January 4, the *New York Times* reported that the rat population of Central Park was exploding ("hundreds of large grayish-brown rats scramble every day through the fallen leaves of Central Park"), even as half the staff of the Pest Control Division of the Parks Department had been laid off.[27] At the end of the month, a bomb exploded at Fraunces Tavern near the South Street Seaport, killing four people who were there for lunch; the Fuerzas Armadas de Liberación, a Puerto Rican national-ist organization, took credit for the attack, proclaiming it a retaliation for a bombing in Puerto Rico earlier in the month.[28]

Governor Carey's January State of the State address did little to lift the mood in the city. Carey made it clear there would not be much aid or comfort coming from the state. "Sudden storms have swept across our economy and all of American life, shattering our hopes and our illusions of comfort," he told the legislature. Only days before, three of Nixon's close associates had been convicted of crimes related to Water-gate, but Carey suggested that the nation's difficulties went beyond the scandal in Washington: the United States was mired in serious eco-nomic problems, and these were especially severe in New York, where business activity had been declining for five straight years. The state government had to adjust to these new conditions, and it had to do so immediately.

In the old days, Carey said, "What we did was limited only by our imagination and our desire. Our buildings were the tallest and most sumptuous. Our civil service the most highly trained and paid. Our public assistance programs the most expensive." Once, the state budget had seemed a "never-ending horn of plenty." But given the deepening economic problems of the state, those days were over. The future held austerity, "deep and painful cuts" that would affect millions of people. "I did not become Governor of this state to preside over the dismantling of its government or of all the programs to help those in need," Carey proclaimed. "But a government without self-control can do nothing and help no one."[29]

The same stern phrases might have been applied to the city government as well. And for the bankers who had helped issue New York City's loans, they must have felt both like a warning—the state would no longer bail out the city—and an invitation to demand changes that had previously been off the table.

Like Wagner and Lindsay, Beame had tried to borrow to cover the budget gap. He had wanted to believe that the city's money difficulties were merely ones of cash flow, of late payments from the state and the federal government, not the manifestation of deeper dilemmas. Borrowing was a familiar solution to an old problem. But Beame had the bad luck of turning to the municipal bond markets just as the rules of city finance were changing. Suddenly, the banks that had facilitated the great expansion of debt no longer wanted to play along.

5. Things Fall Apart

Few events in New York City's government life were more ritualized than the collection of bids for the privilege of underwriting—that is, marketing to the investing public—the city's notes and bonds, its short-term and long-term IOUs. Every month or so the comptroller held a meeting in a conference room on the fifth floor of the imposing gray Municipal Building across the street from City Hall, three floors up from the chapel where over ten thousand people got married each year.

Present at the meeting would be representatives of the city's major banks, which also happened to be the largest banks in the country: First National City Bank, Chase Manhattan Bank, Chemical Bank, Morgan Guaranty, Manufacturers Hanover, Merrill Lynch, and Bankers Trust. Individual banks would usually not buy the debt alone but join into syndicates, with each group combing through the *Daily Bond Buyer* and talking to potential investors to gauge the market. They would meet to discuss what price they would pay for the debt up front, how much each bank would underwrite, and what interest rate the city would need to guarantee in order to make the debt attractive to enough investors. The banks made their money by reselling the debt instruments for more than they'd paid for them, so their profit margins were highly dependent on judging the market correctly.[1]

One by one, a banker from each syndicate would drop a sealed envelope containing a secret bid into a small, weathered box made out of green tin. The comptroller would open the envelopes, disappear briefly into his private office to calculate which offer would give the city the best deal, and re-emerge to announce the winner. The banks that had bought the city's bonds and notes would then get to work, selling them off to smaller banks and to the public.

The meetings had a cheerful, clubby atmosphere. In ordinary times, the municipal bond department was hardly the flashiest part of a bank. Usually the men involved in the day-to-day dealings of municipal finance were lower-level people, mostly in their thirties or forties, up-and-comers but nowhere near the highest-ranking executives. Their business was tidy and lucrative; the interest income earned on the debt was tax-free at the federal level (and often at the state and local levels as well), and it was easy to find customers for the bonds. There was even a pleasant feeling of civic responsibility and boosterism involved in financing a major city like New York. Some years later, one of the men in charge of the muni desk at Chemical Bank observed that the business wasn't driven strictly by "the profit motive." People and banks purchased city bonds out of a sense of social purpose, the feeling that they were helping finance bridges, roads, schools, libraries. "They thought they were fulfilling a valid social role in supporting this big, dynamic, important city."[2]

Municipal bonds were a growing industry throughout the postwar years. As government at all levels expanded, so did its financing needs, and there was a community of bankers eager to promote public debt. Well into the early 1970s, New York City banks aggressively encouraged investors to purchase the bonds the city issued. They marketed them across the country, offering the city their endorsement. No one kept a complete list of the individuals and institutions that held city debt, but the underwriting banks' biggest customers were probably other banks and large institutional investors.[3] Individual investors bought their share of bonds as well; many of them were not especially sophisticated about finance, and bought New York City bonds because the debt of the biggest city in the country seemed reasonably safe.[4] And the under-writing banks also held on to some notes for their own portfolios. Like the other investors, they found the city's debt appealing because of its tax advantages and because New York City seemed eminently secure. By 1975, the banks that participated in underwriting New York's debts, known as clearing house banks, held debt worth more than $1 billion, which gave them a deep financial interest in the health of the city.[5]

The banks were aided in their work by the major bond rating agen-cies, Moody's and Standard & Poor's, which endorsed the city's notes and bonds with an A rating (a few steps below the top grade of AAA, but still denoting high confidence that the debts would be repaid). The banks were helped, too, by the lawyers, known as "bond counsel," who looked over the information provided by the city and approved all of the sales. None of the warning signs—the role of borrowed funds in the budget, the use of various gimmicks to make the numbers come out, the uncertainty about how much money would come from the state and federal governments—seemed to raise a red flag for the ratings agencies, the bond counsel, or the bankers.

But by the midseventies, the situation changed. The financial sector, which had been governed by fairly tight federal regulations through-out the postwar years, was opening up to a wide range of new kinds of investments, both domestically and internationally. Real estate invest-ment trusts and new financial instruments targeting small investors— these tantalized the banks and made them call their old habits into question.[6] Banks were increasingly looking around the world for new outlets: First National City Bank, for example, expanded its overseas business (including loans to foreign governments) from $6 billion in 1970 to $28.7 billion only four years later. Countries with oil, reaping a windfall from the oil embargo, put their new riches into these global banks, which then made loans to developing nations running large deficits because of the energy price spike.[7]

These new opportunities made it less appealing for banks to bother with municipal bonds. Nationally, the proportion of municipal debt held by banks had risen from one-quarter in 1960 to almost half in 1970;

over the 1970s, though, it fell to 37 percent.[8] One of the main selling points for city debt had long been that it generated tax-free interest, but the banks' international income lessened that tax advantage. When First National City Bank, for example, earned money from foreign sources, it paid taxes on that income elsewhere, and could then deduct those foreign taxes from its domestic earnings.[9] Over at the comptroller's office, Jonathan Weiner was especially concerned about the banks' declining interest in city bonds. "Our major banks are now finding it unprofitable to carry, both for trading and holding purposes, tax-exempt debt," Weiner wrote in one memo. "I think this is a structural and long-term difficulty—the banks are finding a variety of very profitable loans and leases which are providing immense tax shelters and are thus eliminating the value in holding our debt." The implications seemed clear: what if the banks no longer wanted to make loans to the city?[10]

The troubled state of financial markets of all sorts added to the anxiety. In the late 1960s, the stock market had reached its highest peaks since 1929—but in the 1970s, stocks entered a slump so severe that by the end of the decade *Business Week* would famously warn of the "death of equities." Likewise, real estate investment trusts, which bundled properties together and then sold shares to investors, briefly seemed a hot ticket in the early 1970s but plummeted in value with the onset of recession in 1973.[11] And while the 1960s had seen companies consolidating in a seemingly endless set of mergers and acquisitions, by the early 1970s this movement began to falter, and management consultants started to advise that the megalithic firms be broken up. In retrospect, the expansion of New York City debt seems of a piece with the broader economic patterns of the late 1960s and early 1970s: a turn to finance and speculation during the "go-go years" at the end of the long postwar boom, followed by a contraction when this bubble popped.

As the recession of the 1970s deepened, the bankers began to hold their intense involvement with New York City up for scrutiny. Although municipal debt is often viewed as a conservative investment, was New York really the blue chip it had once been assumed to be? And was it still worth it to hold and market so much of the city's debt? By the end of 1974, the major banks were starting to sell off their municipal debt.

In the last quarter of the year alone, they cut their holdings of tax-exempt and municipal debt by more than 7 percent.[12]

But the very moment when banks were turning away from the municipal market was when city and state governments all across the country were seeking to borrow more.[13] And in New York City, this contradiction would be particularly acute.

As New York's problems became harder and harder to ignore, banks ceased to regard the municipal desk as a minor part of their operations. Instead, the deepening crisis pulled in the most powerful figures in the banking world.

The men in charge of the city's largest banks had long pondered what role business in general, and banks in particular, should have in politics. Years before the fiscal crisis began, David Rockefeller, the president of Chase Manhattan Bank—and brother to Nelson, the governor of New York State—had advocated for bankers and business leaders to become political activists. In 1958, he had helped to found the Downtown Lower Manhattan Association to "speak on behalf of the downtown financial community," as he later put it in his memoirs.[14] The DLMA pressed for the construction of Battery Park City and the World Trade Center, major development projects that helped to shift the economic geography of Lower Manhattan away from the port and toward finance and real estate.[15] In the late 1960s, shaken by the critique of corporate America advanced by the New Left, Rockefeller took his ideas further. He embraced the ideal of corporate social responsibility, arguing that business should help determine the "form and content of the new social contract," as he put it in a *New York Times* op-ed piece.[16] Rejecting the idea that government had to play the central role in rebuilding inner cities, he argued that "the basic task of urban rehabilitation is one for private enterprise." He urged banks to pool their money and invest in literally creating one hundred "new cities" across the country, so that people living in the overcrowded urban cores could move out.[17]

The major rival of Chase Manhattan in the city was First National City Bank, headed by Walter Wriston. (It would change its name to

Citibank in 1976.) Wriston hated the notion of "social responsibility," considering it a capitulation to liberals and New Leftists who were unlikely to ever place their trust in corporations. Still, like Rockefeller, he believed that business—and banks in particular—needed to play a stronger role in politics to protect their interests. Wriston was an early member of the Business Roundtable, an organization of Fortune 500 CEOs formed in the 1970s to augment the power of business in politics. He liked to cite conservative economic thinker Ludwig von Mises in his speeches, and his letters to government officials contained flights into abstract political theory.[18] In one note to Nixon, for example, he encouraged the president to end a wage and price control program that had been instituted to try to curb inflation, not so much because it would not work but because it was akin to enslavement: "The control of wages and prices, if carried to its logical conclusion, will lead to control over all income and all resources. . . . It is time to end the control program before our freedoms are eroded beyond repair."[19]

By the end of 1974, the whispers that New York might soon be on the edge of insolvency began to preoccupy Wriston, Rockefeller, and their counterparts at other banks. After all, if the city wound up in bankruptcy court, a judge would weigh the legal documents that gave creditors first lien on the city's resources against the other needs of the city, such as paying the police and firemen and teachers. As the man in charge of municipals at Chemical Bank wrote in one memo to the chairman of his bank, he was far from certain that the city would prioritize repaying its creditors if "a choice has to be made between meeting debt service and, say, the public payroll."[20] If the public payroll were to be deemed more important, the banks stood to lose a lot of money.

For Rockefeller and Wriston, there were larger issues at stake as well. The problems of New York went to the heart of questions about the city's government. Did its responsibility lie in providing extensive social services and guaranteeing a set of social rights to all? Or should its main commitment be to make the city an attractive place for businesses and corporations by lowering taxes, relaxing regulations, and fostering economic development?

As 1974 drew to a close, the banks were more persuaded than ever that the time had come to force New York to change. The men who handled the city's debt began to act with a passion almost rivaling that of the protesters who marched outside City Hall, demanding that the city keep firehouses open and colleges free. What the bankers wanted was the opposite: for the city to slash its public sector. As one junior banker at Morgan Guaranty wrote in a memo to his superiors, the bankers had to stop offering New York their "compassionate understanding." They had to insist that the city make cuts and layoffs on a scale never before contemplated—regardless of the "heat that will result." The time to play nice had passed. The mayor and the comptroller "now need some straight talk from us as bankers."[21]

Giving that straight talk, though, was not so easy. Mayor Beame had a very different understanding of the role of the banks in the city. From his perspective, it was their job to represent New York to the financial community of the nation and to help the city sell its debt—not to question the city's priorities.

On December 17, 1974, a small group of men met at Gracie Mansion to talk to the mayor about what was happening to New York. The group included the key members of the "Jersey Mafia" (so dubbed because they all resided in the suburbs of northern New Jersey and commuted into New York), the midlevel executives who specialized in city debt: Thomas LaBrecque of Chase Manhattan, Richard Kezer of First National City Bank, Franklin Smeal of Morgan Guaranty, as well as representatives from Merrill Lynch and Salomon Brothers.[22] Comptroller Goldin was there, and so was Steve Clifford.

At this point, New York City's total debt was $10 billion. But the real problem was less the total amount than the fact that about $5 billion of this was short-term debt. As those short-term loans came due, the city would roll them over—essentially, renew them by taking out new loans to repay the holders of the maturing ones. But this meant borrowing heavily each month just to take care of existing debts.[23] And the interest rates the city had to pay kept on climbing, so that each new round of debt became more expensive to repay. In the late

1960s, the rate had been around 4 percent, but by the end of 1974 it was 8 percent—a difference that translated into millions of dollars more in interest payments each year. (In a vicious cycle, those higher interest rates made the city's debt all the more risky, by saddling New York with higher bills that it had no way to pay aside from yet more borrowing.)

The news the bankers had to deliver to the mayor was not good. The Merrill Lynch executive told Beame that the markets had been a total "disaster" over the past weeks, and that it was not at all clear that any banks would bid to handle the city's debt in January. He reported that out-of-state banks and institutional investors had practically stopped buying New York's debt. The other bankers chimed in, warning that the city had to reestablish its "credibility" with investors and demonstrate that it had the situation under control. The city simply had to stop borrowing so much, so quickly, and Beame had to make it clear that he was serious about balancing the budget.

The mayor responded that "in the real world," all government budgets had to increase every year. New York was no exception. Borrowing, therefore, would have to keep rising too. The banks, he felt, had an obligation to market the city to investors—they should not just "sit by and tell the city to reform." Their support could buttress the city and ultimately help it regain the loyalty of banks in other parts of the country.

The meeting devolved into a testy back-and-forth, as the bankers warned Beame that the city could not operate indefinitely on borrowed money. A city was not a national government that could run deficits with impunity. The mayor was not taking the situation seriously enough: "The whole system could come tumbling down." Beame, for his part, said that he would do all he could to reassure investors, but that it was the job of the banks to stop talking about the city's problems to the press and to do all they could to keep moving the city's notes and bonds.[24]

The bankers wanted Beame to promise cuts that would reassure the market. He wanted them to offer that reassurance themselves. They looked at him and saw a man who failed to understand the city's responsibility to its banks and bondholders. He looked at them and saw a group of men who had the money and power to help New York but who stubbornly refused to do so.

The next time Mayor Beame met with the banks, he tried to bypass the so-called Jersey Mafia and go straight to the top. He called the bank presidents and CEOs to an 8:00 a.m. meeting at Gracie Mansion on a Thursday in mid-January. This time it was the mayor who was exasperated.

Earlier in the week the city had tried to sell $625 million in revenue-anticipation notes. The bankers had responded that they would only be able to sell the notes if the city agreed to interest charges over 9 percent—one of the highest rates in the city's history, and one that would only augment the debt service bill that was quickly overwhelming the budget.

Beame blamed the bankers for the high interest rates. He insisted that the banks had resources and power and money, and should use them—indeed, he repeated once more, they had an *obligation* to use them—to "sell" the city to investors around the country, persuading them to buy city debt. They should act as "good will ambassadors" for New York. Instead, with their talk of deficits and budget gimmickry, they were tarnishing its good name, "bad-mouthing" it in its moment of greatest need.

The purpose of the meeting was to set up a new Financial Community Liaison Group. Beame hoped that if he shared information about the city government with the bankers, they might be more willing to publicize the safety of the city's debt. Ellmore Patterson, of Morgan Guaranty, accepted the invitation to head the group. It seemed like a good sign.[25]

But within a few weeks, Beame was furious again. "I refuse to believe that the financial community of New York City cannot make tax-exempt City obligations attractive to investors," he wrote in a letter to Patterson. That investors were leery of buying city notes was proof of the duplicity of the bankers and brokers, who were warning the public away from New York with their rumors of bad debt and unsustainable expense.

The "peddlers of this nonsense" were "malicious," engaging in "sabotage and disloyalty." Such rumors could sweep "like a prairie fire" through an impressionable, anxious investing class. It was the job—even the moral task—of Patterson and the city's banks to do the "selling job" the city needed, to turn right side up the "topsy-turvy" situation in which the greatest metropolis in the nation could not attract buyers for its debt.[26]

Beame probably did not know that over at the comptroller's office, Steve Clifford had prepared a set of notes for the comptroller and his representatives to use when talking to "influentials"—a group that presumably included the city's bankers. In his notes, Clifford warned that the market for the city's debt might be about to "collapse precipitously"; that the city needed to shed no less than a billion dollars in expenses (which might include closing CUNY, shutting down the public hospitals, and cutting off contributions to welfare); and that the financial community should be prepared for a variety of outcomes, including the suspension of payment on debt.[27]

If anyone was passing even a little bit of this on to the bankers, it was small wonder they were not calmed.

Perhaps the city's situation really might have stabilized were it not for the default of Nelson Rockefeller's Urban Development Corporation, a New York State agency that built low- and middle-income housing using a strange new way of financing government investment.

As governor, Rockefeller was fascinated by developing what he termed the "imaginative use of credit."[28] The New York State constitution mandated that voters approve all new bond issues, and in 1960 voters turned down several Rockefeller-backed proposals. Rather than back down from his building plans for the state, the governor turned to a new device: the "moral obligation" bond. Such a bond did not represent a legally binding claim on state revenues, and therefore did not count against the state's legal debt limit or require the approval of voters. Instead, the state merely asserted its "moral responsibility" for repaying the money that had been borrowed.

The moral obligation bond was the inspiration of John Mitchell, a municipal bond attorney who was an adviser to Rockefeller. (Years later, Mitchell would serve as attorney general under Nixon and go to prison for his role in Watergate.) As Mitchell recalled, Rockefeller reacted to his idea "like it was the salvation of mankind."[29] He used moral obligation financing to build one hundred new hospitals, to construct one billion dollars' worth of highways, to expand the state university system from 38,000 to 244,000 students.[30] And he used it to fund the UDC, which built extremely rapidly, constructing about 30,000 housing units in just three years (including Marcus Garvey Village in Brooklyn and the apartment buildings on Roosevelt Island, then known as Welfare Island).

For revenues that would allow them to repay their debts, UDC projects were heavily dependent on federal housing subsidies. But federal funding for low-income housing dwindled in the early 1970s. As a result, in February 1975 the UDC informed its bondholders that it was unable to pay off $104.5 million in notes it had issued. The revenue was just not there, and banks were refusing to lend it more money. Eventually investors would get paid back, the UDC heads promised, but for the moment there was no way the agency could repay what it owed.[31]

The crisis that developed around the UDC highlighted how dependent government had become on the support of private finance—on the loyalty of bankers who felt no obligation to keep propping up government policies indefinitely when their private interests seemed in jeopardy. The UDC default also directly affected the market for the debt of New York City. Although the UDC was run by the state, the failure of one entity from a government called "New York" scared off investors who might otherwise have wanted to buy the city's debt. Amid growing worries about debt-dependent budgets, the collapse of the UDC seemed like it might be a harbinger of the city's future as well.

The failure of the UDC drew attention to the way that government issuance of public debt was skirting legal debt limits. The state constitution limited New York's indebtedness by requiring voter referendums; it

limited the indebtedness of each municipality within the state, meanwhile, by requiring those debts not to exceed 10 percent of the assessed
value of the municipality's taxable real estate. This raised a question:
Was it even legal for New York City to borrow as heavily as it had?

In February 1975, two young law professors—William Quirk and
Leon Wein—filed lawsuits against the New York City government, arguing that the city's extensive borrowing violated the state constitution.
Quirk and Wein had both been lawyers for the city during the Lindsay
administration, and they had become alienated by what they saw as
Lindsay's willingness to take on debt. "He was borrowing himself into
bankruptcy, and we just sat there watching it."[32] Philosophically, they
resented the undemocratic nature of public debt, the way that it bound
future generations to payments they had never agreed to make.[33] After
they left city government, they decided to do something to challenge the
city. Together, they filed a series of briefs arguing that New York was
borrowing so much that its outstanding debt exceeded the constitutional limit, and that this violated the rights of taxpayers.[34]

The suit was dismissed by a city court in March, and it would later
be rejected by the Court of Appeals.[35] But the damage had been done.
The mere notion that hundreds of millions of dollars of the city's debt
might have been illegally incurred made the city's financiers even
more panicked about its condition. Reports that the city's payroll had
decreased much less than Beame had promised when he announced
that he would lay off thousands of people at the end of 1974 did not
make them feel any better.[36]

The most intense warnings came from First National City Bank. Jac
Friedgut, a young economist there, had been charged with reporting on
what was happening to the city finances. He was troubled by what he
found in the budget, and he reported his fears: the city's revenue-
anticipation notes were backed by revenues that might never materialize. The problem was that New York City had too big a heart: it had
adopted wholesale the priorities of the Great Society, seeking to go
even further than the federal government in its efforts to fight poverty.
Friedgut insisted that massive cuts—not taxes or more state and federal
aid—were the only meaningful solution. He argued that the banks

should push the mayor to radically cut the government's spending while pressing for federal funds to enable the city to repay its debts. "These proposals will, not surprisingly, be unpopular with the mayor," Friedgut wrote. But it was plain that the crisis point had arrived, and in such an extreme situation "many things can be done" even if they might seem unthinkable at first glance. "The time is now."[37]

Throughout the rest of the winter, Friedgut kept producing memos with titles such as "The City's Budget Mess," which circulated throughout First National City Bank and probably throughout the broader financial community as well.[38] His investigations were punched up with moral outrage. A few years after the crisis, he suggested that if there were city officials who had deliberately misled the public (as opposed to those who had made honest mistakes), they should be sent to jail.[39]

As the bankers' anxieties about the city grew, most of the underwriting banks themselves seem to have stopped holding onto the city debt they bought.[40] They were still willing to sell the city's debt on the public market, but they no longer wanted to keep much of it in their own accounts.

Early in the winter of 1975, the city was still able to keep borrowing. Money was getting more expensive, and conversations about the city's future more fraught, but at least the cash kept coming in. At the end of February, though, for the first time a sale of notes fell through.

The man who stopped the sale was Charles Sanford, a young banker at Bankers Trust. Municipals were not typically his responsibility at all; he'd never done a muni deal before. But the man who normally handled them had had to take an emergency leave from the bank for health reasons and had asked Sanford to step in.[41]

Bankers Trust was heading a syndicate that had already agreed to purchase $260 million of tax-anticipation notes, with the money to change hands at the end of the month. Sanford now had to oversee the rest of the transaction—the actual acceptance of the notes and then their resale to the public. Because he wanted to work with lawyers he could trust, he called in the bank's law firm, White & Case, to look over the paperwork and give him the green light to sign off on it. The lawyers were not the ones who usually oversaw the municipal desk, and they were troubled by what they found.[42] Probably thinking of Quirk and Wein's lawsuits, they raised the question of whether the city had exceeded its legal debt limit. They also asked whether it was right to expect that the taxes backing the notes would come in. When the city proved unable to verify that they would—Goldin, the comptroller, said that it was physically impossible to gather the data on such short notice—the lawyers refused to sanction the sale.

Sanford called a meeting. He was worried, nervous about leaving the syndicate and pulling out of the deal. He didn't know what would happen to the banks; he was still less certain what would happen to the city. He had to tell a group of bankers who were older and far more experienced than he that his law firm disagreed with the standard protocol, and that given the questions his lawyers had raised he could not go forward with the sale.

Once Bankers Trust pulled out, the rest of the group collapsed quickly. Sanford had to call the comptroller's office and tell them the sale would not go through; the city would not be able to market its notes to the country. Goldin was incredulous. This had never happened before. He asked Sanford to reconsider, urged him to change his mind. But Sanford refused, and the sale had to be canceled.

For the first time the city had been unable to raise the money it needed through the credit markets—and the very next month it needed still more.[43]

The collapse of the tax-anticipation note sale at the end of February reverberated through the city's banking community. Sanford's disapproval of the deal, which might have been shrugged off as just an inexperienced banker's one-time folly, instead suddenly became the financiers' consensus.

On the morning of Thursday, March 6, 1975, the press assembled in the office of the comptroller. It was the familiar routine for the day when the banks were to bid on the city's bond-anticipation notes. The deadline for bids was 11 a.m. But on that morning the comptroller did not burst into the room, as he always did, to announce the winning bid to all those gathered. The bankers did not wait, chatting and jovial, to hear which syndicate would seize the business. Instead, the little tin box was empty. That morning, there were no bids on the city's debt at all.

The city needed to sell the notes in order to cover its March 14 payroll, and to make a payment on two earlier loans coming due. But the lawyers for the banks, following the lead of Bankers Trust, were insisting that the city provide more information. Picking up again on the issues raised by Quirk and Wein, they wanted the city to demonstrate that the bonds that were supposed to guarantee the BANs could be issued within the legal framework of the city's debt limit.[44]

For Mayor Beame, it seemed unthinkable for the banks to challenge the city in this way. The city set the rules; the banks had to follow them. And because the banks had bought so heavily, the city assumed that the banks had no choice but to continue underwriting future loans—out of self-interest if nothing else. As First Deputy Mayor James Cavanagh put it, "The banks and us are in a community of interests. If we go down, they go down."[45]

Once, many of the bankers had seen their role in the city in similar terms. Even beyond their immense material self-interest in the city's investments, they were committed to upholding its credit, to helping the metropolis operate smoothly and well. As Richard Adams, senior vice president of Chemical Bank, would put it months later to investigators from the Securities and Exchange Commission, his bank had once "owned a very substantial proportion" of New York debt because "we believed in it as a financial community, we had a stake in it, we were a member of the City and we supported it." The bank didn't *want* to "pull the plug" sooner, or to alert the investing public, because it "didn't believe that the City was in as bad shape as it was."[46]

What Beame and Cavanagh failed to realize was that by the spring of 1975, the bankers had changed their minds. Having begun to operate in a global context, they no longer saw their economic and political interests as being inextricably linked to those of the city. Freed from the moral sensibility that had tied them to the particular place, the specific metropolis, they were free to reject not just the city's bonds but New

York itself. Now the municipal debt was, to them, only an economic proposition—and New York's economics did not look good.

After more than ten and a half hours of negotiation, late into the night on March 6 and resuming at 8 a.m. on March 7, the bankers agreed to underwrite the BANs one last time. In return, they demanded the highest interest rates in their history for that type of investment: 8.69 percent. (The revenue-anticipation notes sold in January had carried an interest rate of over 9 percent, but the BANs were regarded as less risky than the RANs.) City Council President Paul O'Dwyer described the agreement as an "outrageous stick-up."[47]

Two weeks later, David Rockefeller, Ellmore Patterson, and William Spencer (the second in command at First National City Bank) went to a secret meeting with Beame to tell him that the city was "out of credit and credibility."[48] Throughout the rest of March, the bankers met often, trying to figure out a plan of action. One memo that circulated inside Chemical Bank proposed a simple solution: "Stop Payment on N.Y.C. Checks."[49] White & Case, the law firm that Bankers Trust had brought in for advice, warned that if the banks continued to market the city's debts without a fuller disclosure of its financial problems they might face legal liabilities. The "adverse information" any such report would likely contain, however, would "in all likelihood render the City securities unsaleable."[50]

By the beginning of April, it was clear that the normal relationship between the city and the banks had collapsed. That's when the fiscal crisis really began.

6. Washington Politics

Once it became clear how wary the banks were about continuing to market the city's debt, the ratings agency Standard & Poor's immediately suspended the A rating it had given the city's bonds. After all, the only way the city could readily pay its debt service was through continued borrowing. So if it could not borrow, the worth of its bonds was immediately in doubt.

Standard & Poor's evaluation agreed with that of Fitch Investor Services, the smaller agency that had downgraded the city's debt the previous year. Amazingly, though, Moody's, the other major agency, continued to uphold its own A rating, noting that the city's problems were nothing new. "For half a century now, it has been widely known that New York City has a revenue problem." The real security of the city did not come from cash on hand anyway, Moody's said. Rather, it was the result of "the City's unique position in the American economy."[1]

In other words, as Moody's saw it, New York was simply too big and too important to fail. The logic of this position was that should the city come close to default, the national government would find a way to bail it out.

Even as the banks' support for the city crumbled, Mayor Beame seems to have held the same faith as Moody's. On Sunday, March 23, he held what the *Times* described as an "extraordinary" press conference at Gracie Mansion. Both the location and the day of the week signaled urgency, meetings with the press rarely being held on Sundays. Yet sitting at the head of a long table in a sun-filled room, Beame insisted on what would have seemed unremarkable only months before: that the city's fiscal structure remained sound. He announced another round of layoffs and a fresh dose of austerity, insisting that with these cuts New York would be able to cover all its payrolls, and make all its debt payments, including interest, on time. "By no stretch of the imagination can this great city, with its unparalleled assets, sink under the weight of the current wave of unwarranted negative publicity attributed to certain segments of the financial community," Beame proclaimed.[2] He followed up with a showy demonstration of putting his own finances on the line, investing $50,000 of his personal savings in city debt.[3] (When Comptroller Goldin heard Beame announce the purchase on the radio, he immediately wondered why the mayor would make such a risky bet: "Has he gone mad?")[4]

In fact the only way the city was actually able to cover its April bills was through the help of New York State, which agreed to borrow $400 million on the city's behalf in order to advance it funds that would normally arrive only in June.[5] Behind the scenes, meanwhile, the Beame administration was putting together a draft of congressional legislation that would grant a bank operated by the federal government the ability to purchase city bonds, giving New York an escape hatch in the absence of the private market.[6] For City Hall to write a bill that would then have to be taken up in Congress was obviously a long shot, but it reflected Beame's sense that federal financing might be key for dealing with the city's problems. Just as Moody's suggested, the city's plans for resolving its crisis hinged on its ability to win aid from higher levels of government.

On April 9, the day after Moody's professed its faith that the city would never be permitted to fail, the mayor gave a speech to an audience of two hundred securities traders, members of a group known as the Money Marketers. There, he lashed out against the financiers who had let the city down, far more openly than he permitted himself to do in his meetings with the bankers. "As Mayor," he said, "I cannot stand by idly and permit this great metropolis to be victimized by a nervous marketplace." Beame denounced the "corrosive negativism" of the banks, which had "tarnished our city's financial image wholly without justification." He accused the banks of holding the city to account for their other difficulties. "Some financial institutions, terrified by their UDC experiences . . . and troubled by other similar purchases of questionable paper, began to pressure the City of New York to pay penance for all the sins of the market," he argued. Waving a copy of one of the First National City Bank memos that criticized the city, Beame told the crowd that fully half of his own wealth was invested in the city's securities, because he had "that much confidence" in New York. Why on earth couldn't the banks show the same faith?[7]

Predictably, the traders responded angrily and defensively. "You've got to get down to basics," said one. "Why should the state support an over-pensioned and over-salaried bureaucracy?" Another told the mayor that he had to come to grips with reality. "The market is looking for a leader."[8]

In late April, Mayor Beame reluctantly announced yet another round of budget cuts, which he deemed "murderous." There would be no more aid to nursing schools that had previously received city subsidies.[9] The research libraries of the New York Public Library would no longer be open on Saturdays.[10] Beame also proposed closing Delafield, the smallest of the city's municipal hospitals, and shrinking the city workforce by 10 percent: 525 fewer policemen, 332 fewer firefighters, 791 fewer sanitation workers.[11] The news was not well received by New Yorkers. In response to the proposed closing of a city hospital on Staten Island devoted to long-term care for patients with chronic conditions, quadriplegic patients organized a demonstration in wheelchairs in front of City Hall.[12] And when Beame suggested cuts of $70 million to the CUNY budget, students responded by occupying the dean's office at Hunter College and the administration building at City College, as well as by organizing a demonstration at Gracie Mansion attended by more than a thousand student protesters, most of them African American.[13]

From the bankers' perspective, on the other hand, even these cuts did not go nearly far enough. By the end of April it was clear that the banks simply would not lead investors back to New York City bonds. The city would have to get help elsewhere, and the only institution with the resources to help was the federal government itself. It would be up to President Gerald Ford and his administration to decide whether New York's role in the national economy and in the cultural imagination was such that it warranted aid.

No one had ever elected Gerald Ford president. He held the office because of the crimes of not one but two of the country's elected leaders: first Vice President Spiro Agnew, who had resigned in October 1973 after pleading no contest to charges of taking bribes, and then Richard Nixon, whose spectacular illegal acts led him to resign in August 1974. When Ford pardoned Nixon only a few weeks after taking office, he was generally assumed to have made his own backroom deal. He was a president no one had chosen, and a leader compromised by his unwillingness to pursue the corruption of his predecessor.

Perhaps because he had never been obliged to campaign for the presidency, Ford was widely seen as a political moderate. He had entered Republican politics in 1948, challenging an isolationist conservative congressman from Grand Rapids, Michigan, who opposed the Marshall Plan. Riding the wave of moderate dissatisfaction with the direction of the G.O.P. following the presidential defeat of conservative leader Barry Goldwater in 1964, Ford became the House Minority Leader the following year. He was regarded as pragmatic, someone who, as one assistant put it, "didn't have a vigorous ideology" because his long congressional career had taught him the importance of compromise.[14]

Even though Ford sought to highlight the differences between his politics and those of the Republican conservatives, many of his ideas actually echoed theirs. He was a staunch opponent of the Great Society, voting down the line against Medicare, Medicaid, subsidized housing, federal aid to education, and food stamps. "A government big enough to do everything for you is a government big enough to take everything

away from you," he liked to say.[15] He denounced the Democratic Party
as the "party of Big Business, of Big Government, of Big Spending, of
Big Deficits, of Big Cost of Living, of Big Labor Trouble, of Big Home
Foreclosures, of Big Scandals, of Big Riots in the Streets and of Big
Promises."[16]

Ford had been preoccupied with balanced budgets and fiscal responsibility throughout his life. Even as an undergraduate at the University
of Michigan, where he studied economics and played football, Ford was
unusually concerned with fiscal rectitude. As house manager for the
Delta Kappa Epsilon fraternity, Ford took on the challenge of straight-
ening out the fraternity's troubled finances, and when he graduated, the
University of Michigan yearbook noted with pride that he had "put
the D.K.E. house back on a paying basis."[17] Later, while serving on the
House Appropriations Committee, he mastered the details of the federal budget, and he consistently framed his opposition to Great Society
programs in terms of how much they were likely to cost.[18] "It is my judgment that fiscal discipline is a necessary weapon in any fight against
inflation," he told Congress in a joint address early in his presidency.
"I do not think any of us in this Chamber today can ask the American
people to tighten their belts if Uncle Sam is unwilling to tighten his
belt first."[19]

This long-standing hostility to the welfare state, organized labor,
and the Great Society inevitably shaped the way Ford thought about
New York City. As he wrote in his memoir years later, in his view
"the problem was New York had a bad policy of paying too much in
pensions, paying too much in salaries to New York City employees.
And the city was going bankrupt because of this irresponsible fiscal
policy."[20]

Ford's thinking about New York was also shaped by the broader economic problems of the 1970s. Unemployment reached 8.9 percent in
the spring of 1975—the highest in the postwar years—while the economy contracted by 5 percent. The automobile industry, the old power-
house of the American economy, was hit especially hard: by the start
of 1975, the country's large automakers had laid off half their combined workforce, more than 280,000 people.[21] To make matters worse,

Americans were not only losing jobs but having to deal with rapid inflation, which ate away at the purchasing power of wages and salaries.

The paired economic difficulties created great stress within the Ford
administration, as the president and his economic advisers struggled to
come up with a coherent political response. Previously, most economists
had conceived of inflation as a problem that primarily affected a growing economy, so there was little clear sense of how to respond to inflation during a recession. At first, Ford attempted to persuade companies
not to institute higher prices and workers not to bargain for higher
wages. But this program, known as "Whip Inflation Now," or WIN,
turned out to be a dismal failure. Next, Ford endorsed a one-year tax
cut of $16 billion, while imposing a one-year moratorium on virtually
all new federal spending in order to restrain the growth of the federal
debt.[22] From an economic standpoint these policies were essentially self-
contradictory: the tax cut was meant to boost the economy by encouraging people to spend more, but the federal moratorium meant that the
government itself spent less than it would have otherwise, slowing the
economy down. And the tax cut was immediately attacked from all
sides: economists warned that the $16 billion reduction would not pro-
vide sufficient stimulus to make a difference, while members of Ford's
administration threatened to quit because the tax cuts increased the
deficit.[23]

The situation was all the more difficult for Ford because he was trying to stitch together an administration that included a variety of different factions. There were holdovers from the Nixon years; people
who had come to Washington from New York State along with Nelson
Rockefeller, now Ford's vice president; and finally his own longtime
friends and allies. A number of these people belonged to the more liberal and moderate elements in the Republican Party. Rockefeller, for
example, had presided over the great expansion of borrowing in New
York and had long been the standard-bearer for liberal Republicanism.
Even people who would later become conservative leaders—such as
Donald Rumsfeld, Ford's chief of staff, and Dick Cheney, his deputy
chief of staff—were linked at the time to moderate Republican circles.
Rumsfeld had gotten his start in politics as a middle-of-the-road con-

gressman representing suburban Chicago, while Cheney's first political job was as an assistant to Republican William Steiger of Wisconsin, who sponsored the legislation that created the Occupational Safety and Health Administration and worked to expand environmental protection for the Great Lakes.[24]

At the same time, Ford was well aware that the Republican Party's right wing was becoming more organized and aggressive. Activists were setting up new conservative think tanks, such as the Heritage Foundation; new groups such as the Business Roundtable were putting forward a more pro-corporate politics; the United States Chamber of Commerce was encouraging businesspeople to support politicians who backed lower taxes and less government. Ford knew if he stood for reelection he would probably have to contend with Ronald Reagan, the governor of California and conservative movement hero, and that without the support of conservatives it would be hard to win his own party's primary, let alone the general election. Ford's cabinet and roster of advisers had its share of doctrinaire free-market conservatives as well. The young economist Alan Greenspan, a devotee of the free market thinker Ayn Rand, whose philosophy sought to invert prevailing moral codes and celebrate selfishness as the primary moral virtue, was chair of Ford's Council of Economic Advisers. The president shared with Greenspan a deep concern about inflation, as well as a commitment to refusing to expand federal programs in response to the recession. Economist Arthur Laffer, meanwhile, held a position in Ford's Treasury Department. He was inspired to draw his famous back-of-the-napkin curve illustrating the central principle of supply-side economics—the erroneous notion that lowering taxes could actually lead to higher government revenues—at a lunch meeting at which he was discussing one of Ford's early tax proposals with Dick Cheney.[25]

Of the conservatives in Ford's White House, the most influential by far was his Treasury Secretary, William Simon. Simon guided the administration's response to the problem of New York, and he also, more than anyone else, told the story of New York to the rest of the world. As it happened, Simon had an intimate knowledge of New York City finances, for he had made his fortune as a municipal bond trader

before going to Washington. He had been the senior partner in charge
of the Government Bond and Municipal Bond Department at Salomon
Brothers, where he was known as ruthlessly competitive. (One associate called him "the Vince Lombardi of Wall Street—to him, winning
was everything.")[26] He had played a key role in overseeing the growth
of the municipal desk at Salomon, tirelessly advocating on behalf of the
industry.[27] Although he worked in the city, he lived with his wife and
seven children on a 64-acre estate in New Jersey. He was deeply opposed
to the power of government, and just as convinced of the superiority of
the free market. "Government is a menace," he told an interviewer for
Playboy magazine. "We love Government spending programs, but these
lead to massive deficits—so we create even more money to finance even
larger deficits." He worried that democracy might never be able to fight
inflation, because entitlement programs were so popular. "I wish the
American people could get a basic understanding of what it means when
government removes your economic freedoms, because shortly thereafter, as happened in ancient Greece, your social and political freedoms
follow." Ultimately, he feared for the national character. "What the hell
happened to the American free-enterprise spirit: *Did the Puritans need
subsidies?*"[28]

Within the Ford administration, Simon, Greenspan, and Rumsfeld
advocated a hard line with regard to New York City from fairly early on,
opposing virtually any assistance for the city. They even suggested that
it might be for the best for New York to declare bankruptcy: this would
send a clear message to municipal politicians, labor leaders, and bankers about the perils of government spending. Rockefeller, on the other
hand, urged the president to remain open to finding some way to aid
New York—using the crisis as a chance to force the city to transform
itself. On both sides, though, everyone in Washington agreed that what
happened in New York would have serious consequences for the country
as a whole. After all, the city had been the exemplar of postwar liberalism. Its failure was not just a local problem or a cautionary tale for
the financial industry, much less a story of the unequal distribution
of resources in metropolitan areas. Rather it called into question the
ideological, economic, and political underpinnings of liberalism itself.

For the Ford administration, the fiscal crisis marked a political opportunity.

In early May 1975, Mayor Beame and Governor Carey met with Treasury Secretary Simon and the chair of the Federal Reserve Bank, Arthur Burns.[29] David Rockefeller, the president of Chase Manhattan, and top bankers from Morgan and First National City Bank were also present. Following the meeting, Simon told the press that the federal government would do nothing to help New York City, since "the fundamental solution to the city's problems does not lie at the Federal level."[30]

Beame and Carey were not satisfied. They insisted they needed an audience with Ford himself. At first the president's office tried to put them off, but the mayor and the governor said that the possibility of default was imminent and that they would not consider any answer final until they saw Ford in person. "Inasmuch as they have already met with your senior officials, and still demand a meeting, I believe it's difficult to turn down such a request from the Governor of New York and the Mayor of New York City," wrote Jack Marsh, a former congressman who was a counselor to Ford.[31]

Ford was not surprised to hear from the mayor and the governor. He had been following the city's problems closely throughout the year. The first warnings had come in December 1974, when people at the Federal Reserve Bank reported rumors that "as early as January" New York would be unable to pay interest or principal on its debt. If that happened, it seemed likely to spread panic through the entire banking system. A midlevel official in the capital markets section of the Fed was so troubled by the possibility that the city would default that he wrote up a memo for the higher-ups. At least one bank, he said, was starting to make preparations for the collapse of the city.[32]

Over the winter and early spring of 1975, New York bankers had begun making concerted appeals to Washington for aid, even as they withdrew from financing the city themselves. (As one Morgan Guaranty banker argued, "There is only one place I know of where one can go for the hundreds of millions, if not billions, that may be required to keep the City running.")[33] The bankers had little interest in preserving social services in the city; their main goal was to enlist the help of the federal government in protecting their investments. Indeed, as they pleaded for help, they did so through a fierce attack on the city's public institutions, playing to Ford's antipathy to government spending by arguing that these could be cut sharply in return for aid.

A week after the failed note sale of March 6, David Grossman, a Chase Manhattan Bank executive who had formerly served under Lindsay as New York's budget director, met with officials at the Federal Reserve. He flat out asked the Fed to loan the city $3 billion. This would provide New York with a cushion so that it would not have to return to the markets to keep borrowing so often. In return, Grossman promised—even though he hadn't consulted with the city's elected leaders—that New York would agree to cut its budget by $2 billion: ending free tuition and open enrollment at CUNY, slashing personnel, cutting salaries. The federal government should be prepared to call out the "militia" in the event of a strike by the municipal employees, Grossman told those assembled, since such cuts were likely to trigger intense social unrest.[34]

A few days later, Jac Friedgut, the economist at First National City Bank who had been charged with monitoring the city's finances, addressed the New York City congressional delegation. His speech was essentially a version of one of his caustic internal memoranda. Little mention was made of the serious economic difficulties the city had encountered: the loss of industry, rising unemployment, the flight to suburbia. Instead, Friedgut blamed the city's mounting crisis on its overweening generosity: the number of people on welfare, the public sector unions, and the "free or 'discount' public services" such as CUNY and mass transit, which were eating up the city's funds and trapping it on a "debt treadmill." In short, the city's "heart" was expanding "faster than its pocketbook." To regain the confidence of the marketplace, he said, New York needed to make massive cuts.[35]

Still, some members of the Ford administration were at first surprisingly open to the idea of providing aid to the city in one form or another.

At the Treasury Department, one of Simon's advisers suggested that a case could be made for the federal government itself to buy New York's bonds. If it seemed that many banks held so much city debt that they would collapse following the city's failure, thus destabilizing the entire national financial system, such aid might be "necessary to avoid a crisis."[36] Simon, for his part, wrote to Ford to ask whether the federal government might consider advancing the payments it made to New York State for welfare and Medicaid, sending the money scheduled for July in early April instead. He told the president that it seemed likely that the city might default on April 14, which would "have a most unfortunate impact on confidence in our economy in general and on the credit markets in particular."[37]

Had Ford been willing to entertain such ideas—advancing some assistance without requiring tremendous cuts in return—it might in fact have been possible to resolve the city's problems without the wrenching drama that followed. But Ford was reluctant to countenance suggestions that he do more to help. He was much more sympathetic to advisers such as L. William Seidman, his old friend from Grand Rapids and director of his Economic Policy Board, who warned that extending aid without demanding budget cuts—even advancing payments that would eventually get sent anyway—would establish "a dangerous precedent."[38] Nor did the former New Yorkers in the administration approve. Richard Dunham of the president's Domestic Council, who had come to Washington with Nelson Rockefeller, complained to the vice president that advancing aid would be a "one time shot assistance" that would do no more than put "a finger in the dike."[39] Most hostile of all was Donald Rumsfeld. "Going along with New York would be a disaster," he wrote in a memo to Ford responding to Simon's idea of advancing some of the money that would be coming to the city in July. "First for N.Y. since they would delay cleaning up their mess. Second, for the precedent it would set. In my view the request is outrageous."[40]

For the president, the problems of the city seemed linked to those facing the entire country, and it would be contradictory and confusing to urge austerity for the nation while subsidizing New York's welfare state. Faced with the specter of the city's default, Ford, Rumsfeld, and many close to them believed that the best thing the federal government could do was nothing at all.

Such was the state of play when the president gathered his inner circle to talk about the "possible insolvency" of the city.[41] Most of Ford's advisers believed New York was shamelessly begging for help to prop up its welfare state. Before it got any aid at all from the federal government, they said, the city should adopt austerity. It should impose tolls on the East River bridges. It should raise the subway fare and lay off 10,000 workers. It should cut the education budget by $100 million. It should slash faculty salaries at CUNY and end free tuition. (CUNY was a particular bête noire of the Ford administration: it seemed the ultimate symbol of municipal largesse, the embodiment of its most utopian promises.)[42] The cold light of default, some of Ford's advisers suggested, might be the only thing that could compel the city to change its ways. "A default," argued Robert Gerard of the Treasury Department, "could trigger the kind of radical action by the city which is required."[43] And as far as the impact a New York default might have on the national economy, Ford's advisers thought the bankers and politicians were exaggerating the risk.

This argument appealed to the president. Its simplicity, fortitude, and stark critique of New York all gave Ford the courage he needed. He would not cave to the scare tactics and pleas for aid. The city's profligacy—the rampant spending of the arrogant liberals—would stop with him. Rather than seek a low-profile way of providing aid to the city and giving it time to restructure its debts, Ford adopted a highly ideologically charged response to the city's fiscal crisis.

A meeting with Mayor Beame and Governor Carey was set for May 13. As the president was preparing for the encounter, he wrote himself a little note: "24 hrs. Must do what's right. Bite bullet."[44]

The weather on May 13 was balmy and warm, a humid spring day in Washington. Beame and Carey arrived at the White House early in the afternoon and went to meet the president, the vice president, and their staffs in the Cabinet Room of the White House. Peter Goldmark, Carey's budget director, had accompanied his boss to Washington, and he recalls seeing the look of recognition that passed between Carey and Ford as they sat down at the long table that filled the room. They were two long-time men of the House of Representatives. No one had thought either would have a career that would go beyond Congress, but one had managed to become governor, the other president.[45]

The aftershocks of the Vietnam War were still reverberating throughout Southeast Asia. It was only two weeks since the last American personnel had evacuated Saigon. The day before the meeting, the Khmer Rouge had captured the *Mayaguez*, an American merchant ship that had been sailing through what the United States argued were international waters. Thirty-nine American crew members were being held prisoner, and Ford had to decide whether to send in military troops to rescue them—a final show of force in the region. As he listened to the leaders of New York, Ford had a great deal on his mind.

The president's briefing notes for the meeting had been prepared by James Cannon, the director of his Domestic Council and a veteran of the Rockefeller administration in New York State. Cannon had urged the president to strike a sympathetic note: "You are up against a hard problem." But he also felt the president should make it clear that Washington could not help New York, because this would open the floodgates for requests from other cities. The city's problems were, at heart, the result of bad local management. They had not developed "overnight" but reflected years of misplaced priorities. The president was obligated to deliver the message that Beame and Carey had no alternative but to cut the city's spending drastically. This was the only real solution to the fiscal crisis.[46]

The meeting began just a little after 2 p.m. Gathered in the Cabinet Room alongside President Ford and Vice President Rockefeller was a team of administration officials: William Simon, Alan Greenspan, L. William Seidman of the Economic Policy Board, James Cannon and Richard Dunham of the Domestic Council, and James Lynn of the Office of Management and Budget. Beame and Carey brought their advisers as well: Peter Goldmark, David Burke, and Judah Gribetz came with the governor, and Deputy Mayor James Cavanaugh accompanied Beame.[47]

The president's opening words might have reassured Carey and Beame that he was open to their case. Ford began by reminding them that as a former member of the Appropriations Committee in Congress, he had a very good understanding of the complexity of fiscal politics. He felt "sympathetic" to the people of New York. Then he opened the floor to the supplicants.[48]

Carey spoke first. The leaders of the city and of the state, he said, felt as though "we are headed for a cliff." He feared that if services had to be abruptly suspended or further cut, conflict might erupt in the city. New York, he said, did not want a "handout." What he wanted was for the federal government to offer to guarantee the city's bonds—in other words, to promise that if the city was not able to pay interest and principal on them, the federal government would step in to do so. Doing this would provide greater security to investors, and they would be willing to purchase the city's debt again.[49]

Then Beame began, and all the emotion he usually kept tamped down flowed into his remarks. He opened with a passionate denunciation of the "boycott" the financial markets were trying to mount against the city. It was unbelievable, "stupid"—a cash boycott against the city of New York! Even though he had been pushing austerity like no mayor before, closing schools, hospitals, and fire stations! "This whole thing," he exclaimed, "has been so damned distorted all over the place!" His budget cuts had already brought the city to the brink of "social chaos." Just the previous week he'd returned to the city from Washington, where he'd been meeting with William Simon, to make a dinner appearance. But it was the day when the CUNY students were holding their demonstration in front of Gracie Mansion, and the mayor hadn't even been able to get into his own home. "I think I've gone as far as I can. Otherwise the city will disintegrate," he said. "I know what's going to happen to me but I don't give a God—I don't give a damn." Why couldn't the president see that New York's fate mattered to the rest of the country, and to how the United States was seen around the world? After all,

Europeans didn't travel to America to visit Detroit or Columbus, did they?[50]

Here, the president laughed at the mayor's touching New York pride, his sense that the city was the heart of the nation. "I'm a good Michigander," he reminded Beame. And Nelson Rockefeller, quiet until then, chimed in: "Don't get carried away, Abe."

The mayor returned to his theme. He didn't ask for much, but what he did want was a bit different from what Carey asked for: Beame hoped that Ford would provide support for congressional action to give the city a $1 billion loan. That money would help tide things over—to push the city through the next three months, during which time it would be able to pass new taxes, make any further necessary cuts, and arrive at a balanced budget. Just the promise of support from the president would be enough to restore the confidence of the banks.

The president took it all in, listening calmly to the mayor and the governor. He then began to ask questions. Why, he wondered, should the city have to turn to the federal government for this financial guarantee—why couldn't the state step in? Rockefeller agreed: the state was a more logical guarantor for city bonds, since its information about the city was likely to be more extensive. Carey grew angry. "We've done all we can," he said. He would not damage the credit of the state to help the city. Ford then asked Beame why he couldn't go back to the banks. Why wouldn't they accept his promise to balance the budget?

"I don't know," said Beame. "I've asked that question a hundred times."[51]

Why, asked Ford, hadn't the city made more cuts? He began to count them off, using the suggestions that his advisers had prepared for him. "Why don't you raise the 35-cent transit fare to 40 or 50 cents?" asked the president.

Beame responded that this would be inflationary, and that the constant upward press of prices menaced the entire national economy. What was more, he had promised to hold the fare steady through the end of the year. And besides, a small fare hike would hardly put a dent in the city's debt. To make a real difference it would have to be raised to 65 cents—even a dollar.

Ford responded with irritation: Beame didn't understand. Raising the fare was symbolic, a way of telling the markets and the banks that the city was changing its ways. The purpose would be more to overcome the city's "lack of credibility" than to raise revenue. He brought up another cut his advisers had suggested: "Why not charge tuition at community colleges?"

For Beame, this was too much. Free tuition, he insisted, was a 128-year tradition in the city of New York, one that went to the heart of the city's social contract. Thousands of student demonstrators were already massing in the streets; tuition might push them over the edge. What's more, he owed his own upward mobility to City College: "I wouldn't be here today if it weren't for free tuition."

Ford then stopped proposing cuts and asked whether the Federal Reserve Board was amenable to aiding the city. Simon responded that this seemed impractical. Out of alternatives, the president finally took up the question that had brought Beame and Carey to Washington. "Let's consider federal help," he said, as though playing out what the scenario would involve. How much would the city require? And for how long?

Beame repeated that he only wanted a loan for ninety days. That was enough time for the state legislature to grant new taxing powers to the city, which it would then use to arrive at a truly balanced budget. Without the help, Carey jumped in, the city would default—and any alternative was preferable to that.

And when did the city need the money? By May 30, Beame replied—less than three weeks away.

Ford quickly began to demur. Realistically, he could not imagine Congress acting quickly enough, even if he were to ask for legislation the very next day.

This meant, Carey said, a "premonition of default." And Congress should be aware that it would affect municipal bonds across the nation, not only in New York.

Ford went on. He could not make—no president could make—a commitment to the city until he saw the "facts and figures," until he had proof that New York would in fact balance its budget. "You have made a plea in general terms. But I have to look at cold figures. I believe you. I'm very sympathetic. You are making an effort at fiscal responsibility. I admire you for it." But he would need to "see it in black and white" before he could do anything to help.[52]

"I go along 1000% or 100%, whatever the figure is," Beame said. But his promise was empty. Everyone present knew the mayor could not guarantee a balanced budget. He would need the support of Albany lawmakers, both for state aid and for taxing powers for the city, and many of the lawmakers were Republicans. Nor had the City Council members seen Beame's plan, and they were the ones who would need to vote to approve it. Ford insisted those steps had to come first. He couldn't just have Abe Beame's word but needed "some iron"—for example, the commitment of the entire City Council to a program of austerity.[53]

Throughout the meeting with the president, Beame presented the city's problems in the narrowest possible terms, reluctant to concede that there was really a problem at all. He claimed the city was just running low on cash while it waited for revenues to arrive. His blinkered vision of the city's problems and unwillingness to acknowledge the severity of the situation, his inability to describe what was happening in New York as the result of broader social and economic changes, made Beame's case to Ford all the less persuasive.

The president ended the meeting by asking his visitors to give him twenty-four hours to think things over, while they figured out what they could do in terms of rallying the City Council around budget cuts more draconian than anything New York had seen before. "For ten years, it was done wrong," Ford said. "You've got to do it right."[54]

After leaving the White House, Beame and Carey hurried to meet with Oklahoman Carl Albert, Speaker of the House, and then with Senator Mike Mansfield, Senate majority leader. Both Democrats tried to side-step the conversation, saying that the mayor and governor had to talk to the chairs of the Banking and Currency Committees instead. In these private meetings, Carey was pessimistic, saying that Ford had made it clear that he thought "no New York bailout bill" could ever pass

Congress.[55] Meanwhile, the city's congressional delegation was also making the rounds in Washington. They met with Arthur Burns, chair of the Federal Reserve, who told them there was no way he could get five of the seven votes on the Board of Governors in favor of having the Fed purchase city debt. "He couldn't have been more bleak," said one representative. "He sounded as though he wished we didn't know the Fed existed."[56]

But in the press conference that followed their conversation with the president, Carey and Beame did their best to sound cheerful and optimistic. Carey spoke of the "warmth and understanding" with which Ford had greeted them. The generous length of the meeting—it had lasted a full hour and a half—underscored how seriously the president was taking the problems of the city, as did his promise of a response the very next day. Beame chimed in: "I was pleased that he had an open mind." When reporters began to ask questions about the possibility of default—how might it affect the nation's bond markets?—Carey brought the press conference to an abrupt close.[57]

Meanwhile, the president was trying to make his decision and figure out how best to convey it to New York's leaders. James Cannon prepared a memorandum for him spelling out the options. Ford could agree to support the city's request for a ninety-day loan from the federal government in the amount of $1 billion. Or he could "flatly deny the request." Or—and this was Cannon's preferred choice—he could deny the request, but "leave a slight loophole which would enable the Federal government to assist the City if disruption of the financial markets did occur as the result of a default; and/or subject to certain conditions and restrictions." In other words, the federal government could refuse to provide immediate help, but keep in its back pocket the possibility of aid should the city's default set off a cascade of bank failures.

Having recommended the last option, Cannon suggested Ford send a letter instead of just conveying the message by phone. A letter that could be publicly released would best communicate Ford's understanding of the "complexity" of the situation, and would "explain to the financial community the care with which you have considered this matter and the reasoning that supports your decision." It would be for the bankers as much as for Beame.[58]

Cannon drafted the "Dear Abe" letter. Although the president was "deeply impressed" by the seriousness of the situation, it said, and by the "extraordinary imbalance" between revenues and expenses, he did not feel that he could aid the city. "It is clear that the City's basic critical financial condition is not new but has been a long time in the making," the letter stated. To have any chance at federal aid—here was the loophole—the city needed first to provide a plan to balance its budget. "Fiscal responsibility is essential for cities, states and the federal government." Cannon took the opportunity to deliver a small lecture on budgeting—one likely directed at the Congress as much as at the city. "Every family which makes up a budget has to make painful choices. As we make these choices at home, so must we also make them in public office too. We must stop promising more and more services without knowing how we will cover their costs."

The letter's conclusion was clear and uncompromising. "In view of the foregoing considerations, I must deny your request for support of your Federal legislative proposal."[59]

Carey and Beame were together at a Brooklyn Democratic Party dinner at the Waldorf-Astoria Hotel when the news came from Washington. Cannon called Beame to alert him to the president's response, reading him the letter over the phone before it was released to the press.[60] Beame fumed with disappointment. "I don't think this shows feeling for us at all," he told Cannon on the phone. It seemed that even Rockefeller had turned against New York. "I always thought Nelson was a friend," he complained. "This is a really bad move. I can understand the President having to take the position he does but I can't tell you I like it. I'm upset about it and I hope you will pass that along to the President and more especially the Vice President."[61]

Beame went back to the dinner and gave the news to Carey. Before an audience of 2,300 party regulars who were more accustomed to boilerplate speeches and political nods than flustered, fiery rhetoric, the mayor and the governor then denounced the Republican White House. Threatening that civic disorder might be the result of the president's position, Carey fumed against the "level of arrogance and disregard for New York" displayed by the federal government. "Have they no heart? Have they no understanding of our problems? Must a city riot?" he asked.[62]

In a hastily organized news conference in the foyer outside the hotel ballroom, Beame lambasted the president for being more responsive to corporations than to the city. Bankrupt companies could get bailouts—why not New York? "It's incredible to me that the President of the United States thinks more about the stockholders of Lockheed or Penn Central than the eight million people of our city," he told the press. "Has anyone told the President that the Mayor is cutting services to the bone? Have his advisers seen the demonstrators pleading to keep us from closing hospitals, libraries, day-care centers, and fire houses?" Asked if he was sure that he would have enough money to cover payrolls and expenses and keep the city from default over the coming weeks, Beame equivocated for the first time, saying only: "All I can say is I will do everything I can."[63]

Beame had always believed that New York City was too big to fail, that its historic place in the country's economy and politics would keep it safe, and that if bankruptcy ever became a real threat the federal government would provide a way out. Such was not to be the case. Gerald Ford and the advisers who surrounded him were attuned instead to the needs and politics of the conservative mobilization that was gaining momentum across the country. New York City was on its own.

PART II

CRISIS

7. Big Mac

In the weeks that followed Beame and Carey's trip to Washington, the clock was ticking for New York City. It was scheduled to pay back $792 million worth of debt on Wednesday, June 11, and it did not have the money. Unless aid came from somewhere, the city would default.[1]

In the days after Ford's refusal of federal aid, there were plenty of suggestions for ways that New York could raise funds. In an interesting twist on privatization, Manhattan State Senator Roy Goodman suggested that the city could sell the Brooklyn Bridge, along with other bridges, schools, hospitals, libraries, and police and fire stations, and then lease them back on favorable terms.[2] Officials of Suffolk County, on eastern Long Island, briefly debated loaning New York City $200 million, as though to compensate for the taxes that had migrated to the suburbs over the previous two decades. Not that the people of Long Island had a deep sense of responsibility: the suggestion caused such outrage that it was quickly withdrawn.[3]

Less daring options were rejected as well. Beame asked Albany for a new commuter tax and other additional taxing authority, as well as $640 million in state aid. The Republican-dominated state legislature quickly vetoed the idea. Warren Anderson, the Republican majority leader in the Senate, said it would be "counterproductive" to give the city additional funds: "I can only liken it to someone addicted to heroin. Do you really help him by giving him more?"[4] Comptroller Goldin, for his part, returned to the bankers to beg them to underwrite one more offering. They responded with a chilly letter, saying that the city's financing requirements went beyond "the ability of the New York financial community by itself to provide," and that they would only become involved in a "total assistance program" that involved fundamental fiscal reforms.[5] Op-ed writers for the city's papers began to invoke the specter of bankruptcy, sometimes advocating it as the best possible solution to the city's difficulties. "The sensible course is to seek bankruptcy now, before a series of spasm reactions by a desperate city government makes New York an impossible place in which to live or do business," advised economics writer Martin Mayer in the *New York Times*.[6]

Some New Yorkers took matters into their own hands. A retired city schoolteacher sent back to the city a $2 tax refund: "The city needs the money more than I do." Another city resident contributed $2.98: "If this keeps one policeman on duty for 15 minutes and saves a life or prevents a crime, it will be the best investment anyone could make." A third-grade girl sent a $1 bill, along with a personal note for Mayor Beame: "I would like you to fix the park on Spring Street. . . . Say yes or no please write a letter to me and fast. I love you." Mayor Beame did write back to some of these benefactors, thanking them for their kind wishes and their futile contributions. "It is a tremendously worthwhile expression of your faith in our city and I wish we had more like you with us," he told one person who had mailed in a check for $100.[7]

As the reality of Washington's refusal set in, the state and the city alike scrambled to find a way forward. But there was no transparent solution, because different people understood the causes of the city's problems in very different ways. Business executives wanted New York to slash its public sector, while the city's labor unions and some local politicians blamed the banks for the city's predicament and insisted they would fight any cuts in city services. Why, they asked, should New Yorkers be punished for the recalcitrance of the financiers?

Each side had a leader. For the businessmen, this was Felix Rohatyn, the Viennese-born Lazard Frères banker who had a knack for the telling phrase and whose fabulous personal wealth coexisted with an underlying pessimism about the stability of capitalism as a social order. For the unions, it was Victor Gotbaum, the executive director of the city's largest public sector union, whose life had been spent trying to organize the most marginal city workers and win them a more decent and secure livelihood. The two men came from opposing worlds, politically and ideologically, and they developed radically different understandings of the fiscal crisis.

Victor Gotbaum had always wanted to speak for the "hungry people"—the ones nobody saw and nobody remembered.[8] These were the workers who toiled under the city in its sewers, washed the laundry in its hospitals, served lunch to the children in its school cafeterias, collected the tickets at the Central Park Zoo, identified the bodies that wound up in the city morgue. They were absent from the tourist photographs of the World Trade Center and the Empire State Building; they were not present in the iconic postcard images of the Chrysler Building and the Brooklyn Bridge. No one thought of them, and yet they were the ones whose work kept the great machine of the city turning, the people without whom the city would grind to a halt.

Gotbaum had grown up in Flatbush, Brooklyn, one of five children in a Jewish household whose fortunes fell with the Great Depression. His father, a printing salesman who hated his work at the best of times, became unemployed in the 1930s. Gotbaum's family went on welfare to survive. The thirteen-year-old boy had to get a job—first as a dishwasher in a luncheonette, then in his uncle's printing shop—to keep his family out of destitution. His high school career was a disaster: he barely eked out passing grades. It was something of a miracle that he managed to graduate, since he hardly went to class at all.

Those difficult years helped Gotbaum find his calling as an organizer. When he was working in his uncle's shop, he recalled later, he found out that the two white workers on the line were making $10 an hour, and the two black workers were making only $8. He organized a strike for equal pay, and won.[9]

After fighting in World War II, Gotbaum, despite his poor academic record, was accepted into Brooklyn College. He and his wife, Sarah, attended the college for free; they lived in public housing and paid for their master's degrees with money from the GI Bill. After a short period with the State Department, Gotbaum found his way to the labor movement and to the project of organizing low-wage workers in public hospitals.

For public sector workers, the 1960s were a decade as transformative as the 1930s had been for factory laborers. Throughout the first half of the twentieth century, the legal climate of the United States had been consistently hostile to the idea of unionization for police officers, firefighters, teachers, and other government employees. These people, political leaders argued, were not really workers at all, in the way that people employed by private businesses were. Rather they were servants of the public good, responsible for the commonweal. Their labor was crucial to maintaining public safety and social order. Were they to act in their own interests, they might destabilize the whole society. Because of this, public sector workers were intentionally left out of the Wagner Act of the 1930s, which granted private sector workers collective bargaining rights. Even FDR had been ambivalent about collective bargaining for federal employees, and he was outright opposed to the notion that they had the right to strike. For decades, Wisconsin was the only state that permitted collective bargaining by city and state workers.

Despite the absence of formal rights, public sector workers in New York City did try to organize during the 1930s and after. They formed a wide variety of unions, and were able to exert some pressure through public demonstrations and campaigns, as well as through backroom deals and private political arrangements. But the city government did not recognize any of these organizations, so they had no capacity to bargain on behalf of their members. Even a liberal such as La Guardia had no interest in negotiating with a unionized city workforce.

This all changed in New York City starting in 1958, when Mayor Wagner pushed through his "Little Wagner Act," the executive order permitting city workers to engage in collective bargaining. Slowly, over the 1960s, city workers—many of them black and Latino, most poorly paid—began to organize. The unions they built were infused with the spirit of the civil rights movement: passionate, militant, committed to justice in a broad sense instead of being narrowly focused on economic problems. They were part of a national upsurge in organizing among public sector workers. Between 1955 and 1975, the country's public union membership grew tenfold, to about 4 million. In a sign of the unions' growing confidence and power, in 1958, there had been 15 strikes by public sector workers nationally; in 1975, there were 478.[10] For city and state governments, as well as the broader public, the rise of a unionized public sector workforce was, in the words of labor journalist Sam Zagoria, as surprising as "an invasion from outer space."[11]

After a stint organizing hospitals in Chicago, Gotbaum returned to his hometown and became the executive director of the rapidly growing District Council 37 of the American Federation of State, County, and Municipal Employees (AFSCME). There, he led the drive for union recognition among the invisible workers at the municipal hospitals: the linen cleaners, the clerical assistants, the janitors, the truck drivers, the watchmen and aides. These overwhelmingly black and Latino workers labored in hot laundries, crowded kitchens, and busy wards, receiving little respect or acknowledgment from the mostly white doctors and nurses. Their wages were low and they had little control over basic conditions of their work: their supervisors could set schedules, establish work assignments, transfer people to less desirable jobs, and fire them at will.

In its first years, DC 37 was quite successful in its interactions with the city. It negotiated strong contracts, turning what had been menial jobs into middle-class work. It also sought to provide social services to its members: health care, legal services, tuition benefits, professional training, even its own college program. Both at the bargaining table and in its union hall, DC 37 gave people a way to improve their lives through collective action—something many of these workers had never experienced.

DC 37 went on to win bargaining rights for school-lunch workers, school aides, and a host of other city employees. It would eventually represent a vast range of occupations, including a variety of professionals who worked for the city: librarians, architects, accountants, physical therapists, court reporters, and others.[12] Different as they were, all these workers were joined in Gotbaum's District Council. But this union, and

the world that it sought to build, would both be called into question by
the fiscal crisis.

Unlike Gotbaum, Felix Rohatyn had spent his early life in privilege,
growing up in Vienna as the grandson of a man who owned several brew-
eries as well as a small credit bank. But he, too, had witnessed political and
economic upheavals in his childhood. Rohatyn's family had fled the Nazis
in the 1930s. Later in his life, Rohatyn claimed that the experience of stuff-
ing gold coins into toothpaste tubes to sneak them over the Spanish bor-
der had taught him how fragile any fortune might be.[13]

Throughout the rest of his life, Rohatyn would remain preoccupied by
the threat of economic disaster. Even as he became a financier, he remained
a firm believer in the necessity of government intervention to assure social
stability. The economic and social order never seemed to him solid, depend-
able, something to be taken for granted. When the United States slid into
recession in the early 1970s, he feared the worst. The bankruptcy of the
Penn Central Railroad and the collapse of the go-go market of the late
1960s seemed to Rohatyn to be of a piece with the National Guard shooting of protesters at Kent State University in May 1970 following Nixon's
invasion of Cambodia. All were signs of a larger social disorder, a creeping
chaos that threatened the stability of the American system itself.[14]

As a financier, Rohatyn became known for his capacity to broker
deals when no one else could. In 1971, he became involved in a "Crisis
Committee" formed by the New York Stock Exchange to help several
brokerages that were in danger of failing (they had not kept sufficient
capital reserves to cover their accounts when the stock market fell). His
role in organizing a fund to bail out these firms solidified Rohatyn's reputation as someone with a gift for calming nerves in the stressful atmosphere of financial panic. The incident also confirmed his underlying
fears about the recklessness of speculators, the duplicity of accountants,
and the rapidity with which the market could come undone.[15] That same
year, he would perform similar financial magic when defense manufacturer Lockheed almost went bankrupt, helping to pull together a bailout package relying on both private and federal funds.[16]

His experiences on Wall Street in the early 1970s convinced Rohatyn that the state had to take a more active role in combating economic and political disorder. In 1974, Rohatyn argued that the federal government should create a new lending agency that could make loans to businesses overburdened with debt and damaged by the falling stock market.[17] Later in life, he observed, "I always thought that somewhere you had to think about whether capitalism is going to work. That is really the real question. And certainly when you look around, the answer isn't at all clear."[18]

Rohatyn's worries about speculation, risk, and their impact on social stability were ironic given that he had worked at Lazard Frères most of his career. Lazard was very different from the behemoth institutions such as Chase and First National City Bank that managed New York City's debt. Even in the middle years of the twentieth century, when banking was generally a staid, predictable business, Lazard was a sleek investment bank specializing in mergers and acquisitions. Its bankers had reputations as the best and the smartest, the "wizards" of finance. Lazard helped to propel the conglomerate wave of the 1960s and to pioneer hostile takeovers two decades before the buyout wave of the 1980s—activities for which its partners earned outsize salaries that also anticipated the compensation windfalls in the decades to come.[19]

It was one of these deals that brought Rohatyn into the public eye, in a rather unflattering light. ITT—the International Telephone & Telegraph Corporation—was among Rohatyn's biggest clients, a massive, sprawling conglomerate with lines in car rentals (it bought Avis), bread making (Wonder Bread), hotels (the Sheraton chain), and other industries. When ITT tried to buy the Hartford Insurance Group, the Justice Department questioned whether this might violate antitrust laws. The company lobbied to be permitted to keep Hartford, donating hundreds of thousands of dollars to the 1972 Republican convention; Rohatyn held personal meetings with officials in the Nixon administration even as the case went before the Justice Department. This lobbying became the subject of a congressional investigation. *Washington Post* writer Nicholas von Hoffman inveighed against Rohatyn, pointing a finger at the "little, stock-jobbing . . . Felix the Fixer."[20] The nickname stuck, insinuating that Rohatyn was somehow connected to a world of backroom dealings and corporate sleaze.

Given all this history, one might have thought Rohatyn would stay far away from the scandal of New York. But his discomfort over his tarnished image may in fact have made the chance to save New York all the more appealing. When he heard of the city's fiscal straits, he was immediately concerned it might lead to international financial collapse, and that increasing difficulties of life within New York might spark destructive riots throughout the city.[21] As Carey cast about for business leaders to serve on what he called a "blue-ribbon commission" to address the fiscal crisis, several different people—including David Burke, one of Carey's longtime advisers—recommended Rohatyn. Burke recalled years later that Rohatyn, a friend, had once opened up to him over lunch about his fears that he would forever be "despised" because of his connections to ITT. He had told Burke that he longed to find some way to honor the nation that had welcomed his family when they were poor refugees from the Nazis. So when the governor went looking for businessmen to take up the charge of finding a solution for the city, Burke gave the financier a call and reminded him of their chat.[22] Rohatyn had never met Carey. Immediately upon walking into the governor's New York office, though, he was impressed that Carey shared his sense that there was no short-term remedy, no set of "bookkeeping tricks" that could rescue the city's finances. They agreed that the only way to save New York was to change it thoroughly, to force it to make the difficult choices needed for reform.[23]

This was a chance for Rohatyn to remake himself and his public image. Could his skills as a dealmaker, which had gotten him embroiled in so much controversy, also rehabilitate the city? Could "the fixer" fix New York?

Gotbaum had known that a new era of fiscal crisis was dawning for more than half a year before Beame and Carey went to meet with Ford. In the fall of 1974, when Beame announced the city's first layoffs, union members had panicked. Letters streamed into Gotbaum's office expressing anxiety about both workers' employment prospects and the impact on the people who used city services. When the city announced that all the aides and counselors for the city's Department of Corrections would be laid off, Gotbaum received a petition signed by people detained at Rikers Island, who said that without the correctional aide program inmates were "vastly impossibilitied" in arranging family life and legal advice.[24] The captain of the Manhattan House of Detention wrote to Gotbaum as well, pointing out that laid-off correctional aides would probably end up on welfare.[25] After these communiqués, Gotbaum sent a telegram to the Commissioner of Corrections urging that the cuts be reconsidered, with a reference to the infamous 1971 upstate New York prison uprising: "We do not need a New York City version of Attica."[26]

Gotbaum tried to stick to a tough line with the mayor, insisting that Beame had to respect the contractual rights of union members.[27] But despite the bluster, Gotbaum knew the unions were in a tricky position. The press blamed their high wages for the fiscal crisis. He was excluded from any of the meetings taking place between the bankers and the mayor. "It is terribly important that we respond to the fiscal crisis on a unified basis," he said at a February 1975 meeting at the Municipal Labor Committee, a long-standing organization that sought to join together the diverse municipal unions in order to present a single front in bargaining with city government.[28]

Solidarity was difficult to achieve within the city's labor movement, which was divided both occupationally and politically. Memories of 1968 schoolteachers' strikes in Ocean Hill–Brownsville—which had pitted the teachers, mostly Jewish, against black parents and activists who wanted more community control of the schools—were still fresh. Albert Shanker, the president of the United Federation of Teachers, had stoked anxiety among the teachers about black anti-Semitism, tapping into their fears of the very students they taught. This particularly rankled unions such as DC 37, which had many black members; Gotbaum had attacked Shanker for feeding the controversy, setting off years of feuding between the two men and their unions. Other city employees were also sometimes at odds with Gotbaum's union. The police officers (who more and more lived outside New York) and firefighters, for example, viewed themselves as indispensable to the city in a way that the teachers and the civil servants of DC 37 were not.[29]

Gotbaum recognized that to unite these competing factions, he would need to direct them against a common enemy. He decided to organize a massive demonstration that would specifically target First National City Bank. Like Beame, Gotbaum blamed First National for the panic about the city's finances, criticizing the bank's representatives— such as Jac Friedgut—for circulating memos detailing the city's problems, going to Washington to complain about New York, and insisting that layoffs and cuts were the only recourse. The union took out a full-page ad in the *New York Times* to call for a rally on June 4, 1975. The demonstration would bring together "hospital workers, police, firemen, engineers, laborers, social workers, clerks," and other city workers "from accountants to zookeepers" to protest "the destructive role First National City Bank has played in fomenting and exploiting the financial crisis in our city." Meanwhile, DC 37 would take all its funds out of First National, and urge its members to cancel their credit cards and withdraw their money as well.[30]

Although many unions representing different groups of city workers joined the effort, not all union leaders agreed. Stephen Crowley, the president of the Detectives Endowment Association, for example, wrote to Gotbaum personally to argue that the bank couldn't be blamed for the city's problems. As he saw it, New York had high welfare costs because its generous policies had "attracted the poor from all over the nation," while students receiving free tuition drove to "tax-supported colleges in expensive automobiles." A better solution to the crisis would be to tell President Ford that New York would no longer be able to issue checks to welfare recipients after July 1—at which point the president might designate the city a disaster area, the "victim of the winds of inflation and the floods of recession," and so take over its welfare bills.[31]

The language of Crowley's letter highlighted the distinctiveness of what Gotbaum was trying to do on June 4. Crowley wanted to see the city's plight as something akin to a natural disaster, as though a hurricane had swept through the city, leaving devastation in its path. He also painted a picture of a city being taken advantage of by its poorest citizens. By contrast, Gotbaum and the other unions sought to create a moral drama out of the developing crisis, to argue that the banks were not simply reflecting the rational preferences of a market of anonymous investors but acting according to their own values, choosing to use their power to force cuts in services and to restrain the power of public workers. The unions, therefore, had a responsibility to fight back—in the interests of their members, but also for the city as a whole.

Aside from Rohatyn, the committee that Carey put together to explore ways the city might avoid default included three other members: Macy's CEO Donald Smiley; Metropolitan Life president Richard Shinn; and former Federal District Court judge Simon Rifkind, one of the city's most prominent and politically connected lawyers. Almost everyone involved in the discussions agreed that there were two parts to what the city needed to do. The first was finding a way to reorganize its debt, so the city could borrow money again and pay it off at lower interest rates, instead of the punishingly high rates it had been forced to accept in 1974. The second was persuading—or compelling—the city's leadership to drastically cut services and costs, so that investors would again believe that New York City was a safe bet.

Rohatyn and his colleagues proposed to create a new agency, controlled by New York State, to market long-term bonds on behalf of the city. The bonds would be backed by a dedicated stream of revenues from the city's sales tax—the same sales tax the city had always levied but now would be sent directly to the new state-controlled agency instead of to the city government. The agency would be named the Municipal Assistance Corporation, or MAC for short. Its board, appointed by the governor, would have the power to assess the city's progress toward a balanced budget and, if warranted, release the money that MAC raised through its bond sales. If its members deemed that the city's elected leaders were not doing enough, MAC could withhold the funds New York needed to cover its bills.

Establishing the MAC would have a double purpose: it would help raise cash while also giving the state a way to press New York City to slash its public sector. But there was no guarantee that the plan would work. Would investors who had just rejected the city's debt be willing to buy MAC bonds? And—just as important and just as unknown— would the city government accept such a radical diminution of its power?

There was some historical precedent for such an arrangement. In the 1930s, when the Great Depression and the stock market crash battered New York, the city government had faced a serious budget shortfall. Under pressure, the mayor at the time, John L. O'Brian, had accepted a "Bankers' Agreement," which the governor had negotiated with the banks. According to its terms, the banks would loan the city $70 million if it agreed to balance its budget by firing workers from the city payroll instead of raising real estate taxes. Although the Bankers' Agreement had not in fact solved the city's problems in the 1930s (only Mayor La Guardia's taxes on business and federal grants of the New Deal era had closed the budget gap), memories of this compromise still hovered over the city. Four decades later, as people in the financial community and the comptroller's office cast about for possible solutions to a new budget crisis, they would occasionally bring up that deal from a previous age.[32] It was far from clear, though, whether 1970s New York, a city far more politicized and unionized than it had been in the 1930s, would tolerate such a loss of autonomy.

If the plans for the June 4 demonstration at First National City Bank were any indication, it would not.

"What should we do if the demonstrators crowd into the branch? Should we have plywood handy in case of broken windows?"[33]

The memo distributed to First National City Bank managers aimed to prepare them for the possibility of mayhem at the approaching union rally at 111 Wall Street, the bank's check-processing center. The bank planned to station thirty-three extra guards, armed with clubs, in the lobby, and to make medical assistance available, if needed, on the twenty-third floor. "If there is violence at the rally, that will work in our favor," one executive noted.[34] The bank prepared itself in the arena of public relations as well, organizing a press conference to be held before the rally. It also contracted with the polling company BBDO to conduct public opinion surveys both before and after the demonstration to see whether New Yorkers really blamed the banks, and specifically First National, for the city's problems.[35] Every bank employee received a detailed, multipage letter from bank president William Spencer, defending the bank's actions and insisting that New York's fiscal crisis was of its own making. "Choosing where to cut will be painful," Spencer wrote. "But it's the only way to fiscal survival."[36]

Exactly how painful was detailed by Mayor Beame a week before the planned demonstration. In a televised evening address delivered before the City Council, the Board of Estimate, all the city's department heads, the leaders of all the major unions, and four hundred members of the general public, the mayor presented two budgets: one that was predicated on the city's receipt of state aid and new taxing powers, the other detailing what would happen should the city not get such help from Albany. In either case, the mayor anticipated ample austerity. Even should the city get all the aid it requested, he would need to make deep cutbacks with serious consequences. Thirty thousand city workers (out of the current workforce of 338,000) would lose their jobs, meaning 20,000 fewer students at CUNY, the closing of libraries and school programs, and fewer garbage pickups. But should the city *not* get the aid it was asking for, the consequences would be far more dire: the city's payrolls would be cut by 67,000 people, meaning mass layoffs of police officers, firefighters, schoolteachers, social workers, prison guards, sanitation workers, and more.[37]

In the address, Beame celebrated the city's long tradition of public services, especially its stellar educational system, which had produced thinkers and artists such as Felix Frankfurter and Jonas Salk, George Gershwin and James Baldwin. (For the sports fans, he also mentioned Sandy Koufax and Kareem Abdul-Jabbar.) This proud history, he warned, was now threatened because the banks were "poisoning our wells." The mayor called for a congressional investigation of the banks: because of their attacks on New York's reputation and the resulting "cash boycott," he said, the city had been forced to "move from programmed recovery to shock therapy."[38] Beame promised that despite the difficulties the city faced, he would stand strong and fight for the interests of New Yorkers. "I am very much a part of this city," he said. "It is my life, and given your support, I will not fail you."[39]

Reading news coverage of the speech, some tourists expressed their shock at the scale of the cuts. "Fifty-thousand layoffs?" said a doctor visiting from University City, Iowa, in fact understating the "crisis" scenario numbers. "That's more than the population of our whole town."[40]

The weather on Wednesday, June 4, was breezy and warm, a perfect late spring day. Getting off the subway at Wall Street, rally-goers found a swelling crowd, estimated by the newspapers at 10,000. They were packed so tightly in the canyon-like streets of Lower Manhattan that those at the back of the throng could not see the sleek granite bank building at its front. The narrow alleys between skyscrapers overflowed with people waving placards bearing messages such as "People Before Profits, Mr. Wriston," "Don't Help People Who Hurt You: Don't Bank at City Bank," "First National City Short Changes New York City," "Down With the Banks," and "Dump the Debt." Some carried brightly colored balloons, oddly festive given the grim messages of the day. From a flatbed truck bedecked with patriotic red-white-and-blue bunting, Gotbaum thundered against First National as the "chief villain" of the crisis, insisting that the banks should not be able to determine the city's social policies. Ken McFeeley, the president of the Patrolmen's Benevolent Association, got the day's largest ovation when he announced that his union would remove its pension investments from the villainous bank. "First National City can have its profits, but they're not going to have it on the backs of cops!" Frank Sisto, speaking for the sanitation workers, warned of "hundreds of thousands of tons of garbage in the streets." Barry Feinstein of Teamsters Local 237 spoke of the hospitals becoming a "mechanism for moving people to the morgue." To the roars of the crowd, he shouted, "We'll be living in rubble and ruin!"[41]

From their tinted windows high above, First National's employees peered out at the scene below. Executives paced back and forth, muttering into walkie-talkies. The violence the bank had braced for did not arrive, and its assiduous polling suggested that the protest had only a small impact on public opinion. Still, the demonstration signaled the beginning of something larger and more threatening.[42] It suggested that a gulf was opening between the people on the streets—whose neighborhoods would be swept by fire and crime, whose subway trains would now run more slowly, whose children played in the parks falling into disrepair and attended schools that would lose teachers—and the people who watched from above, whose lives in the hard-edged city would be cushioned by wealth.

Beleaguered by protests and frustrated with the banks, Mayor Beame was growing angry and tense. He was gripped by insomnia, going to bed after midnight and rising again before 7 a.m. Even when he managed to get into bed early, his wife would wake in the middle of the night to find him up and restless.[43] The *New York Times* reporter Fred Ferretti noted that the mayor's sour mood was evident in his physical tics: he bounced up and down in his seat during meetings with uncontainable irritation, and stretched up on his tiptoes to emphasize a point when speaking. He was still furious at Washington, complaining that the Soviets had been given a warmer reception than the one he'd gotten. Sometimes, he made bitter jokes about his problems. Stopping to chat with the owner of a newly opened shop on East 89th Street, he quipped: "I hope you don't experience the same cash flow problems I have." In the Albany airport, a woman rushed up to him and reported that she'd dreamed the city had been given a large amount of cash.[44] But in waking life, no such windfall seemed likely to appear.

A few days before the union demonstration, Governor Carey had announced the proposal for the Municipal Assistance Corporation. The state would release $200 million in outright aid to the city (and the banks agreed to roll over $280 million in debt)—but only if the City Council agreed to turn over its sales tax revenue and cut its budget as mandated by MAC. The city's elected leaders immediately denounced the plan, pointing out that MAC was raising money to repay creditors, not to preserve city services. MAC was a "bail-out for the banks," said Brooklyn Borough President Sebastian Leone. Donald Manes, the borough president of Queens, insisted the city jettison the state and act alone: "What we ought to do is create our own corporation." Paul O'Dwyer, the radical Speaker of the City Council, dismissed the idea of MAC outright: "We're back to the bankers' agreement of the nineteen thirties. Only worse. We'd be solving their default problems, not our own." Bronx Borough President Robert Abrams also suggested that the city did not have to accept MAC: "It's one option. Default is another."[45]

The rebellious attitude of the city politicians put Beame in an even more trying position. Was he, the leader of the city, to be the sellout who granted a state agency so much control over the city's finances? Beame knew that if MAC did not go through, the city would default, but it felt terrible to be mayor of a city that was in the process of radically curtailing its own autonomy and power. He persuaded Carey to call a meeting with his blue-ribbon panel and the City Council leadership and borough presidents. Although Beame only telephoned Rohatyn and his fellow counselors at midnight on June 3, they arrived at 9:30 sharp the next morning at City Hall. They gathered in the Blue Room, the formal meeting room in City Hall across from the mayor's private office, decorated with portraits of celebrated New York politicians from centuries past. Rohatyn explained to the city's elected leadership that without MAC, there was no hope of any money from the banks or the state. "This is not a game of chicken," he warned. "If by Monday Big Mac is not in business, you're finished."[46] By the end of the hour, most of the borough presidents and the local politicians were persuaded that "there is no alternative," as Manhattan Borough President Percy Sutton put it.[47] With this, much of the organized political resistance to MAC stopped.

Meanwhile, the city was about to get its first boost of aid from a different source: its business class. Lewis Rudin, one of the city's top real estate moguls and one of the founders of the Association for a Better New York, campaigned to persuade the owners of city real estate to prepay their property taxes. In exchange, the city would give those landlords a discount of 8 percent. By early June, Rudin had commitments from such companies as New York Telephone, Con Edison, Rockefeller Center, Chase Manhattan, and of course the Rudin Management Company itself, for a total of $140 million.[48] Even First National City Bank agreed to participate. "As I am sure you know (despite some comments to the contrary)," bank president William Spencer wrote to Rudin, First National "has always worked and will continue to work for New York City in all its major aspects."[49]

Unions contributed money to the city too, although they could not match the dollar amounts of the corporations and landlords: the radical labor union District 65, for instance, professed its "great faith" in the city and prepaid real estate taxes worth $12,500. Beame expressed his profound gratitude for the gesture of "good citizenship" during what he was still describing as simply a problem of cash flow.[50] The money came not a moment too soon, as the city needed it to cover bills coming due. Carrying checks worth $18.5 million, city aides dashed through the streets to get to the banks by closing time to deposit the money.[51]

The City Council—which had to file a formal "home rule" message endorsing the creation of the new agency—and the State Legislature spent a week hashing out the details of the law. They paid special attention to the advice of bankers whose support would be needed to sell the MAC bonds. At 2:02 a.m. on Tuesday, June 10, the message arrived in Albany that the City Council was finally ready for the legislature to vote on the bill creating MAC. At 2:45 a.m. the State Senate approved the legislation. Governor Carey signed it into law before dawn.

Beame was uneasy down to the last minute. Waiting in Gracie Mansion to hear word from Albany, he turned to Felix Rohatyn. Was he quite sure that "what we are doing is legal and in our authority?"

Rohatyn smiled and patted the mayor on the shoulder. With no small condescension, he ribbed Beame about the many questionable ways he had already stretched the borrowing power of the city: "Don't worry, Abe, you've done it plenty of times before."[52]

The board of the newly established Municipal Assistance Corporation wasted no time in meeting. It gathered in the afternoon on June 10, the very day MAC had been created, at the midtown conference rooms of the executive offices of the State of New York—its meeting place a symbol of how insulated the agency was meant to be from the influence of City Hall.

The board was dominated by businessmen. Along with Felix Rohatyn and Simon Rifkind, it included accounting executive Thomas Flynn, brokerage partner and former NYSE President John Coleman, president of the New York Telephone Company William Ellinghaus, investment banker George Gould, and Francis Barry, president of the Circle Line sightseeing boat company. There was also Robert Clifton Weaver, the president of Baruch College and the first secretary of the Department of Housing and Urban Development under Lyndon Johnson; he was MAC's only African American member. The sole woman on the board was Donna Shalala, a professor at Columbia's Teachers College who had served on Carey's transition team. She was asked to be the group's treasurer, a selection that reflected her expertise in municipal finance, but also indicated the desire of the bankers and financiers to avoid anything that could expose them and their firms to financial scrutiny: none of them wanted to bear legal responsibility for MAC. The thirty-three-year-old academic—who was excited to be part of a group that included, as she put it in later years, the "top lawyers, bankers and finance people in the world"—had no such concerns. As a result, it became her responsibility to sign off on all of MAC's financial documentation.[53]

MAC confronted a formidable task. For the city to meet its debts, the agency had to sell massive quantities of bonds to the same investors who had refused to buy city debt throughout the winter and spring. On July 7, $750 million in notes would come due, then $500 million on August 1, $1 billion on August 22, and $750 million a month later. Standard & Poor's gave MAC debt an A+ rating, but its president observed that "selling $3 billion notes and bonds in 90 days is a tall order for any issuer."[54]

Raising money for the city was only part of MAC's job, though. To win back the credit markets, MAC would have to compel the city to change its spending habits, to cut social services, and demonstrate that it was undergoing fundamental changes. As Assistant Secretary of the Treasury Gerald Parsky put it in Washington, "Whatever long-term benefits MAC provides are likely to derive from its pervasive role in the city's budget process."[55]

This was MAC's situation: it was technically a financing vehicle, but its real purpose was political. It had to force the city and its unionized workers to accept a staggering array of budget cuts, at the very moment when New Yorkers were beginning to rise up in protest. As the summer of 1975 began, New York was poised for a showdown.

8. Fear City

The leaflets were emblazoned with the gothic image of a smirking skull gazing out of a dark shroud. "A Survival Guide for Visitors to the City of New York," the cover read. "WELCOME TO FEAR CITY."

On the inside pages, tourists were warned to postpone any trips to the Big Apple: "The best advice we can give you is this: until things change, stay away from New York City if you possibly can." If a visit was absolutely necessary, tourists were advised to stay off the streets after 6 p.m., to avoid public transportation at all costs, and above all, to limit their sightseeing only to Manhattan. "In the South Bronx, which is known to police officers as 'Fort Apache,' arson has become an uncontrollable problem." The pamphlet closed with a sardonic warning, illustrated by another winking skull: "Good luck."[1]

The leaflets caused a tremendous uproar, receiving press attention not only in the city but around the country, with coverage in the *Washington Post*, *Chicago Tribune*, *San Francisco Chronicle*, and *Los Angeles Times*. The notion of a campaign to keep tourists away was lurid enough, but what was truly unsettling was that the leaflets had been produced by a coalition of unions representing New York's own police officers and firefighters. The group planned to distribute the leaflets at the city's airports, and to hold a concurrent demonstration at City Hall. "HOW MUCH IS YOUR LIFE WORTH?" read a full-page ad in the *New York Times* advertising the protest. "Don't give the city up to muggers, rapists and arsonists! It's your city . . . it's your life and safety. Attend this mass people's rally and help save a life. . . . *It could be yours.*"[2]

Beame exploded when he heard about the planned action, denouncing the campaign as "an act of rank disloyalty" and condemning the unions' efforts to arouse "fear, panic and trepidation among the city's citizens and visitors."[3] When Ken McFeeley, the president of the Patrolmen's Benevolent Association, traveled out to Kennedy International Airport early in the morning of June 13 with a stack of leaflets, he was intercepted by officials of the Transit Authority, who served him with a restraining order that the Mayor had obtained. Abandoning the notion of leafleting the airports, police officers instead drove sound trucks decked with American flags and red-white-and-blue bunting around the city, blasting out warnings about the threats to public safety.[4]

The police protests were just one of the many demonstrations roiling New York. Beame's "crisis" budget, with its "horror list" requiring the layoff of tens of thousands more city workers, was to take effect by the end of June, and much of the city seemed to be gearing up to stop the cuts. On Monday, June 9, the Board of Education held a citywide "day of mourning" for the public school system. Flags at schools were lowered to half-mast, students, parents, and teachers wore black armbands, and at 10:30 a.m. classrooms observed a five-minute period of silence. Principals then led lines of students from their classrooms as though in a fire drill, to dramatize the emergency facing the school system.[5] Later in the month, parents on the Upper West Side organized a one-day boycott, keeping their children home from school; they set up a mock overcrowded classroom to show what conditions would be like should the cuts go through. Meanwhile, the city university system simply stopped processing the last 15,000 applications it received, and senior citizens marched on City Hall to protest the closing of senior centers. The city's four largest charities objected to the plans to shutter forty day care centers, fire two thousand employees from the city's welfare department, and close mental health facilities.[6] And when a few sanitation workers were suspended, several hundred of their colleagues walked off the job, leaving tons of garbage to rot in the summer heat.[7]

The protests grew more desperate as the July 1 deadline approached. Two days before the cuts would take effect, a crowd of two hundred on City Island, at the tip of the Bronx, blocked the island's sole bridge for two hours, furious about plans to close their only fire station. "Nero fiddled while Rome burned," read one of their hand-lettered signs. The next day, eight hundred people gathered on the Lower East Side outside the Engine Company 15 firehouse, forming a "bucket brigade" to pass buckets up and down the line as though to show how the community would have to fight fires after the budget cuts. At 113th Street and Amsterdam Avenue, five hundred people marched to the local fire station to drop off petitions to keep the firehouse open. The firefighters there were lingering around Engine 47 just "waiting for the ax to fall."[8]

The sanitation workers union filed a legal challenge to stop its members from being laid off. When this was turned back in court, John DeLury, the union president, warned the newspapers that wildcat strikes (that is, strikes unauthorized by the union leadership) would be the inevitable result. "There's nothing I can do, there's nothing the court can do, there's nothing the Mayor can do to head it off. I, the Mayor, Christ Almighty is not going to stop this."[9]

As the last hours of the fiscal year ticked away, the Beame administration set the mass layoffs in motion. Shortly before midnight, the teletype in police stations all over the city tapped out a message: "Due to the fiscal crisis, it is necessary to lay off 5,034 police officers and detectives. Commanding officers shall notify members appearing on the revised list that their services are terminated as of 2400 hours, June 30th, 1975."

Those on the list were expected to turn in their badges and guns immediately. "We've known all along that it was coming," said one commander. "But when it comes, it hits you like a guillotine."[10]

New York had long been seen as "a laboratory for liberal assumptions about the proper scope of government," as George F. Will put it in the *Washington Post*.[11] But the July layoffs were a lab experiment in a different way. How much resistance would there be to the plans to restructure the city as the banks demanded? Would popular protests against the cuts change the position of Albany or Washington? How far would the city's labor unions go to protect the city's public services and the union members' jobs? And how would the newly formed Municipal Assistance Corporation respond? As the message that the layoffs were beginning went out at midnight on June 30, the entire city—and much of the country—seemed to be watching, waiting to see what would happen next.

On the first day of the new fiscal year, July 1, New York awoke to a new reality. Throughout the boroughs, city employees who were usually there had vanished.

The city, perhaps hoping for a last-minute infusion of aid from Albany, had made no contingency plans to cover for the laid-off workers, so they were simply missing from their posts. Traffic jams clogged the Manhattan streets because no traffic police officers were on duty at the bridges and tunnels. Fifteen firehouses were padlocked, and twenty-two day care centers closed.[12] Seven of the city's drawbridges were left frozen in the "down" position; cars could get across, but marine traffic was blocked.[13] The Parking Violations Bureau on Staten Island was shut; anyone who wanted to pay a parking ticket had to go to Brooklyn.[14] Even when offices were open, staff shortages meant that many people were turned away. One elderly woman, who had come down from 157th Street to 34th Street in an attempt to get her Medicaid card, told a reporter that she was too weak to make the trip again: "I don't know what I'll do."[15]

By the afternoon, the city was in chaos. As soon as the layoffs were confirmed, ten thousand city sanitation workers walked off the job, just as their union president had predicted. (He continued to insist that the strike was unofficial and not coordinated from above, although the Sanitation Commissioner described it as "the best organized wildcat strike I've ever seen.") Piles of garbage rose in Harlem, the South Bronx, Astoria, and Bay Ridge. On the West Side, trash spilled out of overflowing plastic bags, cascading across the sidewalk and blocking foot traffic. On Park Avenue there was talk of hiring private trash collectors, or else of hiding the refuse in the basements and spraying it with chemicals to keep down the smell—anything to keep the streets clean. In Red Hook, heaps of paper bags filled with garbage rose almost six feet tall outside of public housing projects by the end of the strike's first day.[16] The sanitation workers joked that they planned to dump loads of trash on the lawn at Gracie Mansion.[17]

The normal order of things was reversed. The laid-off workers, invisible when they had been doing their jobs, were suddenly visible all around the New York streets. The people who had been charged with maintaining public order became unruly themselves, turning against the city that had turned against them. At about 2 p.m., hundreds of laid-off police officers began to mass around City Hall, carrying handmade signs bearing such slogans as "Burn Baby Burn" and "Beame Is a Deserter, a Rat. He Left the City Defenseless." They milled about the park and City Hall, waiting for Ken McFeeley, the union president, to arrive. A few dozen walked onto the Brooklyn Bridge, briefly halting traffic. Then about three hundred stormed onto the bridge's entrance and exit ramps, blocking them with wooden police barricades. Some marchers carried American flags; one officer on a horse was heard encouraging the demonstrators to "get the flags in front." Once McFeeley arrived at the rally, his speech was punctuated by shouts of "Strike! Strike!" as the crowd called out for him to join the demonstrators on the bridge. He refused to do so, pushing, sweaty, through the angry throng, encouraging people to wait before taking any drastic action. But as soon as his speech ended the rest of the crowd—hopped up on emotion and alcohol—ran onto the bridge. One protester popped the tire of a car with the staff of a flagpole; others were throwing beer bottles, threatening to flip cars over, and shouting at their brethren in uniform who were trying to maintain some semblance of order. The on-duty cops were overmatched, as became clear when they tried to seize one especially raucous protester. A fight immediately broke out between the cops in uniform and those who had been laid off, and the crowd dragged the arrested man from the police car that was trying to take him away; eventually he escaped into the streets. For five hours, the protesting cops blocked the bridge, roaming around and spilling into the streets of Lower

Manhattan.[18] They eventually dispersed, sodden and exhausted, drifting through the streets in the still-hot early evening.[19]

Protests swirled throughout the rest of the city as well. One officer, never identified, broke into the North Brooklyn radio system, urging police to refuse to answer emergency calls as a protest against the firings. At the city's asphalt plant in Flushing, Queens, two city officials conducting an inspection were assaulted—one kicked in the groin, the other punched in the face and ribs—by a furious group of Highway Department laborers who had been laid off.[20]

The next day, July 2, ten times as many firefighters as usual called in sick. Garbage fires blazed throughout the city, but there was no one to respond to them. Fire companies had to be called in all the way from Staten Island to come to the Bronx.[21] One Brooklyn fire dispatcher estimated that there were at least 125 small garbage fires "in every neighborhood" in the borough. In East Harlem, the streets were turned into what one reporter described as a "vast incinerator of flaming garbage," leaving charred and blackened piles lining the streets.[22] Some people saw setting trash on fire as a form of neighborhood service, keeping their own streets clean when the city would not. Elsewhere, young men spilled garbage into the streets and vacant lots, setting it ablaze and then adding cherry bombs and firecrackers to heighten the flames as a kind of free-form protest. "If we're going to burn, let the whole city burn," said one young man at 103rd Street and Lexington Avenue in Manhattan.[23]

Neighborhoods rallied around their fire stations. In Bayside, Queens, the owner of a hardware store, whose business had once been saved by a fire company now slated for closure, pasted up signs on lampposts: "We have just begun to fight."[24] In Bushwick, hundreds of people blocked the doors of the local firehouse to prevent the fire equipment from being removed.[25] When police came to clear them away, they refused to dismantle the barricades they had set up. Fourteen firefighters were trapped within the station—and as one lieutenant put it, they were not exactly "unwilling hostages." The neighborhood, he said, had seen 2,200 fires the previous year: "They don't call it Wood City for nothing."[26]

In the afternoon, another police protest took place downtown. Older officers—the ones whose seniority had let them escape layoffs—ran around chasing the younger, laid-off cops in a game of cat and mouse to try to stop them from blocking traffic in Lower Manhattan. They could not, however, stop laid-off highway workers from taking over the Henry Hudson Parkway, halting traffic for miles in yet another wildcat protest.[27]

The events of early July resonated throughout the United States. New York was not the only city to see public workers out on strike that summer. Although the scale of the city's problems was unique, the general issues that New York confronted were not. All across the country, cities had been hollowed out by white flight, suburbanization, and the movement of manufacturing to the South and overseas in search of lower wages and more compliant local governments. These changes had been hidden at first by economic growth, but the recession that had started in 1974 left governments everywhere scrambling to fund their public services. The public sector workers who had organized during the 1960s, meanwhile, were eager to find ways to keep pressing forward, to win a more secure position in what seemed to be a rapidly eroding middle class.

On July 1, while the New York City workers were beginning their actions, 76,000 state employees struck in Pennsylvania, demanding 10 percent wage increases—three times what the state was offering. Rumor had it that when the Democratic governor refused to grant the wage hike, saying he needed to keep taxes down, the leader of the employees' union retorted: "Let's go out and close down this God-damned state." In Seattle, July 1 marked the day when voters went to the polls after firefighters angered by the mayor's budget-cutting plans collected enough signatures for a recall election.[28] And in August, San Francisco police officers and firefighters went on strike, despite a California law prohibiting them from doing so. They were pressing for a wage increase of over 10 percent to cope with inflation and keep up with wages paid for similar work in other California cities.[29] The city's Board of Supervisors initially resisted their demands. "The spectacle of New York is too well known to all," warned Mayor Joseph Alioto: "San

Francisco can go the route of New York unless we call a halt to unreasonable expenses right now."[30] But after a tumultuous few weeks—the firefighters threatened to picket the city airport, striking police officers began shooting out streetlamps, and someone left a small bomb to go off on Alioto's lawn—the mayor seized emergency powers and granted the workers the wage increase they sought.[31]

It was clear that the stage was set for protracted conflicts. Newly unionized public sector employees were not going to sit still for budget cuts that undermined the economic position they had only recently carved out. Their militancy, though, was breeding a fierce reaction—not only from the conservative activists who had long opposed public sector unions but also from mainstream liberals. The *New York Times* bemoaned the "power-giddy unions" that stood in the way of necessary retrenchment, while the *Philadelphia Inquirer* insisted that the time had come to "protect the public" from the "excessive exercise of power by unionized civil servants."[32] John Rousselot, a conservative California congressman who had served for a time as the national public relations chairman for the John Birch Society, proclaimed: "If government is to maintain its sovereignty, it cannot share this responsibility with a handful of professional union men who are not answerable to an electorate."[33]

As demonstrations raged nationwide, the federal government and the Municipal Assistance Corporation were keeping a close eye on New York City. On July 1, the same day that layoffs were announced and the police officers stormed the Brooklyn Bridge, the MAC board also convened. They heard a report that MAC bonds were meeting with a "very cool" reception, as investors wondered "what changes were going to take place within the City of New York's budgetary procedures" and whether there would be "some visible indication" that the city was changing its course.[34] In Washington, Treasury Secretary William Simon and Domestic Council adviser James Cannon wrote Ford a memo warning that MAC needed to do even more to "force" changes in the city. They wanted New York to make far-reaching reforms such as closing hospitals and starting to charge tuition at CUNY, in addition to making further job cuts and extracting wage concessions from the unions.

Simon and Cannon advised the Ford administration to establish a liaison with MAC to push for such changes. This connection, of course, could not be allowed to become public: "Nothing would play more into the hands of the unions and the City Administration, which could claim—to a highly responsive audience—that the Ford administration was threatening and bullying the City into actions designed to harm the low and middle classes." Nonetheless, Simon and Cannon advised, the federal government should contact MAC board members to urge them to lean on Beame.[35]

The anxiety at MAC grew more intense when, within days of the layoffs, Albany allowed the city to raise some taxes, and Beame immediately announced that he would rehire 2,000 of the laid-off police officers and 750 firefighters.[36] Meanwhile, the sanitation workers union hashed out a backroom deal whereby its laid-off employees would return to work, with the union temporarily putting up the money to pay their salaries. The implication was that more funding would be forthcoming, and the rehiring would become permanent.

From the perspective of the MAC board, it seemed that the worst scenario was coming to pass. The protests had shown how uncontrollable the city was, how far it was from accepting retrenchment. And the money from Albany indicated that the city did not have to accept it—that there might even be a reward for protest. The members of the MAC board decided that it was time for them to confront city officials directly.

The man charged with establishing MAC as a more forceful presence in city affairs was Herbert Elish, who had served as Sanitation Commissioner in the Lindsay administration.

Elish was chosen for the job because it was thought that his background in the Department of Sanitation would enable him to reach out to the city's unions. He had grown up in the Midwood neighborhood of Brooklyn, and as a young man had even considered himself a "socialist" thanks to the influence of his uncle, a high school principal who'd loaned him such books as Edward Bellamy's utopian classic, *Looking Backward*. When Elish went to Williams College he left his old politics, like his old neighborhood, behind. But he was still idealistic enough that when Lindsay had contacted him he was happy to leave a career as a Washington lawyer to work in city government. After Beame was elected, Elish departed City Hall and went to work at First National City Bank.

Like most people at the bank and in the city's elite political circles, Elish felt there was no real alternative to MAC. He recognized the need to calm the unions. But over time, he would become less than entirely comfortable with the trend represented by the organization. To him, such state agencies would come to represent "a substantial diminution of democracy," with just "half a dozen people" who had not been elected taking charge of decisions about the city's future.[37]

Following through on the plan to pressure city officials in person, Elish and the MAC board called in Mayor Beame and his Deputy Mayor James Cavanagh to meet with them on July 17. It must have seemed a long way from City Hall: MAC's board had begun gathering at the cushy midtown offices of Simon Rifkind's law firm, on the twenty-eighth floor of a skyscraper at Park Avenue and 52nd Street. The conference room windows offered panoramic views of the city grid.[38]

Cavanagh and Beame were not MAC's first visitors that day. They were preceded by a group of bankers, including David Rockefeller and William Spencer, who warned that the mayor had lost all credibility because of the decision to rehire some of the workers he'd laid off at the start of July. Such acts, they insisted, represented "business as usual," and they were directly responsible for the "apathy" of the credit markets regarding the MAC bonds. MAC needed to reestablish that it was in charge and force real change in the city. Nothing that Beame did, Rockefeller argued, would make the investing public have any faith in him again.[39]

The bankers left before Beame and Cavanagh arrived for their meeting. The mayor might have thought that he had come to MAC to negotiate. But after their conversation with the financiers, Rohatyn and the others were not inclined to yield an inch. William Ellinghaus, the president of New York Telephone, told Beame that the financial community was looking for clear evidence that New York was committed to a more "Spartan type of living." Yes, the city had laid off thousands of employees, but that was not enough: the layoffs were haphazard, it appeared that the city was willing to reverse course if only more money came in from Albany, and all the cuts Beame had made were still not sufficient to balance the budget. What was needed was deeper structural change. Rohatyn said the only chance Beame had to persuade the credit markets to become friendly again was to reshape the city so drastically that there could be no doubt about New York's new direction. This was why MAC had decided it was imperative to cut services even more dramatically: only then would the financial community be persuaded that the city had truly changed its ways. "Overkill" was needed to have the necessary "shock impact" on the markets.[40] Investors, Rohatyn believed, were shying away from New York because the "city's way of life is disliked nation-wide."[41]

When the MAC board told Beame to impose tuition at CUNY, he seemed "stricken," as one observer put it. He objected that the money tuition would raise—about $32 million—would only be a drop in the bucket of what the city needed, while the poor and working-class population that the university served would find the fees a real burden. Rohatyn told him that he didn't get it: it wasn't the money that mattered but the symbolism of it, the evidence that the city was changing its "lifestyle" for good.[42]

After he left the meeting with the MAC board, Beame announced that he would have to renege on the deal he had cut with the rehired sanitation workers: 1,434 of them would be dismissed right away, with another 750 to follow by the end of the month. The city simply did not have the money to keep them on. The union president was furious: "They lied, they absolutely lied," he said, fuming that he had been told there would be no more layoffs in July.[43]

Sanitation Commissioner Robert T. Groh reported that garbage pickups would be cut by half in the city's most congested areas. In some parts of the city, street sweeping would halt altogether—Groh hoped that New Yorkers might clean the gutters themselves, "out of a sense of civic responsibility."[44] But such community feeling could go only so far. By early the following week, more than a thousand tons of garbage, rancid in the summer heat, had piled up around the city. Garbage cans swelled with trash; bulging bags sat out in front of buildings. In Crown Heights, Brooklyn, where one-third of the sanitation workers for the district had been laid off, frustrated residents began to throw mounds of fetid refuse into the middle of the street. "The garbage was just piling up and going into the ninth day and it was just laying there, so we put it out where they had to pick it up," said one woman. People in Park Slope did the same thing, and residents of Canarsie were thinking about join-ing in. "This is the only way the city responds," one of them said.[45] On July 30—the final day of work for those 750 sanitation workers—the city had almost three hundred garbage fires, as people sought to simply incinerate the waste themselves. The burning piles of trash in the middle of the street were like signal flares, as though every neighborhood was trying to make its plight visible, impossible to ignore any longer.[46]

But City Hall was no longer looking only at the streets of New York. Instead, as MAC insisted, Beame was directing his gaze farther afield.

A few days after the showdown with Beame, the MAC board held a meeting with the presidents of the city's major labor unions, who had privately told Elish about their irritation at being shut out of MAC con-versations.[47]

Rumors were flying in labor circles that union members would be asked to accept a wage freeze because of the fiscal crisis, and the response of the city's labor leaders had been fierce. Albert Shanker of the UFT said he would "rather see the city default. That way everybody would be affected, bankers, utilities, oil companies, and not the workers alone." Ken McFeeley of the police officers' union agreed: "Then nobody gets paid, the unions, welfare, the bankers—we'll all be in the same boat together." Victor Gotbaum gave a verbal shrug: "If the city defaults, it defaults."[48]

Behind the scenes, though, the divisions in the city's labor move-ment were growing. And Gotbaum's own ideas about the fiscal crisis were changing. Initially, in June, he had seen it as a political smoke-screen, and felt skeptical that it was real at all.[49] But by July he was gen-uinely worried about bankruptcy. While at first the crisis might have been "manufactured by the banks," he said at a DC 37 Executive Board meeting, it had developed so far that "the threat was real and chaos imminent as the situation got out of hand."[50] He had also disliked the "Fear City" campaign, which he thought served the interests of the uniformed services but no one else. At a meeting of the Municipal Labor Committee, he called for unity: "We must decide whether we will be an organization moving together or individual groups moving in terms of self-interest."[51]

Gotbaum's real fear was that public sector unions might lose collective bargaining rights as a result of the fiscal crisis. It had always been his inclination to avoid outright confrontation; he preferred mediation and bargaining to strikes. He knew well that if the city went into bankruptcy there would no longer be any way to bargain. The union contracts could be voided by a judge, and the union itself weakened or broken altogether. For Gotbaum, any settlement, no matter how bad, was preferable to that.[52] This emphasis on protecting collective bargaining above all else set Gotbaum apart from some of the other union leaders, such as McFeeley of the PBA and Richard Vizzini of the Uniformed Firefighters Association. Facing election challenges within their own unions, they were far less willing to accept wage cuts or freezes that were sure to be unpopular with members.[53]

When Gotbaum, Vizzini, McFeeley, Shanker, and other union leaders arrived at the Park Avenue skyscraper on July 21, they expressed their frustration with the development of events and the way they were perennially blamed for causing the crisis. Gotbaum, who had been designated the unions' spokesman for the meeting, said the labor movement had been made into a "scapegoat." Fifteen thousand city workers had already lost their jobs. The situation could hardly be worse if New York did default.[54]

Just as Gotbaum was speaking, however, news arrived that the price of MAC bonds had fallen 10 percent over the course of their first day of public trading. (The initial offers had been privately placed with banks.)[55] The meeting ended on a grim note.

The fear that MAC might completely fail to raise the money needed by New York prompted the bankers to press ever more aggressively for the evidence of change they believed was necessary to create a market for the bonds. David Rockefeller wrote a letter demanding a "definitive program" without delay. Representatives of Chase and Merrill Lynch sent their own letter: "The city is on trial for its life. Its chances are slim and mere words will not suffice."[56] Rohatyn said that he saw a 70 percent chance that the city would default by July 29—and that the result would be complete chaos.[57]

The floundering bond sales gave more weight to MAC's insistence that the layoffs were not enough. Beame announced that the unions had until July 29 to agree to more layoffs or a wage freeze, and that if they did not, the city would impose such conditions unilaterally—even though a freeze clearly violated the union contracts. He also said he was going to support a transit fare hike, and that he thought it would be necessary to start charging tuition at CUNY. Such changes came hard to Beame. "I've said time and again I couldn't be Mayor if it wasn't for my opportunity to go to the tuition-free college," he said mournfully. "I know it's no good politically. I don't give a god-damn politically. We've got to get the funds to run the city."[58]

The labor leaders who met with the city to discuss the wage freeze proposal included Gotbaum, Shanker, Barry Feinstein of the Teamsters, and John DeLury of the Sanitation Workers. An unusual new figure also attended the negotiations: Jack Bigel, a labor consultant who worked closely with DeLury. Earlier in his life, Bigel had been a man of the left, an organizer for one of the first public sector unions in the city, the United Public Workers, which was accused of being Communist-led. But Bigel had come to see himself as a pragmatist, someone who retained his "social viewpoint" but didn't care what label was applied to it. As he told the *New York Times* in 1976, "I am not an anti-Marxist, I am not a Marxist."

Bigel knew all the labor leaders in the city because he ran a consulting service, the Program Planners, which analyzed statistical data about wages, cost of living, health insurance, and other economic facts to help the unions craft their negotiating strategies. His familiarity with economic statistics made him comfortable working with city finances, and he was perfectly suited to acting as a go-between, connecting Rohatyn and the bankers with people from the world of labor. Even though he did not represent any particular union—indeed, perhaps because of this—he would become one of the main people the city and the banks consulted to understand the labor perspective throughout the crisis.[59]

The talks, held at the Americana Hotel, had a few moments of drama. (Gotbaum once stalked out of a meeting, slamming the door, only to return minutes later when he remembered that it was being held in his own room.)[60] But despite these episodes of heightened emotion, it soon became clear where the talks were heading. A clear split had emerged between Gotbaum and the others. He no longer wanted to lead a movement against the banks. His main goal now was to encourage his members to accept the wage freeze, which had only recently appeared entirely unthinkable. On July 31, he agreed to defer for one year the increases his members were contractually entitled to. He was not "thrilled" with it, he said, but it was preferable to any of the disastrous alternatives. "We will be living in a City in trouble, but with this package, we will, at least, continue to live."[61]

The members of DC 37 voted to accept the deal. But the police and firefighters unions did not, and neither did the teachers' union, which was in the midst of contract negotiations with the city. Unity within the city's labor movement—however flimsy it might have been—was shattered.

The same day that Gotbaum agreed to the wage freeze, Beame once more convened the members of the City Council to lay out his proposal for retrenchment. All the unions that had not accepted the terms of the freeze would have it imposed upon their members, despite the dubious legality of that maneuver; city employees in management, too, would have their salaries frozen. The capital budget would be cut by $275 million, the CUNY budget sliced by $32 million, and the fare for subways and buses hiked from 35 to 50 cents. "There is nothing I have done in public life that has been more bitter than recommending these slashing economies that affect each and every one of us," Beame told the City Council. "We will sacrifice and change our life style, but we will not cripple or hobble our great city."[62]

It was an effort at a commanding performance. But no rhetoric, no gesture could disguise the reality: the city was no longer under Beame's control. The very same day, the MAC board issued its own statement, emphasizing the need for New York to undertake a "fundamental rethinking" of the "quality and level of services" the city could provide. "We believe that to balance the budget, to restore the confidence of the financial community whose resources we need in order to survive, to guarantee the survival of New York there is an urgent need to alter the traditional view of what city government can and should do."[63] The MAC board was careful to insist that it did not want to infringe on the city's self-governance: "We do not wish to govern New York. We hope only to assist the elected leaders of the city through a very difficult crisis."[64] But the unmistakable message was that locally elected leaders were subject to the demands of the bond market—the people across the country who bought the city's notes and bonds. As one city official said to the *Times*, "Our problems have reached the point where we have to consider the money lender in Chicago and Los Angeles, and not just the homeowner in Queens."[65]

The city workers losing their jobs, the parents concerned about the size of their children's classes, the neighborhood residents angry about garbage piling up on the sidewalks, the people in fire-swept neighborhoods afraid of losing protection had not taken into account whose needs really counted in making decisions about their city. The marchers and protesters could not affect the people who had real power: those around the country who had purchased the city's debts. These investors were now Beame's constituency as much as the residents of New York, and perhaps more so.

9. The Facts of Life

Throughout the summer of 1975, the national press debated the problems of New York. Many editorialists compared New York to a bankrupt corporation, though the *St. Louis Post-Dispatch* jeered that "unlike a company that goes broke and whose assets are sold off to pay creditors, New York presumably will not be put on the auction block. After all, who would buy it?"[1] The *Washington Post* mocked the "myth so deeply embedded in New York's politics that things are 'free' if government provides them."[2] The *Miami Herald* compared New York City to "a drunk in the family who loses most of his paycheck on the way home every Friday."[3] For the *Chicago Tribune*, the city's public sector unions were to blame: "New York City is writhing in financial agony—some say it is dying—but the municipal unions that have been carving their pounds of flesh out of the city's emaciated body for years are unwilling to make the slightest sacrifice to help the city now."[4] And the *Baltimore Sun* anticipated President Ford's comparison of New York to the nation as a whole: "The day may come when the federal government will face a crisis similar to the one New York faces now. And no government will be able to bail Uncle Sam out."[5]

Yet not all the editorial writers were so hostile to the city, and some

suggested that despite its problems it should not be pushed into bankruptcy. What if New York's collapse were not an isolated instance of
poor management and fraudulent accounting, but rather a harbinger of
a wave of municipal bankruptcies? What would the impact be on cities
across the nation, and even on the financial system of the country as a
whole? The *Boston Globe* suggested there was nothing particularly distinctive about the situation: "New York's problems are not so very different from those of other big cities—it is just suffering them earlier and
harder."[6] The *Washington Post* recommended some kind of federal bailout for the city, warning that unless the government was willing to act
as a "lender of last resort" the entire municipal and state bond market
might collapse.[7] Even the editors of the *Baltimore Sun* allowed that "the
consequences of a New York bankruptcy could be so harmful for other
state and local governments which borrow to live, the federal government has some responsibility here."[8]

The problems debated in the national press raised the question: What
options did New York have in the summer of 1975?

Some local political leaders argued that it was time for the city to
break free of the finicky investors who were starving it for funds. Instead
of trying to reshape its policies so that it could borrow money again,
they said, New York City could simply require the banks, pension funds,
and insurance companies located within its borders to buy the city's
bonds. City Council President Paul O'Dwyer, Manhattan Borough
President Percy Sutton, and Bronx Borough President Robert Abrams
wrote a letter to Governor Carey and the majority leaders in the State
Senate and Assembly arguing that the time had come for the city to stop
relying on "the whim of distant investors . . . We must act like a government, not a beggar in search of funds."[9] Forcing banks to buy bonds
would have been unlikely to pass legal muster, though, and Carey never
gave a serious response to the proposal.

Others argued, once more, that the federal government should share
the burden of paying for the city's services. Mayor Beame, along with
political and social leaders to his left, made the case that New York City
provided inestimable economic and social benefits to the country as a

whole. Historically, it had offered a vast program of social benefits to African Americans, who had come north because they were fleeing the violence and exclusion of Jim Crow; in other words, the city had picked up the bill for the sins of the American South. Likewise, as a magnet for immigrants, the city bore the weight of global poverty that brought people from around the world to the United States. These were not problems of the city's making, yet they took a toll directly on New York's budget. Felix Rohatyn joined the mayor in arguing that Washington should pay for Medicaid and AFDC, instead of demanding that the city take up a full quarter of the bill. One letter-writer to the *New York Times* made the same suggestion: instead of attacking the city's social programs, the federal government should take them over and replicate them throughout the country, their cost borne by the entire American population instead of by individual urban centers.[10]

But even as some of the city's elites pressed for federal aid, they also kept agitating for cuts in city services. They sought to get old-time politicians out of the city's budget office, encouraging Beame to bring in new deputies who would reflect the expertise and values of the corporate sector. The most dramatic structural change that they pushed through was the creation of a new state-level agency that removed final authority over the city's finances from New York's elected politicians, giving it instead to people who could be trusted to impose cuts. Such a plan could never have succeeded at an earlier time: no one would have approved handing authority over the budget to a council of seven people, the majority of them picked by the governor. But in the crisis the unthinkable became real.

A muggy heat wave gripped New York in the first weeks of August. People broke the law to open thousands of fire hydrants in neighborhoods throughout the city.[11] Two thousand young people—mostly black and Puerto Rican—employed in the city's summer jobs program blocked traffic in Harlem for four hours one afternoon, crowding into the streets around a Youth Services Agency pay office, protesting they had not received their paychecks.[12] "I haven't been paid for three weeks," one young man said. "This is crazy. The slavery days are over."[13]

At a speech dedicating the Federal Hall National Memorial in Lower Manhattan, Beame found his words drowned out by the angry boos of the crowd and calls to "shut up!" Sweating and shaken, he stepped back from the podium, briefly silenced, before insisting on finishing his speech over the roar.[14] After working full days, the mayor and his aides spent their nights huddled in a windowless room in the basement of the Municipal Building, where relentless air conditioning kept temperatures around 50 degrees despite the stifling heat outdoors.[15]

The prevailing mood was summed up, perhaps, by a grim letter to the editor that appeared in mid-August in the *New York Times*. The author, an urban planner, suggested the time had come to "depopulate" the city of New York. The city was more crowded and noisy every year, its housing stock dilapidated, its number of jobs too small. "Ostentatious wealth" and "slums that rival the worst in Calcutta" jutted up against each other. Even if a return to fiscal solvency were possible, it would not solve these problems; the only solution was to flee "this death-like urban environment." The writer, it seemed, had already taken his own advice, having decamped to North Long Beach, New Jersey.[16]

Meanwhile, New York's financial needs seemed inexhaustible. Even after all its layoffs, the city needed to come up with about a billion dollars more for September payrolls, welfare, and debt service.[17] There was no getting around the fact that the Municipal Assistance Corporation was having trouble selling its bonds. The small banks around the country, which had once seen New York City debt as a secure investment, no longer wanted to purchase anything bearing the words *New York*. "If there is one theme to the questions the salesmen get, it's 'what happens to the MAC bonds if the city defaults?'" one banker told the *New York Times*.[18] The brokers at the bond department at one Philadelphia-based brokerage started telling their clients that New York City would default on its debt sometime in the winter. The city had to be forced to live "within its means," they said, and the conflict between "the world of reality vs. the world of politics" meant that this was unlikely to happen in time to stave off collapse.[19]

Despite his intense interest in New York's fate, President Ford had made no public statements about events in the city since his meeting with Beame and Carey in May. He chose an August visit to Belgrade, in the Communist country of Yugoslavia, to break his silence.

The City Hall in Belgrade had the same pretentious trappings of officialdom as city halls in the United States—red drapes, marble floor, a hundred chairs, forty-foot-high ceilings. Perhaps the sheer familiarity of this studied grandeur inspired Ford to open up about New York. "They don't know how to handle money," he complained about the city's elected leaders. "All they know how to do is spend it." They had been pressing the president for funds, but he had refused "until they get their management straightened out." The Yugoslav politicians expressed their sympathy, observing that it was tough to run a big city. Ford heartily agreed.[20]

When reports broke in New York that Ford was complaining about their city in the Communist bloc, the city's politicians reacted with scorn. "I never thought I'd see the day when the President of the United States would go around the world talking disparagingly about any part of this country," complained Mayor Beame. His office issued a "tongue-in-cheek" statement that New York should open talks with the Soviet Union: "That appears to be the fastest way to get aid in Washington."[21]

The propriety of their location aside, Ford's comments reflected the rising concern within Washington about New York's possible bankruptcy and its impact. With MAC's bond sales faltering, it seemed increasingly likely that the city was going to wind up unable to pay its debts. Some officials believed the collapse was very close indeed. On August 1, Richard Dunham, the former Rockefeller adviser, wrote a report for Ford and James Cannon stating that the "central question" was whether the city would be forced into default in August—or whether the inevitable might at least be postponed until the fall.[22]

For Felix Rohatyn and others on the MAC board, the struggling bond sales made it clear that the city's only real chance of survival was through loans from the federal government. No other lender would have the financial might to rescue the city. Rohatyn had traveled to Washington at the end of July to talk to Treasury Secretary William Simon and to Arthur Burns, the chair of the Federal Reserve; even a tentative commitment from them to consider loans to the city, he felt, would go far toward reassuring investors that New York would remain solvent, and thus would help with marketing the MAC bonds.[23] But no commitment was forthcoming. While he was in Washington, Rohatyn also argued again that the federal government should cover far more of the city's share of its welfare bill. "If a Federal takeover [of welfare] could be accomplished, I know damn well we would have a viable city financially," he told the press.[24]

Ford and his advisers did not appreciate the haranguing. Simon had appointed Edwin Yeo, a young undersecretary of the Treasury, to chair a steering group that would follow events in New York. In mid-August, Yeo reported that the outlook for the city was the worst it had been for months. Far from whipping the city into shape, MAC had devolved into "an impotent and divided group, the most vocal faction of which seems to be lobbying for a 'federal involvement.'"[25] Ford's economic adviser L. William Seidman complained that the city had not carried out its austerity plans as promised, citing Beame's decision to rehire the laid-off police, fire, and sanitation workers after the "disruptive actions" of early July. Nor had it presented a three-year budget plan or a plan to remove operating expenses from the capital budget.[26] Simon himself was especially scathing about Carey, whom he viewed as trying to shift the blame onto the banks and the federal government.[27] When Peter Peyser, a Republican congressman from Westchester, contacted the White House to attempt to set up a meeting between Ford and the New York congressional delegation, Donald Rumsfeld instructed him to contact Simon instead. "I told him to call you—that you were the single-stop, all-purpose plug point for the Administration on New York City," Rumsfeld wrote to Simon, adding a sarcastic "Congratulations."[28]

But even as Ford and his closest circle tried to distance themselves from developments in the city, Yeo was busy trying to imagine what would happen once New York went under. It was hard to believe that the federal government could remain completely uninvolved if the city actually declared bankruptcy. For example, a general strike might spread among firefighters and police officers if the city were unable to make payroll, and while the state might be able to handle that situation, Washington also needed to be prepared to step in. Bankruptcy could also mean that welfare and Medicaid payments would cease, cutting off money that desperate people needed to survive. The New York Stock Exchange might be closed for days—or longer—"in the event of civil disorder."[29]

Even the nationwide financial system seemed to be more susceptible to events in New York than Simon had believed at first. Although Treasury officials insisted that the main challenge was merely "psychological," surveys conducted by the Federal Reserve showed that a sizable number of medium-sized and small banks across the country were extremely heavily invested in New York's debt. Looking at bank capital, for example—the difference between a bank's assets and its liabilities—showed that there were fifty-one banks across the country that had more than half their capital tied up in New York City debt. Six of those banks owned city paper worth more than 125 percent of their total capital, meaning that they had effectively borrowed money from elsewhere to invest in New York.[30] All these banks would be likely to fail if the city declared bankruptcy. Even if the total number of outright bank collapses was fairly small, such "potential failures" and the general uncertainty "could cause a worldwide lack of confidence in the major U.S. institutions." Yeo argued that the FDIC and the Federal Reserve had to be ready to issue credit and help impaired banks recover—even if this opened the Ford administration anew to the charge that it was willing to "bail out" the banks but not the city.[31]

By the end of August, the Ford administration had conjured a scenario in which the New York Stock Exchange was shut, the city police were on strike, welfare checks to New Yorkers had stopped, and bank failures were ricocheting around the country. Yet it still refused to aid the city, insisting that the best thing the federal government could do was stay out of New York's affairs.

———

In the absence of aid from Washington, banks lost interest in the MAC bonds, which suddenly seemed almost as risky as those issued directly by the city itself. At the end of August, the top executives at First National City Bank, Chase, and Morgan Guaranty met with Rohatyn and Carey to say that they would do nothing else to help MAC raise the money the city needed to cover its bills and debts through the end of the year.[32]

Governor Carey was now growing anxious about the solvency of the state, not just the city. His director of the budget, Peter Goldmark, had written a memo describing the extent to which the city's problems were becoming a drag on New York State. The state, like the city, was running a persistent budget deficit, which was coming under increasing scrutiny. "It is not an exaggeration to say we are at a point where the danger to the State is as great as the danger to the City," Goldmark warned. "We have all seen how the passage of time limits choices and erodes the confidence a government enjoys. We face a clear set of dangers; the time for us to get moving is now."[33]

The problems of MAC and the deepening fears about the state's finances led Carey to take action, convening a special session of the state legislature to press for the creation of a new state agency: the Emergency Financial Control Board, charged with developing a plan to lead New York City to a balanced budget by the end of 1978. The board would be empowered to order the city to reduce its spending, to evaluate and audit the city's records, and to override labor contracts agreed to by the city's elected officials. To justify the loss of the city's autonomy, the statute establishing the EFCB proclaimed a "state of emergency," saying that "to end this disaster," New York State needed to use its "police and emergency powers" to exercise control over the financial affairs of New York City.[34]

Democratic lawmakers pulled out all the stops to bring vacationing assemblymen and senators back to Albany to vote on the new law. Two upstate Democrats were difficult to locate, having gone together on a canoe and camping trip in Canada; they made it, unshaven, just in time to vote. One Bronx Democrat on vacation in Puerto Rico could not be found even after Carey called the governor of the commonwealth.[35] But even without him the Democrats had the numbers, and the State Senate approved the Financial Emergency Act by a 33–26 vote at four o'clock in the morning on Tuesday, September 9.

The city's financial elites liked what they saw in the new legislation. With the EFCB in place, the city's major banks once again agreed to buy and hold MAC bonds. This made it possible for the city to raise the money it needed for the month of September. Led by Victor Gotbaum and Jack Bigel, the city's public sector unions, too, agreed to support the act and to use their pension funds to buy MAC bonds. The alternative, Gotbaum warned, was even more massive layoffs and perhaps the loss of collective bargaining altogether.[36]

The EFCB wrested control over the city's finances out of the hands of the mayor and the City Council. The seven-member board included four public officials: the governor and comptroller of New York State, and the mayor and comptroller of New York City. The remaining three members would be private citizens appointed by Governor Carey. He chose William Ellinghaus, the president of New York Telephone Company, who had also served on MAC; Albert Casey, the president of American Airlines; and David Margolis, the president of firearms manufacturer Colt Industries.[37] The corporate slant was so obvious that the *Village Voice* ran a series of profiles of EFCB members titled "Meet Your Junta."

There was no labor representative on the EFCB. Nor did the board include anyone who could represent the black and Latino communities in the city. The director of a Fort Greene, Brooklyn, community group wrote a letter to the governor's office arguing that it was "incumbent" on Carey to appoint a black representative to the EFCB, given the general sense that government officials were trying "to solve the fiscal problems of New York City on the backs of blacks and other minorities."[38] But the governor chose not to do so. After all, he saw the agency's main job as forcing the city to accept service cuts, no matter what residents themselves might want. The only way to restore New York's fiscal health, he believed, was to make its government less democratic.

It was an opinion widely shared by the city's elites. As one MAC director told the *New York Times*, "The city is insolvent. To ordinary

men and women, any outfit that has a huge deficit, that has used up its
reserves and that can't borrow any money is insolvent. There has to be
some sort of receivership by the state. It's not an assault on home rule.
It's the facts of life."³⁹

The shifts in power went beyond just the creation of the EFCB. Behind
the scenes, Beame was also being pushed to fire two close friends and
longtime political allies: his deputy mayor, James Cavanagh, and his
budget director, Melvin Lechner. Both were widely seen in the financial
community as old-style machine politicians, men with little professional
expertise in municipal finance, who balanced the budget through sleight
of hand. Cavanagh in particular came in for scorn: it was often said that
he walked around with "the budget" on little slips of paper in his pockets,
that he explained his accounting practices by saying that he took a little
from here and a little from there and somehow it all magically balanced
out, and that he viewed the success of the city government in terms of
how many more jobs it was able to offer each year.⁴⁰

Beame resented the humiliating loss of control that the EFCB represented, and released a statement protesting that a plan to rescue the city
did not necessarily have to "include a takeover of the city by the state."⁴¹
He was also aware that many of the bankers were pressing for the ouster
of Cavanagh and Lechner as a stand-in for their real desire: a new mayor.
The *Daily News* reported that MAC had tried to persuade Carey to pass
legislation that would strip Beame of his powers.⁴² The mayor was desperate to hold on to his allies; even as he tried to present himself as the
model of pliability, saying that he would "do anything" to avoid default,
he refused to accede to the demands that Cavanagh and Lechner be
forced to resign.⁴³ Instead, Beame decided to remake City Hall by appoint-
ing new people, corporate executives who would meet with the approval
of the business world and the EFCB. The first of these was Kenneth Axelson, a senior vice president and finance director at J.C. Penney, whom
Beame brought in to serve as deputy mayor for finance.

Axelson lived in the neighborhood near Lincoln Center, in a ten-
room apartment on Central Park West. His major claim to civic par-

ticipation was the work he'd put into raising money for renovations of the 67th Street Playground in Central Park. He presented himself as an efficient, professional, skilled, and above all apolitical executive who would bring the city's finances under control. He would accept only a dollar a year from the city in payment, while continuing to collect a $143,000 salary (the equivalent of $630,000 today) from J.C. Penney.[44]

Axelson's swearing-in ceremony at City Hall made clear who his real constituency would be. The event was so well attended that it had to be moved to a larger room than was originally expected. It glittered with financial executives such as Ellmore Patterson of Morgan Guaranty, as well as the "Jersey Mafia" bankers. Axelson acknowledged them in a short speech after being sworn in: "I see the banks of New York City here. I see the investment houses. The brokerage houses. My friends on the Securities and Exchange Commission. My friends in the accounting profession."[45] Jac Friedgut spoke for many when he said that Axelson's presence in City Hall symbolized a "new fiscal discipline."[46] It also promised financiers a sympathetic ear. For the first time, there was someone in City Hall whom the bankers could trust.

It wasn't clear, though, that this closer relationship would be enough to keep the city out of bankruptcy. Behind the scenes, the Beame administration was already preparing for default—and in ways that might have frightened the very people who were welcoming Axelson's arrival and pushing for Cavanagh to leave.

Early in September, Cavanagh sent Beame an outline of a plan for how New York might proceed if it was no longer able to cover its bills. Should it default, the city would be cut off from the credit markets; it would have to function entirely on the cash it took in from the federal and state governments and the revenues it could collect. Cavanagh made a list of what this might cover: payroll, welfare, Medicaid, the Health and Hospitals Corporation, day care, and transit. Notably, the payment of interest on the city's debts was absent from the list.[47]

To handle planning for default, Beame pulled together a Contingency Committee. It included Beame, Cavanagh, and Axelson, along with the president of Union Savings Bank, the CEO of Saks Fifth Avenue, the publisher of the African American newspaper *New York Amsterdam*

News, and the president of Metropolitan Life (who had also served on the Carey committee that created MAC). Beame brought in lawyers from Weil, Gotshal & Manges, one of the city's top bankruptcy law firms, to advise the city on how to handle what might come next. Like Edwin Yeo and others in the Ford administration, the Contingency Committee members tried to picture what the city would look like if bankruptcy came to pass. They imagined city workers paid in scrip instead of cash, the likely need to call on the National Guard and the auxiliary police to keep social order, the state of the city after a massive snowstorm without money to pay for cleanup, the suffering that might result from closing hospitals, day care centers, and homeless shelters. One meeting's agenda ended with the topic "Return to Normal?"—with the question mark suggesting that the members of the Contingency Committee were far from sure this would ever happen.[48]

Ironically, one major legal and political problem that immediately became clear was that it would be extremely difficult for New York to declare bankruptcy under existing federal law. The regulations required that 51 percent of all creditors of a municipality agree to the terms of a repayment plan before the municipality would be allowed to declare bankruptcy. But in New York, there was no comprehensive list giving the names of all the creditors, who probably numbered in the tens of thousands. The city could get stranded—unable to pay its creditors but also incapable of formally declaring bankruptcy and gaining the protection of the courts. To avoid this possibility, the federal law would have to be changed. To build support for that change, attorney Ira Millstein said at the first meeting of the committee that perhaps it would be best to refer to Chapter IX not by the ugly name of "bankruptcy" but by something more neutral-sounding, such as "adjustment of debts."[49]

This deepening resignation in the Beame administration about the prospect of bankruptcy belied its public position, but it was hardly a surprise. No matter how often the city's leaders insisted they were committed to avoiding default, people in the national financial community believed it was coming. When the American Banking Association held its centennial convention in New York early in October, Mayor Beame hosted a City Hall reception with champagne and sandwiches. (The champagne was local and the sandwiches plain—as the city's Economic Development Administrator put it, the time was wrong for "lavish" parties.)[50] A poll of bankers at the convention revealed that 60 percent of them thought default was imminent. Referring to the city's spending on transit, libraries, and universities, the president of a small Kentucky bank wagged his finger at New Yorkers: "When politicians make wild promises to get elected, the public must pay." Nor had the outsiders' attitude toward New York particularly softened. Asked whether Washington should aid the city, one Midwestern banker responded, "Hell, no."[51]

New York's elite circles were mobilizing in other ways as well. As the summer of 1975 drew to its close, the two New York senators, Jacob Javits and James Buckley, began to assemble a group of notable citizens— the "cream of the city," as Buckley put it—to rally support for New York. Javits and Buckley had little in common: the former was a liberal Republican who had represented New York in the Senate since 1957, the latter (brother of *National Review* founder William F. Buckley) a conservative who had only won election to the Senate in 1971. But when Javits reached out to Buckley, the junior senator readily responded across ideological lines.

Javits wanted to create an organization of New York luminaries who could persuade investors around the country to buy MAC bonds. He thought that such businessmen might be able to win promises from their colleagues to commit to New York and not leave for greener pastures. Perhaps they could even pool their wealth and buy some bonds themselves! He also hoped that if wealthy, powerful New Yorkers spoke out in defense of their city, it might be harder for Congress to say no.

Buckley's approach was different: New Yorkers should not wait passively for federal aid, he believed; instead, they should take action to help their city. Civic-minded volunteers could take over the work that municipal employees had been performing. As services were cut and city workers were laid off, private citizens could fill the gap. Such was the spirit in which journalist Theodore White responded to an early appeal, writing to a leader of the new organization as though he were a medieval knight answering the call to defend his besieged city: "Men of my blood and our tradition can do nought else but answer when the horn winds from the Great Keep and our city is beset by pestilence, inflation, default, and disaster. I and the old grey; my son; my daughter; my wife; and whatever of the yeomanry I can gather on the South Walk of Sixty-fourth Street will be at your service, sire, when the day and time of assembly is heralded to me."[52]

The organization that Javits and Buckley created included such men as real estate magnate Lew Rudin (who was still rallying property owners to prepay their taxes), hotel giant Harry Helmsley, and of course Felix Rohatyn. They held their first meeting in early September at the corporate headquarters of Bristol-Myers. The mood was intense: in a discussion about what they should call themselves, one person suggested the "Pallbearers for New York."[53] The group rejected "Citizens Committee to Save New York City" because it sounded as though New York were terminally ill, and settled instead on "Citizens Committee for New York City." Javits read aloud a statement that President Ford had sent in to express his pleasure that the business leaders were gathering. He did not mention that Cheney and other advisers had toned down the original draft of the statement and had been strongly opposed to the president's sending any acknowledgment at all, feeling that it might give investors the impression that the federal government would aid the city.[54]

Only one person present at the early meetings suggested there might be something unseemly about the city's rich gathering in support of cuts that would hardly affect their own lives: Episcopalian Bishop Paul Moore. For years, Moore had been an impassioned advocate for the city's poor. He had castigated the city's corporations for their disinvestment from New York, reminding them that such abandonment was a moral and not a purely economic choice. He insisted that the problem of poverty in the city was not local in its origins—that it was a national story of black Southerners who had come to the northern cities to escape Jim Crow and found themselves stranded in metropolises that were being drained of jobs. Rejecting the program of austerity advocated by the others, Moore asked the group to imagine what poor New Yorkers might think if they knew that a group of businessmen "tried to save New York by making their lives even more miserable." Perhaps there was a way to reach out to these communities and discuss how to "refine" their services rather than making them feel that "the fat cats of this city are trying to save the city by dumping them down the drain." For Moore, this was not simply a question of morality, but of stability and social equality. "If we cut back further on the welfare and social services that some people feel are cut-backable, not only will there be a tremendous human tragedy involved for millions of these people, but there will be an enormous reaction sooner or later, whether it be in riots or more anti-social activity, who knows?" If anyone there had driven through the South Bronx recently, they would understand what he was talking about, he said—knowing, of course, how unlikely it was that anyone present had.[55]

While the elites of the city were forming their various committees and making forecasts, New Yorkers, as Moore pointed out, were finding themselves the subjects of a new regime of austerity.

The subway fare was increased from thirty-five to fifty cents, an increase that was met with bitterness and rage. "It's going to cost you more to get to work than to eat breakfast," said one Bronx commuter. On the day the new price went into effect, someone chained open the gates at the 8th Avenue and 23rd Street station so people could enter the subway without paying. A hundred noisy demonstrators leapt the turnstiles at Times Square. A young assemblyman named Charles Schumer stood outside the Broadway and 42nd Street entrance, selling two hundred 50-cent tokens at the old 35-cent fare in what he termed a "token protest" against the hike.[56]

The cuts to public health also drew the ire of city employees and patients alike. Doctors at the city's public hospitals threatened to strike, and workers at an addiction treatment program held a raucous sit-in at the Department of Health to protest the layoffs, breaking windows and damaging furniture.[57]

In the ongoing conflict over schools, meanwhile, the city had laid off about 7,000 teachers. The United Federation of Teachers spent the summer in contract negotiations with city officials, and at one point it looked like the union was willing to give up salary increases if the laid-off teachers were hired back. But the city refused, aware of how unhappy MAC and investors would be if any layoffs were rescinded. As Deputy Chancellor Bernard Gifford remembered, "The city was being attacked because of its lack of credibility. . . . The bankers wanted blood on the streets."[58]

Thanks to the layoffs, class sizes shot up to 45 or 50 students per class, far above the contractually agreed-upon number. In some cases, classes had as many as 60 kids. Support staff was at a minimum. School assistants and lunchroom aides had been let go, and school guards had been laid off even in neighborhoods where drug addicts were often spotted near the schools. After one day back at school, the teachers went on strike.[59]

The picket lines that formed around the schools were at once outraged and melancholy. Striking teachers said that with the immense class sizes, they were being asked to be "nothing more than babysitters."[60] They carried signs, often handmade: "45 Kids Per Class Is No Class," "We'd Rather Resign Than Teach in Substandard Schools," "Killing Our Schools Is Killing Our Children,"[61] and "Interest in Children Before Interest for Banks!"[62] Parents joined teachers on the picket lines. "These classes are unspeakable," said one mother at P.S. 9 on 84th Street. "Forty in a class, and 40 percent of the staff dismissed—it's simply unspeakable."[63] The strike ended after a week, but only because Shanker, the president of the UFT, pushed teachers to go back: he recognized that the city had relatively little incentive to make concessions, since striking teachers did not need to be paid.[64]

But even the settlement of the strike was a sign of how much had changed. The union and the city could no longer simply hammer out a deal. Their proposed contract went to the Emergency Financial Control Board, which decided that its terms were too expensive, and forced the city and the union into further negotiations to lower the cost.[65] The same day that the EFCB struck down the preliminary UFT contract, Judge Irving Saypol (who in the 1950s had been the U.S. Attorney responsible for prosecuting Julius and Ethel Rosenberg for espionage) ruled that the UFT had broken the law by striking and was in contempt of court. But the ruling did not end the school protests. Early in October, approximately 20,000 students walked out of their classrooms to register their objection to overcrowding and the elimination of sports programs. More than 2,000 boycotted classes at Sheepshead Bay High School in Brooklyn, holding signs demanding more teachers and smaller classes: "Walk Out, Don't Cop Out!"[66]

The fall of 1975 was a turning point for the city. The creation of the Emergency Financial Control Board, the appointment of Kenneth Axelson as deputy mayor for finance, and the formation of the Citizens Committee for New York all pointed to different ways that various social and economic elites were joining forces to transform New York.

Almost everyone in this cohort agreed that drastic budget cuts were necessary to keep New York from bankruptcy, which they regarded as the ultimate nightmare. This desire for cuts was not the result of any abstract ideology, or carefully planned political program to slash the state and promote the private market. The elites did not dream up the EFCB because they had read the free-market critiques of economist Milton Friedman or the antigovernment philosophizing of University of Virginia professor James Buchanan, or because they were moved by the speeches of California governor Ronald Reagan. Instead, people at the top of the city's social hierarchy came together in a gradual way, pushed by the failure of their earlier efforts, looking to find others whose outlook they could trust. Only a few months earlier, creating an entity such as the EFCB—with its explicit mission of undercutting the fiscal authority of democratically elected politicians—would have been inconceivable. But now the dynamic of crisis made these upper echelons look to each other. They might not know exactly what to do, they might not know exactly how to do it, but they were sure that the only hope lay in giving greater power to people like themselves.

10. On the Brink

Throughout the summer and fall of 1975, the threat that New York City would go bankrupt hovered over the city and the nation. Fear of failure was so great in the city's elite circles that it became a powerful way of forcing consensus. Bankruptcy's symbolism, its connotations of emptiness and collapse, were nearly as terrifying as whatever the reality might be, and instilled the notion that default must be avoided by any means necessary.

Just about the only people who were unfazed by the prospect of New York's financial collapse were Alan Greenspan, William Simon, Donald Rumsfeld, and President Ford himself. All of them saw New York's default as something the free market should be able to take in stride. When companies failed, they went bankrupt; why not New York?

During the first week of September, as the New York State Legislature debated the city's fate, Gerald Ford was on the other side of the country, in Ronald Reagan territory, laying the groundwork for the 1976 primary campaign. On the morning of September 5, he was visiting Sacramento, California, preparing to deliver a speech in the Capitol building. He planned to talk about violent crime in America, a crisis he often likened to war. ("One man or woman or child becomes just as dead from a switchblade slash as from a nuclear missile blast," as he put it.)[1] But while Ford was walking the 150 yards from his hotel to the Capitol, a petite red-haired woman wearing a long red dress and matching turban burst from the crowd, waving a .45 pistol and pointing it at the president. A Secret Service man grabbed it from her hand and wrestled her to the ground, even as she shouted, "Don't get excited! It didn't go off! It didn't go off!"[2] The woman, Lynette Alice Fromme, was a follower of Charles Manson, and had brought the gun to the rally to threaten the president in the name of defending redwood forests.

Two and a half weeks later, as Ford emerged from a fundraising speech before 2,000 Republicans at the St. Francis Hotel in San Francisco, he was again ambushed by a woman with a gun. Sara Jane Moore, a single, five-times-divorced mother of a nine-year-old son, was a paid informant working for the FBI and the Bureau of Alcohol, Tobacco and Firearms. When her contacts in the Bay Area left-wing scene grew suspicious that she was spying on them, Moore hatched a plan to shoot the president—partly to prove her loyalty to the political cause (even though in truth she had been doing exactly what her friends feared), partly out of the anguish and anger she later said she felt about being used by the security state. Firing at Ford from across the street with a .38 revolver, she narrowly missed. Afterward she told Secret Service agents that she had been waiting for the president a long time, and that if he had been any later she would have canceled the assassination attempt to avoid being delayed in picking up her son at the end of the school day.[3]

Alan Greenspan, who had accompanied Ford on his California journey, was deeply troubled by the two wild incidents. Such violence seemed to him evidence of a nihilistic mood emerging in contemporary America. Violence, he concluded, was "ever more condoned" in American society, especially if it claimed allegiance to "revolutionary ideas." And he believed that the radical violence was linked to a broader skepticism about the virtues of capitalism and the free market, which made such acts seem morally acceptable, even righteous. The challenge had to be met on the level of political ideology: the Ford administration needed to offer a robust, articulate defense of the American economic system, to justify it in ethical and moral terms. "If we cannot say that our society, granted its imperfections . . . is not a moral society," he wrote in a letter to Dick Cheney and Donald Rumsfeld, then "all the physical well-being that our economy can create for our citizens will be unconvincing."[4]

Greenspan saw the New York City fiscal crisis in similar terms. The metropolis appeared to him the epitome of a nation and a culture that had veered into chaos, and needed to be taught the terms of a new moral politics. "There is no short cut to fiscal responsibility," he wrote to Rumsfeld in a long memorandum about the city and its problems. "There is no alternative for New York City except to rapidly put its affairs in order."[5] From Greenspan's perspective, there was little that the federal government could do to aid New York without entrenching still more deeply the problems that had brought the city to the brink in the first place. As a true believer in the free market, Greenspan was committed to the idea that the city and its investors should have to face the consequences of their irresponsible ways. "Hoping for some miracle is scarcely an act of responsibility," he told Rumsfeld. It was time to face reality: "A default of New York City seems virtually inevitable."[6]

Ford himself had a different set of reasons for refusing to help the city. With the fight for the 1976 Republican presidential nomination heating up, he was eager to prove that he could win the presidency on his own merits, that he wasn't just the man who had pardoned Nixon. But he was painfully aware of the threats he faced from the right, especially from Ronald Reagan. To appeal to Reagan's constituency, Ford had taken a hard line against all new spending programs that would contribute to the deficit and vowed to stop the "tremendous growth" in federal spending.[7] Accordingly, he felt that it was essential from a political standpoint to oppose virtually all federal aid to New York City. Any assistance not only risked being perceived as signaling approval of New York's social policies but would also clearly extend the reach of the federal government. In other words, it would amount to endorsing government spending on both the municipal and federal levels—the very spending that Ford had committed to reining in.

William Simon and others at the Treasury Department supported Ford's hard line, advocating for bankruptcy over federal aid. "Direct

Federal aid, a guarantee or a partial guarantee might avoid default. But it would also begin the Federalization of state and local affairs," Simon wrote in one memo.[8] The president's close advisers tried to minimize the sense of fear brought about by the idea of bankruptcy, arguing that it was a normal economic event, not a crisis. Simon testified before Congress that there was far too much anxiety about the word "bankrupt": after all, New York would of course continue to *exist* even if it was in default on its debts.[9]

But other people in the Republican Party and even within the Ford administration itself feared the president was hurting his chances by downplaying the possible financial collapse of the country's largest metropolis. The Republican majority leader in the New York State Senate, Warren Anderson, lobbied the president for aid, warning that the city's bankruptcy might spin into a "national catastrophe." This would not only be a disaster on its own terms but would surely doom Ford's prospects in the election. None other than Hugh Carey (with his populist, Catholic appeal that could win over "Kennedy loyalists") would emerge from the calamity an unbeatable opponent, Anderson argued.[10] Economic advisers prepared memoranda for Ford enumerating the pros and cons for various different mechanisms whereby the federal government could aid the city if it chose to do so—direct loans, guarantees, advancing welfare or Medicaid payments.[11] Even William Simon was wary of Carey, fearing that the governor was outmaneuvering Washington with his "adroit" handling of the crisis, setting up a scenario in which the federal government—and not Albany—would be blamed if the city collapsed.[12]

As fall went on, the voices of warning from Ford's friends became more urgent. Charls Walker, a lobbyist and business consultant, wrote the president a personal note at the beginning of October, expressing his fear that the issue would be political "dynamite" in the election year: "I am getting very, very worried about the New York City financial problem." Walker suggested that rather than allowing New York to default, the federal government should create a Municipal Reconstruction Finance Corporation to lend money to cities in desperate straits (modeling it on the Depression-era agency that lent money to failing businesses). This agency, he said, should be headed by a "hard-nosed, take-charge financial type accustomed to driving hard bargains and making them stick."[13]

Businessmen, bankers, and financial lobbyists also expressed their deep concern about a New York City bankruptcy and reiterated their support for some form of federal aid to keep the city from collapse. The president of Bank of America told the Senate Committee on Banking, Housing and Urban Affairs that "the effects of a New York City default may well be grave and enduring, not only in terms of our economy and financial markets, but also of public confidence in government and loss of international prestige." Default, he said, "most certainly must be averted in the national interest."[14] The president of the Standard & Poor's rating agency said New York would certainly default without federal intervention, and predicted that this would probably lead to civil disorder and a "revolt" in the city.[15] The chairman of Con Edison wrote to Ford to plead with him not to allow New York to go bankrupt, citing the appointment of Axelson as deputy mayor for finance as a sign that the city was serious about reform. "Governor Carey and Mayor Beame already have placed management of the City's finances in the hands of some of the ablest business executives in the country."[16]

Even in rural parts of the country where there was little political sympathy for New York, local government officials found themselves caught between their desire to punish the city for its profligate ways and their own reliance on the municipal bond market. At a meeting of the National Association of Counties, one official from Indianapolis complained, "I'm really in a dither. I'd like to protect the bond market . . . but I'll be damned if I want to support bad government." Many feared that if New York collapsed it might take the bond market with it, or that Congress might seize on the evident need for greater regulation to begin to tax municipal bonds.[17]

New York City's troubles made news even beyond U.S. borders, as the city's crisis was cast in the stark terms of Cold War politics. A possible collapse seemed to be a sign of the inner weakness of the United States—and by extension, of Western democratic capitalism itself. *Pravda* ran articles on the garbage strike; the *New York Times* reported that in the Soviet Union, Beame's name was mentioned in the press "at least as often as that of President Ford." In October, the *New York Law Journal*, a daily publication for lawyers and judges, took out a full-page ad in the *New York Times* to promote a special issue of the journal devoted to the crisis. Large headlines ran across the top of the ad—"New York City Defaults; Market Collapses; Bond Prices Plunge; Creditors Sue; Emergency Declared"—followed by the rhetorical question: "How Would Russia Look If Moscow Failed?"[18]

The foreign leader most outspoken on the subject of the city's crisis was Helmut Schmidt, the chancellor of West Germany. When Schmidt visited the United States in early October for a private lunch with Ford, the German leader was blunt about his fears that New York's financial collapse might challenge the security of both nations. He was deeply worried about William Simon's blithe attitude. Should New York go under, Schmidt warned Ford, it would be a "Black Friday" around the world, and might well lead to panic in all kinds of markets. Ford responded as he always did, insisting that the problem was the city's because it had been "mismanaged for ten years." But Schmidt's concerns were widely reported in the press, reinforcing the sense that Ford did not fully appreciate the threat of the city's collapse.[19]

Schmidt's criticisms emboldened Vice President Nelson Rockefeller to break with the president.[20] Rockefeller, too, was skeptical of Simon's nonchalance and probably recognized that as New York's former governor he was significantly implicated in the city's fate. Over the summer he had written to the president to say that the federal government could not simply ignore the crisis: "If the Federal government stands by while New York defaults on its obligations, the political consequences could be severe."[21] At a Waldorf-Astoria banquet the Saturday of Columbus Day weekend, Rockefeller rose from a table he shared with Beame to deliver a speech calling for President Ford to find a way to help New York "in time to avoid catastrophe." He defended the city's social programs, saying that the old message from Washington in the days of the Great Society had been that "we were an affluent society with unlimited resources that could abolish poverty by statutory fiat." Those days were over forever, he acknowledged, and of course New York must be forced to "take stock" of its resources and to chart "a more realistic course"—but the city should not be punished just because it had once believed.[22]

The White House appeared unprepared for Rockefeller's sudden departure from the party line. A journalist immediately asked Ron Nessen, the press secretary, whether Rockefeller and Ford were now in disagreement about New York. Nonplussed, Nessen responded, "I'll let you be the judge of that."[23] Reports circulated that Donald Rumsfeld was "beside himself" with rage when he read about Rockefeller's speech the next morning.[24] But Rockefeller's defection from Ford's line opened up space for more dissenters—a few days later, Ford's transportation secretary wrote the president a long memo calling on him to keep New York out of default.[25]

Even Simon was starting to feel the heat, as he found himself bombarded by critical mail from friends in the financial world. If the city stopped welfare payments, one wrote, there would be "riots in the streets." Businesses would flee the scene and it would become a "disaster area." And the problem was not all New York's fault, but a national issue: "Certainly the fact that high welfare payments have attracted so many people from Puerto Rico and the South should not be a cause for punishing New York City and its bond holders."[26] Such correspondence may have been on Simon's mind at the senior staff meeting the morning after Rockefeller's speech. As the other staff members buzzed about the news, Simon seemed resigned: "New York City is going to win," he told the group. After all, it was the media capital of the country, and no matter what, the press would always side with New York.[27]

The Ford administration's official line was still one of no aid for New York. But that resolve would be sorely tested just a few days later.

At 12:25 in the morning on Friday, October 17, 1975, an aide for Mayor Abraham Beame placed a desperate telephone call to Ford. He was not permitted to wake the sleeping president, though the mayor's office had serious news. That day, New York City had a massive debt of nearly $453 million coming due, and it had only $34 million on hand. Without immediate access to more money, the city would be forced into default.[28]

As the day dawned, reports on what was about to happen in New York spread around the world. Currency trading nearly halted in Europe; the price of gold climbed; the Dow Jones plummeted. Dozens of people who owned city bonds lined up in the Municipal Building early in the morning, clutching notes they wanted to redeem; they were turned away and told to come back later on.[29]

For most New Yorkers, life that day went on as usual. The trains ran, people went to work, the streetlamps turned off as the sun came up. But for those who knew what was happening, it was as though the city was about to enter a strange new land, where nothing could be taken for granted any longer.

The previous evening, the city's economic and political leadership had been gathered at the political pageant known as the Alfred E. Smith Memorial Dinner, held every year at the Waldorf-Astoria Hotel in Midtown. This formal assemblage to raise money for Catholic charities had begun in 1945 in honor of Alfred Smith, the 1920s governor of New York State and the first Catholic candidate for president. The fiercely anti-Communist Archbishop Francis J. Spellman organized the first gathering the year after Smith died. The dinners quickly became a "ritual of American politics," to quote journalist Theodore H. White. In presidential election years, it was a tradition for both major candidates to attend and to share a stage for the last time before voters went to the polls. Instead of serious debate, they would trade short, jokey speeches poking fun at themselves and at each other, as though to reassure all present that no matter who won in November everyone still belonged to the same club. In past years, Kennedy, Nixon, Eisenhower, Johnson, and Hubert Humphrey had all been featured speakers.

Despite the desperate mood in the city, no one thought of canceling the 1975 event. Ella Grasso, the first woman governor of Connecticut, was the guest of honor. But her speech was to be the least-remembered aspect of the dinner on October 16.

When Hugh Carey left his New York office on Thursday afternoon to attend the Smith dinner, he was aware that the city did not have the money to cover the next day's debt payments, but there seemed to be a plan to assemble it in time. The trustees of the Teachers' Retirement

System, the pension fund for the teachers' union, were gathering that same evening to authorize the purchase of a round of MAC bonds. That purchase would, in turn, give the MAC board—scheduled to meet at 10 p.m.—the legal ability to release money for the payment of city debts.

Carey had fully expected the Teachers' Retirement System to approve the MAC bonds. He had not, however, accounted for the intense unhappiness within the union about the direction of the city. The previous day, October 15, Mayor Beame had made public the first version of the city's new financial plan as required by the EFCB. It proposed to shrink the public sector in almost every way—closing hospitals, day care centers, fire companies, and senior citizen centers, ceasing addiction treatment services, and limiting other social programs.[30] According to the plan, the city could no longer afford an "expansive university system," a "large and under-utilized hospital system," or the spending that had grown out of the "federally sponsored social services revolution of the 1960s." It could only accomplish the bare minimum expected of all city governments: police and fire protection, sanitation, sewage, and the provision of potable water. "We can take no pride in the plan," Beame wrote in a public letter to Carey, "because it places a higher priority at this time on the grim economic realities confronting the City, rather than the needs of our citizens. Unfortunately, this is a course that must be taken at this time in the interests of our economic survival."[31]

The mayor's announcement was hard for the city's labor leaders to swallow. Among other issues, it would necessitate the layoff of thousands of union members without even the pretense of negotiation with the unions, which seemed an ominous sign for the future of collective bargaining. The Municipal Labor Committee immediately issued a fierce public statement, saying that the only people who really understood what these cuts would mean for the city were the city workers themselves. "In the schools, hospitals, precincts, parks, libraries, youth centers, social, recreational and other agencies of New York City, we see firsthand how the fabric of life in this city is being irretrievably torn." The city would be destroyed by service cuts of this magnitude, the statement charged, for "the fiscal crisis is far less dangerous than the social crisis confronting New York City."[32]

Amidst this mounting anger, it must have been hard for Albert Shanker of the United Federation of Teachers not to notice that the city's plans for getting through October 17 revolved around the teachers' pension fund purchasing $150 million in city debt. The UFT members had struck against austerity in September; their contract was still under review by the EFCB. Why should the union now lift a finger to help?

Indeed, Deputy Mayor Kenneth Axelson was sufficiently concerned about Shanker that he had contacted the Treasury Department earlier in the month to alert them to the possibility that the UFT might hold out on the bonds until its contract was signed. And on the morning of October 16, Felix Rohatyn noted with some concern that the UFT pension fund trustees had not given their "firm binding commitment" for the bond purchase. All the other union pension funds had already bought their share of the notes—but not the teachers.

Following this conversation, Governor Carey spoke to Shanker to emphasize that negotiations with the Board of Education had to be considered "completely separate from, and unrelated to" the use of the teachers' pension moneys to fund the city.[33] Still, no one thought the teachers would actually refuse to come through. When Carey left the office in the afternoon of October 16 to go to the dinner at the Waldorf, he told his staff not to expect him back until the next day.[34]

Much of the Al Smith dinner proceeded as usual. The raised platform seating the city notables was so packed with tables that it took up nearly half the room. William Ellinghaus was there, as were Richard Shinn and Hugh Carey, Arthur Ochs Sulzberger and Mrs. Vincent Astor, James Cavanagh and Mayor Beame. The 1,700 assembled guests consumed their "bicentennial menu" of Maryland terrapin soup, oysters, steak, and steamed baby Maine potatoes, and listened to New York's legendary urban planner Robert Moses reminisce about Smith.[35]

But as the night went on, Comptroller Goldin noticed something odd. It seemed to him that the dais was emptying out, the notables seated there melting away. A bit before 10 p.m., a waiter stopped by the comptroller's table. Mayor Beame, he said, was requesting Goldin's presence at Gracie Mansion immediately.[36]

By the time Goldin arrived, the city's bankruptcy lawyers had already been meeting for hours in the basement rooms; the ashtrays were filled to overflowing. The teachers' union, he was told, had voted against buying the MAC bonds, citing fiduciary responsibility. As pension fund trustee Reuben Mitchell put it, "We must watch that investments are properly diversified, that all our eggs aren't put in one basket."[37]

The members of the MAC board, arriving back at the governor's midtown office to sign off on their part of the deal, many still in formal dress from the dinner, got the news at the same time. Felix Rohatyn burst into the room carrying the press release from the teachers' union. The UFT had done enough to help the city, it proclaimed; now New York would need to come up with the money on its own.

Up at Gracie Mansion, the mayor and his team of lawyers were getting ready to figure out how the city could declare bankruptcy and still keep running. Sidney Frigand, the mayor's press secretary, later recalled the debates about which workers were indispensable to the city's operation. "Bridge tenders who raise and lower bridges were essential. Teachers weren't life-or-death."[38] Despite the lack of legal precedent for the default of a city like New York, the city's lawyers, working through the night, drew up a bankruptcy petition to file in State Supreme Court that would protect the city's assets from immediate seizure by its creditors. Mayor Beame signed it, as did attorney Ira Millstein and the city's corporation counsel, W. Bernard Richland.[39]

Meanwhile, Beame's old friend and public relations counselor Howard Rubenstein prepared a press release in the mayor's name that the banks would have found chilling. "I have been advised by the Comptroller that the City of New York has insufficient cash on hand to meet debt obligations due today," the statement began. "This constitutes the default that we have struggled to avoid." The document then went on to present the case for a formal declaration of bankruptcy. Unless the city made this declaration immediately, it would be legally required to use all of its remaining money to pay for debt service "rather than life support and other essential services." Under bankruptcy, on the other hand, it would be up to the courts to adjudicate what to do with the resources that remained.

What followed was a list of the city's priorities in the state of default, in keeping with what the Contingency Committee had suggested. At the top were police and fire protection, sanitation, and public health. Next were food and shelter for those who depended on the city, hospital and emergency medical care for people without other resources, and payment to any vendors who provided these services. Then the city would pay for the public schools, primary and secondary alike. Only after these basic city services were met would interest on the city debt be paid.[40]

At Carey's office the mood was morose. Shortly after the governor heard that Shanker was pulling out of the deal he spoke to Richard Ravitch, a wealthy real estate developer who had helped Carey cope with the collapse of the Urban Development Corporation. Ravitch was personally acquainted with Al Shanker—they had been connected through the democratic socialist and civil rights leader Bayard Rustin. Later in the evening, Carey phoned again as Ravitch was climbing into bed. After the call he prepared to go meet the governor.[41]

After they consulted briefly, Carey dispatched a police car to drive Ravitch to Shanker's apartment. There, the two men talked late into the night. Ravitch recalls that their conversation ranged from the immediate to the existential. According to him, Shanker was primarily concerned with the question of whether it really was in keeping with any concept of fiduciary responsibility to use pension funds that retirees were depending on to purchase the debt of a near-bankrupt city. He never raised the question of the teachers' contract and the EFCB, even though it must have been on his mind.

Ravitch went home in a police car at five o'clock in the morning, charged with a feeling of tremendous responsibility. Anxious and excited, he wondered whether one man—Shanker—could make a difference in history. Sleep was out of the question. After all, the morning television stations were reporting that the city was about to go bankrupt, and no one knew what would happen after that.[42]

Felix Rohatyn, meanwhile, had called President Ford's adviser L. William Seidman shortly after midnight. "Looks like a default tomorrow," he told Seidman, blaming the teachers for backing out of the financing deal.

"Absolutely certain?" asked Seidman, pressing him on whether the city had any other options.

Rohatyn responded that he thought New York was out of alternatives, though of course they'd keep trying. He promised to keep in touch with Washington throughout the day.[43]

When Ford woke up at 5:30 a.m., he got the news from Seidman and convened a meeting of those within the administration dealing with New York City.[44] The federal government was kept closely informed about developments, but it seemed unlikely to step in with credit or aid. As Ron Nessen, Ford's press secretary, told reporters, "This is not a natural disaster or an act of God. It is a self-inflicted act by the people who have been running New York City for a long time."[45]

On the morning of October 17, as luck would have it, Mayor Beame was supposed to be honored by the city's Optimist Club. Thirty-seven members of the organization came to City Hall, attempting to present the mayor with an award to recognize his "optimistic attitude" in coping with New York's difficulties.[46] They were turned away. "Only a miracle can prevent default now, and I don't expect any miracles," City Council President Paul O'Dwyer told the *Daily News*.[47]

The city's collapse was the top story on every television news program, and the drama inevitably put a spotlight on Albert Shanker and the teachers' union. Early in the morning, Shanker met with Beame and former mayor Robert Wagner at Gracie Mansion. A few hours later, Shanker called Ravitch at Carey's office. He wanted to talk again, but he had no desire to go to the governor's office, to walk in past all the reporters.

They agreed to meet at Ravitch's Upper East Side apartment. Shanker came down from Gracie Mansion, while Carey and Ravitch, riding in an unmarked police vehicle to elude press attention, traveled up from the governor's office. There was no regular food in the house to eat, so the governor, the head of the teachers' union, and their aides and friends snacked on some matzos that Ravitch had lying around. At around noon, after three hours of conversation—and reassurances that should the city default, MAC bonds would get priority—Shanker agreed to recommend to the trustees of the teachers' union that they agree to the bond purchase. No one else was coming forward to save the city, and if New York collapsed, who knew what terms a bankruptcy judge might declare for the teachers' union? It was easy to imagine that teachers might be fired en masse, or their pensions raided to pay back debts.[48]

Shanker went back to the governor's office to meet the press around two in the afternoon. As he spoke to the reporters, looking worn and exhausted, he made it clear he was under pressure far more intense than he had ever anticipated. He still thought the mayor and the governor had been "extremely destructive" to the school system and the entire framework of collective bargaining through their unilateral cuts. His union, he insisted, had been the victim of "blackmail." But it was an unusual sort of coercion, for no single individual could be blamed. "Look," Shanker told the crowd, "the pressure is not from the Governor, and it's not from the Mayor. The pressure is from the situation."[49]

Once the union voted to make the purchase, the city's normal mechanisms cranked back into gear. The throng of creditors who had gathered early in the morning at the Municipal Building began to collect checks at 3:10 in the afternoon.[50] Manufacturers Hanover stayed open past its closing time to accept the money from the teachers' union and to process requests to redeem notes.[51] New York, it became clear, would not default that day.

Ever after, there would be questions about the events of October 17. It seemed surreal that the city had come so close to bankruptcy. Perhaps the teachers' union had never been serious about not making the purchase, but had only sought to show the EFCB that its compliance should not be taken for granted. Perhaps if the UFT had held out and refused to buy the debt, some other union—maybe Victor Gotbaum's District Council 37 or John DeLury's Sanitation Workers—would have swooped in at the last minute, unlikely as it was for one of them to put up yet more cash. More than anything else, the chaotic events of that night and day demonstrated the theatrics of default: the threat of bankruptcy and its unknown consequences could be used to make people do all kinds of things they had earlier insisted were completely out of the question. Yet even if the near-default was half performance, it made clear how chaotic the reality would be: how bankruptcy would slow the financial markets, gum up the ability of other cities and states to borrow, and affect the international strength of the dollar.

In the event, the bankruptcy petition was put away, as was Mayor Beame's draft press release. Never made public, they were part of an alternative reality, one that had not in the end come to pass but which would hover over the city throughout the rest of the fall. That it had come so close to happening brought bankruptcy from the realm of speculation into the realm of the entirely plausible, and there it would stay.

11. Drop Dead

Throughout October, Congress heard testimony about whether—and how—it should provide aid to New York. The president of the Bank of America argued in favor of a new federal agency to give loans to troubled cities, similar to that imagined by Ford's friend Charles Walker, while the vice president of bond research at Moody's warned that "a City default could be the last puff of wind that causes the entire house of cards to tumble."[1] Although most big-city mayors backed aid for New York, some city leaders came to Washington to argue the opposite: the mayor of Spokane, Washington, for example, insisted that helping New York would only "condone excesses" and "underwrite irresponsible demands by unions."[2] Congressmen themselves were divided on the topic. Many, such as Senator James Allen of Alabama, complained that federal help might endanger "the survival of local self-government."[3] Still, it was clear that momentum in Congress was building in favor of some form of assistance. Some representatives supported a series of federal loans to New York, with interest rates much lower than those charged by the banks. Others proposed to encourage investment in MAC bonds by providing a federal guarantee for them, so that if the city went bankrupt Washington would cover the bond investors' losses.

On October 24, Gerald Ford gathered his senior staff in the Cabinet Room of the White House for a somber discussion. They were acutely aware of the mood on Capitol Hill, but it did not shake their resolve. Even with the potential collapse of New York City staring them in the face, they were certain that the federal government should do nothing to forestall it. Ford opened the meeting by asking: "Does anyone think that we should support any legislation to prevent default?"

The room was silent. Then Donald Rumsfeld spoke. "Not just 'No.' But 'Hell No.'"[4]

Ford's cabinet was adamant: there would be no federal aid to keep New York from going bankrupt. The major item on their agenda, instead, was the question of whether the federal government would provide financial assistance to the city *after* it declared bankruptcy. As the president was starting to realize, there was no way for Washington to remain at a distance forever. If New York could not pay its creditors, it would still need to pay its firefighters and police officers, teachers and park keepers, transit workers and welfare recipients. Yet the city might run out of the money to cover those bills. What would happen then? The threat of complete social breakdown in New York would force the federal government to become involved.

The president and his advisers were also becoming increasingly concerned that inaction on their part would open up space for the president's political detractors. One internal administration memo stressed the need for a media plan to confront the "scare tactics" of the city's leadership and influence coverage of the crisis in a way that would be favorable to Ford. The memo also recommended contacting all "fence sitters" in Congress to firm up their support for the president's position. Its most urgent recommendation was that Ford deliver a major public speech about New York City that would clarify his position and rally the nation behind the idea of denying aid to New York.[5]

It was not immediately evident what the right forum for such a speech might be. Ford was already planning another West Coast trip for the last week of October, to raise money and build support among conservatives for his 1976 campaign. His overtures to the right had had a setback earlier in the summer when his wife, Betty, told *60 Minutes* that she "would not be surprised" if her eighteen-year-old daughter was having an affair, nor would she be completely shocked if she learned that her children had tried marijuana. It was clear to Ford that his policy on New York had to appeal to conservatives, and his views would need to be couched in language they could understand. It was imperative to downplay New York City as a subject of national concern: the whole justification for the president's steadfast denial of aid was that the city's problems were local and had little potential to affect other parts of the country. But, paradoxically, the very gesture of giving such a speech could be self-defeating. As Republican Senator Hugh Scott put it, by giving a national address on television or before a joint session of Congress, "the President would be admitting that New York City is a national issue and that its default could cause a ripple effect."[6]

If delivering the speech before Congress was imprudent, then where should it be given? The president's advisers fretted about an alternative. Speaking in New York City itself—perhaps at a meeting of the National Association of Businessmen or the Investment Forum of New York—was no solution. Talking to an audience of business leaders would open Ford to the charge that he was ignoring the humanitarian dimension of the crisis. What was more, at any location in New York there was a "potential demonstrator problem," plus the delicate question of what to do should Mayor Beame insist on greeting the president, which might be "embarrassing." But speaking about New York City at a California fundraising dinner seemed equally disastrous. How would it look to dismiss New York's problems before a bunch of "fat cats" at a partisan function?[7]

Finally, Ford settled on a luncheon at the National Press Club in Washington, D.C. He could talk about the city before an audience of journalists, the people responsible for narrating the city's problems to the rest of the nation. The speech was scheduled for noon on Wednesday, October 29. Immediately after, Ford would travel by helicopter to an Air Force base, and from there he would fly to the West Coast to address rainmakers in Los Angeles and San Francisco.

Knowing where the speech would happen did not make deciding what to say any easier. Ford and his speechwriters worked on it for at least nine days. The first draft was written by Robert Hartmann, Ford's longtime speechwriter. (He had coined the line "our long national nightmare is over," which the president delivered when announcing his pardon of Nixon.) This was then extensively edited by L. William Seidman of Ford's Economic Policy Board, Treasury Secretary William Simon, and James Lynn of the Office of Management and Budget, as well as by Ford himself.

As he prepared the talk, Ford was aware that he was seeking to balance fundamentally contradictory political aims. He wanted to appeal to conservatives by emphasizing that he had no intention of approving any Congressional proposals to extend fiscal aid to keep the city from defaulting. His sole concession was to revise the bankruptcy law so that the city could file for bankruptcy and draft a plan to settle its affairs under judicial supervision. But at the same time, the president did not want to be perceived as overly punitive. He needed to be seen as generous, tolerant, and sympathetic to ordinary New Yorkers, and to make it clear that he did not think they should suffer because of their leaders' irresponsibility.

These conflicting imperatives led Ford and his staff to rewrite the speech at least five times. The earliest versions excoriated bondholders and bankers almost as fiercely as the city's politicians. In the first version of the speech, Hartmann suggested the president say, "To me, it is clear that those who made the choice to invest their money should now bear the risk, not the 200,000,000 Americans who never made such a choice."[8] By the time the speech was done, the emphasis on the financial community had been significantly toned down, so that the brunt of Ford's criticism rested squarely on the city leaders.

Most challenging for Ford's team was finding some way to reassure New Yorkers that they would not be left without police or fire protection. One draft assured the people of the city that "their governments, city, state and Federal, will not punish them for the fiscal sins of others."[9] This was cut, replaced by: "There must be policemen on the beat, firemen in the station, nurses in the wards, and teachers in the classroom. Life must go on."[10] Then in the next version, the "teachers in the classroom" disappeared—after all, the Ford administration had not yet determined whether the public schools were an "essential public service" that should be maintained if the city was in default.[11]

The most striking line in the speech was added only in its fifth draft: "I can tell you now that I am prepared to veto any bill that has as its purpose a Federal bail-out of New York City to prevent a default." In contrast to the evasive tone of some of the earlier drafts, it was as blunt as could be. This sentence would be quoted in all the news reports the next day.[12]

The events in the days leading up to Ford's speech did not assuage concerns about the city's future, nor did they lend credence to the idea that its problems were a local affair that would be calming down soon. The threat of fiscal collapse appeared to be spreading to other cities and states, such as Yonkers (directly north of New York) and even Massachusetts.[13] The Senate Banking Committee was collecting testimony from people who wanted to support the city—the day before Ford's speech, George Ball, a former undersecretary of state and a partner at Lehman Brothers, warned the committee that Moscow would see New York's bankruptcy as a "symptom of the weakness of American capitalism."[14] At the same time, protests were mounting in the streets of New York. Thousands of Chinese immigrants and Chinese Americans marched to City Hall to demonstrate against the planned closure of the Fifth Precinct police station on Elizabeth Street. "If we lose the Fifth, it will kill the whole community. There will be no Chinatown," the leader of one community group told the press.[15]

Ford knew what he was going to say, but he was still wavering about exactly how to say it. In a sign of how concerned he was about striking the right note, the day before he delivered his address Ford met with the leadership of the city's police and firefighter unions. The meeting was brokered by Senator James Buckley, the very type of conservative leader whose support Ford was desperate to win. Buckley's position on the city was different from the typical line on the right, though. He had been in touch with Ford's aides to urge the president to "minimize his rhetoric" on New York and to "talk more about the need to assist the millions of innocent citizens" whose city was failing through no fault of their own. He thought Ford could blame the city's leaders while not "totally

alienating" New Yorkers. Ford's advisers were excited by these overtures from Buckley, which they hoped might indicate his willingness to
support the president in the Republican primary, and they encouraged
Ford to find a way to "join forces" with Buckley on New York.[16]

The union leaders begged the president to promise that if the city
defaulted, the federal government would step in with money for police
and fire protection before anything else. Confronted by their emotional
pleas, Ford expressed solidarity and support, promising to do all he
could to make sure that "essential services" were not disrupted by the
default. Finally, he tried to reassure them that his speech the next day
would be "very sympathetic to the people of New York."[17]

If that really was Ford's intent, rarely has a political speech had an
impact more divergent from its aim.

When Ford arrived at the National Press Club on October 29, he was
greeted by William Broom, the president of the journalists' club and a
Washington bureau chief at Knight-Ridder newspapers. He said hello
to the luncheon guests at the head table: reporters from the *Washington
Post*, the *New York Daily News*, the *Daily Oklahoman*, and a few other
newspapers and news services such as Reuters. At exactly noon, Ford
rose to address the 450 luncheon attendees.

In his speech, Ford strove to juxtapose his own "straight talk" and
good moral values with the city's extravagant and flagrant irresponsibility. He opened by saying that his goal was to "sort facts and figures
from fiction and fear-mongering." New York, he said, was an orphan,
left on the doorstep of the federal government, "unwanted and abandoned by its real parents." He rehearsed the standard portrait of the
profligate city, repeating that the wages and salaries of its workers were
"the highest in the United States," even though his own budget office
had just released a report saying this wasn't so. He complained that the
city's municipal hospitals were too generous and that it operated "one
of the largest universities in the world, free of tuition for any high school
graduate, rich or poor, who wants to attend." Yet now that the city had
fallen on hard times it wanted America to foot the bills instead of mak-

ing cuts. "Why," he asked, should other Americans "support advantages in New York that they have not been able to afford for their own communities?"

Ford implored the country not to give in to "panic" about the impact of a New York bankruptcy. Such fears, he said, were being stoked by the city's bankers and politicians. Giving the city aid to help it avoid default would set a "terrible" precedent for cities across the country.

Instead, as planned, Ford proposed a revision of bankruptcy laws to make it easier for New York to file. Bankruptcy, he suggested, would enable the city to restructure its finances in an orderly fashion. And while that process was under way, the court could issue debt certificates so the city could sustain its essential services—which, Ford assured the country, would not be halted just because the city was in default. In short, Ford's message for New York was that the best he would do was open the way for an orderly collapse.

In the last few minutes, Ford broadened his view of the city to the country as a whole. "There is," he warned, "a profound lesson for all Americans in the financial experience of our biggest and our richest city." The United States might be the wealthiest nation in the world, but there still remained "a practical limit" to "our public bounty." Other cities, other states, even the federal government itself were not immune to the sickness that had enveloped New York. In a sense, the entire nation bore responsibility for what had happened, for New York had simply done what Washington had been doing throughout the 1960s: borrowing money and expanding the deficit in order to provide services for poor people. And what was happening to New York anticipated what Ford feared would be the fate of the entire country. Standing fast and refusing aid to New York meant taking the entire nation in a new direction, leading it away from the reckless spending of the Great Society.

Ford had initially planned not to accept questions. He wanted to leave as soon as he was done speaking.[18] But in the end, he agreed to take a few preselected questions from the National Press Club president. The last of these pointed toward the upcoming presidential election: After this speech, did Ford see any hope of winning New York in 1976? Ford was perhaps not underestimating by much when he replied, "I think I'll have a friend or two in New York City."[19]

The president then left for the White House, where he met briefly with Alan Greenspan and Donald Rumsfeld before departing for the West Coast. On his trip, Ford would speak at Republican Party events large and small, at banquets and luncheons attended by hundreds and also at more intimate gatherings with just a few dozen wealthy individuals. In his remarks, he frequently returned to the subject of New York, seeking to spin the city's plight into his own political gold. He pointed to New York's budget as an example of how the country had gone wrong: "Too many things have gotten out of balance, including too many budgets."[20] In San Francisco, he cited the 1906 earthquake as an example of a real urban disaster—a crisis, he said, that the city had surmounted on its own, without federal aid.[21] Stopping in Milwaukee on his way back to the east, Ford referenced New York once again: "It is neither responsible nor compassionate to spend a city or a nation into bankruptcy."[22]

From his fundraising tour, it is clear how Ford hoped to integrate his rebuff of New York into a broader political narrative. The reaction to his speech, however, was far stronger than he had probably anticipated.

The story of the headline that would forever sum up Ford's attitude toward New York passed into legend only weeks after it was written. As the *New Yorker* told the story, *Daily News* managing editor William Brink had been mulling over the cover story on Ford's speech all afternoon. Its headline would be printed in 144-point type, the largest possible, so it had to be short. Brink scrawled one phase after another on the pad in front of him, all lackluster variations on the theme of "No." His colleagues rejected each one.

Then it came to him, all of a sudden: DROP DEAD. He wrote it down, then scribbled FORD TO CITY above. His editor, Michael O'Neill, pronounced it "terrific." The rest of the team was delighted.[23]

Before the speech, Ford's advisers had carefully considered the press coverage, planning how to best answer questions about the possibility of a "ripple effect" and whether the federal government would do anything to aid the city after default.[24] But they were not prepared for the wave of outrage that followed. The *Daily News* headline itself became news worldwide. Inside, the paper reported that, according to "White House officials," no federal money would go to maintain essential city services—and that Ford's administration did not consider public schooling to be among the "essential services" in the first place.[25]

The *Daily News* coverage set the tone for the city's response. "It's tragic that this Midwesterner who hasn't been able to administer his way out of a paper bag is dogmatically telling New Yorkers what we have to do, and worse, talking to us as though we were children," said Victor Gotbaum.[26] Carey accused the president of "fiscal illiteracy," arguing that his proposals were "an open invitation to public bankruptcy" and represented a "plan for federally supervised martial law."[27] Moody's downgraded the city's debt once again, saying that "elements of default are now predominating."[28] The *New York Times* editorial page—which had hardly been sympathetic to the city's leadership—excoriated the president's position, deeming his focus on the constitutional separation of powers (according to which the federal government should not get mixed up with municipal budgets) hopelessly outmoded. "Like a bemused stranger from another time and place, President Ford yesterday addressed the contemporary crisis in urban America's largest city in terms of the political and economic dogmas of an 18th-century rural confederacy," wrote the editors. The newspaper accused Ford of indulging in "moralistic posturing" from his "shaky pulpit" and turning his back on the city in need.[29]

Mail critical of the speech poured into the White House. "These are desperate times, Mr. President, and I sincerely believe our economic recovery is far too fragile to withstand a New York City default," wrote one Pennsylvania manufacturer.[30] "Your performance today at the National Press Club was a shameful and irresponsible stab in the back," read a telegram from a Brooklyn rabbi.[31] "If Ford 'spared' (and pardoned) Nixon, how dare he sentence and condemn New York City?" wrote one constituent to her congressman, Ed Koch.[32] A "life-long Republican" told Ford that he was "disgusted" with the president's "very political position" on New York, which, he said, sought to revive "small-town bigotry about big cities."[33] Another angry writer wished she could "understand how you can 'bail' out a corporation such as Lockheed and refuse to help a city."[34]

The city's plight began to inspire local bards. One poet suggested that the president's "lordly indifference" to New York's plight demanded a revision of Emma Lazarus's famous lyric:

> Spare me your tired, your poor,
> Your baffled leaders yearning to breathe free,
> The wretched refuse which has sought your shore.
> Keep these, the weary, tempest-tossed from me.
> My veto stands beside the golden door.[35]

Another poetic intervention was published in the letters section of the *Times*:

> No town is an island,
> Entire of itself.
> Any town's default diminishes me,
> Because I am involved in that town. . . .[36]

Even the editorial page of the *Times* got in on the poetic act, running a poem titled "Gotham Roundelay" that humorously traced Federal Reserve Chair Arthur Burns's deepening concern about the city:

> Three months ago, three months ago,
> My heart was young and gay;
> I told the Chief Executive,
> New York has got to pay!
>
> Three weeks ago, three weeks ago,
> My mien had grown more sober.
> I worried more but still was sure
> Default would soon blow over.

By monotonic rates of growth
I'm now three times less sure
Than e'er I was three weeks ago
And twelve times three months more.

Where will I be three months from now
If defaulting ain't scare talk?
With sprinkling can 'midst growing grass
On the sidewalks of Noo Yawk.[37]

Ford received more measured feedback from Capitol Hill. His office carefully contacted congressional representatives and senators to gauge their reactions. Some were strongly positive. "Great speech. It is a shame the networks did not carry it," commented Michigan senator (and Republican) Robert Griffin.[38] Massachusetts Democrat Tip O'Neill described it as the "biggest damn political statement ever written." Republican representative Robert Michel of Illinois pronounced it "damn good, right on target." Others condemned Ford's do-nothing approach. Democratic representative Thomas Ludlow Ashley of Oklahoma strongly criticized Ford for joining the "conspiracy of 'irresponsibility,'" saying he believed "there is no doubt we will experience both severe national and international adverse economic consequences if and when New York City actually defaults."[39] If Ford hoped that his threat of a veto would preempt legislative proposals, he was mistaken: none of the congressional committees preparing bills to aid New York withdrew them.

Within Ford's inner circle, Rumsfeld and Simon, not surprisingly, were quite satisfied with the speech. They thought it would prompt the city to take serious action at last instead of relying on Washington as a safety net. At the first senior staff meeting following the speech, on Monday, November 3, they remarked that there finally seemed to be "considerable movement" in the city to stave off collapse. Simon reported that he was meeting "sub rosa" with a banker from Morgan Guaranty, who told him the state was debating a tax hike. (Simon believed the priority should be budget cuts, but he saw tax increases as essential to getting the city out of debt.) James Lynn observed that over the next few months, more cities would be "tightening their belts." Simon noted that the threatened default in Massachusetts had been averted—once the banks realized there would be "no NYC bailout," they pressed the state to find a way to balance the budget. Rumsfeld concluded on an optimistic note: "The discussion of New York is going to have a good effect on other cities."[40]

The quest for their approval may have been what really motivated Ford to take such a hard line in his address. Whatever else the speech accomplished, it showcased the ascendance of the conservatives in Ford's administration. That same evening, Ford announced that he was over-hauling his cabinet, promoting Rumsfeld to Secretary of Defense and Cheney to Chief of Staff. (He also replaced his Commerce Secretary and the head of the CIA, while Henry Kissinger stepped down at the National Security Agency.) Although the press mocked Ford as confused and irresolute for the suddenness of the reorganization—it was dubbed the "Halloween Massacre"—the changes highlighted the growing power of the right in Ford's White House.[41] November 3 also saw Nelson Rockefeller announce that he would withdraw his name from consideration as Ford's running mate in 1976. This was a sign of the deepening split between the president and vice president over New York City, but also another indication that Ford's campaign advisers saw Rockefeller's liberal Republicanism as a liability.

The approval of his inner circle aside, Ford was stung by the general hostility to the speech. The next day, reporters were already asking him about the *Daily News* headline: Had he really told New York to drop dead? "Not at all," the president said to one television news station. "I have great sympathy for the people of New York."[42] For years to come, Ford would insist the media had been far too tough on his speech and distorted his real meaning.[43]

But this was dissembling. Ford's real position was exactly as harsh and strict as it appeared: by the end of October, the dominant voices in his administration saw no way forward for the city but default and bankruptcy. Their certitude on this point blinded them to the difficulties that bankruptcy might involve, and even pushed them to ignore the reality of how municipal crises had been dealt with in the past. When journalists looked into some of the claims from Ford's speeches in California, for example, they found that Republican president Theodore Roosevelt had, in fact, sent federal aid to earthquake-stricken San Francisco back in 1906.[44]

12. Pastrami and Rambouillet

In the days after Ford's speech, observers throughout the country and around the world focused intently on New York City. Without federal aid, it was widely assumed that default was inevitable—the only question was when. Believing that the Ford administration's denial of aid was final and that there was no other way out for New York, Senator James Buckley called on the city to "face the facts," stop wasting time, and simply declare that it was bankrupt.[1]

Not everyone was so resigned. Despite the president's insistence that aid was impossible, a poll done by the *New York Times* showed that the country was evenly split on the question.[2] In Oklahoma City, a local author started a "Grassroots for Gotham" campaign, proposing that everyone in the country send one dollar to New York.[3] While giving a talk in Chicago, the executive head of the American Jewish Committee expressed his fear that the economic consequences of default—workers competing for ever-more-scarce public sector jobs, bondholders losing their investments—would lead to "attempts to scapegoat" minority groups such as Jews.[4] New York's Catholic leaders framed the issue in moral terms. "This present crisis is not simply a fiscal crisis. In its true dimensions, it is a human problem as well," read a statement by Brooklyn bishop Francis J. Mugavero and the city's Cardinal Terence Cooke. "If New York City goes bankrupt, where will the poor and those who cannot find jobs obtain food and clothing and a roof over their heads?"[5]

Internationally, the press and politicians were horrified and transfixed by the possibility of the city's bankruptcy. The *Times* of London published an editorial denouncing Ford's "monumental folly," saying that he had failed to understand the "nature of a modern financial system" and the way that the city's collapse would reverberate around the world. A financial analyst who was in touch with the Ford administration reported that the European financial community believed that New York's difficulties suggested that Washington itself was unstable—why else would it refuse to help?[6] Bond sales for cities outside the United States slowed sharply in November, and international clients began to move their money out of New York banks.[7] One London politician said it would be a "massive tragedy for Western democracy" for New York City to default.[8] The mayor of Rome observed, "A city should never die." The mayor of Moscow expressed relief that he was not running New York: "Under the system that exists in your country, if I were offered such a post I would not accept it."[9]

Back in the States, the press kept demanding answers to the question of what "essential services" the federal government would cover if the city declared bankruptcy. Schools? Jails? Police and fire? Welfare and Medicaid? William Simon advised Ford to avoid clarifying his position—to "make no further announcement and take no action until default"—so as to leave himself room to maneuver in such a scenario.[10] But the ambiguity only provoked greater anxiety, as all the city agencies jockeyed to be deemed essential. The head of the Board of Education wrote to Kenneth Axelson, the deputy mayor for finance, saying that while he would "pray" that default could be averted, the schools had to prepare "should the unthinkable become reality." There were many questions: Would special education be continued? Would the schools be cleaned? Would the school buses run? Could the schools purchase fuel for heating, books for classes, toilet paper?[11] The Community Council

of Greater New York—a coalition of groups devoted to easing poverty—
compiled a list of services for the poor, including food, shelter, clothing,
and emergency medical aid, whose loss might jeopardize "the lives of
those dependent on these services."[12] The State Health Commissioner
petitioned for water supply employees to be included on the essential
list. "You couldn't fight fire without a water supply system," he said before
a meeting of the State Public Health Council.[13] The chairman of the
board of Con Edison begged the president to deem electrical services
"essential," and pointed out that if the utility were not able to collect the
$120 million the city owed it annually for the electricity that powered
its streetlamps, hospitals, fire stations, elevators, and subways, it would
be unable to pay its taxes to the city or the state.[14]

The Contingency Committee that Beame had assembled sought to
prepare for whatever might follow default. The lawyers predicted "vast
and continued confusion and uncertainty," with thousands of creditors
petitioning the city in lawsuits that might drag on for years. The city
would be blocked from the credit markets, while judges, creditors' committees, the EFCB, and maybe a federal board would take any remaining power away from elected officials. "Running the City in these
circumstances is hard to imagine," lawyer Ira Millstein drily noted.[15]
The members of the Contingency Committee were so desperate that
they contacted bankers at First Boston to investigate how and whether
a "scrip" system of payment might work in the city if it ran out of cash
to pay workers and vendors. But their efforts were hamstrung by the difficulty of getting clear information about expenses from Beame. "We
are frustrated and helpless and need guidance and direction from you
as to what is wanted from us," Robert Rivel, the chairman of the committee, wrote to the mayor.[16]

Beame himself felt publicly humiliated by the president's speech. The
cover of Newsweek the following week featured a caricature of Beame
swaddled like a baby, being spanked by Ford.[17] He tried to strike back,
giving his own address at the National Press Club on November 5, where
he insisted that the city's economic and political importance—as well
as the taxes that it paid to the federal government—made it worthy of
aid. But he was sufficiently afraid himself of what would happen to the

city that he did what he had sworn he'd never do: he forced James Cavanagh, the first deputy mayor and his closest associate, out of the city government.

Whether anyone compelled Beame to push out Cavanagh remains unclear, but in the financial community and on the MAC board it was an article of faith that the mayor's old guard needed to be replaced with new leaders—men such as Axelson, trained budget professionals with close ties to the business world. Only this type of person would have the will to make painful cuts to the city's budget, put through layoffs, and restrain spending. As long as the likes of Cavanagh were in power, those factions reasoned, the city could not be trusted to do what was necessary. After Ford's denial of aid, Beame finally decided that he had no choice. Keeping Cavanagh meant putting the entire city—and his own mayoralty—at risk.

Beame and Cavanagh met at Gracie Mansion late in the afternoon on Friday, November 14, for a short, painful conversation. Both kept their suit jackets on. Beame told his old friend that he'd taken care of him: a job was waiting at the Fund for the City of New York, which had inquired whether Cavanagh might be available to direct a program aimed at developing middle-management talent for the city. He could even keep his pension. As the *Times* reported, Beame said, "Jim, this is up to you. I'm not going to ask you to get out."[18]

Cavanagh understood. "If there's truth to these pressures, it's just as well."[19] The two men looked at each other, and then hugged for a long time.[20]

Cavanagh repaired to City Hall, where he shared white wine and scotch with his assistants. He later told the papers that his critics had never confronted him directly—that was part of the problem. "It was like punching pillows," he said. "All of those pillows smothered me."[21]

Beame was determined to make it look as though Cavanagh had chosen to retire of his own accord. One month later, he held a lavish dinner in Cavanagh's honor, attended by a thousand guests. Joe Papp spoke in praise of Cavanagh, saying that "bankers and financiers" could not provide the "human leadership chosen by the people. Efficiency and economic considerations alone will lead only to a fascist desert."[22]

Cavanagh's departure marked a turning point for the city. For the bankers, for the people at MAC, Cavanagh embodied the old way of doing things—free-spending, with little sense of the consequences, and not averse to budget manipulation. But their objections went beyond his advocacy for the practices that had obfuscated the city's worsening financial situation for so long. Cavanagh also exemplified what increasingly seemed like an antiquated view of city government, one that celebrated municipal generosity and provision of services rather than corporate-style success.[23] "A city is not a business," he told the *Daily News*. "If you run a private business, and don't make a profit, you can shut down, like an airline that lays up planes and lays off workers if the flights are empty. I told them at meetings, we can't do that. We have to fly the plane, loaded or unloaded."[24] Even after the fiscal crisis had unfolded completely, Cavanagh remained defiant, almost proud of the ways he had managed to procure the money the city needed—the "gimmicks," as he described them. All the layoffs, all the firings, all the cutbacks: his New York would not have done such things. That was why he had to go.

He would be replaced as first deputy mayor by John Zuccotti, the chairman of the City Planning Commission, a graduate of Princeton and Yale Law School who had served in the Lindsay administration and advocated tax abatements to support converting old industrial spaces into housing. Zuccotti's appointment, more than anything else, seemed proof that a new order was in place at City Hall.

The early weeks of November were an anxious time for Governor Carey as well. Not just the city but the entire state was in deep trouble. Peter Goldmark, Carey's budget director, had been warning Carey that if the city collapsed, several important New York State agencies would also be pushed to the edge of bankruptcy, since investors would be unlikely to purchase their bonds.[25] And there was still concern about the city of Yonkers, which was approaching a mid-November debt redemption deadline that might put it into default.

As the tumult surrounding New York City increased, Carey made his own private appeals to Washington. "I sense, Mr. President," he wrote to Ford, "as do many others across the country, that we are at an economic crossroads unparalleled since those final moments in the darkest Depression. Whatever points you thought necessary to make about the past mistakes of New York have been made."[26] He hoped the president might convince the Federal Reserve to act as a lender of last resort for state agencies (perfectly responsible ones, he insisted) that had been blocked from credit markets by the panic that Ford's speech unleashed.[27] In response, Carey received a chilly little note from one of Ford's economic advisers, reminding him that the Federal Reserve was an independent body that the Ford administration did not direct or control.[28]

Carey was so afraid of what would happen to New York State if the federal government did not come through that he began to consider previously unthinkable solutions. Not only was he finally willing to agree to a round of state tax hikes, but he hatched a dubious plan to allow New York City to halt repayment of its debts without officially defaulting.

Years later, Carey recalled that he had come up with the idea over pastrami sandwiches with an old friend, the former judge and lawyer Simon Rifkind. Both felt rather gloomy and pessimistic—Felix Rohatyn had told the governor there was little to do but prepare for bankruptcy. But as they ate, Carey asked Rifkind a series of pointed questions about New York political history. During the Great Depression, Carey said, Franklin Roosevelt, then governor of New York, passed an emergency law declaring that homeowners would not have to repay the principal on their mortgages for the time being—only interest. FDR, he noted, would often sign laws and then wait for their constitutionality to be determined after the fact. Carey asked his friend the judge: Would a financial crisis such as the one facing the state and city of New York be sufficient grounds to pass an emergency measure similar to Roosevelt's—a law suspending the city's repayment of principal to its creditors? And how long would it take such a law to be challenged in court? Rifkind guessed that it would take about a year for the courts to hear and rule on such a case.[29]

For Carey, this seemed like plenty of time. Whether or not the law was constitutional, a year free of panics and collapse sounded like bliss. Carey decided to bring before the legislature a plan allowing the city to pay only interest (no principal) to creditors whose notes were due to mature in the next year. The creditors would also be given the option of exchanging their notes for MAC bonds that matured in ten years.[30] Carey liked to refer to the arrangement as the "pastrami agreement."[31]

In theory, that agreement would relieve the city from the immediate burden of the debts coming due, saving it from having to pay $1.6 billion to its creditors in 1976. But the plan would first have to pass the state legislature, and in any case it was not a long-term solution. That, Carey was sure, would require federal aid. Along with Rohatyn, he kept trying to rally the major banks and pension funds for one more infusion of cash, while making sure that Washington knew about their efforts.[32] On November 11, Carey and Rohatyn sent Ford a proposal asking once again for assistance. They promised to cut the city's welfare and social spending, raise taxes in both the city and the state, and enact the "pastrami agreement" to help the city restructure its debts.[33] A few days later, Rohatyn followed up by sending Ford a packet of letters signed by the heads of the eleven clearinghouse banks, along with union presidents Shanker, Gotbaum, and DeLury. Each letter contained promises to convert current holdings of short-term MAC and city debt into ten-year bonds, giving the city a much longer period of time to repay what it owed. The banks and unions also promised to invest an additional $2.5 billion in short-term city notes.[34] Taken together, these pledges from the banks and the union pension funds meant that a much smaller assistance package from federal government would suffice.[35]

The state legislature passed Carey's law on November 14, declaring that the normal expectation that bonds represented the "full faith and credit" of New York City had to be suspended in light of the "dramatic" worsening of the city's fiscal plight and the potentially "disastrous consequences" of bankruptcy.[36] The phrasing was designed to echo Roosevelt's Depression-era legislation on mortgage payments as closely as possible, in the hope that this would enable the law to survive constitutional challenge.[37] (Some of FDR's debt moratoriums had indeed been ruled constitutional during the 1930s.) Still, as law professors around the country observed, the new law looked a lot like default under another name. Spokesmen for the state, including Rifkind, fell over themselves insisting that it wasn't: the noteholders were able to exchange their notes for MAC bonds, and they could still collect interest on their debts, which the state would, in fact, eventually redeem—the only question was when.

Even with the city's debt redemptions postponed, however, federal aid remained crucial. The unions and the banks, still afraid that the city might default, would only help with financing if the federal government agreed to offer some form of assistance.[38] Carey traveled to Capitol Hill to press the city's case with his former colleagues in Congress. Walking from office to office, he peeked in to chat with politicians from Louisiana, Ohio, California, and Wisconsin, asking one surprised representative: "Can you help us get the poor old broken-down State of New York back on its feet again?"[39]

All eyes were on Washington. Would Ford finally move to help the city, now that the banks and unions had committed their support, now that the state was willing to raise taxes and restructure debt, now that the city was ready to cut back on everything and throw out old-fashioned politicians? As one of Ford's aides wrote, "The New York City thing is rapidly building to a climax."[40] The president found himself entertaining possibilities he had once insisted he never would consider.

Throughout the fall, Ford had come under mounting pressure from Congress. Both the House and the Senate banking committees had endorsed legislation that would provide a federal guarantee for debt issued by the city, while placing the city government under stringent federal control: a new control board, headed by Simon, was to oversee the city's finances and ensure a balanced budget within two years.[41] Representatives from across the country rejected the idea that New York's problems were simply local. Ohio Democrat Thomas Ashley—the chair of the House Economic Stabilization Committee—wrote to Ford personally, calling him "the first friend I've had in the White House in a long time" and urging him not to block the proposed legislation. "If you do . . . and if New York City subsequently requires Federal help by your own standards, your access to the Congress then will be on terms and at a price which we both understand."[42] Ashley even published an op-ed in the *New York Times*, arguing that the city had been made to suffer enough already to be an object lesson for the country: "Is the pound of flesh really necessary?"[43]

Ford appeared unmovable. "I'm not going to change my position," he had said. "I will not be locked in a corner to buy a bill that is unacceptable. The other way"—meaning bankruptcy—"is clear, quick and sound."[44] As he told a group of congressional Republicans, his position was the only one consistent with his larger desire to contain federal spending on domestic programs, a trend that had to stop "if we wish to avoid the fate of New York City."[45]

Yet Ford began to telegraph that his seemingly firm view was at least in part a bargaining position, a way to force the city to make changes. On November 17, the day before he received Rohatyn's packet of letters from bankers and union leaders, he had met with five Democratic senators, who warned him that if the city collapsed it would be unable to borrow money "for a generation" and that time was scarce. Ford demurred—but he also said that "if Congress and I had capitulated two months ago, we wouldn't have [the] results achieved so far." This offered a tantalizing possibility: perhaps Ford was only threatening to condemn the city to make sure that Beame went through with the budget cuts.[46] Ford told the senators to say nothing to the press—it would be "very ill advised" to give anyone the impression that he was modifying his views at all. Nonetheless, two days later an aide told Ford that Capitol Hill was "awash with rumors" that the president was changing his mind. Nelson Rockefeller did his best to stoke this impression as well, even going so far as to tell an audience at one of his speeches that Ford was finally rethinking his stance.[47]

An even more explicit admission came when Ford traveled to Rambouillet, France, for an economic summit with the leaders of Germany, France, Italy, the United Kingdom, and Japan. Helmut Schmidt—who had been so critical of Ford's position on New York—opened the conversation by warning of the economic perils of "psychological uncertainty." He was referring to Europe's long-term problems, but Ford, unprompted, brought up New York City. In a stunning reversal, he told those assembled that he would approve legislation permitting federal guarantees for New York's debt—even if the state legislature could not come up with a package that he deemed acceptable. His tough stance, he said, had been a negotiating strategy. "The only way we have achieved results is to be difficult," he said. "This has been a sort of brinksmanship by the Administration forcing New York City and New York State to take responsible action." Schmidt and the others expressed their relief, and Schmidt even apologized for taking his concerns about New York to the press. Ford told him that "patience and firmness" had been needed to make sure the city adopted retrenchment, and asked all those present to keep the conversation absolutely top secret and to leak nothing to the press. "If there is advance information we are caving, necessary action will not materialize."[48]

As the speculation and debate over aid swirled through Washington and Albany, New York City had reached the limit of its promises and was running out of cash. Even with the funds freed up by the moratorium law that Carey had dreamed up, by the end of November it would be short $60 million it needed to pay its employees and contractors.[49] On December 5 it would need $100 million for another payroll; on December 11, $440 million in short-term notes would come due.[50] As had so often been the case throughout the year, it seemed that New York was about to simply be out of funds.

But now there seemed to be a real possibility that help might arrive in time. With rumors circulating that Ford would reverse himself, Carey's moratorium suddenly seemed less like a euphemism for default and more like a potential part of an actual solution.

Yet the legislation proposed in Congress was contingent on the state government's approving a package of tax increases that would help the city move toward a balanced budget. And despite the urgency of the situation, Republicans and Democrats in Albany continued to bicker over what kinds of taxes would be best: the Republicans wanted to prevent an increase in the commuter tax, the Democrats sought to head off a hike in the sales tax. Each side wanted to pin responsibility for new taxes on the other. (As Peter Goldmark wrote to Carey, "Samuel Beckett wrote a play called *Krapp's Last Tape*; the measures necessary now can accurately be called Rockefeller's Last Tax.")[51] Ford was furious at the inaction. If the state could not pass the package, he insisted (despite what he'd said in France) that New York would get nothing. He told his cabinet that the state legislature had "bombed out," saying, "I thank the Good Lord that we didn't commit aid to New York City."[52]

Finally, on Tuesday, November 25, the state legislature pushed through tax increases that raised the city income tax by 25 percent, increased sales taxes on a host of items such as cigarettes and haircuts, and imposed a 50 percent surcharge on an estate tax in the city. Carey wrote to Ford, reporting that the "financial and legal requirements requested as a precondition to any Federal involvement in the fiscal crisis of New York City have been accomplished, and achieved in full."[53]

The next day, Ford made good on the promises he'd made at Rambouillet. He proposed legislation to provide $2.3 billion in a series of short-term "seasonal" loans to the city through the state, made at the start of the fiscal year and due at the end of it. The city would have to pay the federal government 8 percent interest on the loans (one percent higher than the current rate for Treasury bills), and its progress toward a balanced budget—a goal it would have to achieve in three years—would be closely monitored. None other than William Simon in his role as Treasury Secretary would be empowered to stop the loans if it seemed likely that the federal government would not be repaid.[54] As Ford put it to his senior staff in a meeting on November 28, "They are totally under the gun to perform." This funding proposal, he swore, was his absolute final offer, his last concession. "Come Hell or high water, this is it."[55]

No more was needed. On December 9, with little fanfare, Ford signed the bill into law. He insisted that there was no reversal of his earlier promise to deny aid, that the city and the state finally had demonstrated that they had done all they could to help themselves. "New York City has bailed itself out," he proclaimed. The federal government would be protected from any possible loss of funds, he said, because it would have first lien on the city's income, and taxpayers wouldn't lose any money on the deal.[56] Meanwhile, perhaps with an eye to the future, Congress also approved Ford's revisions to the federal bankruptcy code as it applied to cities, amending it to allow municipalities to file for bankruptcy without the approval of their creditors.[57]

New York had needed to line up a total of $6.8 billion in financing to cover the period between the end of 1975 and June 1978, the year the city was supposed to achieve a balanced budget according to the act that had created the EFCB. At last this was secured. The most important piece came from the unions, whose leaders agreed to purchase $2.5 billion in city debt with their pension funds. They also agreed to forego interest payments and instead reinvest the money in city securities. The banks and other institutional investors consented to roll over $1 billion in city debt. The moratorium on repaying principal to owners of city bonds—the "pastrami agreement"—meant the city would save another $1.6 billion. Owners of MAC bonds agreed to accept lower interest rates and a longer time to repay the principal. The state agreed to advance the city $800 million, while new taxes would generate $500 million.[58]

But none of those pieces would have fallen into place without federal support. The federal loans were what spared the city from having to borrow any more money while it waited to collect taxes or receive other transfer payments. And it was the assurance of these loans, plus the moratorium, that persuaded the banks and the pension funds to agree to make their purchases. The difference that federal help made was remarkable. Indeed, once Ford did extend support to the city, it became clear that the hostility of the federal government had played a central role in turning the city's fiscal shortfalls into a full-fledged panic.

For the time being, the crisis had been averted. There was no immediate threat of default; the day of reckoning had been postponed. New York would not go into bankruptcy court. There would be no creditors' meetings in Shea Stadium, no judge settling the city's affairs, no tedious years-long battles hashing out who got what. The markets of the world would not be roiled by collapse; municipal bonds could be traded without their owners' blanching at the spectacle of default. On the global markets, the value of the American dollar immediately rose.[59]

Underneath all the technicalities of the refinancing agreements, though, was a promise to fundamentally restructure how New York City worked—to drastically cut the budget and shift spending away from social services. As Felix Rohatyn put it, in the years ahead the city would be forced to undergo "the most brutal kind of financial and fiscal exercise any community in the country will ever have to face." The pain, he said, was "just beginning."[60]

And the New Yorkers who would feel that pain most acutely experienced none of the financiers' contentment. The week before the state legislature passed the deal, protests had flared throughout the city once again. Thousands of people representing the city's grassroots antipoverty organizations marched through Harlem, Brownsville, and the Lower East Side, blocking traffic at intersections and stopping cars from passing through the Brooklyn Battery Tunnel.[61] A jailhouse riot, triggered by deteriorating conditions, exploded at the House of Detention for Men on Rikers Island. Because of budget cuts the number of guards at the jail had been reduced to 340 from the recommended 500, while the jail's population had increased by 50 percent over the preceding year, so that inmates were held three to a cell. Prisoners took over two cell blocks, holding several guards hostage to bargain for better and safer conditions in the jail.[62]

As the *Catholic News* had put it, and as Bishop Paul Moore had remarked early on, the fiscal crisis all along had masked an underlying social calamity. From the perspective of North Williamsburg or Bushwick or Harlem or Hunts Point, the Upper West Side or even Greenwich Village, the meaning of the crisis looked very different than it did in City Hall or Albany or Washington, D.C.

PART III

LEGACIES

13. State of Emergency

The bad news arrived for the Chelsea Children's Center, on Ninth Avenue, in the middle of the summer of 1976. The center was one of more than four hundred publicly funded day care centers in the city, which offered free or subsidized child care to poor and working-class families.[1] This day care network had expanded during the 1960s, when it had looked as if the federal government might approve the creation of a universal system of early child care. President Nixon had vetoed that legislation in 1971, but money for day care and early childhood education was still available from both federal and local sources.

In the spring of 1976, though, the budget of the Agency for Child Development was cut by $31 million as part of the federally mandated cost-cutting regime. As a result, forty-nine day care centers lost their funding, on top of twenty-eight that had already been defunded the previous year. The Bronx borough president, Robert Abrams, wrote Beame an outraged letter: "We have just heard that mailograms have been received by a number of day care centers with the opening words 'we regret to inform you' and telling them that they will be closed. Perhaps it is appropriate to echo the chilling telegrams sent to the families of service men."[2]

The director of the Chelsea Children's Center was appalled by the
news. "You don't just break up a home for no reason," she told the newspapers. The mothers whose children attended the day care didn't know
what they would do without the familiar, cozy space. Would they be able
to keep their jobs? Would they have to go on welfare? Would they rely
on grandmothers, sisters, aunts, friends, babysitters? Would they, in
desperation, leave their young children at home alone?[3] It seemed better for the center to try to keep going for the moment—the staff members volunteering their services while they collected unemployment, the
parents scraping together what funds they could, the directors hoping
that the Church of the Holy Apostles, which rented space to the center,
would not move to evict it quite yet.[4]

Because of the budget cuts, about a thousand day care workers lost
their jobs. In addition, the city and state tightened the eligibility rules
so that women unemployed for more than four months lost the right to
place their children in a day care center, even if they were still seeking
work.[5] Four thousand people marched near City Hall in defense of day
care in June 1976, chanting slogans such as "We want day care! No more
welfare!" Supporters of the programs pointed out that day care enabled
poor women to keep working, and that it brought together people from
different racial and ethnic backgrounds.[6]

With the support of Congresswoman Bella Abzug, a coalition of day
care advocates filed a lawsuit challenging the city's choice of which particular centers to close as arbitrary and unjust.[7] The suspect nature of
the closures was highlighted later in the summer of 1976, when reports
revealed that the city was paying exorbitantly high rents to certain
politically connected day care landlords, and that those centers were not
the ones the city moved to close.[8] Still, such revelations did not change
the funding difficulties—if anything, they helped to weaken political
support for the day care system overall.

The uncertainty surrounding the future of the Chelsea Children's
Center was replicated on a grand scale throughout the city in 1976 and
1977, as money that had previously been available for libraries, parks,
schools, playgrounds, health care, and police and fire services simply
vanished. Over the three years that followed the fiscal crisis, the city's

public workforce shrank by 69,672. The cutbacks affected the entire spectrum of city services.[9] Fewer people were seen in the public clinics and public hospitals. Streets were cleaned less frequently. Restaurant inspections and inspections for lead paint declined.[10] Transit fares were raised from 50 to 60 cents, even as the number of subway breakdowns tripled and the bus fleet aged.[11] The number of students at CUNY dropped by a quarter. Capital improvement projects ground to a halt, though the City Planning Commission warned that the city's bridges, sewers, water tunnels, and parks were becoming so dilapidated that they might collapse—invoking the West Side Highway debacle on a much larger scale.[12] The layoffs fell with special force on the city's black and Latino workforce, and on women—workers who often had less seniority and thus less protection.[13]

The Beame administration and the Emergency Financial Control Board tried to make the case that the cuts had been accomplished with minimal reduction in services, that they simply corrected inefficiencies and made the city run more smoothly. In an essay in the *New York Times Magazine*, Roger Starr, Beame's Housing and Development Administrator, provided the most controversial justification for the cuts in February 1976, when he proposed what he termed "planned shrinkage"—the intentional removal of city services from the poorest and most dysfunctional neighborhoods.[14] He reasoned that people were fleeing anyway. Large swaths of the city, he wrote, "have been so reduced in population that block after block of apartment buildings stand open to wind and sky, their roofs burned, their plumbing pilfered." Since the residents were already leaving, why should the city keep sending in the fire engines, maintaining the subway stations, operating the libraries and schools? Starr concluded: "Better a thriving city of five million than a Calcutta of seven, destroyed by its internal wrangling."[15]

Many New Yorkers responded to Starr's proposal with horror. Members of the Black and Puerto Rican Caucus of the City Council denounced the idea of "planned shrinkage" as "outrageous," and their chairman released a statement calling it "nothing short of racial genocide."[16] The Beame administration rejected the plan—Deputy Mayor John Zuccotti commented that it didn't seem "practical" to shut down large sections of the city, and Starr resigned his city office over the summer.[17] None-theless, even though it was never the Beame administration's official policy, "shrinkage" seemed to provide a rationale for making cuts, a way to see them as part of a plan that could serve the larger good. Felix Rohatyn echoed Starr's general thesis, suggesting that blighted areas of the city should be bulldozed to make space for industrial expansion.[18] In response to Starr's essay, one reader wrote in that the South Bronx might better be turned into wheat fields.[19] The argument heard over and over was that rather than providing services to poor neighborhoods and poor people, the city should husband its scarce resources for economic development—finding ways to make New York attractive to business and private investment once again.

In practice, the intense pressure from the EFCB and the federal gov-ernment to cut the budget left little space for reimagining how the city might function. The city's expenditures shrank by 20 percent in real terms between 1975 and 1981, leaving public services stripped to the bone.[20] What's more, decisions about the cost-cutting seem to have been made in a rather ad hoc fashion. The city's agreement with Washington did not specify how the required savings were to be achieved, and offi-cials ordering budget cuts gave departments little time to plan for how they might be put into effect. One round of cuts would often be quickly followed by another, so adjustments were constantly being made and then rendered obsolete; the city wound up repeatedly reducing the num-ber of employees without making clear decisions about how to reassign the work they had been doing. The result was a sense of slippage and chaos, a constant downward spiral. The disorganization itself seemed to prove that the city could not be relied on any longer.

The public sector often tried to work around the cuts. Simply battling to stay open, as the Chelsea Children's Center did, was one way to resist.[21] Another was to make creative use of the funding provided through the 1973 Comprehensive Employment and Training Act (CETA), which pro-vided federal money for hiring out-of-work people temporarily—for a year or two—in order to help them gain employment experience. Although rehiring laid-off city workers was clearly not the purpose of CETA, in some cases the city was able to use the money to do this for a time.[22]

On occasion the conflicts burst into the open, becoming protracted fights over what the city owed to its poor and working-class residents. In February 1976, an op-ed in the *New York Times* made the case that what was really at stake was the question of how much its residents would tolerate. "Whether or not the promises of social and economic entitlements of the 1960s can be rolled back to a lower order of magnitude without social upheaval is being tested in New York City," the writer suggested.[23] It was far from clear that such social unrest could be avoided. Rather than quietly tolerate retrenchment in the name of saving New York, the people who stood to lose clinics, hospitals, libraries, and day care centers fought to protect the services that sustained their communities—to make clear that their lives were something more than numbers on a budget sheet.

Although the Beame administration (with Zuccotti and Axelson in place) was formulating the city's financial plan and carrying out the budget cuts, the mayor and the City Council were no longer the final arbiters of the city's finances. That role fell to the Emergency Financial Control Board, the state agency that Carey had created at the end of the summer of 1975 and staffed with executives Alfred Casey of American Airlines, William Ellinghaus of New York Telephone, and David Margolis of Colt Industries.

Everything about the EFCB was designed to ensure its insulation from the politics that had supposedly been driving the city's spending. The board met every few weeks in a windowless back room at Carey's midtown offices, not in a city building.[24] In addition to the board's seven voting members (the governor and lieutenant governor, the mayor and comptroller, and the three business executives), a small group of the governor's aides were regulars at the meetings, as was Felix Rohatyn.[25] At the request of the municipal unions, labor consultant Jack Bigel was also invited as a nonvoting "observer." The heavy representation of the corporate sector, the absence of any community or labor representatives aside from Bigel, and the fact that the city's elected officials held only two of the seven votes all made it clear that the EFCB was to stand apart from the scrum of city politics.

Not surprisingly, the board pushed for the city to take a tough stance
with its unions. Ellinghaus and Casey, in particular, urged the city to
collect fines from public workers who had gone on strike in 1975, especially the sanitation workers and the teachers.[26] The three corporate
executives were also concerned that the city might seek to shrink its labor
force merely through attrition rather than through layoffs and broader
restructuring.[27] The city responded by creating a new Management
Advisory Committee to recommend appropriate ways to "streamline"
its functions, headed by Richard Shinn, the president of Metropolitan
Life and an early member of the Business Roundtable corporate lobbying organization.[28] Still, even after Shinn's appointment, Ellinghaus
warned the other board members that the city had to confront the
perception that nothing was happening, that it was taking too long to
make the needed cuts and changes.[29]

The sense that the city had to restructure and rethink all its operations, not merely continue with a shrunk-down version of the status
quo, was already in the air when thirty-five-year-old Stephen Berger
took over as the executive director of the EFCB in the spring of 1976.
Brash and tough-minded, Berger saw himself as a very different kind of
leader from his predecessor, Herbert Elish, who had come to EFCB
after his time at MAC.[30] Elish, he recalled years later, was "very smart,
and basically a reasonably decent human being. And I'm not."[31]

Berger considered himself a liberal, but one whose integrity and
desire to save the public sector led him to challenge almost every tenet
of the old faith. He was concerned with the same issues as other
liberals—poverty, inequality, economic injustice. But he was equally
obsessed with fiscal practicalities, which had a tendency to put him at
"political odds with people who have, in theory, the same social goals."
He prided himself on being willing (unlike old-school liberals) to challenge organized labor. He would close inefficient hospitals even if neighborhoods clung to them, claiming that they had a "right" to health care.
He would shake the faith in free tuition at CUNY, which he likened to
a "secular religious" certainty.[32] His willingness to butcher any and all
sacred cows was, he believed, why Governor Carey had put him in charge.

HARRY HAMBURG / NY DAILY NEWS ARCHIVE VIA GETTY IMAGES

In December 1973, an 80-foot section of the West Side Highway collapsed under the weight of a truck carrying asphalt for needed repairs on the road.

Garbage lies strewn across 57th Street on the first day of the sanitation workers' strike, July 1, 1975.

FRANK LEONARDO / NEW YORK POST ARCHIVES / NYP HOLDINGS VIA GETTY IMAGES

THE CARLOS ORTÍZ COLLECTION, ARCHIVES OF THE PUERTO RICAN DIASPORA, CENTRO DE ESTUDIOS PUERTORRIQUEÑOS, HUNTER COLLEGE, CUNY

Union members protesting the planned budget cuts outside the headquarters of First National City Bank in June 1975.

PAUL HOSEFROS / THE NEW YORK TIMES / REDUX

Policemen who had been laid off by the city block traffic on the Brooklyn Bridge in angry protest, July 1, 1975.

RICHARD CORKERY / NEW YORK DAILY NEWS VIA GETTY IMAGES

Felix Rohatyn, the Lazard Frères investment banker who was the first chairman of the Municipal Assistance Corporation, and Governor Hugh Carey meeting with reporters.

BETTMANN VIA GETTY IMAGES

Treasury Secretary William E. Simon speaking into a microphone aboard Air Force One. Alan Greenspan, the Chairman of the Council of Economic Advisers, lounges on the floor of the airplane next to the reporter. At center is Henry Kissinger, Secretary of State.

Mayor Abraham Beame, in front of Gracie Mansion, holding up the famous *Daily News* cover.

BILL STAHL, JR. / NEW YORK DAILY NEWS VIA GETTY IMAGES

JANIE EISENBERG

Residents of the North Brooklyn neighborhood of Williamsburg protesting in front of Engine Company 212, the People's Firehouse.

WALLACE EDGECOMBE / GERALD J. MEYER COLLECTION, HOSTOS COMMUNITY COLLEGE
ARCHIVES AND SPECIAL COLLECTIONS / CITY UNIVERSITY OF NEW YORK

Rally to Save Hostos in front of the Chase Manhattan Bank at 149th Street near Third Avenue in the Bronx, November 19, 1975. This large rally was the first major activity of the Community Coalition to Save Hostos.

People young and old alike taking goods from an A&P grocery store in the Bronx during the blackout of July 1977.

BETTMANN VIA GETTY IMAGES

WHITE HOUSE PHOTOGRAPHERS / NATIONAL ARCHIVES AND RECORDS ADMINISTRATION

President Jimmy Carter and Secretary of Housing and Urban Development Patricia Harris touring the South Bronx with Mayor Beame in October 1977.

ALLAN TANNENBAUM / GETTY IMAGES

Children playing amid the rubble of abandoned buildings in the South Bronx in March 1979.

"Time to cut the crap; the world has changed; we are going to do things differently."[33]

The members of the EFCB repeatedly said that their role was not to set the priorities of the city but merely to guarantee that it would execute a financial plan to achieve a balanced budget within three years, as had been established by Washington in the legislation extending loans to the city. They sometimes fretted over whether the board really had the power to give policy recommendations to the city at all. They presented themselves as neutral, apolitical, the arbiters of fiscal reality rather than ideology. Nonetheless, they had a clear idea of how they wanted the city to change. What they sought was not simply budget cuts but a shift in priorities, a move away from the city's long-standing commitment to social welfare spending.

The board wanted the city to concentrate its efforts on providing the traditional urban services—fire, police, sanitation, and primary and secondary schools—rather than health care, higher education, and cash grants to aid the poor. No longer trying to be an engine of redistribution, it should instead emphasize core city functions. Any additional resources that might be left over should be pushed into "development"—reviving New York's economy by cutting taxes, issuing industrial bonds, and otherwise attracting private investment. "The city should not only cope with financial emergency," Berger wrote in one report in the summer of 1976, but think about "redesigning its government, so as to provide better service that costs its taxpayers less."[34]

There was little sense on the board of the potential problems that might result from curtailing services or programs aimed at poor people. Jack Bigel was alone in insisting that "someday this board would be held responsible" for the social suffering brought about by austerity.[35] When riots broke out at Rikers Island in fall 1975, and when the *Times* reported that heroin use was rising as drug treatment programs were cut, Bigel argued that there needed to be not one but two plans—both a fiscal plan and a social one. As the city hit its fiscal milestones, he said, the EFCB should also take account of what the social cost might be.[36] The other members of the board had little to say in response.

As 1976 began, the board anxiously noted that New York City did not seem to be taking part in the mild economic recovery that was brightening prospects elsewhere in the nation. If the city's tax revenues did not improve, the whole laboriously constructed financial plan—the promised federal aid, the deferral of debt payments under the "pastrami agreement," the cuts to social services—might turn out to be insufficient to avoid disaster. As Margolis put it, "if the revenue base erodes too drastically, everything planned thus far will have to be torn up and we will have to begin over again."[37] Such anxieties only made more intense the imperative to restructure, retrench, and reshape the administration of New York.

Though the city government often chafed at the EFCB's relentless cost-cutting focus, there was a subject on which the Beame administration and the board were in complete agreement: some of the city's nineteen public hospitals had to go. This was one area, Comptroller Goldin said, where cuts were not only tolerable, but where in fact "superior service was consistent with retrenchment."[38]

The municipal hospital system had been the subject of political controversy going back to the 1950s. Critics both inside and out of the city government had long accused the hospitals of being under-utilized and inefficient, and argued that many of them should be turned into much smaller outpatient facilities if they were to continue to exist at all. There were, indeed, numerous problems. Many of the city hospitals struggled to deliver high-quality care. Despite their high city subsidies, they still suffered from a chronic lack of funds; studies suggested that only 70 percent of inpatient beds were in use at any given time.

But it was difficult even to discuss the problems in a candid way, since hospitals were major sources of employment in poor neighborhoods, and many hospital workers were terrified of losing their jobs.[39] What's more, regardless of their many flaws, the municipal hospitals served millions of people each year who lacked health insurance or were on Medicaid. The hospitals were a key line of defense against symptoms stemming from the ongoing health crises in the city's poor neighborhoods—asthma, lead poisoning, cancer, heart disease, venereal disease, tuberculosis, sickle cell anemia, violence, and mental health problems. A program of "reform" that centered primarily on closing hospitals would mean turning away from the city's real health needs.

During the 1950s and 1960s the city had sought to address the issue by developing a program of "affiliations" that linked public hospitals with the city's premier academic medical centers, such as Columbia and Cornell. The idea was that these schools would send their students to the municipal hospitals for clinical training. But these relationships were often fraught. Even though affiliation might bring new resources, the patients at the public hospitals—mostly poor people, often black and Latino—feared they were being used as guinea pigs, their health secondary to the educational needs of the medical schools. Public hospital doctors felt condescended to by the academics.[40]

In 1970, trying to respond to the perception that the public hospitals were overly politicized, Mayor Lindsay created the Health and Hospitals Corporation, a semi-independent agency with the power to determine its own budget and float its own bonds. Just as the Board of Education employed the city's teachers and CUNY was in charge of its professors, the HHC would be the official employer for the 40,000-plus workers at the city hospitals. It had its own director and board of trustees, and was supposed to be insulated from some of the pressures on the city government.

The creation of the HHC did very little, however, to ease the tensions in the city hospital system.[41] And now the fiscal crisis brought long-standing disagreements over the future of that system into the open. Fiscal necessity provided a new rationale for closing hospitals, as the system's critics had long desired. Delafield Hospital in Washington Heights, near the top of Manhattan, was the first to go, in the summer of 1975. It was hard to make the case that Delafield was a model facility: it had had just a 50 percent occupancy rate, and numerous violations of the city's health code. Still, it was the only municipal hospital in Manhattan above 137th Street, serving communities that were mostly low-income, African American, and Latino.[42] One *Village Voice* reporter spoke with a few of the patients waiting there. "I'm lost if they close this place down," said one eighty-one-year-old woman, partly blind, suffering from diabetes. "The doctors treat me like a human being, not a poor person." The respiratory clinic at Delafield handled more than 260,000 visits per year; a woman with chronic asthma who was a regular patient said she wanted to keep working with her doctor there, not change to some new person in a less equipped clinic. "The Mayor doesn't care if I suffer or die."[43]

Other city hospitals came to take away Delafield's dental chairs, microscopes, and beds. The executive director of the hospital said, "How the political powers of the city can sleep at night is beyond me."[44]

More hospital closures followed in short order. Fordham Hospital and Morrisania Hospital, both in the Bronx, were shuttered in 1976. Part of Sea View Hospital on Staten Island was also shut down, as was a neighborhood family health clinic in the Bronx.[45] Gouverneur on the Lower East Side continued to provide some outpatient care but ceased to function as a hospital, its emergency and inpatient services eliminated.[46] Even the staunchest critics of the public hospitals felt their disappearance as a loss. A community activist in the Bronx who once called Fordham Hospital services "totally inadequate" now said, "If we lose the Fordham we'll lose all chances of getting a new Fordham. Once you close an institution, it's all over."[47]

The conflict between the EFCB and the city hospitals was crystallized in a nasty fight over the president of the Health and Hospitals Corporation—John "Mike" Holloman, a black physician and civil rights activist who was strongly opposed to closing the city hospitals and to the cuts to health services more generally. Holloman had the slogan "Health Care Is a Right" embossed on the back of his nameplate on his desk at the HHC, and quotations from Dr. Martin Luther King Jr. hung on his office walls.[48] He demanded that the city press forward with opening the North Bronx Central Hospital, a new facility largely completed before the fiscal crisis began but whose future was now thrown into doubt. He spoke out publicly, denouncing the EFCB and the cuts more broadly: "We are seeing now the devastating effects upon human services as social policy is being made under the guise of fiscal constraints by men who are not answerable to an electorate," Holloman said in one speech to the Brooklyn TB and Lung Association.[49]

The EFCB and the Beame administration became increasingly hostile toward Holloman. The management of the HHC, they agreed, was so "inept" and "incompetent" (as Rohatyn and Ed Koch, respectively, put it) that fiscal reorganization would require a change in leadership. Even though the board could not technically tell HHC "who should run it and how it should be run," its members agreed that when HHC presented a new financial plan to the EFCB, it should also include a plan for restructuring its management so that the agency would be run by people more mindful of the city's fiscal imperatives.[50] In response, Holloman and his supporters accused the board, the city, and Congressman Koch of racism.[51] This only made the city's reaction all the more hostile. Lowell Bellin, the city's commissioner of public health, an advocate of shutting hospitals and consolidating services, wrote in one memo: "The problem is not ideology. The problem is not racism. The problem is not insensitivity to the poor by the city's Health Commissioner. The problem, rather, has been and continues to be the managerial incompetence of the current Health and Hospitals Corporation staff."[52]

As 1976 wore on, the EFCB and the Beame administration pressed Holloman to resign. He refused, insisting that he would never agree to step down. In the end he was fired by the HHC Board of Trustees by a vote of nine to seven at an emotional meeting in January 1977. Holloman left the meeting with tears running down his face. Shortly after the vote, the only black member of the HHC board to vote in favor of Holloman's dismissal was surrounded by angry activists calling him an "Uncle Tom"; one of them punched him in the face.[53] In place of Holloman, Beame proposed (and the HHC board approved) the creation of an eight-person committee to run the hospital system and to oversee its restructuring, to be headed by Donald Kummerfeld, a former banker who was serving as the city's new budget director and deputy mayor.[54]

Because closing hospitals was such a dramatic and visible withdrawal of resources, these struggles received intense press attention, but the crisis was also felt in other parts of the city's public health network. Anything dedicated to serving the most socially vulnerable was especially likely to be cut. Prisoners in the city's jails lost health services, as the budget for prison health fell by 25 percent; this meant seven fewer doctors and fifty-two fewer nurses, while psychiatric services were pared down so drastically they almost ceased to exist at two of the city's largest correctional institutions.[55] The city also closed three nursing schools at the city's public hospitals, one of which, the School of Nursing at Kings County Hospital, had been open since 1897.[56]

For many years, New York had operated one of the most innovative public health departments in the country. It had pioneered many strategies for bringing primary and preventive health to poor and working-class New Yorkers: routine examinations and dental care in public schools, a nutrition education service, and labs to screen for venereal disease. These efforts, too, were all greatly diminished as a result of the crisis. Between 1974 and 1977, the workforce of the Department of Health shrank from 4,400 full-time and 1,600 part-time employees to 3,300 full-time and 1,000 part-time workers. Its staff of nutritionists fell from 23 to 5.[57] The city had run twenty District Health Centers, which provided primary care free of charge; by 1977, seven had closed. The Health Research Council, which collected data and conducted research on urban public health, was eliminated.

Children were especially affected by the cutbacks. The city had operated seventy-six Child Health Stations, which provided infant and newborn care, evaluations, assessments, and checkups for children; twenty closed during the fiscal crisis. The number of dental clinics (both in health centers and in schools) dropped by a third during the mid-1970s. Eye clinics, which provided vision screening for children, lost half their funding, and fourteen of twenty-one closed.[58]

The list of closures went on and on. Five of ten general immunization clinics closed; two of five lead-poisoning screening clinics were shut down, as were two of the six sickle-cell anemia testing clinics. The city had operated twenty-seven chest clinics that performed X-rays and examinations for pulmonary diseases, especially tuberculosis; ten were closed between 1974 and 1978, even as the number of new TB cases was beginning to climb.[59] Justifying threatened cuts to family planning, well-baby, and podiatry clinics, a city spokesman said that services like birth control were "not life-saving" and therefore could not be prioritized.[60] But the city's suicide hotline, too, was cut back; sometimes people would have to call multiple times before anyone picked up the phone.[61]

Drug treatment programs were also significantly curtailed by the cuts. In 1967, seeking to respond to rising heroin use in New York, the Lindsay administration had established the Addiction Services Agency to coordinate drug treatment. The programs it ran included both methadone treatment centers and "drug-free" treatment programs that did not use methadone. But at the end of 1976, the ASA was eliminated as a separate agency, its drug-free treatment programs dismantled, and the Department of Health took over the methadone clinics that remained.[62] The city discontinued its 24-hour drug abuse hotline.[63] All this took place only a few years after New York State had passed the Rockefeller drug laws, which instituted stringent new penalties for drug possession and dealing. It also coincided with a marked increase in heroin availability in the city: reports estimated that about five tons of heroin would be smuggled into the city in 1975. Compounding the problem, the narcotics division of the police department had also undergone budget cuts, and its ranks shrank from 450 to 312 officers from 1974 to 1975. Most of those laid off were black and Latino undercover agents who worked in the markets where heroin use was growing.[64] The reduction in treatment programs coupled with the harsh Rockefeller drug laws added up to a new way of dealing with drug addiction: through the criminal justice system and punitive policing, rather than rehabilitation or therapies that might bring addicts back into mainstream society.[65]

The ASA, like the day care system, had been plagued by reports of fraud. Still, the city government received a great deal of mail expressing anger over the cuts. The president of a PTA on Staten Island, for example, wrote that the drug treatment agencies filled an "absolutely vital need for our youngsters."[66] In the spring of 1976, hundreds of recovering drug addicts—most from residential drug-free (non-methadone) programs that were slated for closure—staged a nine-day sleep-out in front of Gracie Mansion. For some, the closures meant they would have to return to prison; others would most likely be forced to live out on the streets. "This is Forgotten City and these are forgotten children," read posters at the vigil.[67]

For the city's poorest, the meaning of the cuts was plain. The city wanted them to disappear.

Instead of running public services through the city government, the new idea was that they should be taken up by volunteer New Yorkers. "The city should be asking its citizens to assume more responsibility for their own well-being, because tax revenues are no longer available to sustain the levels and breadth of service that have heretofore been provided," Berger, the EFCB's executive director, proclaimed.[68]

The leading organization encouraging volunteering in the city to replace services that had been cut back was the Citizens Committee for New York City, the group that Senators Javits and Buckley had started in the fall of 1975. The committee's primary goal in 1976 was to work with the Beame administration to recruit 10,000 volunteers who would work for free (on a "temporary" basis, the mayor assured everyone) to provide services the city could no longer afford. In February 1976, Beame rolled out a program intended to do just that, calling on all agency heads to give serious consideration to how they might use free labor. Libraries in danger of closing or operating on reduced hours could use volunteers; the Health Department might turn to "thousands" of volunteers to do everything from lab work to clinical services; auxiliary police and citizen patrols could make up for cuts in the police force if their numbers were doubled. To cope with the sanitation cutbacks, local self-help groups were to be encouraged to sweep the sidewalks. Local business groups were joining forces to purchase their own private mechanized street-sweepers.[69]

The liberal former editor of *Newsweek*, Osborn Elliott, became the head of the Citizens Committee. When he came down to City Hall to join Beame in introducing the program, he handed Beame a button that read "I'm a New Yorker Fighting the Crisis—Ask Me How." Beame joked: "Any time anybody wants me to sweep the sidewalks, let me know, will you?"[70]

The committee did in fact recruit many volunteers for the city—about 1,500 people were placed in the first few months of its operations.[71] The auxiliary police reported an increase in phone inquiries, as did the school volunteers association.[72] Yet it was not always clear that the city had the resources even to organize these new volunteers. In the schools, for example, the staff of the program that organized volunteers was cut from eight to two, making it difficult to coordinate the very people the city was encouraging to donate their services.[73]

The Citizen Committee's self-help gospel went beyond urging people to make up for laid-off public sector workers. The organization also fostered the creation of block associations, in the hope they would take responsibility for street-sweeping, general cleanliness, and tree maintenance. The committee planned to distribute 2,500 street brooms to volunteers, and it placed a full-page ad in the *New York Times*, picturing a group of New Yorkers grinning widely and bearing brooms under the headline "A Call to Arms."[74] The Citizen Committee also encouraged the creation of Merchants' Associations, which they hoped would undertake collective security projects, improve physical infrastructure, and generally involve business owners more deeply in their neighborhoods.[75] In 1977, the committee published a massive "self-help" handbook, cataloging dozens of public-spirited projects that people could undertake without waiting for action from the city or the federal government—everything from forming bike patrols to replace police service to removing graffiti to handing out brooms and litter baskets to the neighborhood street sweeps.[76]

Local activists appreciated the efforts of the Citizens Committee, and especially the small grants it dispensed. "May God in his infinite Wisdom continue to bless and keep you, that you may continue to find ways and means to get recognition for the *little* person," one member of a tenants' association wrote to the group.[77] As significant as the grants was the public relations message. "The Citizens' Committee overall program to encourage community self-help and more volunteers also has as its objective the improvement of New York City's negative image in other parts of the country," read one internal document. Over the course of late 1975 and 1976, Elliott met with more than a hundred newspaper and magazine editors from publications around the country. The local boosters made the case that self-help was replacing angry protest as a way to respond to the crisis. "I believe New Yorkers have developed more of a sense of small-town community spirit," Elizabeth Barlow—one of the earliest advocates for raising private funds to help repair Central Park—told *U.S. News and World Report*.[78] The organization paid for billboards in Grand Central and elsewhere proclaiming "NEW YORK, NEW YORK, YOU'RE STILL A HELLUVA TOWN!"[79]

From an early point, many of the people who joined the Citizens Committee argued that the city needed to imagine a completely different approach to urban government—one that relied on "citizen participation" and self-help to "sustain, as well as to supplement, services seriously crippled by layoffs and attrition," as the *New York Times* put it.[80] But even as it called for a new public spirit, the Citizens Committee was reimagining the very nature of the public sphere. The public sector was tired and broken; the private economy was the only viable source of initiative and strength.

At the end of 1976, Elliott left the magazine world altogether to take a post in the Beame administration. His new job: New York's first Deputy Director of Economic Development, charged with attracting new businesses to the city. He would be paid only $1 a year—becoming a model of altruism and self-help for a city in despair.

Sadly, all the volunteer efforts did little to counteract the impact of the cuts. Haphazard, steep, and enacted over a short period that magnified their impact, they not only affected the poor but also shrank the resources that had long defined middle-class life in New York. Cuts to fire and police protection, at the very moment when crime was rising and the number of fires surging, made the city feel palpably less safe. The sanitation cuts made it dirtier. But among the most contentious were those that affected education and culture—raising the question of who could have access to knowledge and under what conditions.

Almost every aspect of the public school system was touched by the cutbacks. The number of people employed by the Board of Education fell by almost 20 percent between 1975 and 1978. There were thousands fewer teachers by the end of 1976 than there had been a year earlier, not to mention fewer guidance counselors, assistant principals, and other support staff.[81] The result was larger classes at all grade levels, fewer classes in art and music, and a shorter school day. The funding for extra-curricular high school activities such as orchestra, band, newspapers, and magazines was cut in half, and funding for athletic programs was likewise cut, leading to less support for some sports and the complete elimination of others (including handball, golf, fencing, and dance teams).[82]

Basic aspects of school safety were neglected. Crossing guards, whose salaries came from the police budget, were eliminated throughout the city.[83] Building repairs and maintenance stopped almost completely. One city councilman in Brooklyn visited an elementary school in his district to find bricks and plaster falling from the walls, an infestation of roaches, and windows that refused to close, leaving rooms so drafty that they were too cold for students.[84] The schools cut back on custodial services by about 40 percent, so that classrooms, offices, cafeterias, and outside spaces were cleaned every other day instead of daily, while window washing was done only once a year. Schools could not purchase sufficient toilet paper and paper towels, conditions "bordering on a health hazard," as one administrator complained.[85] Cuts in security left many schools less safe, and reports of robbery, extortion, larceny, and drug use in the schools rose sharply.[86]

Prior to the fiscal crisis the city had operated a set of additional programs—such as high school classes in the evenings, trade schools, continuing education for adults, and summer school—that reached out to nontraditional students. But in the wake of the crisis all of these programs were scaled back to the bare minimum. Summer school ceased to exist except for high school seniors who would be unable to graduate without the additional classes. Continuing education for adults was sharply curtailed.[87] The city had run five high schools for pregnant girls; all of these were threatened with closure.[88] The budget for evening high schools was cut by 89 percent, and the number of students in those programs fell from 30,000 to 10,000, as the city's sixteen evening schools were reduced to one full-time and two part-time schools.[89]

Schools throughout the system were affected, in both middle-class and poor communities. The prestigious Midwood High School in Brooklyn saw class sizes rise as its teaching staff contracted from 130 to 100. Advanced courses were eliminated, as were a range of electives in subjects such as constitutional law, bacteriology, ecology, and world classics. Yet the situation was even more difficult at the Louis D. Brandeis High School in Manhattan—a school on the Upper West Side with 6,000 students, the majority nonwhite—which lost 56 of its 272 teachers. I.S. 70, a middle school on West 17th Street, lost all its guidance counselors, eight teachers, two "deans of discipline," and a number of school aides, assistant principals, and school secretaries—despite an enrollment of 1,550 students, the largest in the school's history.[90] The loss of security guards was especially worrisome to parents. At one school, P.S. 33 in Chelsea, several hundred children spent recess in a park without a fence and only two school aides.[91] Therapeutic services, such as speech therapy and school dental clinics, were cut back.[92] One principal at P.S. 11 in Chelsea said to the local paper, "It is one thing to tighten belts; it is another thing to cripple, and that is what they are doing to the schools."[93]

The school cuts angered parents and families all over the city. Sometimes this led to protest. In the West Village, for example, cutbacks had led to a loss of 280 teachers, with the cuts falling especially heavily on young instructors: virtually every teacher hired after 1970 was laid off.[94] Class sizes hovered between thirty-six and forty students per teacher, well above the contractually mandated maximum of thirty-two; in some schools, they went as high as forty-two students per teacher.[95] "We have no enrichment programs, one counselor for every 3,000 students and barely enough teachers for the already overcrowded classes," the district superintendent told the neighborhood paper.[96] In the fall of 1976, the Community School Board representing the Village voted for a boycott of the schools to protest the cuts. The board was promptly suspended by the Board of Education, and the boycott proved difficult to pull off, as many parents complained that it only created the new difficulty of organizing alternative care for children. Only at one school in the district, P.S. 3, was the shutdown successful, with a mere handful of the school's 440 students showing up on the day the action was called. Whether a coincidence or not, a few weeks later the Board of Education threatened to shut down P.S. 3 altogether.[97]

There was also a wave of protests in Harlem, where parents demonstrated against the loss of teachers, the shortening of the school day, and the plans to close schools. Some parents slept in schools that were threatened with closure, in a symbolic gesture to keep them open. Others organized boycotts, keeping the children home to protest the cuts that seemed to endanger their ability to gain a meaningful education at all.[98]

The deterioration of the public schools imperiled a beloved resource that made it possible to raise children in the city rather than moving to the suburbs—one of the main points of connection between middle-class New Yorkers and the city government. One editorial in the local Greenwich Village newspaper bemoaned the cuts to the neighborhood schools: "No kindergarten at the beginning—no college at the end. . . . Is this kind of public education worth staying in New York for?"[99] An op-ed in the *New York Times* complained about the elimination of music, art, and poetry programs at the elementary school as well as swelling class sizes: "New York is forcing middle-class children out of its schools and providing precious little education to those that remain."[100]

Echoing the conflict over the schools was the battle over the city's public libraries. The library system had always been a hybrid public-private effort: while the branch libraries were supported almost exclusively by the city and the state, the research libraries (including the famous library at 42nd Street) relied on a mix of public funds and private donations. Both the branches and the research division had faced serious problems in the early 1970s. In 1972 and 1973, the city had threatened to close several branch libraries, including the Jefferson Market Library in Greenwich Village, citing budget shortages. Branch library hours were cut by 55 percent between 1971 and 1975.[101] At the same time, the research libraries were undergoing their own budget crisis, which reflected the declining value of their endowments. In 1971, the executive director of the research libraries, John Cory, wrote that the New York Public Library was confronting a budget shortfall so serious that it would have to contemplate steps that could lead to its eventual "limitation or elimination"—soon it would become a "moribund and inaccessible archive useful only if transferred to some other institution."[102] In a 1971 article about the cuts at the 42nd Street building, architecture critic Ada Louise Huxtable, an avid user of the library, noted the slowdown in collecting new books, the decline of maintenance, and the shortened hours. "What is being quietly cut back," she wrote, "is not the conspicuous consumption of an affluent society, but its civilized and liberating foundations."[103]

The fiscal crisis gave new weight to such warnings. The leadership of the library had long seen it as "truly everyman's university," open to anyone engaged in inquiry regardless of university affiliation.[104] As one library handbook described the democratic sweep of the institution, "The New York Public Library, being truly public, serves everyone, from the toddler at his Picture Book Hour to the scholar at his tome, and as soon as a person can write his name he is eligible for a borrower's card and may begin to bring books home."[105] The fiscal stress made this seem an impossible dream. In 1976, Cory's successor, James W. Henderson, penned a pessimistic projection for the future, titled "Whither the Research Libraries?" He opened with a short description of the aim of the library: "to collect and preserve as much as possible of the record of man's endeavor and to make it readily accessible." But was this still possible? Henderson laid out several courses of action the 42nd Street library could take—including entirely ceasing to collect in subject areas such as the social sciences, science, technology, and the performing arts, thus becoming a history and humanities library only. Other proposals included merging research libraries with branch libraries to consolidate operations.[106]

These drastic reorganization plans did not come about, but the more quotidian cuts continued. The research libraries reduced their hours of operation and the scope and pace of their collecting. The manuscripts and archives division annex saw its staff cut back to one person, which made it almost impossible to function. Researchers in need of collections located in the annex were, in most cases, out of luck.[107]

The branch libraries, meanwhile, were threatened with outright closure. Eight of them—three in Manhattan, three in the Bronx, and two on Staten Island—were slated to be shut down in January 1976, eliminating fifty-two jobs. Eight more branches were to close over the summer, including such venerable institutions as the Hudson Park branch in the West Village and the Muhlenberg Branch in Chelsea. Yet other branch libraries were placed on barebones three-days-a-week schedules, making it difficult for people to use them at all.[108]

Fierce neighborhood protests met these cutbacks. At the Tremont branch in the Bronx and the Columbia branch in Morningside Heights, neighborhood residents occupied the libraries to keep them from being shuttered. In Morningside Heights the sit-in began as soon as the library officially closed on January 16 and continued for forty days. Protesters slept in the library and organized media events to call attention to the library closings. They met with representatives from the Tremont branch to organize a city-wide effort to keep the libraries open.[109] Under pressure, Beame announced in February that he would postpone the library closings for the time being.[110] Despite the temporary relief, morale at the libraries was predictably low; as one staffer put it, "We are like a dying fish washed up on the beach."[111]

The pattern of events at the library branches—where cuts were threatened, then postponed or reversed in response to protests—unfolded for some other city services too. In 1977, for example, some money was restored to the schools, leading to the rehiring of several thousand teachers and the restoration of the full school day. But even when cuts were rescinded, they had deeply affected the political culture of the city. There was a profound sense that New York was no longer truly committed to the services it had once been proud to provide.[112] As a neighborhood newspaper put it, in 1975 "the budget knife cut right through the heart of city life. Garbage piled up; libraries shortened hours; wallets emptied faster in the subway token line and tiny tots and senior citizens were left wondering whether or not they'd have a center to go to next week."[113]

In those neighborhoods and areas where the fight with the city became most desperate, the experience of loss was transmuted into something else: an insistence that there was no alternative for people but to resist. Such was the case in the fight to keep open the city's firehouses—especially those in poor neighborhoods such as Greenpoint-Williamsburg.

14. The People's Firehouse

Before the autumn of 1975, Adam Veneski never saw himself as a political activist. It's not that he was apathetic; he had once even tried to organize a union at the soda bottling factory where he worked. But he wasn't political or ideological as much as profoundly sociable. He was the kind of person who always had people around him, a big man with giant arms and a smile that split his wide face. As one friend remembered years later, when Veneski spoke, "you paid attention to every word he said."[1]

Veneski had grown up in Northside, the northernmost part of the Brooklyn neighborhood of Greenpoint-Williamsburg. In the half-residential, half-industrial community, it was possible to walk almost to the edge of the East River and see Manhattan across the water, the buildings rising above the cars that sped up and down Franklin Delano Roosevelt Drive. Northside was a tight-knit ethnic enclave; most of the people who lived there were of Polish descent, in contrast to the east part of the neighborhood, which was mostly Italian, or the south, which was primarily Puerto Rican and Hasidic. Despite the myriad ways in which Northside life was shaped by the decisions made in City Hall, it was a world unto itself, a neighborhood of narrow streets and low apartment buildings and single-family homes painted in pastel shades. Many of the homes had been in the same family for generations; as the neighbor-hood's state senator would later testify, it was not at all uncommon for a person to be "born, christened, married and administered the Last Rites all in the same house."[2] Northside had a way of folding a person in, and Veneski's roots were deep there. He was the oldest of four brothers, born and raised in the community, and he never wanted to leave. When he met and married his wife, Brigitte, they found a small apartment in Northside to raise their four children. Both Veneskis always worked: she in a meat market, he bottling sodas. He had little formal education, but he possessed a sharp, intuitive intelligence about people and a capacity to draw them to him.

Were it not for the city's plan to shut down Engine Company 212—the fire station that served the Northside—Veneski might never have become interested in politics at all.

For many New Yorkers, the city's willingness to cut back on fire protec-tion was the most shocking aspect of the fiscal crisis. Nineteen seventy-seven was a particularly brutal year for fires in the city, with several very large and lethal blazes that brought the total number of fire deaths to 330 (up from 232 the year before).[3] Fire had become a social emer-gency, especially acute in the city's poorest neighborhoods. But instead of devoting additional resources to the fire crisis, the city was cutting back on the fire department: between 1974 and 1977, the city would lose more than 1,500 firefighters.[4]

Fire service in the city had been the subject of fierce contention even before the fiscal crisis. Looking to find ways to quantify city services and to weaken public sector unions, the Lindsay administration had con-tracted with the RAND Corporation in the late 1960s to study the fire department and come up with a technical metric that it could use to make decisions about which fire stations to maintain and which to close. The goal was to ration this expensive service on the basis of facts and numbers rather than sentiment and emotion. Based on an analysis of the amount of time it took a fire company to get to a fire, and on a division of the city into different "hazard categories" determined by the likelihood of fires, the RAND researchers proposed closing or relocating 35 fire companies between 1972 and 1976.[5] Over the course of the 1970s, 32 of the city's 114 fire companies were indeed disbanded.[6]

The RAND analysis also advocated replacing the old alarm boxes with telephone-style alarms, so the person calling in could actually speak to the dispatcher. The idea seemed like common sense, but in practice it led to a dramatic rise in the number of false alarms. To deal with that problem, RAND then ruled that if a dispatcher could not make out what the person on the other end of the phone was saying, only a single truck should be sent to the scene. Eventually the policy became even more draconian, so that some "no voice" alarms received no fire company response at all.[7]

Whatever efficiencies the RAND studies might have accomplished were soon overwhelmed. Between the mid-1960s and the late 1970s, the number of serious fires in the city rose from 160 to 500 per year.[8]

The South Bronx was the most infamous of the fire-plagued neighborhoods, but the nightmare of fire and the destruction it could wreak was also evident in the Brooklyn neighborhood of Bushwick, directly south of Veneski's Greenpoint-Williamsburg. Over the late 1960s and early 1970s, the Italian and German working-class neighborhood of Bushwick had been rapidly transformed into an extremely poor black and Latino one. "Blockbusting" real estate speculators exploited racial fears, encouraging white homeowners to sell their houses cheap because black people were moving into the neighborhood—leaving flyers with slogans such as "Don't wait until it's too late!" in mailboxes—and then reselling the houses to black and Latino homebuyers at inflated prices.[9] Bushwick's population declined from 200,000 to 134,000 in only a few years as the original white population left the area, moving farther out into Brooklyn or to the suburbs on Long Island.

Soon, fires began to burn throughout the neighborhood, some set intentionally by landlords who wanted to collect insurance payouts, others accidental blazes that simply grew out of control before the fire trucks could arrive. By 1975, entire blocks were filled with rubble, empty shells of buildings without windows or doors. Newspapers carried stories of tragedy and horror: an eight-year-old incinerated in a fast-moving conflagration; a fire in a deserted knitting mill that burned down a church and twenty-two houses; teenagers who set fires for "fun and profit." "It looks like there has been a war here, a very bad war," said the neighborhood's City Council representative to the *Daily News* in 1977. One firefighter described Bushwick as consumed by a "holocaust."[10]

Because the consequences of fire for a neighborhood were so severe, almost every one of the RAND-driven proposals to close or relocate a fire company met with intense resistance and protest, both from neighborhoods and from firefighters themselves. "Don't let Mayor Lindsay, Fire Commissioner Lowery, Chief O'Hagan, Budget Director Grossman and the RAND Corporation rob you of the fire protection you need and pay for!" read an ad taken out by the firefighters' union in 1972, urging New Yorkers to join a mass rally at City Hall against the cuts.[11] "This neighborhood is a bomb," said one SoHo firefighter whose station was slated for shutdown in 1974, describing the flimsy lofts and inadequate construction that left buildings vulnerable to fire.[12] As closures were announced in the summer of 1975, there were protests at nearly every one of the threatened stations. But no communities saw as lengthy a struggle as Northside in Greenpoint-Williamsburg, where local residents would wind up occupying their fire station for a remarkable stretch of sixteen months.

Even before the fiscal crisis, Greenpoint-Williamsburg had spent years preparing for a showdown with City Hall.[13] The residents had long felt that city government saw their presence along the waterfront as a hindrance—they were occupying land that could be put to more valuable commercial and industrial use. (In this context, Roger Starr's rhetoric of "planned shrinkage" was particularly troubling to the locals.) The history of tension went all the way back to the construction of the Brooklyn-Queens Expressway in the 1950s. Despite substantial community resistance, two thousand housing units and two churches had been torn down to make way for the highway. And in a tragic accident in 1956—a memory that lingered long after as an example of City Hall's neglect—six young children playing at a construction site for the highway were killed when a wall caved in on them, crushing them under twenty-five tons of gravel and sand.[14]

The conflicts between the city government and the Greenpoint-Williamsburg neighborhood intensified in 1969. As part of its efforts to retain industry in the outer boroughs, the Lindsay administration had claimed the right of eminent domain to demolish ninety-seven homes in order to provide additional space to a neighborhood manufacturer, S&S Corrugated Paper Machinery, which was threatening to move to New Jersey. People fought for four years to stop the takeover of the land, in the process forming a new community organization, the Northside Community Development Council (NCDC), which received federal funding during the War on Poverty. With the support of faculty at Pratt Institute, they managed to work out a plan to relocate many of the families to new city-built brick apartment buildings in the neighborhood. Still, holdouts remained, and in September 1973 bulldozers came in to raze their homes. Police and city marshals dragged out the last families, carrying them down the street and throwing their furniture after them.[15]

The houses that these families sought to protect—which were typical for the neighborhood—might not have appeared to others to be worth very much. Their structural weaknesses made them, among other things, susceptible to fire: they shared common walls, they had no fire stops between the floors, and their frames were wood instead of sturdy stone.[16] As one firefighter said of similar buildings in neighboring Bushwick, they could "go up like tinderboxes."[17] For residents of Greenpoint-Williamsburg, the firehouse on Wythe Avenue—Engine Company 212—was all that stood between their family homes and the kind of conflagrations that were consuming other parts of the city. They saw the fire station as a symbol of the city's commitment to protect the wood-frame houses and the families who lived in them, a counterweight to the anxiety about the government's desire to claim the land for more profitable uses.

In a declining city, the simple fact of the existence of Engine Company

212 was a tacit promise that Greenpoint-Williamsburg would not be allowed to fall too far. So when the city first moved to close the station, in the summer of 1975, it seemed a sign that the neighborhood was being cut loose, consigned to despair. "If you cut sanitation, the streets stink," read an article in the local newspaper. "If you cut education, children don't learn to read. But if you cut fire protection, *people burn*."[18]

Adam Veneski was among those who were waiting for the ax to fall on Engine Company 212. Early in the year he'd been injured in an accident at the bottling company when a conveyor belt started moving at the wrong time. (Though they had no evidence, his family always wondered whether the accident had anything to do with Veneski's participation in a union drive at the plant.) He was collecting workers' compensation, waiting to see what would happen to the neighborhood.

Rumors that Engine Company 212 was on the chopping block had circulated through the neighborhood over the summer. At the first warning, a group of Boy Scouts who were friendly with the firefighters took up a petition to save it.[19] The Northside Community Development Council—which included both volunteers from the neighborhood and full-time staffers, many of whom were veterans of the housing and civil rights movements—helped organize protests at the firehouse, reaching out to the press, the firefighters, and the community. In the middle of the summer, and then again in the early fall, the Beame administration said the firehouse might be slated for closure. Both times, the mayor's office rescinded the order before it went through.

But over Thanksgiving weekend came the news that Engine Company 212 would finally be shut. Only a few days after Ford declared his support for federal loans, Fire Commissioner John O'Hagan announced that eight fire companies would be disbanded—two in Brooklyn, two in Manhattan, two in Queens, and one apiece in the Bronx (City Island) and Staten Island. Five of the firehouses would be closed altogether. He admitted that "the cuts will result in an increase in loss of life and property," but insisted that there was no choice. Under the new terms set by the Emergency Financial Control Board and the federal government, the Fire Department had to cut its budget by $8.3 million. To make that happen, Engine Company 212 had to go.[20]

On the Friday after Thanksgiving, Adam and Brigitte Veneski were in their apartment when they heard sirens blaring in the cold autumn night. The alarms were set off by the firefighters at Engine 212, who had talked to the Northside Community Development Council and neighborhood residents ahead of time, and agreed that they would alert people to come to the station if it was threatened—Northside was in danger. The Veneskis rushed to the firehouse. One of the firefighters told them that the city was coming to steal the fire truck from their neighborhood, right in the middle of the holiday weekend. The truck would be removed on Saturday morning at 9 a.m. and the station shuttered.

Veneski went back to his apartment. As his family remembers, he got a battery-operated bullhorn and went through the streets of Northside, calling on his neighbors to defend Engine 212. It was like Paul Revere, one firefighter said, warning that the enemy was on its way.[21]

About two hundred people showed up at the fire station on Wythe Avenue, and a raucous protest took shape, with demonstrators staying outside all night, drinking vodka, singing, dancing, and chanting. There were kids and elderly women, mothers and students, people not only from Northside but from Greenpoint and South Williamsburg as well. They streamed into the fire station, taking it over; the firefighters willingly remained in the back, the crowd's nominal hostages. Bob Roher, a young New Yorker who had trained as an organizer and came to work for the NCDC, remembers talking to Veneski. The two of them made a plan: when the police arrived in the morning, the people stationed at the firehouse would ask the churches to ring their bells. Residents would then occupy the station and surround it as well, to show that it belonged to the community and not to the city. The fire truck would stay inside.

Early in the morning a contingent of police and firefighters arrived to reclaim the station and remove the truck. As Roher recalls it, he asked Veneski what he wanted to do. Both knew that if they left the truck would be taken, but staying meant a serious risk of arrest. Veneski said that he wanted to stay. The church bells started to ring. More curious people came down to the station. They formed a human chain, facing down the police, daring them to come in to remove the demonstrators. After a brief standoff, the local congressional representative, Fred Richmond, took up negotiations with the police. The fire department agreed for the moment to let the engine stay where it was, though the firehouse was no longer in service.[22]

Three days later, a fire blazed through two buildings on Dobbin Street, right around the corner from the station. The residents escaped without serious injury, but their homes were destroyed. "If this isn't proof that we need 212 back, I don't know what is," said one woman whose home was lost in the fire. "Let Mayor Beame come and see what he's done. This city don't care about poor people at all."[23]

The fire strengthened the resolve of the protesters occupying the firehouse. Knowing the city would remove the fire engine if everyone left, Adam Veneski began to sleep in the station. The Veneski children slept at home during the week, but Brigitte cooked the family meals at the firehouse, and they ate their meals and did their homework there. On the weekends the kids would lay down mattresses in the fire truck and sleep on top of the hoses. Other people in the neighborhood joined in. Veneski believed that their presence acted as a moral reminder that the firehouse belonged to the community—it was not merely a line on the budget that could be struck out at will. They placed a sofa in front of the fire truck, turning domestic comfort into a barricade. "We'll block the fire house as long as we humanly can," one woman who had lived in the neighborhood for sixty-five years told the New York Times.[24]

Many such struggles dwindle away after a few months, and this might have happened in Northside as well. But people from all around the city, including a number of young activists who had been radicalized in the civil rights and antiwar mobilizations of the 1960s, were drawn to the moral vision of the neighborhood activists, to the immediacy and intensity of the fight. At a time when many on the left saw the white working class as hopelessly conservative and retrograde, the fight over the firehouse seemed to be an example of a different political tendency: a white ethnic working class that looked outward to challenge the distribution of power within the city, rather than blaming nonwhite people for their embattled position.[25]

Sometimes the firehouse activists turned to the techniques of street theater to make their case. In one skit, the script called for a chorus to perform behind cardboard flames, singing to the tune of the Beatles anthem "Help!":

Help us if you can, we're burning down
And we really need 212 to hang around
Don't let Northside burn to the ground
Won't you please, please, please help us?[26]

In a different scene, the activists imagined Mayor Beame calculating with Big MAC: "Just look how much money is being wasted on services for the public! We can cut some here, a little there, some more out of this . . ." The skit was framed with another bit of protest verse, this one based on the old rhyme about ax-murderer Lizzie Borden:

Mayor Beame had an axe
Gave the city 40 whacks
When Big MAC saw what he had done
They told him make it 41.[27]

The firehouse activists drew on many strategies to keep the struggle going. Auxiliary firefighters ran training for local women on how to fight fires, set up hoses, and use chemical fire extinguishers.[28] They held polka parties at the firehouse, screened movies such as the labor classic *Salt of the Earth*, and ran Tuesday-night "action meetings" to strategize about what the next steps might be.[29] They collected their own statistics to challenge the official rationale for closing the firehouse, carefully charting how long it took to respond to fires and how much more quickly the firehouse activists could get to the scene than the fire company from the next neighborhood over. The walls of the fire station were covered with charts and graphs about fire response time, in contrast to the opaque evidence the city provided about how it determined what to cut and where.[30] In the spring of 1976, Beame announced that he would consider reopening Engine Company 212 if the activists could clearly demonstrate that its closure threatened public safety. Rising to the challenge, the NCDC organized fact-finding panels at the firehouse, where volunteer researchers presented their findings about increased delays in fire response times.[31]

The clearest demonstration of the danger posed by decreased fire service came soon enough. In April 1976, a fire broke out across the street from the Veneski home, leaving nineteen families homeless. People gathered at the firehouse that evening for the regular Tuesday-night action meeting, shaken and emotional. Engine Company 212 was becoming a center for those displaced by fires; twelve people, including a pair of fourteen-month-old twins, had come to sleep at the station earlier in the month after their building burned. The mood was angry, especially since the latest fire could easily have been contained had the old fire truck been active—it was so close to the station.[32]

Early the next morning, Veneski led about seventy Northsiders onto the Brooklyn-Queens Expressway during the morning rush hour. They went up the ramp with six cars in front and two behind. At the top, they blocked traffic and unfurled a protest banner. For about forty-five minutes they stopped traffic, causing a jam that extended all the way back to Long Island. Eventually the police arrived and walked the protesters off the expressway, declining to make any arrests.[33]

The demonstration on the BQE highlighted one of the unusual aspects of the firehouse protest: the close alliance between the demonstrators, the firefighters (and their union), and the police. According to one story, a fire department official who had been present on the first day of the sit-in refused to carry out the plan to remove the people who had flocked to the station. After all, Engine Company 212 belonged to the neighborhood, he said. It was the "people's firehouse."[34]

As Veneski camped out in the firehouse month after month, his mood swung from ebullient to grim. He was worried that he didn't have enough support: Why weren't even more people out in the street or at the station? Some in the neighborhood were actively hostile, complaining that Communists and other radicals were manipulating residents for their own purposes.[35] The NCDC split as conservatives in the organization grew alienated from the left-leaning students.[36] Veneski believed that he and his family were being harassed for their political participation. "I gave up three months of my life—will you listen for five minutes?" Veneski complained at one restive meeting.[37]

But despite their frustration and exhaustion, Veneski and the other activists were determined to save the firehouse. "We believe that the fiscal reforms adopted by the City Government are an attack against the poor and working people," read one editorial in the NCDC newsletter.[38] The activists refused to accept the city's rhetoric of fiscal necessity at face value and insisted that closing the firehouse violated their Fourteenth Amendment rights to equal protection.[39] They described themselves as hardworking members of society who paid their taxes and fulfilled their obligations. Why, then, would the city not fulfill its obligations in turn? The "working people" and "taxpayers" of Northside—blue-collar, middle-class, and poor alike—only wanted their due, said an NCDC organizer.[40] "Do you know that two hydrants were out of service, adding to the delay in extinguishing the fire in your neighbor's home? Do you know they had to special call fire companies from great distances to extinguish this fire?" read a flyer that was distributed after a fire. "How long must we continue to play 'Fire House Roulette?' Demand the fire protection you always had and still pay taxes for."[41]

The closure of the firehouse posed both a literal and symbolic threat to the community. People feared that with more fires burning because of decreased service, more buildings would be abandoned, banks would become more aggressive in their redlining, and fire insurance rates would skyrocket—as had happened in neighboring Bushwick. More broadly, the residents believed their existence as members of a stable working-class community was under assault. They framed their struggle in the terms laid out by Roger Starr. One banner hanging in the firehouse read "Planned Shrinkage Means Planned Genocide," and another pronounced: "Planned Shrinkage Stops at Northside."[42]

Over the course of 1976, there were more than one hundred fires in the neighborhood, killing eight people.[43] On the one-year anniversary of the firehouse occupation, an occasion for both celebration and mourning, activists began the day with a mass and memorial service to commemorate the victims. A sixteen-car motorcade then drove to the home of Fire Commissioner O'Hagan in Bay Ridge to hold an hour-long demonstration. Picketing the houses of those in city leadership was a new tactic for the firehouse protesters. They believed it was especially infuriating to those at City Hall because it reminded them of the presence of a scruffy working class in the city—as Veneski said, "I think [Deputy Mayor Zuccotti] doesn't want us to picket his beautiful house."[44] In the evening the firehouse became the scene of a rowdy party, supplied by local supporters with pans of lasagna, piles of kielbasa sausages, soda, and kegs of beer.

The firehouse struggle depended on community connections, ethnic ties, and local solidarities. This intimacy was its strength, but also a weakness. Focused on their own neighborhood struggle, the activists made few efforts to reach outside Northside, to form alliances with other neighborhoods throughout the city that were facing similar cuts.

A complex racial politics was at work in the firehouse struggle. Greenpoint-Williamsburg had never seen the blockbusting characteristic of Bedford-Stuyvesant and Bushwick, but many private landlords in the area refused to rent to people of color. Neighborhood residents had protested the construction of public housing in the 1950s and 1960s, and there was a long history of hostility to the projects' African American and Latino residents.[45] In the firehouse conflict, the white ethnic demonstrators benefited from their whiteness, receiving a degree of support from police and fire officials that would have been almost impossible to imagine in minority neighborhoods at the same time. Their claims on the neighborhood were treated as legitimate in a way that black and Latino demands on city resources often were not.

To Northside's credit, though, the theme of race—which rose so readily to the fore in other neighborhoods—never became the focus of the firehouse campaign. Whatever the private sentiments of neighborhood residents may have been, the leaders of the group sought to articulate their struggle in terms that avoided racial stereotypes and conflicts. In many other social debates of the time, white working-class people, feeling themselves under siege, turned to attacking welfare recipients, single mothers, criminals, and other "unproductive" elements of society, all stereotyped as nonwhite. A few hints of such rhetoric did emerge in the firehouse protests, as when demonstrators invoked the category of "taxpayers" to insist on municipal services—an implicit contrast with people on welfare who simply took from the city. But in Northside the demonstrators also talked about themselves as the poor. They saw their enemies as City Hall and the Emergency Financial Control Board, not other ordinary New Yorkers. They made their claims to city resources in the language of taxpayers' rights, but also in a communal frame— staking out the right of their neighborhood to survive and endure as a working-class space.[46]

When the city did begin to make proposals to solve the Northside problem, its initial offers involved transferring resources from other neighborhoods to Greenpoint-Williamsburg. But the people at Engine Company 212 were reluctant to be pitted against people in other parts of the city. A few weeks after the one-year anniversary of the occupation, the city proposed reassigning a Queens fire company to Northside, a move blocked by Queens residents who filed a lawsuit to prevent the relocation. City officials next proposed to transfer to Northside a fire company from Fort Greene, a majority African American neighborhood. Although it was the middle of the winter when the announcement came, protests broke out in the snow outside the Fort Greene fire station.[47] A few days later, Veneski and others from Engine Company 212 brought their red People's Firehouse banner to disrupt a town hall meeting organized by the new Brooklyn borough president at his swearing-in ceremony, demanding that he keep fire protection in Fort Greene. "We want the Borough President to back the Fort Greene people. We want him to take a stand," Veneski said.[48] There was no sense that the people of Greenpoint-Williamsburg deserved fire service any more than those of Fort Greene.

In March 1977, the Northside firehouse reopened, but with a smaller company. The protest continued, and in June 1978 Engine Company 212 was fully restored. "We waited. We sacrificed and . . . we got it. We got the whole thing," Veneski told a crowd of several hundred who gathered at the firehouse to celebrate and hear a reading of the names of the many community residents who had participated in the protests over two and a half years.[49]

But even this victory was tinged with loss. Fire department officials made it clear that the restored fire company, with the same staffing level as before, would now be expected to cover three times as much territory.[50] The Northside activists had succeeded in saving their local firehouse, but they could not fight the overall logic of budget cuts across the board.

Still, for those most deeply involved in the People's Firehouse, the experience was sweet. One man who spoke at the reopening ceremony had lived in the neighborhood for seventy-one years. "Thank you," he told the crowds. "You can look around and see. The neighborhood is coming back into its own."[51] Veneski's own life had been transformed by the firehouse struggle. He had gone from working in a soda company to being a recognized community leader, participating in a struggle that he knew had national implications. Suddenly he was in the limelight. People from the media came to him, looking for interviews and photographs. He began to travel to other cities facing fiscal crises to talk about what they might do to resist firehouse shutdowns. He became known and beloved by many of Brooklyn's politicians, and kept working for better conditions in the neighborhood—for tenant protection, health services, education, classes in English as a second language. The People's Firehouse became a community organization, advocating for tenants' rights as well as better public services for the neighborhood. Veneski's life circumstances improved, too: while he was living in the fire station, he and his wife took over a grocery store across the street and became small business owners.[52]

His new social status did not make him forget the firehouse, though. Should the city ever again plan to close Engine Company 212, Veneski joked, he would organize his people to block the New York City marathon as it came through the neighborhood—the ultimate act of civil disobedience he'd dreamed up but never been able to put into practice during the long sixteen months he had slept on the firehouse floor.

15. The College in the Tire Factory

The people of Northside had gone to battle for a fire station. In the South Bronx, a neighborhood racked by fire, they fought instead for a college.

Eugenio María de Hostos Community College of the City University of New York was hardly a grand structure—nothing at all like any of the classical limestone buildings that formed the imposing quadrangle of Columbia University at 116th Street. Instead, the school was housed in an abandoned tire factory in the South Bronx. The school administration had scrambled to ready the building, located at the corner of 149th Street and Grand Concourse, in time for the first Hostos classes in the fall of 1970. The school had no blackboards or chalk, and what was supposed to serve as the library had no books. "We walked into school the first day and saw what we had—a renovated factory," one student told the *New York Times*.[1]

Hostos was an unusual educational experiment. The two-year community college was expressly designed for a bilingual population, offering classes in Spanish and English. The students were hardly a conventional group, including many single mothers, older students, Vietnam veterans, former inmates, and students struggling with addiction.[2] Many faculty members were on the left politically, committed to teaching a working-class Puerto Rican, Dominican, and African American population.[3] One of its goals was to train students for careers in the health professions; it also sought to provide the potential for a path to the four-year senior colleges of the CUNY system. Beyond those educational ambitions, Hostos served as a community center that offered free dental services, helped people prepare income tax returns, and hosted Latino theater, opera, choir groups, and local meetings. Its location in a space created by capital flight seemed, in a way, appropriate: it represented the possibility that the neighborhood's devastation could be turned in a hopeful direction. From its earliest days, people saw Hostos as a rare example of city investment in the South Bronx. As one professor put it, "Hostos was like an oasis, it was like a chance to start over again."[4]

Protest and political agitation marked the school from its earliest days. During its first year, Hostos students led a boycott and sit-in to demand more black and Puerto Rican faculty, the creation of a student council, the establishment of black and Puerto Rican cultural studies centers, better facilities, and improved access to reading materials— books for the library, for starters.[5] The students also wanted to fly black liberation and Puerto Rican flags atop the building. The college president, a doctor from Lincoln Hospital, agreed to do so, though he noted that by law the American flag had to fly higher than the rest.[6] In the autumn of 1975, the fiscal crisis threw both CUNY and Hostos into turmoil. The founding premise of CUNY—free tuition—came under threat, as the city's fiscal overseers called upon it to make the students pay. And as that struggle progressed, it became an open question whether Hostos would continue to exist at all. The people who had welcomed the school into their neighborhood only a few years earlier suddenly had to confront the possibility that soon it might no longer be there.

The City University of New York dated back to 1847, when the president of the city's Board of Education, an autodidact named Townsend Harris, pressed the state legislature to fund a "Free Academy" that would be open to all qualified applicants in the city regardless of their financial status. "Open the doors to all—let the children of the rich and the poor take their seats together, and know of no distinction save that of industry, good conduct and intellect," he wrote in a letter explaining his proposal.[7] Originally located at 23rd Street and Lexington Avenue, the Free Academy moved up to 138th Street in 1866, when it was renamed the College of the City of New York. It expanded early in the twentieth century to include Hunter, a women's college that was originally intended to train high school teachers, and eventually Brooklyn and Queens Colleges as well. The system grew again in the postwar years, driven by the GI Bill and by increased interest in higher education as a means of creating a skilled workforce. In addition to the four-year senior colleges, during the 1950s and early 1960s the city opened several two-year community colleges; more schools, both two- and four-year, would be added in the late 1960s to create a network spanning all five boroughs. In 1961, Nelson Rockefeller authorized the creation of a Graduate Center, with the ability to confer doctoral degrees, so that the system truly became the City University of New York.[8]

For most of the postwar period, any full-time student at the municipal colleges could obtain a bachelor's degree free of charge. The view of higher education as a right that could be claimed by any New York resident was among the most striking aspects of the city's social policy. It articulated a conception of citizenship that was much more expansive than any to be found at the national level. CUNY was at once utilitarian and utopian, a means to upward mobility as well as an extension of the promise of intellectual life for all, regardless of their ability to pay. Its distinctiveness was precisely what led the city's critics, including President Ford, to focus on CUNY as a symbol of the city's excessive generosity overall. That CUNY was free was key to its identity; charging tuition would thus be a way for the city to demonstrate that things had fundamentally changed.

To be sure, the popular notion of a "free" CUNY was somewhat oversimplified. Students did have to pay library and laboratory fees, and graduate students and part-time undergraduates had to pay "instructional fees," which were tantamount to tuition and which generated a substantial amount of income for the university.[9] The city and state had tussled over whether CUNY should start charging tuition and just offer tuition aid to the poorest students—who often had to attend part-time and were thus already paying instructional fees.[10] And in the early 1970s, the situation of CUNY became especially complicated because of a new "open admissions" policy. Adopted following student protests at City College about the small proportion of black and Latino students at the four-year schools, the policy guaranteed placement in one of the system's colleges to every high school graduate in the city.

Many older professors saw open admissions as a threat to the educational quality of their institution and their status. They worried that the new students would dilute the caliber of a student body that had been made up of well-prepared students, many from the premier schools in the system. On the other hand, the more politically radical teachers saw open admissions as a way to fulfill the deepest promise of an urban university by including minorities not previously served. As the poet Adrienne Rich wrote in an essay about teaching literature to underprivileged students at City College, she chose to do so because of "a need to involve myself with the real life of the city . . . to ally myself, in some concrete, practical, if limited way, with the possibilities" of the multicultural metropolis.[11] The shortage of resources available to pay for the growth of CUNY after the adoption of open admissions was a further grievance. With the new policy in effect, student enrollment grew dramatically, from 118,000 in 1969–70 to 212,000 in 1974–75, straining both the faculty and the physical capacity of the schools.[12] In 1970, the first year after open admissions began, teachers held classes in coat rooms, copy centers, an indoor ice-skating rink, a bingo hall, and a synagogue. One campus president set up his office in a trailer.[13] Even before the fiscal crisis, CUNY was split, stressed, and uncertain about the future.

In the fall of 1974, the city announced that by the following year CUNY had to cut its budget by nearly 9 percent. The faculty immediately began to protest the cuts, holding teach-ins on the budget crisis and warning students about the "wholesale firing of adjuncts."[14] Some teachers framed the directive as an effort to turn back the "grand victory of Open Admissions," only five years old.[15] "We must not panic and we must remain cohesive," read one letter from the union representing

CUNY faculty and staff, the Professional Staff Congress. "The easiest course of action in any unusual situation is to turn against each other as a means of self-defense. We must NOT become cannibalistic and we must work toward our mutual goal of maintaining the integrity of the total educational process at this college."[16]

Even with the announcement of the budget cuts, though, there was at first little appetite in the city for ending free tuition, long regarded as a bedrock of New York's liberalism. When Hugh Carey was campaigning for governor in the fall of 1974, he reiterated his support. "I will do all in my power, whether I become Governor or not, to preserve free tuition at the City University," he wrote to the chairperson of the University Student Senate. "I believe that the state, not the students, must bear the burden of financing higher education in these days of inflation and higher costs."[17]

Soon, all that would change.

In October 1975 the president of City College, Robert Marshak, issued a report proposing the "restructuring" of CUNY. To lower costs while creating "a diverse, lean, responsive, urban, public institution of the highest quality," Marshak envisioned keeping only two of the existing eight community colleges, merging the others into the four-year senior colleges, and also merging some senior colleges with each other to create research-driven "university centers."[18] Hostos was among the community colleges that Marshak proposed to eliminate.[19]

Although intended as an alternative to across-the-board cuts, Marshak's proposal implicitly suggested that closing campuses such as Hostos might also be a way of preserving the quality of CUNY, which some already saw as compromised by open admissions. One adviser of Marshak's had written him an anguished letter in the summer of 1975, complaining that coming budget cuts would mean killing graduate programs (and "whatever hope there is that research would be one of our missions") or else laying off tenured faculty, which would lead to a drop in morale so severe that the university system would never recover.[20] Marshak himself suggested that his plan to rationalize the campuses and fold programs into each other might make it easier to persuade the state to increase its support for CUNY—that closing some campuses could mean more funding for the school overall. But this underestimated what the local colleges meant to their communities—for instance, what Hostos meant to the South Bronx.

Students and faculty at the South Bronx institution were well prepared to defend the school. The previous year, they had organized a successful campaign to win more space for Hostos, adding another abandoned building to the original repurposed tire factory. When news began to circulate that the very existence of Hostos might be threatened by the fiscal crisis, campus activists who had participated in the drive for the new building were poised and ready. In November 1975, the Hostos faculty senate moved to create a Save Hostos Committee to "mobilize the forces of the students, faculty, staff and community." They sought to guarantee that the school would survive as a "separate entity," not be closed or "absorbed into any other institution."[21]

The SHC—which was chaired by Gerald Meyer, a historian of New York City politics who was also the chapter chair for the Professional Staff Congress, the staff and faculty union—consisted of various subcommittees, including ones for letter-writing, petitioning, voter registration, and community outreach. As the SHC became active, letters from Hostos professors began to appear in the *New York Post*, the *Daily News*, and eventually the *New York Times*.[22] Congressman Charles Rangel pledged his support for the school, and a group of Latino state politicians wrote a letter to the Board of Higher Education: "No budget crisis can ignore the devastating impact which the closing of this college would have on the Puerto Rican population which has received the least services from the public education system of this city."[23] Even the head of the Manhattan/Bronx division of Bankers Trust wrote to the CUNY chancellor to express his hope that the "imminent state of crisis" facing New York would not mean the "complete abandonment" of Hostos.[24]

In addition to the Save Hostos Committee, a separate, more overtly radical group, the largely Puerto Rican Community Coalition to Save Hostos, also sprang up. Ramón Jiménez, a young Harvard-trained lawyer teaching courses on law and sociology at Hostos, helped get it started. An activist since his teenage years, Jiménez was highly involved with left Puerto Rican circles in New York, although he was far more concerned with the conditions of his community in the Bronx than with political independence for the island commonwealth. Thanks to his participation, the Community Coalition had useful connections with local groups such as United Bronx Parents, an organization focused on improving public schools, as well as with St. Ann's Church of Morrisania, whose progressive reverend was friendly with Bishop Paul Moore. In contrast to the Save Hostos Committee, which emphasized lobbying the City Council and other politicians, the leaders of the Community Coalition argued that the only way to successfully pressure the city was to target the banks. As one flyer put it, "the banks, through 'Big MAC,' are responsible for all the cutbacks which threaten to close all the services that our community needs." The group held a late November demonstration at Chase Manhattan Bank: "Join your neighbors in the struggle to protect our right to a better life."[25]

But the organizing made no difference. In February 1976, CUNY Chancellor Robert Kibbee announced a plan to remake CUNY largely in line with Marshak's initial proposal. Hostos would be shuttered. So would John Jay College, a school created to train people for jobs in the criminal justice system, which catered particularly to students from the city's police force. Two more schools—Medgar Evers, located in Brooklyn's Crown Heights, and York College, in Jamaica, Queens, both with overwhelmingly black student enrollments—were to be converted from four-year to two-year schools. New York City Community College would cease to offer any liberal arts curriculum, instead becoming a technical school.[26]

Protests broke out immediately. It seemed hardly accidental that three of the four schools slated for closure and cutback were schools that served mostly nonwhite populations. Medgar Evers faculty members described the plan to reduce their college to a two-year school as "blatantly racist."[27] Many suspected it was the first step toward closing the school altogether. "Those who control the purse strings don't give a damn" about the city's working poor, said one professor involved with the Student-Faculty Coalition to Save Medgar Evers College.[28] The president of York College called for an "all-out war" on the reorganization plan.[29] One police officer studying at John Jay wrote an op-ed for the *Times* arguing that a school focused on civil servants was especially important given the new demands to restructure services in the fiscal crisis.[30] New York City Community College promised a campaign of "massive resistance" to this "latest attempt to destroy the City University of New York."[31] More than three thousand people came to a demonstration against the restructuring, at which angry students hanged the CUNY chancellor and chair of the Board of Higher Education in effigy.[32] One state senator from the Bronx lamented that his vote to "save" the city had been a mistake, since in practice this had meant bailing out the banks but letting the people drown. "If I could vote again, my vote would be for default."[33]

For young people just arriving at the university, the moment felt politically alive: their schools were poised for upheaval. There was profound skepticism about the city's claims: it didn't seem plausible that a city with New York's wealth could really be out of money. With the right priorities, students insisted, it would be possible to make different decisions. "People were like, Oh yeah? You're going to take this away from us? Well, we're going to fight for it," one student recalled.[34]

Nowhere was the protest more intense than at Hostos, where the organizing efforts engaged many students and professors. Students insisted that Hostos was the only place they could imagine going to school—because of the welcoming atmosphere and the Spanish-language instruction that made it possible for them to earn a college degree. "They seem to be saying that the students will have to pay for a mistake made by the bigwigs who didn't know how to keep a budget," one student, a former bank security guard, told the *New York Times*.[35] The chair of the Social Sciences Department at the school penned a furious letter to John Zuccotti: "Why close the only college in the economically depressed area of the South Bronx?"[36] In a subsequent letter, he wrote that the creation of Hostos had been a major victory for the people of the South Bronx and Harlem. "When their interests are so callously cast aside, the city loses, and our precious democracy and equality become empty symbols. Our future lies in opening such colleges, not closing them."[37]

Over the winter, students and faculty collected 8,000 signatures in the Bronx on a petition to save the school.[38] Activists tallied and publicized the number of Hostos students in the district of each city legislator.[39] Stephen Berger at the Emergency Financial Control Board noted that he had received four hundred letters in support of Hostos, while one state senator wrote that "the mail on Hostos is so heavy that it is impossible to answer each letter personally."[40]

Still, there was no clear sign of progress, and increasingly frustrated students and faculty opted for more aggressive tactics. Their first step was to block traffic on the Grand Concourse—the major highway that ran through the Bronx and past Hostos—using classroom chairs dragged out into the street. One faculty member recalls fire trucks coming and threatening to hose the protesters, who had set up their chairs at an intersection and were blocking traffic in all directions while holding "classes" in the street.[41] In the end, the trucks moved on.

The success of that action proved an inspiration. Early in the morning of March 25, a small group of students and professors arrived at the Hostos building. Using locks and long chains, they closed the gates to limit access to the school, so that people could only come and go through the main entrance guarded by student leaders. The protesters seized the keys from custodial staff and used filing cabinets and desks to barricade the exits. They removed mouthpieces from the phones. Their message was clear: the school—their school—was now in their possession.

The organizers' initial idea was that they would keep classes running and the school in order while the sit-in was going on. "This cannot be construed as a lockout," wrote two student leaders, because "professors would come in and teach their students."[42] Women set up a child care center in the college president's office. A core group slept in the school each night.[43] People from the student government provided security, watching from the roofs to make sure the police were not massing to arrest those inside.[44] Activists from the People's Firehouse came to visit.[45] One day neighborhood parents brought more than five hundred children to encircle the school, chanting: "Save Hostos, we too want to go to college!"[46]

The spirit of rebellion went beyond just keeping the school open and running. The occupiers screened films such as *Black Power*, and held teach-ins on the fiscal crisis for the broader community. They began to talk not only of saving the school but transforming it, kicking out the current president (described as a "traitor") and bringing in a new and more radical administration that would topple all manner of academic hierarchies.[47] "We, the different student, worker, and community organizations have seized our college and fired the incompetent, corrupt administration," read one open letter written shortly after the occupation began. "There has never been a takeover like this one."[48] For his part, Cándido de León, the college president, returned the paychecks of faculty members who were participating in the shutdown to Comptroller Goldin, saying he thought there was no legal basis for paying the very people who were preventing the school from functioning.[49]

De León was not alone in objecting to the takeover of the school by the protesters. At a college-wide faculty meeting, professors criticized the occupation for disrupting classes, and the group voted in favor of a resolution to clear the building "using force if necessary."[50] The relationship between the Community Coalition to Save Hostos, focused on direct action, and the Save Hostos Committee, with its emphasis on lobbying elected officials, grew strained.[51]

On April 4, the Board of Higher Education voted (over the objection of its one African American and two Puerto Rican members) to merge Hostos with Bronx Community College. Meanwhile, the college administration obtained a court injunction against the occupation of the school. On April 12, police entered the building and arrested forty protesters. Several hundred people gathered outside the school while the arrests were happening, and marched to the police precinct following the students and faculty who had been arrested.[52] The handcuffed protesters made for some dramatic photographs on the cover of the *Daily News*— Jiménez tried to keep his mother from seeing the paper that day, knowing she would be miserable to find her Ivy League–educated son in handcuffs—but all the charges were eventually dropped.

The occupation left the organizers exhausted and the Hostos faculty riven by internal dissent. Still, efforts to save the school continued through the spring. In early May, the Community Coalition to Save

Hostos organized a mass protest targeting the Emergency Financial Control Board. (One flyer for the rally featured mug shots of the members of the EFCB, along with text reading: "We Accuse the Members of the Emergency Financial Control Board of CRIMES against the COMMUNITY!")[53] A large, mostly Latino crowd marched several miles down to the EFCB offices, with fifty people carrying a block-long Puerto Rican flag. "Unless we stop the Emergency Financial Control Board, Hostos College, open admissions and free tuition will not be available to the vast majority of Latins, Blacks and working people," a flyer read.[54] As one eighteen-year-old student put it, "Losing Hostos would be like somebody burning down your house."[55]

While the fight over closing the Hostos campus continued in the Bronx, the entire CUNY system was falling apart. With the state refusing to extend further funding to the school as long as tuition remained free, the university was running out of money.

CUNY's leadership tried to postpone the inevitable. In mid-April 1976, Chancellor Kibbee announced that he was going to stop submitting receipts from vendors for payment so he could conserve money to pay faculty and staff.[56] He also suggested that he might defer paying two weeks of teachers' salaries for two years. Upset faculty members filed simultaneous lawsuits against the school and the CUNY staff union, saying that the threatened wage deferral was equivalent to robbery, a unilateral pay cut by other means.[57]

These plans were obviously short-term measures. From Albany, Governor Carey offered his preferred long-term solution: reversing his support for free tuition, he called for the Board of Higher Education to charge students to attend the school. If the board refused, he said, he would not grant CUNY any increase in state aid. The school would simply have to spend down its funds until it could no longer operate. The university system was in a bind: without charging tuition it could not get state aid, and without state aid it could not function.

There was an immediate outcry—a protest march of one thousand City College students, a three-day boycott of classes at City College, and a short hunger strike by faculty there.[58] At the end of May, Sandra López Bird, a Puerto Rican member of the Board of Higher Education, submitted her resignation. She cited the closing of Hostos, "the only institution specifically oriented toward the needs of New York Hispanics," as well as her sense that the restructuring plans would keep them and black students in second-class institutions. The imposition of tuition was the final straw, a "death blow" to the "goals for which the City University was originally established."[59] Following Bird's departure, the chairman of the board and three other board members resigned as well, all of them saying that they could not support Carey's proposal to impose tuition. Governor Carey lashed out against them all, accusing them of being "unable to cope with the harsh realities of the fiscal crisis" and evading their responsibilities.[60]

On May 29, just a few days after the resignations, CUNY reported that it did not have the money to cover its June payroll. The university shut down completely. It was the middle of exam period, many students had not yet completed their final tests, and none had gotten grades for the spring semester. Graduation ceremonies were canceled, as were summer programs.[61] To some extent, the university was gambling that the state and city would blink—that they'd find the situation intolerable and come up with the money CUNY needed to operate. But the school was also simply unable to go on without funding.

Faculty and students responded to the shutdown in different ways. Some organized impromptu protests. At Manhattan Community College, students and professors set up tables in the street, collecting signatures on a petition urging Carey to bring funding back. "We need your help," one professor shouted. "There's no City University as of 4 o'clock today."[62] Others argued that the CUNY staff union should insist that the university reopen immediately: the alternative was "default in what is owed to students who have completed a year's work."[63] Some tried to go on in whatever way they could; one physics professor held a final exam on the Staten Island Ferry. The union told the faculty not to report for work as long as there was no money to pay them, and denounced the city for its refusal to pay: it was "no less pardonable, legally or morally, for the city to default on its payments to its workers than it is to default on its payments to its creditors."[64] Hundreds of faculty members applied for unemployment insurance, begging for extensions on phone bills and rent.[65] Some students, making light of their derailed plans, gathered at local bars to jokingly toast the shutdown—"No more exams!"[66]

The closure of the school wore away support for free tuition. As the *Times* editorial page put it, without tuition "the ax would fall so heavily on so many departments and people that former staunch free-tuition supporters have rushed to accept tuition as the lesser evil."[67] On June 1, the Board of Higher Education—with new members hastily installed to replace those who had resigned in protest—voted seven to one to start charging tuition at CUNY.[68] The lone dissenting vote came from Vinia R. Quinones, a Puerto Rican hospital administrator who was now the sole nonwhite member of the Board.[69]

Once the BHE ruled in favor of tuition—which ranged from $387 to $462 per semester for city residents, the equivalent of about $1,635 to $1,950 today—Carey and the state legislature approved an infusion of fiscal aid for the school.[70] The money permitted it to reopen, but it was still not sufficient to fully resolve the financial crunch.[71] Five thousand part-time and a thousand full-time CUNY employees were terminated—mostly counselors, higher education officers, nontenured lecturers, and tenure-track faculty. (Tenured faculty were threatened with layoffs as well, but in the end all of them kept their jobs, although ten people who had been promised tenure were let go.)[72] The American Association of University Professors censured the Board of Higher Education, calling the mass layoffs "a cataclysmic event in American higher education."[73] Class sizes rose as a result of the layoffs, climbing on average from twenty-five students per class to thirty, and in some cases rising as high as fifty or sixty per class.[74]

The CUNY staff union did what it could to help people who were fired as a result of the crisis. It was able to get some people reinstated and insisted that senior faculty who had been laid off should be first in line to get their jobs back.[75] Two of the colleges that had originally planned to cut tenured lines—Brooklyn College and Queens College—eventually decided against doing so.[76] The union filed a class-action lawsuit on behalf of members who had lost their jobs, and there was some talk of forming a coalition to restore free tuition.[77] But nothing came of it.

The introduction of tuition at CUNY marked the beginning of a change in the financing of the city university overall. Tuition made up a significant new source of revenue: the payments contributed $135.5 million, while the state gave $170 million and the city contributed $160.5 million. In 1979, the state would agree to take over paying the majority of the costs for the senior colleges—a significant expansion of state aid.[78] Politically, though, winning this aid had required giving up the principle of an inclusive, tuition-free college for all.

By the fall semester, the number of students in the entering freshman class at CUNY had declined by 17 percent, while the number of graduate students had fallen by a quarter.[79] The annual welcome-back letter from the chancellor to the faculty, usually an opportunity for boosting morale, instead sounded the notes of a dirge: "You have borne the major burden of last year's catastrophe."[80] Many students, too, felt that their school had been diminished. As one student told the *New York Times*, "Everyone I know is depressed or in despair. They feel so abandoned. There's no spirit any more."[81]

At Hostos, the events of the summer of 1976 were not all grim. The bill that provided money for CUNY once the Board of Higher Education agreed to charge tuition included $3 million to "protect the unique educational needs of Spanish-speaking students at Hostos Community College in the South Bronx."[82] The school would not be closed after all.

Those who had been involved in the mobilization to save Hostos took great pride in what they had accomplished. Many were acutely aware that they had been instrumental in rescuing the school. Organizing continued over the following two years, and some of the breaches that had opened during the spring of 1976 between radical students and the more moderate faculty were healed. The remaining members of the Community Coalition to Save Hostos joined with Meyer and other faculty activists who had participated in the Save Hostos Committee to work to win funding for the renovation of the new building that had been purchased in 1974 so the school could finally move out of its sub-standard quarters.[83] Years later, Ramón Jiménez, the Community Coalition founder, recollected the impact the experience at Hostos had had on him: "It affected my political life all my life because I got to see that people could win, and sometimes you don't see that."[84]

Yet even though Hostos had survived the plans to close it, the rescue came in the context of CUNY's broader transformation. Like other CUNY colleges, Hostos was forced to retrench. It closed its nursing department and reduced the number of full-time faculty from 170 to 100. Two professors who had been closely associated with the mobilization to save the school, including Ramón Jiménez, were among those who lost their jobs.[85] And like all the other CUNY students, those at Hostos had to start paying tuition, a significant burden for a working-class student population.

Throughout the city, the end of free college tuition was treated as a real loss. Although the city's establishment had been virtually unanimous about the need to charge tuition, once the change actually happened many felt nostalgic for the old model, which saw public universities as a way of extending both social mobility and democracy. The *New York Times* compared the soaring rhetoric that had marked the foundation of the school—"let the children of the rich and the poor take their seats together and know no distinction save that of industry, good conduct and intellect"—with the sorry bureaucratic language that had ended free tuition due to "non-availability of funds." The arrival of tuition at CUNY seemed to be in keeping with national trends toward much more expensive college bills that would soon set higher education apart as the province of the elite.[86]

One *Times* writer lamented that free tuition might soon be treated as a relic of an earlier era. It should, he suggested, rather be conceived of as an idea that was merely put aside for the moment due to difficult conditions. When times grew easier, it could be resurrected. It could become not just a memory from the past but the way of the future, "a sensible and realistic option for a more affluent, more confident and more generous day."[87]

As it turned out, though, neither the city nor the country was moving in that direction.

16. A New New York

Even as CUNY students and faculty, and residents of communities such as Northside, struggled to hold on to the promises the city had once extended to its residents, a transformed New York was beginning to take shape.

One place it could be glimpsed was the Commodore Hotel, at 42nd Street and Lexington Avenue. The magnificent twenty-six-story building, named in homage to nineteenth-century railroad magnate Cornelius "Commodore" Vanderbilt, had been a midtown landmark since its opening in 1919. Owned by the Penn Central Railroad, the hotel fell into disrepair after the railroad declared bankruptcy in 1970. Its management stopped paying property taxes, and Penn Central was eager to sell the property.

The Beame administration was frightened of what would happen if the hotel shut down: What would be the impact of the closing in such a high-profile area of town, right across the street from Grand Central Terminal and just a few blocks away from the main building of the New York Public Library? Would the neighborhood go the way of Times Square? To save the Commodore, the city decided to experiment with a development strategy that seemed at odds with calls for fiscal rectitude.

If a buyer agreed to purchase the Commodore and redevelop it into something new, the city would waive a portion of the site's real estate taxes for years to come.

The developer who won that deal was a young man named Donald Trump. Twenty-nine years old in the spring of 1976, Trump was known for his lush lifestyle, embodied by his silver Cadillac limousine bearing license plates emblazoned with his initials. He lived on East 65th Street in a penthouse apartment, held season tickets to the Knicks and the Rangers, and frequented deluxe nightspots such as the 21 Club and El Morocco. He loved to flaunt his wealth, to show everyone how much he was worth.[1]

From his earliest days, Trump saw the city as a billboard to advertise his glory. As a teenager he'd attended the opening of the Verrazano-Narrows Bridge; later in life, he remembered that the engineer who had designed the structure failed to get public recognition, while politicians were applauded even though they had once opposed the project. "I realized then and there something that I would never forget: I don't want to be made anybody's sucker." His buildings would bear the name of the man who built them.[2]

This mix of bravado and insecurity echoed the embattled populism of Donald Trump's childhood milieu in Queens. His father, Fred, was a developer too, the owner of some 22,000 apartments in the outer boroughs, most of them occupied by whites. In 1973 the federal government sued the family corporation for refusing to rent to African Americans. Rental agents were told to affix a piece of paper with a large "C" for "colored" to the applications of prospective tenants who were black, or simply to put them aside and not consider them.[3] (Rumors of racism had long circulated around the Trump family: in 1927 Fred Trump was arrested at a Ku Klux Klan rally in Queens, and in the 1950s Woody Guthrie—a tenant in a Trump building—wrote lyrics denouncing the racial hostility stirred up by "Old Man Trump" in his apartment complexes.[4]) Donald Trump took a belligerent stance toward the lawsuit, hiring Roy Cohn (the viciously red-baiting former aide to senator Joseph McCarthy) and proclaiming that "the government is not going to experiment in our buildings to the detriment of ourselves and the thousands who live in them now." With an air of moral indignation, he insisted that he had no problem renting to black families—but that renting to "welfare clients" who lacked income guarantees would lead to a panicked exodus of tenants. Eventually, Trump settled the case out of court, agreeing to provide civil rights organizations with lists of vacant apartments as soon as they became available to make sure that black tenants could apply.[5]

Now, Trump was offering to buy the Commodore, strip it down to its iron frame, enfold it in gleaming glass, and rebuild it as a branch of the Hyatt Regency. The plan was elaborate. Trump would be allowed to purchase the property from the railroad for $9.5 million. Then he would sell it for a dollar to the Urban Development Corporation—the same state agency whose failure had helped to trigger the fiscal crisis and which was enjoying new life financing commercial developments, far from its roots in low-income housing. Finally, the UDC would lease the property back to Trump and the Hyatt Corporation for ninety-nine years, allowing the developers to pay taxes far below the normal rate for four decades—a windfall worth hundreds of millions of dollars. (As of 2016, Trump's tax break has cost New York City $360 million in uncollected taxes.)[6]

Trump worked his political connections—his father Fred was a longtime friend and supporter of Mayor Beame—and lobbied the city government as the Board of Estimate prepared to vote on the deal. He also hired Hugh Carey's chief fundraiser to aid in lobbying the Urban Development Corporation. "As you may be aware, Local Community Board No. 5 has voted overwhelmingly, twenty-two to two, in favor of our presently pending proposal to create a Hyatt Regency Hotel at the site of the existing Commodore Hotel," Trump wrote to Deputy Mayor John Zuccotti. "I look forward to your assistance in proceeding with this important development." Trump cited the support he'd received from the *Daily News* and other local media as well as the Hotel Association.[7] In reality, not all of these endorsements were exactly ringing. Many hoteliers opposed the plan, which they thought would give Trump an unfair competitive advantage. As one local television broadcast put it, "The old expression 'beggars can't be choosers' might well apply when it comes to encouraging new construction and business in New York City. . . . If the Trump bid is rejected, the Commodore will shut down—probably this summer—and lie vacant, taxes unpaid, a monument to urban failure."[8] According to this reasoning, the city didn't really have much choice.

But whether or not this was really the case—after all, given Penn Central's eagerness to unload the building, the railroad might have been willing to sell it so cheaply that another buyer would have made the purchase even without the tax break—the city wanted to make the Commodore plan a model for other developers and executives. As Alfred Eisenpreis, the city's Economic Development Administrator, put it, the deal—the first under the city's new Business Investment Incentive Program—was meant to give a "signal to the business community that there has been a change."[9] Soon enough, the old stone façade of the Commodore came down, and in its place rose a "flashy hotel" that seemed, as one architectural critic put it, "an out-of-towner's vision of city life."[10]

It was a harbinger of things to come. In the late 1970s, even as most middle- and working-class New Yorkers were finding it more difficult to live in their city, a glittering new world of wealth was starting to take shape. Throughout Manhattan, new buildings were going up, designed to cater to the city's elites—and, indeed, to elites from around the world who might be enticed to come over. As Felix Rohatyn put it in one address, the city needed to appeal to Europeans "who view with alarm the leftward drift of their respective governments. This time around, New York City should look to Europe and say, 'Give me your rich!'"[11]

Developers fought over air rights in a race to construct ever-taller towers.[12] The new high-rises housed luxury condos and co-ops, whose prices rose as high as $11 million per apartment (the equivalent of about $32 million adjusted for inflation).[13] With the help of a tax abatement from the city, Harry Helmsley built the tallest hotel in the city's history—fifty-one stories and more than a thousand rooms—on Madison Avenue. The city's art auction scene was thriving, too, drawing the dollars of the rich and fashionable ready to spend $750,000 for a Brancusi ($3 million in today's dollars).[14] The stock market was still mired in the bear sell-off of the decade, but glimmers of the day when it would drive the wealth of the city were already starting to become evident at the end of the 1970s, in reports of generous end-of-year bonuses for every employee at Wall Street brokerage firms.[15] The city built a new convention center (on land owned by Trump, in a deal he orchestrated) to lure out-of-town businesspeople to come to the city and spend their money. It worked, and not just for conventioneers: 1979 marked a record year for tourism in New York.[16]

The new New York took shape slowly, and, as the story of the Commodore Hotel suggests, it did not come out of nowhere. Its growth was stimulated by the city's new priorities and the reorientation of the city government toward policies that might help developers and the wealthy. Over the years that followed, the city would become far more generous in offering tax breaks to private businesses wanting to invest in New York City. This helped to spur the emergence of New York as a home for the new global elite, one centered on the financial markets but pointed toward international horizons. Key to the rise of this new city was the rejection of an earlier style of social politics. Public hospitals, free tuition, cheap transit, and a city that ran in the interests of its working class belonged to a past best forgotten. Now, in the parlance of the times, New Yorkers had to learn to help themselves, and they would do so by relying on favors from the rich.

The summer of 1976 was kind to Mayor Beame. In early July, New York hosted a massive bicentennial celebration, complete with a display of tall ships sailing up the Hudson River, a Philharmonic concert on the Great Lawn in Central Park, a confetti parade of cadets and sailors up Broadway, and a fireworks display over the Hudson. (Some onlookers even climbed up onto the still-closed West Side Highway to watch the spectacle.) Just two weeks later, the Democratic National Convention came to Madison Square Garden. City workers scrambled to fix potholes and arrest prostitutes in the vicinity, making New York presentable to delegates from across the country. In what seemed a minor miracle, both the bicentennial and the convention came off with no major hitches—

no wave of delegates being mugged, no headline-grabbing homicides, no strikes or protests disrupting either celebration. The simple absence of disaster was a triumph for the mayor. The *New York Times* even opined that a "new" Beame had "risen from the ashes."[17]

Beame's string of good luck continued into the fall. In early November, President Ford went down to defeat, losing his bid for reelection to Democratic challenger Jimmy Carter. New York State played a major role in the election. Although it had gone to the Republicans in 1972, this time around its forty-one electoral college votes went to Carter, providing much of his fifty-seven-vote margin of victory. The worst fears of Ford's advisers during the fiscal crisis were realized: the infamous "Ford to City: Drop Dead" headline in the *Daily News* had helped deliver the state to the Democrats. With a Democrat replacing Ford in the White House, Beame hoped the federal government would finally be more sympathetic to the city.

After the election, Beame traveled to Israel for the first time. He had been invited to lead a delegation of American mayors there, perhaps a reward for his refusal (which had greatly annoyed the State Department) to welcome Egyptian president Anwar Sadat when he came to speak to the United Nations in the fall of 1975. Beame had never before been to the Middle East, or even to Europe, and he was delighted to be able to make the journey. He joked that he would bring shovels to dig for gold in the ancient cities of the Middle East to help with the city's bailout.[18]

While he was visiting Jerusalem, Beame, like millions of other tourists, went to see the Wailing Wall, the wall in the Old City that is thought to have once belonged to the Temple. There, he participated in the common custom of writing a prayer on a piece of paper and sticking it into the crevices of the wall. What he wrote, however, might have surprised the people of his city. Instead of offering a prayer for long life for his wife and children, or even for the people of New York, the seventy-one-year-old Beame wrote one word on his slip of paper: "Help."[19]

Only a few days later, he received an unsettling telephone call. The Flushing National Bank, a small bank in Queens that had been heavily invested in city paper (the amount it held in city bonds was more than double the rest of its capital) had sued the city, challenging the "pastrami agreement" moratorium on debt repayments.[20] In November 1976, the New York State Supreme Court ruled in favor of Flushing National, throwing out the moratorium. The city had ninety days to settle with its noteholders. There was one loophole: the court said that the noteholders were "not entitled" to repayment until it was clear that this would not be "unnecessarily disruptive" to the workings of the city. But it was still obvious that New York would have to come up with a new financial plan.[21]

One might have thought that Beame would regard this as a setback, his plea for divine help going unanswered. Surprisingly, though, he claimed the opposite, saying that he was relieved to have the moratorium repealed. He insisted that he had never wanted the city to default on its debts. His position had always been that New York City had a constitutional duty to repay its bondholders. After all, he himself was a bondholder who had bought the city's debt believing that New York could never default, and even though the city had never formally gone into bankruptcy, the suspension of debt payments was default by another name.[22] Beame felt particular sympathy for small bondholders, working-class New Yorkers who had invested in the city's notes—sometimes buying tens of thousands of dollars' worth to pay for their children's college educations—and were faced with financial hardship when the moratorium went into effect.

In the city's financial community, the rejection of the agreement was also greeted with delight. Lawyers for the city described the court's decision as a boon for New York, since it would make the city's debt "the most gilt-edged in the Nation." After all, the city was now the only place in the country where a court had ruled that repaying creditors legally trumped any other obligation.[23] The president of Standard & Poor's proclaimed: "This ruling should make the market bullish on all New York securities. It renews our faith in the sanctity of a contract. It shows what we've been saying all along—that the Legislature cannot completely displace the principle of debt repayment."[24]

At the same time, though, the court decision left the city's fiscal future once again in grave doubt. New York now needed to come up with $1 billion to pay the holders of its short-term notes. Desperate for funds, MAC executives even held a few meetings with shadowy investors who claimed to have "$1 or $2 billion of Eurodollars" that they wanted to immediately invest in New York City. (The deal ultimately proved too questionable for MAC even in the circumstances the city faced, and went nowhere.)[25] Most observers thought that more federal aid would eventually be necessary. The only question was when. As Carter's adviser Orin Kramer wrote, "The self-help posturing aside, forging a $1 billion solution without federal aid is unrealistic."[26]

Bankers seized the moment to press for even more control over the city's finances, asking for an extended term for the Emergency Financial Control Board and for an independent trustee "to serve as guardian over revenues from the city's property tax."[27] Once again they insisted that their sole goal was reassuring investors "on the west side of the Hudson" and making New York a place in which they wanted to invest. As one financial executive put it, "Those people can buy Lincoln Continentals or yachts or triple-A rated California bonds. And all the work we have been doing is just about how to fashion a financial plan that will encourage those people to buy the paper of the City of New York."[28]

Instead of giving in to the banks' demands, however, Beame worked out a deal to raise money by asking creditors to exchange their city bonds for MAC debt—essentially a voluntary version of the "pastrami agreement." The plan also relied on the goodwill of the city's labor unions, which agreed to delay collecting the principal for MAC bonds they had purchased with city workers' pension funds. Finally, to cover the gap that still remained, the city came up with some extra cash by moving money from other places in the budget—a maneuver that one banker deemed worth of James Cavanagh.[29]

Beame's choice highlighted an unexpected commonality between the city's public sector unions and its banks: both were now among New York's largest creditors. And because of that, union leaders turned out to share with financial executives many of the same basic goals for the city, such as the desire for a more "efficient" city government.[30] Both groups favored a proposal to build a massive underground highway, known as the "Westway," to replace the crumbling West Side Highway.

Both agreed on the importance of creating a public-private Economic Development Corporation, whose job would be to "coordinate means of achieving a better business climate."[31] And both wanted to see the federal government take over a larger share of New York's welfare payments to lessen the strain on city finances.[32]

By the end of 1977, former adversaries DC 37 president Victor Gotbaum and First National City Bank executive Walter Wriston were meeting regularly to discuss the city's future. Meanwhile, private sector union leaders had been rallied by David Rockefeller to form a Business/Labor Working Group. They endorsed lowering business taxes to make the city "more competitive" with surrounding areas, giving tax abatements (such as those Trump won for the Commodore) to stimulate real estate development, cutting personal income taxes, offering tax credits to keep companies from moving out of the city, and granting tax credits to lure businesses to come in. Little was said about how all these tax cuts might affect the city's revenues—the assumption was that they would lure enough new business to make up any revenue that was lost.[33] It was a far cry from the raucous protest outside of First National City Bank's offices in the spring of 1975.

With the public and private sector unions both securely on board with business interests, neighborhood groups were left without any coordinated resistance to the city's budget cuts. As Rohatyn would later write in the *Harvard Business Review,* "We in New York City found ourselves at war and created the equivalent of a coalition government to manage an austerity program."[34]

The Beame administration's new program for economic development, released in December 1976, likewise represented a startling turnaround from the city's previous priorities. The program, Beame said, represented "the City's commitment to improving the business climate, and its recognition that job-creation must be at the very top of its list of priorities."[35] In this reframing of urban liberalism, support for business was the central goal. Without the private sector, after all, there would be no wealth to support the public. Economic growth was the answer to the fiscal crisis. And this could only be achieved, apparently, by showing corporations that the city would do anything to win the investments that it needed.[36] Being a good liberal, in other words, meant advocating for business.

Despite the holes that still remained in city finances, Beame now insisted that the city should cut taxes that bothered business: "This Administration believes that other tax pressures on private businesses should be stabilized or even lessened."[37] He wanted to undertake a professional campaign to market the city to the rest of the nation, enlisting New York executives to act as an "Ambassador Corps" personally promoting the city as a business-friendly place.[38]

Beame made it clear that should businessmen want to talk, City Hall would listen. Business leaders flooded the city's new Office of Economic Development with letters explaining what they wanted from the government. A vice president at the New York Stock Exchange met with city officials to complain about the "particularly irritating" nature of taxes on the securities industry.[39] Other spokesmen from the financial industry warned that they did not want to be treated as a "captive industry," and that if the city taxed the financial sector then the "goose could be killed."[40] Nor did the business leaders concern themselves solely with taxation. One businessman, for example, wrote that New York should avoid adopting an affirmative action program because doing so would have a "chilling effect": "This City, already suspect for harboring a hostile business climate, will gain an even worse reputation."[41]

City officials tried to reassure executives that they would respond to their demands with alacrity. Osborn Elliot, the former president of the Citizens Committee for New York and now Beame's deputy mayor for economic development, wrote to one concerned businessman that he himself would be personally "instrumental in presenting the 'business point of view' in the highest councils of city government."[42]

Perhaps the clearest expression of the city's newfound determination to win friends in the business world came in a report released in early summer 1977 by the Temporary Commission on City Finances, a group of business leaders and economic policy experts first convened by Beame in the fall of 1975. The group met for a year and a half, discussing strategies to rejuvenate the city. The key, its final report suggested, was "a broad plan for political action that will increase private investment in New York City by first increasing public investment." The city had to gain control over "slack resources" that it could then turn toward the project of economic development.

The participants on the TCCF were not simply proposing austerity. The TCCF called for shifting some of the city's costs to higher levels of government—for the federal government to assume more of the cost of Medicaid and welfare, for the states to take over the senior colleges in the CUNY system. But it also emphasized tax cuts that could make the city more attractive for corporations and for wealthy individuals, since their investment was the key to revival. Should the city be able to shift its most burdensome expenses to the state or federal government, this should not go to preserving social services. Instead of being used to "maintain an inherently imbalanced local governmental system," any funding increase should be focused on spending that would "promote the economy."

The conclusion of the report included a brief meditation on the transformation of New York. There was no point, it said, in waxing nostalgic about old priorities and urban dreams. The task confronting policy makers was to "recognize change as inevitable," since "policies that attempt to recapture the past or even maintain the present are doomed to failure."[43]

The TCCF report, along with Beame's efforts to remake himself as a business advocate, signaled the new direction of the city's social policy following the fiscal crisis. No longer would the city government concern itself with social inequality; no more would it try to use its resources to aid the poor. Instead, the city would adopt strategies of development that focused on tax breaks, and run campaigns designed to market the city to people who didn't live there: tourists, executives, companies that might come and do business in New York. There was an ideological symmetry between these development programs and the worldview of the wealthy developers, whose building projects catered to an emerging class of people who might jet in and out of the city—their luxury New York apartment merely one more domicile in a portfolio spanning the world.

Donald Trump and the developers who exploited the city's despera-tion to build their towers had little interest in the rest of New York. The fact that millions of dollars went to subsidize their building projects instead of restoring public services or promoting recovery in the poor and working-class neighborhoods of the city never registered as a moral concern. Quite the contrary: the mood among the city's new elite in the wake of the fiscal crisis was confident and upbeat.

Later in the decade, hotel king Harry Helmsley told a reporter that he had little interest in seeking the economic revitalization of Harlem, which didn't seem to him something likely to be profitable. "I think I'm performing a very valuable service, providing the best luxury hotel in the world, providing luxury office space," he said.[44] As the seventies drew to a close, Trump commented to the newspapers that he believed things were looking up for the city—it was clearly on the road to recovery. "I'm not talking about the South Bronx," he elaborated, perhaps unneces-sarily. "I don't know anything about the South Bronx."[45]

Trump might not have known about it, but the suffering of the people there was real enough. In the summer of 1977 that would become dramatically clear.

17. Blackout Politics

The lights went out just after 9:30 p.m. on July 13, 1977. It took a few minutes for people to figure out what was going on. Some New Yorkers thought first about their unpaid bills. "What the hell happened? Did they close my electric again?" wondered one Bronx housewife.[1] Others were more afraid than perplexed. A teenager at the movies in Queens later remembered she had started to scream, believing that the Son of Sam, the serial killer who was terrifying the city that summer, had turned out the lights in preparation for bloody mayhem. A sixty-four-year-old woman thought she'd suddenly gone blind.[2]

The darkened city was surreal, unfamiliar, and, some thought, strangely beautiful. As columnist Pete Hamill wrote in the *Daily News*, "The Brooklyn Bridge was dark, the sky light was gone, and the only light came from the dull glow over New Jersey. Over to the left you could see the Statue of Liberty, still lit up in the harbor like a small green toy. You could see nothing else."[3] One police officer driving in from Queens described the scene: "The Rockaway Peninsula looked like a sparkling bracelet and Brooklyn was a big black abyss."[4] Slowly, people recognized that the blackout wasn't just in one neighborhood or even just one borough. At Seventh Avenue in Brooklyn, Hamill heard someone shout: "Fantastic! It's the whole city! It's the whole goddamned world!"[5]

The normal entertainments of a New York night suddenly stopped. The Mets-Cubs game at Shea Stadium had to be halted in the sixth inning. The ballet at Lincoln Center stopped. The cast members of the risqué musical *Oh! Calcutta!*, unable to get to their dressing rooms, were stranded onstage in the nude until generous audience members lent them clothes so they could leave the theater.[6]

Mayor Beame was delivering a political speech at Co-Op City in the Bronx when the blackout began. At first he, too, thought the sputtering of the lights was a short-lived malfunction.[7] Aides whisked the mayor out of the housing complex for a hasty drive through unlit streets to Gracie Mansion and then to City Hall. There, he met with fire commanders in a stifling room illuminated by battery-operated lamps.[8] "This is bad indeed," Beame commented with characteristic understatement.[9]

For people all over the city, the sudden darkness seemed at once surprising and opportune. One minute the streetlamps were on, illuminating the muggy, moonless night with a hazy yellow glow. The next they were off, and not just the streetlamps but the neon signs of the stores, the traffic lights, the lights from the apartment windows—everything gone black except for car headlights and the stray flashlight or candle fished out of the closet.

There is, of course, no complete record of the names of the people who broke into the stores. No one knows whose feet kicked out the panes of glass. Although numerous academics have written about the blackout, there are not many oral histories that capture the perspective of the people who were in the streets that night. One of the few first-person accounts comes from an interview conducted by a Ford Foundation researcher, who spoke to a an unemployed twenty-one-year-old African American Marine veteran living in Brooklyn with his mother and siblings. The young man told his interviewer that he was not someone who regularly broke the law; in fact, he hoped someday to go to college, study law, and become an attorney. But that night in July, he recalled, there was a feeling of carnival thrill when the lights first went off: "I was

charged . . . with the excitement of the moment." Suddenly he could just
stretch out a hand and take sneakers, stereos, jewelry, color televisions—
all the things that beckoned daily from store windows but were always
out of reach. He ran off when a store owner started shooting into the
crowd, but as the lights stayed off for one hour, then three, then five,
and into the early dawn, that initial queasy exhilaration gave way to
calculation. He went back to the stores that lay open, their goods spilling out on the sidewalks, and quickly picked out the consumer products
he knew he'd be able to resell the most easily. He figured that most of
the merchants were white, and that none would be badly hurt anyway.
They'd just collect some insurance and go on.[10]

In some wealthier neighborhoods, the blackout was the occasion
for bonhomie. Guests at a ritzy birthday party at the St. Moritz Hotel
thought it was just part of the festivities, the lights turned off for the
cutting of the cake.[11] On the Upper East Side, restaurants that had lost
air-conditioning set up tables outside for al fresco dining, while helpful drivers parked their cars facing them and left the headlights on
for illumination.[12] The scene was very different elsewhere in the city. At
least thirty-one neighborhoods experienced property damage during
the blackout—some of them historically poor African American or
Latino neighborhoods such as East Harlem, Morrisania, and Bedford-
Stuyvesant, but also much more racially and economically mixed neighborhoods, including Sunset Park, Coney Island, and Flatbush in Brooklyn,
the Upper West Side in Manhattan, and Stapleton on Staten Island.
No borough was left untouched. Of those arrested for participating in
property damage and theft, 65 percent were black, 30 percent Latino,
and 4 percent white. Only 8 percent were over 40; only 7 percent were
women.[13] But the ones arrested were not the only people to help themselves to things. Theft of goods became a much broader phenomenon,
with thousands of people participating who were completely law-abiding
under normal circumstances. Once the storefronts were smashed, anyone
could—and did—come in. All through the next hot summer day, people
picked through piles of rubble and broken glass, looking for something to bring home: women's slacks, blouses, a bottle of wine. Police
officers watched hundreds of women and children milling around an

A&P food store in Brooklyn, scrambling to collect what food remained on the shelves. "How can you shoot anybody here?" one asked.[14]

There were so many people out in the streets taking things from the stores that there was hardly any point in making arrests. As one Harlem woman put it, the streets were filled with an "avalanche of people."[15] Writer Ernesto Quiñonez, who was an eleven-year-old kid in Spanish Harlem that summer, later recalled the scene in his neighborhood: "For every 20 looters the cops locked up, 50 more would take their place."[16]

In much of the city, people took what they wanted from the stores and then went home. In some neighborhoods, though, such as Bushwick in Brooklyn, after carting off the goods people came back to torch the storefronts, as though they wanted to leave nothing behind but ashes.

The city's hospitals stayed open throughout the blackout, even without power. When backup generators at the hospitals failed, doctors and nurses pumped air bags by hand to keep artificial respirators going. At Brooklyn Jewish Hospital, doctors set up a makeshift emergency room in the parking lot, patching up patients—many of them young people whose faces and arms had been slashed by broken glass—under spotlights powered by Fire Department generators. "It's weird, uncanny, like I'm caught up in a M.A.S.H. nightmare and can't wake up," one nurse wearing a blood-spattered smock told a reporter.[17] When morning came, the New York Stock Exchange stayed silent, the trading floor illuminated only by sunlight.[18] Walter Wriston of Citibank walked to work, answering his own phone because no receptionists came in to the office.[19]

Charles Luce, the chairman of Con Edison, had insisted only four days before the blackout began that the chances of such a thing happening in New York City were "less than they have been in 15 years."[20] That lightning striking power lines north of the city should have disabled New York's entire electrical power system seemed to Luce a freak event—an "act of God."[21] In truth, the blackout had as much to do with Con Ed's protocols as it did with natural disaster. But Luce's rhetoric found an echo in the words of the young veteran from Brownsville who took part in the looting, and for whom the sudden dark seemed almost miraculous: "It was like the man upstairs said I'm gonna put the lights out for twenty-four hours and you all go off . . . and get everything you can."[22]

The technical reasons for the electricity outage—the heat wave, the lightning storm in Westchester that shut down two generators, the ensuing overload of the rest of the grid—were heavily debated in the press in the weeks that followed. But the real mystery of the blackout, and the reason it has remained so fascinating for so long, was political. Why did it lead to massive theft and property damage throughout the city? Why did thousands of people take part in robbing stores, an action similar in some ways (as historian Herbert Gutman noted at the time) to the food riots of earlier centuries, when poor people broke the law in ways that their communities found morally acceptable? But although it was possible to see the blackout looting as an expression of the frustration of poor New Yorkers in the wake of austerity, the blackout would soon come to serve a different political purpose. The experience of the city during the blackout would occupy a key place in conservative narratives, a way of justifying why the welfare state had to end.

Comparisons with the blackout of 1965 began almost immediately. During a power outage that began in the late afternoon of a cool November day and stretched through the moonlit autumn night, there had been almost no looting. Now, twelve years later, more than 1,600 stores in neighborhoods all over the city were robbed—everything from clothing stores, food markets, and drugstores to jewelry shops, furniture stores, and even car dealerships—at one Pontiac dealership in the Bronx, people shattered the plate-glass windows and drove away fifty new cars. Grocery and apparel stores, though, were the places most often struck. As one young mother who'd taken some food told an interviewer later, "Maybe a long time ago there weren't too many looters because people had jobs then and you know they didn't do too bad; the city wasn't low of money; but now it's like that." Rising unemployment, deepening poverty, and the awareness of retrenchment during the fiscal crisis established a profoundly different context.[23]

For the first few hours after the blackout began, there was little police presence in the streets. Only 7 percent of all the arrests made after the blackout occurred between 9:30 p.m. on July 13 and 12:30 a.m. on

July 14—even though this was when people began breaking into stores and when the greatest quantity of merchandise was stolen.[24] Whether because of poor morale, lingering anger at the cutbacks to the police force, or simple fear of the crowds, some 10,000 of the city's 25,000 active-duty officers failed to respond to the police commissioner's orders to report immediately for service.[25]

Even had there been more police, it would have been hard to contain the crowds filling the streets without resorting to massive use of force. There were no police shootings on the night of the blackout, but some police officers did respond with violence: in Bushwick, several took off their nameplates and shields and began to "beat up the looters with ax handles and nightsticks," one officer later recalled.[26] And some firefighters turned their hoses from the flames to douse looters.[27]

Early in the morning the police finally began to make arrests and to seize people who came to pick over stores that others had broken into. The next day saw the largest mass arrests in New York City history, with more than 3,700 people jailed. Mayor Beame called for a severe legal response to anyone suspected of theft during the blackout. "Crimes committed during a state of civil emergency must be dealt with most harshly," he wrote to Administrative Judge David Ross.[28]

There was nowhere to put all the prisoners, as the city's jails were crowded almost to the breaking point. The dilapidated Manhattan House of Detention ("the Tombs") had been closed after the inmate uprising there in 1970, when it was deemed unsafe. Now it was abruptly reopened to hold suspected looters, who were chained to one another and jammed into airless rooms that lacked mattresses and were only intended to hold people for a few hours. A dozen men at a time were stuffed into cells crawling with rats. The tiny rooms had no fans, and the heat rose, becoming sweltering and unbearable.[29] Because the courts were understaffed, it took several days to process and charge all those arrested. Many were kept for days, some for a whole week, unable to call their homes and speak to family.[30] Some of those held had not even been involved in the looting but had simply been swept up in arrests. Matters were made still worse by an incident at the Bronx House of Detention, where prisoners had started fires, broken furniture, and tried to smash through walls, with the result that 145 men had to be transferred—crowding other jails still more.[31] Some of the arrestees wound up in basement holding pens at the Brooklyn Criminal Court, which had never been intended to be occupied overnight; one thirty-nine-year-old man died of cirrhosis while in custody there.[32]

Public denunciations of the people who had broken into stores were fierce and relentless. Beame spoke of what had happened in the city as a "night of terror."[33] Picking up his words, the New York Post blared "24 Hours of Terror" on its front page. Store owners described people who had broken into stores as less than human. "The animals are out," one shopkeeper told the Daily News.[34] The owner of an ice cream store at the corner of Fulton Street near Adams Avenue in Brooklyn also called the kids in the street "animals,"[35] as did a merchant who owned a jewelry store in East Harlem.[36] Meanwhile, Soviet papers bragged that Moscow was virtually "blackout-proof," describing the New York blackout as "an inevitable result of capitalist relations, where users of electric energy are dependent on the goodwill of a private company."[37]

The daily papers filled with angry letters, many of them advocating a violent response to the wave of theft. Racism was rarely far from the surface. "The warning should have gone out that every looter would be shot on the spot," one man wrote in to the Times. "The Puerto Ricans can go back to P.R. They belong there anyway and if the blacks do not shape up they can go back to the South. It would probably be an educational lesson for them."[38] Someone from the suburb of Syosset complained that liberal concern about poverty and other social ills ultimately enabled looting: "Let us stop analyzing the problems of the wolves while they are slaughtering the sheep. Rather, let us treat the wolves like wolves while there are still more of us sheep." And a man from Far Rockaway wrote in: "Looters are born, not made."[39] Many people said that a harsher response from the state was in order. "The National Guard should have been called in as soon as the lights went out," wrote one person to the Daily News. "What does it take to get the guard out: an invasion from New Jersey?" Anywhere other than America, "looters are shot on sight," another one chimed in.[40] Perhaps most chilling was the letter that said, "After experiencing all that violence and looting during the blackout, I have just one suggestion: Bring back police brutality."[41]

Not all of the anger about the looting came from white people. The property damage and theft had been worst in black neighborhoods, and black merchants were among the most enraged. One black Harlem shoe store owner told the *Amsterdam News* that the "animals" that had destroyed his shop deserved immediate punishment: "This blackout brought out some of the scum of the earth from our communities; they should be locked up, and the key thrown away."[42] Other shopkeepers were simply sad: "These are just people in the neighborhood who took advantage of an opportunity and broke into stores and destroyed other black people's lives," said one thirty-four-year-old black woman who owned a clothing boutique in Bedford-Stuyvesant.[43]

At the same time, some black leaders expressed a certain degree of sympathy with the people who had participated in taking things from the stores, seeing a chance to make the case for a greater level of social involvement, for public spending and investment that could offer a measure of hope against the alienation revealed by the blackout. The *Amsterdam News* condemned the looting as "suicidal" for black neighborhoods, but the paper also argued that the "white-dominated government" had not comprehended the "depth of despair among our young people."[44] The minister of the First Baptist Church in Crown Heights said that it was not the lights going out that had led people to steal—the real cause was "the lack of jobs, money and a sense of frustration in the minority community."[45] The looting had been a "chance for the poor people to strike back against their oppressors," the pastor of another Baptist church in Manhattan observed.[46] One writer for the *Amsterdam News* described the hopelessness of those who thought that taking TVs or food would help their situation: these were people who had "no Harvards, no Yales, no City Colleges to look forward to, no American dream to chase."[47] Another community activist wrote that the people who had stolen were those who found themselves "tossed on the junk heap of the welfare state."[48]

The many people who had stolen goods did not necessarily see their own actions through this politicized lens, but they often regarded what they'd done as rational and legitimate under the circumstances. Even many of those who were caught in the act of taking groceries, clothing, and appliances from smashed-in stores did not necessarily believe that there was anything morally wrong with what they were doing. They were poor; they were on the margins of society; they lived with an uncertain future in a city where opportunities were contracting all around them. "They couldn't understand why we were arresting them," one police officer recalled. "They were angry with us. They said, 'I'm on welfare. I'm taking what I need.'"[49]

Some of those interviewed on the street also said they understood why people took things. What the papers called "looting" expressed a certain vision of what British historian E. P. Thompson—writing about the bread riots in England in the eighteenth century—might have called the moral economy. "People have no jobs and the golden opportunity presented itself and people took advantage of it," one woman told a reporter.[50] "The people in this neighborhood don't have much money," another one said: "no jobs and [they] suffer other indignities visited on them and when the lights went out, it was just what the doctor ordered. Poor people have been waiting years for those lights to go out."[51]

For conservative intellectuals around the country, the blackout provided an opportunity of a different sort: it was a chance to bolster their case against New York's ineffectual liberal elite, and to make the argument for a more draconian approach. The social order of New York had collapsed as thoroughly as its fiscal politics, and a strict new discipline seemed the only possible solution. Pat Buchanan—then a conservative activist just a few years from his stint in the Nixon White House—fulminated against the idea that the looting had been motivated by material need. "If hunger was at the back of it all," he wrote in an especially nasty column published by the *Daily News*, "how come some of the welfare mommas filmed ripping off jewelry, clothing and liquor stores lumbered about like overfed heifers who could use six months on a liquid protein diet?"[52]

The antiliberal point of view was summed up by the neoconservative writer Midge Decter in the September 1977 issue of *Commentary*, in an article titled "Looting and Liberal Racism." Decter wrote that while young black men had carried out most of the looting and should be held accountable, their actions in fact had been enabled by liberals who refused to hold black youth to the same standards they would expect of their own children. Not poverty but a naked, ugly material-ism, she said, had driven the looting—people were not motivated by "anger or frustration but simple greed." Yet liberals kept making excuses for the black poor, sending the implicit message that they were inferior. Locking them up at least recognized them as members of the same moral community. The criminal justice system could reintegrate them into mainstream society in a way that no other institution would.

Decter's own words, though, presented the black youths as perma-nently alien, impossible to accommodate within the community of the city. For Decter, even the epithet of "animal" was too generous. The looters seemed to her akin to a more primitive life form, resembling nothing so much as cockroaches. "For anyone watching them at work, surging out of the shadows like a horde and scurrying back into the cover of darkness as the police came by, the imagery suggested is one taken from insect life—from urban insect life—rather than from the jungle or the forest."[53]

Other conservative activists joined Decter and Buchanan in reflect-ing on New York in the late 1970s. For a generation of intellectuals, the Great Society and the entrenched poverty of African Americans and Latinos living in the urban core raised the largest political questions about what government could accomplish. Could an activist state help to redress the problem of racial inequality in American cities? To what extent could government action create greater economic equality gen-erally? Even though the percentage of Americans living in poverty did in fact fall during the War on Poverty years, conservative intellectuals still pointed to the problems of cities as evidence of the futility of using the state to change social arrangements. Edward Banfield's *The Unheav-enly City*, published in 1970 and reissued in 1974, made the case that cities were in fact growing better in many ways and that social policy aimed at helping the poor—such as welfare—only made conditions worse. If there was any crisis at all, Banfield argued, it was one brought about by rising expectations that led activists to constantly escalate their demands on local governments beyond what any city could be expected to sustain. Moreover, the constantly increasing demands for more public resources threatened the viability of democracy itself. University of Virginia economist James Buchanan argued that the fatal flaw of democratic government was that in order to get reelected, politicians had to promise ever more benefits to the electorate, no matter whether or not the resources existed to cover these benefits.[54]

Among these various voices, no one was more prominent in the effort to reframe the story of New York as a parable of liberal failure than former Treasury Secretary William Simon, who had played such a central role under Ford in seeking to deny the city federal aid. After Ford lost the presidency, Simon departed Washington and moved back to Wall Street. He also became the president of the John M. Olin Foundation, a once-somnolent family wealth trust that became politically active in the 1970s as Olin—Simon's neighbor in the Hamptons—grew anxious about America's direction. "My greatest ambition," Olin told the New York Times, "is to see free enterprise reestablished in this country. Business and the public must be re-awakened to the creeping stranglehold socialism has gained here since World War II."[55]

Soon, Simon was spending much of his time stumping around the country, speaking to corporate audiences and urging business leaders to do more to promote free market ideas. He became known as the "Billy Graham for capitalism."[56] The foundation helped start a law and economics program at the University of Miami, economic centers at the University of Chicago and Cornell, and a program at UCLA. It also assisted in underwriting Milton Friedman's famous public television program, Free to Choose.[57]

While at the Olin Foundation, Simon finished writing a book outlining what he saw as the dangers of liberalism and unrestrained government spending, drawing on his experiences in Washington—especially the showdown with New York. He had started the project while still Secretary of the Treasury, corresponding about his ideas with friends in the business world and with economists such as Friedman. Friedman had responded with enthusiasm to Simon's initial description of the project, emphasizing that he should stress that "the issues involved are by no means narrowly economic" but rather concerned basic principles of social stability. However benign the intent of government spending, Friedman wrote, it would only hurt low-income people, reduce social cohesion, and threaten the basis of free government.[58] A friend of Simon's who worked at investment bank Jennison Associates, meanwhile, sketched out for him a nightmare scenario of growing government bureaucracies, in which state and pension funds were forced to bail out one bankrupt city after the next: "I think New York may be the pivotal issue, the catalyst which points public opinion in one direction or the other."[59]

Simon worked closely with a ghostwriter named Edith Efron, who had been (along with Alan Greenspan) among Ayn Rand's closest acolytes until Rand became irritated with her and expelled her from the Objectivist movement, the political and philosophical circle devoted to Rand's ideas.[60] Efron interviewed Simon throughout the winter and spring of 1976 and used that material to create a rough draft of a manuscript for Simon to review. Early responses from friends and colleagues were positive: Friedman proclaimed the work "magnificent,"[61] and fellow free-market Nobelist Friedrich von Hayek agreed to pen a short preface. The book was published in 1978, under the title *A Time for Truth*.

A Time for Truth was a jeremiad, warning against an impending economic and political apocalypse. Much of the book was a call for businessmen to take a far more activist role in political life, following the model of Olin and his foundation. But perhaps its most memorable chapter was on New York, for *A Time for Truth* did more than any other source to popularize the conservative interpretation of what had happened to the city. Simon argued that New York had "carried to its fullest expression" the "philosophy that has ruled our nation for forty years." The city's collapse, therefore, marked a "terrifying dress rehearsal of the fate that lies ahead for this country if it continues to be guided by the same philosophy of government."[62]

In the book, Simon fiercely defended his position during the crisis, which he was well aware had been pilloried in the press as sadistic. The unions, the banks, and the city government had all conspired to make it appear that the financial collapse of the city would be a disaster, Simon insisted, but he still believed that this had been "hysteria" and "political blackmail"—that the city would have been able to ride out a bankruptcy without the dire consequences predicted.[63] The city's unions were to blame for bleeding New York's finances with their outrageous salaries and benefits. The city's spending had gone to benefit them, not the poor. The city's taxes had forced the "productive population" out of New York. "Liberal politics, endlessly glorifying its own 'humanism,' has, in fact, been annihilating the very conditions for human survival," he wrote.[64] The city's response to the fiscal crisis had been "rage, rage, rage— and an almost oceanic self-pity."[65]

For Simon, the problems of New York City were not isolated; on the contrary, the city was "America in microcosm." The "philosophy, the illusions, the pretensions, and the rationalizations which guide New York City are those which guide the entire country." Now the task of conservative political leadership was to rally people against the pretensions of liberalism. "If they do not repudiate the ideas that justify this system of government, if they continue to be Mau-Maued by a small political and communications elite with 'moral elephantiasis,'" then New York's present would inevitably become America's future.[66]

To Simon's surprise, *A Time for Truth* became a best seller. By the end of 1978 it had gone through eight printings and sold 200,000 copies.[67] Some Republicans tried to start a "Draft Simon" movement for the 1980 election, writing down his name as a candidate in the New Hampshire primary.[68] But Simon's arguments were most influential in New York itself, where they built on years of criticism of the local welfare state. In 1978, British conservative Antony Fisher worked with Wall Street lawyer (and future CIA director) William Casey and supply-side activist and politician Jeffrey Bell to start the International Center for Economic Policy Studies. This organization would later become the think tank known as the Manhattan Institute for Policy Research, which promoted a "new urban paradigm" that focused on the free market rather than government to solve social problems. In place of the Great Society there would be welfare reform, privatization of city government, stringent fiscal policy, establishment of charter schools, opposition to civil servant unions (especially teachers' unions), and the introduction of broken-windows policing strategies (which focused on arresting people for minor infractions, on the theory that willingness to commit petty crimes anticipated more serious infractions of the law).[69] In the 1980s, the Manhattan Institute would become known as the home of Charles Murray, the author of the anti-welfare broadside *Losing Ground* and later the coauthor of *The Bell Curve*, which argued that the real explanation for racial inequality was that blacks had lower IQs than whites. Roger Starr, the Beame housing administrator who had come up with the idea of "planned shrinkage," also joined the group.

Purporting to cut through the sentimental romanticism and naïve do-goodism of the liberal elite, these conservative thinkers followed Simon in proposing a different agenda for cities. Under it, city governments would no longer aim to aid the poor. They would, instead, focus on "job retention and job creation"—aiding businessmen and corporations in return for their investment in the city.[70] The rising conservative movement joined the city's newly right-leaning liberal establishment in repudiating the old social welfare politics of the city—but whereas the liberals presented a sad resignation about limited resources, the conservatives brought a punitive savagery to their recommendations. In the emerging new consensus view, it was necessary to cut loose the people in the city's burned-out neighborhoods—and should those people refuse to go quietly, they should be met with the harshest punishment available. The politics of fiscal crisis and retrenchment went hand-in-hand with a turn toward jails and prisons as the ultimate response to the problems of urban poverty.[71]

After the blackout, New York politicians pleaded with the federal government to name the city a disaster zone, which would have enabled it to get more federal assistance more quickly. "We can ill afford to lose these individuals from Bronx County, many of whom have lost their life savings due to larceny, arson and vandalism without making an effort to try and assist them to get back on their feet," wrote one assistant district attorney in a telegram to President Carter, warning that without government help local businesspeople would be unable to reopen their stores and might be forced to move out of the Bronx altogether.[72] Congressman Fred Richmond urged Carter and Vice President Walter Mondale to visit the city and see for themselves how things stood; "there is a strong probability that another riot may occur."[73] But the president was reluctant to grant the city the assistance it sought, fearing that this would be interpreted as somehow rewarding the looters.

Some people in Carter's circles expressed concern that this was a mistake. Advisers felt that a failure to respond sympathetically could be politically damaging, that the president would be painted as an "uncaring manager" whose Southern background meant that he didn't "care about cities generally or New York particularly."[74] Others pointed out that extending disaster relief assistance to the city was within the law, and suggested that perhaps the disaster declaration could be limited "solely to the damages following the power shortage, excluding such a declaration for the damages resulting from the subsequent looting."[75] But in an echo of the Ford administration in 1975, Carter refused to deem the city a "disaster area," which would have opened up a variety of different forms of direct federal aid. (Carter did authorize roughly $11 million in grants and loans to help with cleanup and repairs.) The administrator of the Federal Disaster Assistance Administration sent a letter to Governor Carey reminding him that "local and state governments have the primary responsibility for disaster relief."[76]

Implicit in the denial of the "disaster area" status was the idea that New Yorkers had brought their suffering on themselves—this time through their criminal activities. The denial of aid seemed again a way to paint the city as outside the mainstream of America, a space of entitlement and unlawfulness unworthy of federal assistance. "Is New York City, after all, a failed ultra-urban experiment in which people eventually crack, social order eventually collapses, and reason ultimately yields to despair?" read an editorial in the *New York Times* in early August 1977, in the aftermath of yet another Son of Sam murder. The paper counseled against "such despair," and expressed hope that the public "passions" would soon subside. But its description of "a shared sense of outrage and of impotence" captured the city's mood all too well.[77]

18. The Final Storm

The mayoral election campaign of 1977 began with the *Daily News* publishing an editorial that urged the incumbent to withdraw from the race: "We Need a Great Mayor—Beame Should Not Run."[1]

All of the city's ambitious politicians seized the moment to challenge Beame. The candidates in the Democratic primary included Manhattan's first black borough president, Percy Sutton; the pugnacious Congressman Ed Koch; the intellectual Secretary of New York State, Mario Cuomo; and the New Left feminist former Congresswoman Bella Abzug. Yet Beame surprised them all, performing remarkably well in the polls throughout the first half of election season. Even the July blackout, a disaster for the city, proved something of a coup for Beame. The mayor stayed up all night in crisis mode, holding press conferences, meeting with firefighters, scribbling countless notes and memos, and driving through the city's broken neighborhoods to survey the damage.

The blackout helped Beame present himself as a confident leader in the city's new war on lawlessness and crime. The mayor lambasted looters for having "mutilated our communities and assaulted our City," and upbraided judges who let looting suspects out of jail: no one, he declared, should accept "slapping on wrists" when "slapping in irons" was demanded. He declared that all methods were justified in the "never-ending war" against crime.[2] Only a few weeks after the blackout, a Puerto Rican nationalist organization set off two bombs at midtown office buildings. One person was killed, two seriously injured. Beame was on the scene immediately, speaking to reporters on the sidewalk strewn with glass shards, and proclaiming that a reintroduction of the death penalty (something over which New York City's mayor, of course, had no power) would provide a "deterrent to terrorism" in the future.[3]

As late as the end of August, Beame held strong in the polls, tied with Abzug at 17 percent of the vote. But the mayor could only escape the fiscal crisis for so long. The previous year, the Securities and Exchange Commission had opened an investigation into the events of 1975 to establish how the city got into such extreme difficulty. The SEC had conducted interviews with bankers and politicians, bringing David Rockefeller and others in for hours of deposition, but no report had yet been issued. In late spring 1977, though, Joel Harnett, one of Beame's more marginal challengers, filed a lawsuit demanding that the SEC release the results of its investigation into the fiscal crisis, arguing that it contained information of vital importance for the mayoral race.[4] President of the business-oriented City Club and a marketing executive at *Look* magazine who specialized in developing ways for advertisers to target wealthier readers, Harnett was certain the report would support his view that New York's public sector had atrophied into an overgrown bureaucracy, controlled by unions and ruthlessly pursuing its own interests, levying taxes so high that they drove the affluent to depart.[5]

The SEC had seemed in no rush to complete its work, but once Harnett filed his suit, the Washington office of the agency took an interest. The chairman of the agency summoned Stanley Sporkin, the head of enforcement at the national SEC, and told him that the New York office was moving far too slowly. Sporkin was charged with getting a report completed in thirty days, collating hundreds of thousands of pages of testimony and documents into a coherent document. He was dispatched to New York City with a team of staff members, where they holed up in the Plaza Hotel, ordered to work until they were done.[6]

As it happened, the report was completed exactly two weeks before the Democratic primary. High drama surrounded its release at the end of August. For twenty-four hours prior to its official distribution, journalists were not permitted to be unattended in the SEC headquarters, with staffers even accompanying them to the bathrooms. Before the report was publicly available, Beame accused one of its authors (who had recently resigned from a law firm that supported Cuomo) of being connected to the Cuomo mayoral campaign. This drew an angry response from the SEC chairman, who wrote a letter admonishing Beame for the "unfounded attack" on the commission's integrity.[7] Beame also attempted to blunt the report's impact by preemptively releasing all of his own testimony to the SEC, even though he didn't always come off well: at one point, for instance, he had told the financial investigators that "the Mayor has got enough things to do besides sitting down with a pencil and estimating revenues for the city."[8]

Once the report was out, it was clear why Beame was so defensive. Over 800 pages long, based on 12,000 pages of sworn testimony and 250,000 subpoenaed documents, the report was a lawyerly dissection of the city's acts leading up to the crisis. Beame and Goldin, the SEC investigators wrote, had engaged in "deceptive practices masking the city's true and disastrous financial condition," and had "misled" investors.[9] Beame was outraged. He railed against the commission, condemning the report as a "shameless, vicious political document" that was no more than a "hatchet job." He had not willfully misled anybody, he insisted.[10] The perilous condition of the city had not been clear at the outset of the crisis. Instead, it had worsened in the absence of support from the state, the banks, and Washington. Beame's crime had simply been that he was certain New York would make it through the maelstrom. "Can you imagine, I am being accused of expressing confidence in my city."[11]

The other candidates seized on the report. Governor Carey, who was backing Cuomo, told an audience of Jewish community leaders that he had tried to find "integrity" in Beame but that there was none.[12] Abzug accused Beame of "coverup, collusion and conspiracy," promising that should she become mayor she would bring transparency back to the office.[13] Koch had been criticizing Beame's spending throughout the race, but he piled on even more after the report came out. "The City of New York cannot be a W.P.A.," he proclaimed in one of the mayoral debates.[14]

The report finished Beame. It now seemed possible that, even if he should manage to win reelection, he would be embroiled in legal challenges over the next four years. (Although there was no plan to prosecute the mayor and comptroller for defrauding the investors who had purchased city debt, the very existence of the SEC report seemed like an indictment.) "Whether or not he is guilty of all the alleged wrongdoing, he will be fully occupied with his defense against civil class actions for damages and administrative and possibly criminal investigations," one angry New Yorker wrote to the *Times*.[15] "The Mayor should withdraw his candidacy for another term." In the final mayoral debate, Beame himself seemed to want to get off the stage as soon as possible: "Oh, let's not have final statements. Let's just wind it up."[16]

Primary day brought no last-minute redemption for the exhausted mayor. He came in third, behind Koch and Cuomo. In postelection surveys about what issues mattered most, the fiscal crisis ranked number one, higher even than crime. Beame waited until almost 2 a.m. on primary night to concede. Before a crowd of supporters, his wife, Mary, on one side and his son Bernard, a close adviser, on the other, he bade farewell to the city, saying that he had given all he could: "I've not let this city down."[17] Normally so business-like in public, so buttoned-down and detail-oriented, in defeat the seventy-one-year-old Beame found himself on the edge of tears. At one point he had to stop speaking. Mary hugged and kissed him, giving him the strength to finish.[18]

While Koch and Cuomo slugged it out in a nasty primary runoff, Beame started looking for a new place to live. His old friend and public relations adviser Howard Rubenstein wrote a letter of recommendation for the co-op board: "He would make a superb neighbor."[19] After the mayoralty, Beame took up a new career as, of all things, an investment adviser.[20] Working in finance and living in a co-op, Beame found himself in his old age a resident of an entirely different city than the one he'd grown up in.

———

Mayor Beame's departure did not mean the end of the city's fiscal problems. As Mayor Koch took office, Felix Rohatyn was worried—even more so than usual.

As 1978 began, New York was still shut out of the credit markets, unable to borrow money. The impact of the crisis was visible everywhere. The city's physical plant was crumbling because of delays in investment in public infrastructure—there was no money to fix subways, school buildings, or roads, because capital funds were still being diverted to pay for operating expenses. What was more, the federal loan program that Ford had authorized was coming to an end in June 1978, while the city employee pension system was running up against a legal limit to the amount it could invest in city securities. Without new federal aid it seemed likely that New York would again face default. In January 1978, Rohatyn wrote a confidential memorandum to the directors of the Municipal Assistance Corporation, warning them to fasten their seat belts: "We are about to enter a storm fully as dangerous and unpredictable as any we weathered in 1975."[21]

While there were good reasons for Rohatyn's concern, the political situation had changed significantly since 1975, in ways that made it impossible for the fiscal crisis to be repeated in the same dramatic way. New political leaders occupied Gracie Mansion and the White House, and a completely new dynamic operated in both.

For one thing, Koch was determined to reject the welfare state politics of earlier years. Even before becoming mayor he had embraced a scrappy, populist persona, one that was defined against the image of an elitist "limousine liberal." During the Lindsay years Koch was severely critical of the "richies," as he called them, the "exotic liberals" who would "impose standards on others that they don't want for themselves" in the interests of "some philosophical concept."[22] This was an obvious allusion to the city's racial politics. Koch opposed school busing, and gave his vocal support to the homeowners of Forest Hills, Queens, who revolted against the Lindsay administration's plans to place public housing in their neighborhood. Despite the ugly tone of the protests—

the lower-middle-class Jewish residents of Forest Hills threw rocks and flaming torches at construction trailers, raging against the "welfare recipients" who they feared were sure to move in and destroy their community—Koch insisted there was no racist politics here, simply a "rational fear of increased crime and loss of property values."[23]

During the 1977 campaign, Koch played up this image of himself as a man willing to flout liberal orthodoxy. He promised to take on the unions, the people who administered War on Poverty programs (whom he accused of profiting from their work, calling them "poverty pimps"), and the unruly protesters in order to do what the city needed done.[24] He made his support for the death penalty the centerpiece of his campaign in the outer boroughs, showing up at subway stations to greet riders: "I'm for capital punishment. Are you?"[25]

In keeping with this everyman image, Koch took the bus to his own mayoral inauguration. The speech he delivered there laid out an agenda for a new urban policy. He criticized the city for making "mistakes of the heart"—running antipoverty programs that were ineffectual and expensive at best, fraudulent and corrupt at worst. "Experience has shown that Utopia cannot be conjured up with a magic formula of more services, more agencies, more plans and more programs." Instead of looking to the government for more aid and assistance, he said, New Yorkers should give more of themselves to their city. They should seek their own solutions, find their own ways to aid the metropolis: "Government cannot do what the people will not do." At the end of his address, Koch described New York as the new frontier, a haven for entrepreneurs, a place where the self-reliance and ingenuity that had once been the province of the West could once more become core values. Issuing an invitation to people who wanted to carve out their own rugged futures, Koch proclaimed, "Come East and grow up with the new pioneers, grow up with the new City of New York."[26]

In Washington, Carter, like Koch, represented a new movement within the Democratic Party—one that was more skeptical of government power, less connected to organized labor, and less committed to civil rights. It was a style of politics predicated on projecting support for business and for reinventing (and shrinking) the role of the public sector. Like many within the party as it sought to combat a resurgent conservatism, Carter defined himself as a Democrat who represented a break from the past.[27] "Government cannot solve our problems," he said in his 1978 State of the Union address. "It cannot set our goals. It cannot define our vision. Government cannot eliminate poverty or provide a bountiful economy or reduce inflation or save our cities or cure illiteracy or provide energy. And government cannot mandate goodness."[28]

It hadn't always been that way. On the campaign trail, Carter had promised an ambitious new urban agenda: money for states to let them provide more aid to cities, counter-cyclical spending to help cities get through recessions, an expansion of the Comprehensive Employment and Training Act that New York had used so well. In October 1977, in the middle of the mayoral race, the president had visited rubble-strewn Charlotte Street in the South Bronx, where he walked the burned-out blocks and met with community activists as well as businesspeople and the Bronx borough president.[29] The images of the president touring the post-blackout Bronx were aired on television stations across the country. They raised hopes within the borough, too. As Cardinal Cooke wrote to the president after his visit, "Considering the fiscal plight of New York City and New York State, there does not appear to be any [source of] stimulus other than the Federal Government which can really turn the South Bronx around and make it a living space worthy of the God-given dignity and respect of its struggling people."[30]

But those hopes were quickly dashed. The president reacted sharply against the suggestion that the federal government was the only entity with the capacity to help the troubled borough. Instead, he emphasized how important it was to draw on the private sector to solve the Bronx's problems.[31]

This was the climate in which Koch went to Washington to ask for a renewal of federal aid. The challenge was formidable: any request would have to go through the Senate Banking Committee, chaired by Senator William Proxmire, a Wisconsin Democrat who had built his career on opposing excessive government largesse. Proxmire had cast his vote for the federal loan program in 1975 but had promised he would do so only once. He was not pleased to see the city back asking for more. After holding a few days of testimony on the New York situation in late 1977, he wrote a letter to President Carter stating that he saw no reason why New York City should receive another bolus of federal support: "There are resources available to New York City and New York State which should be sufficient to maintain solvency regardless of what the Federal Government does." Proxmire argued that New York State, the state workers' pension funds, and the commercial banks could and should all play a greater role in financing the city; extending the federal loan program would be "a continuing crutch for a patient that should be made to walk again."[32]

But Koch's approach managed to neutralize the objection. When Beame had gone to Washington in 1975, he had asked for aid in part to protect the city's social programs. Koch had no such intentions. For him the fiscal crunch was a chance to demonstrate his toughness. Called to testify before Congress, Koch proudly enumerated the cuts the city had made: reducing its workforce by 20 percent, lowering the welfare rolls by several hundred thousand, closing nineteen fire companies, defunding seventy-seven day care centers, raising transit fares by more than 40 percent—and, of course, imposing tuition at CUNY.[33] These moves had not yet been sufficient to balance the budget, but Koch described his plans to do so as quickly as possible, including such measures as tighter controls over city workers to boost their productivity. "What happens when I do these things?" he asked the committee. "There are picket lines around City Hall and in front of Gracie Mansion, but those things—the measures that I take—won't be deterred simply because there are people who are upset. There is a change going on because the change is intended to use our city dollars, our state dollars and our federal dollars better than ever before and to remove the incompetence."[34] To get the city where it needed to be, Koch said, he would need just one more round of federal support.

Koch's willingness to present himself as a man resistant to public and democratic pressure helped him to win over Proxmire and the rest of the Senate committee. Here was someone with the fortitude to make the needed cuts, to drive the tough bargains. By the end of the negotiations, even Proxmire was arguing in favor of federal support for the city. "It is cruel that it has to come out of the hide of the workers, but that's the way it is," he told the mayor.[35]

Carter, though he had by then abandoned the most ambitious aspects of his urban program, was determined not to allow the fiscal crisis to recur in New York.[36] ("As you know, I have previously stated that bankruptcy is not a viable option for the City of New York," he wrote to Proxmire.)[37] To deal with the looming problem without giving more federal loans to the city, Carter's Treasury Department proposed that Washington raise the limit on how much city pension funds could invest in city debt and provide New York with long-term loan guarantees. In other words, the federal government would supply backup collateral to secure any loans that the city took out from other sources. These guarantees would allow the city workers' pension funds to safely expand the total amount they were loaning the city and offer an incentive for the state workers' pension funds to join in as well.[38]

The Carter administration lobbied hard for the loan guarantees, keeping close track of Congressional support and even picking particular undecided members of Congress for the president to contact personally.[39] Throughout, Carter aides were deeply aware of the city's political value. "Your involvement will be heavily publicized in New York and will heighten your personal identification with an effort which will probably be victorious and can be a great political victory for the Administration in New York," two advisers wrote the president.[40] In the end, both the House and Senate voted in favor of extending the loan guarantees to the city, passing the necessary aid legislation by margins far larger than in 1975.

Carter treated the passage of the loan guarantee bill as a personal victory. In August, with great fanfare, the president came to City Hall for a signing ceremony. (The visit was actually Vice President Mondale's idea: as one aide put it, Mondale believed "it could have a dramatic effect if the signing ceremony were in New York City itself, and could do a great deal to cement our relations with all kinds of people up there.")[41] Five thousand people showed up in the cramped downtown park on a hazy August afternoon to see Carter affix his signature to the legislation, using a mahogany desk that had belonged to George Washington back when New York was the capital of the United States.[42] In preparation for the gala occasion, Koch had ordered a thorough cleaning of City Hall, sprucing up the chandeliers and soaping down walls grubby with years of neglect. The Association for a Better New York paid for a catered lunch.[43]

The loan guarantee, Carter said in his remarks, was a crucial step in New York's climb back toward "solvency and independence." It was "not a handout" nor a "band-aid," but a way of buying the city time and space to work out its problems. Carter praised the "tough discipline" of Mayor Koch and the cuts that the city had already made: there were 60,000 fewer people on its payroll, and the budget deficit had shrunk by over a billion dollars. These reductions had only been possible, he said, because of a spirit of common sacrifice. "Groups that are usually thought of as natural enemies, or competitors, have worked together toward a common goal: Labor and business, bankers and bureaucrats, Democrats and Republicans, politicians and ordinary citizens, all have joined together to take care of long-neglected problems." And this kind of common purpose was exactly what the nation as a whole needed in order to grapple with other problems, such as oil shortages and inflation. New York might even provide a model for the nation when it came to reforming and restraining an out-of-control bureaucracy. "We can take control of the problem of inefficiency, and fat, and waste, and poor management in Government—as New York City has already begun to do."[44]

Despite the president's portrayal of a unified city, not everyone at City Hall that day was there to celebrate. A small group of demonstrators—a hundred or so—were also in attendance. The newspapers reported that they were chanting "something" about human rights, but the festivities easily drowned them out.

The loan guarantees did not make New York's fiscal problems suddenly vanish. "New York City continues its slide into bankruptcy," Senator Daniel Patrick Moynihan wrote to the president in October 1978. Despite all the budget cuts, Moynihan warned, the city still had "no prospect" of balancing its budget—"at least not in this generation"—without even more federal aid.[45] Mayor Koch promised to redouble his efforts but also complained that some federal spending the city had been counting on had failed to materialize. "There is no doubt in my mind nor in the minds of knowledgeable observers" that the city lacked the resources to cover its budget gaps alone, Koch wrote to Carter. "It remains for the Federal government to fulfill the commitments that we feel were made and which are evident in the record."[46]

But by this time Carter was reluctant to provide the city with further assistance. He wanted to see even deeper budget cuts—urging Koch to make more "structural changes" in the city's expenses, especially at the hospitals and at CUNY—and more help from New York State.[47] His aides complained that New York officials were naively assuming that the federal government had no choice but to provide still more help. After Koch publicly criticized Carter for revising his urban policy and not delivering spending he had promised, someone in the administration leaked an internal memo warning that there would once again be "serious discussion" of bankruptcy should New York not take greater strides toward eliminating its $1 billion budget gap. The administration would be taking a new "get tough" policy toward the city, aides told reporters.[48] Carter's adviser Orin Kramer reported to Carter's chief of domestic policy: "The Mayor now has a clearer sense of the potential costs of using the president as a whipping boy."[49]

Still, these lingering tensions between the city and Washington never threatened the Carter administration's commitment to New York, and the city gradually returned to fiscal normalcy. It also worked on changing its image in the public mind. The New York State Department of Commerce hired designer Milton Glaser to come up with a new city logo, resulting in the famous "I ♥ NY." The New York Board of Trade began "Project Appleseed," in which traveling executives would give symbolic gifts—a blade of grass from Central Park, a golden thread from the curtain at Radio City Music Hall, a packet of New York apple seeds—to congressmen across the nation to thank them for voting in favor of aid to New York.[50] And in January 1979, the city reentered the credit markets, selling short-term notes for the first time since March 1975 (it was still not able to sell its bonds). The sale was a success. "We had more orders than we could handle," said a banker from Merrill Lynch, the financial institution in charge of the underwriting consortium.[51] In other ways, too, the era of the fiscal crisis seemed to be ending. In August 1979, almost exactly two years after its initial report, the SEC issued a statement that the facts of the case did not support criminal charges or civil lawsuits against Beame, Goldin, or the city's top bankers.[52]

In fact, New York seemed to be becoming a model for other cities in financial trouble. Yonkers, the fourth-largest metropolis in New York State, nearly defaulted on its debts shortly after New York, but avoided doing so thanks to a stringent program of budget cuts that involved laying off 300 teachers (almost a third of the city's teaching force), under the strict observation of its own financial control board.[53] Similarly, when Cleveland defaulted on $15 million in debt in December 1978, the first major U.S. city to do so since the 1930s, Ohio state officials sought to establish a financial control board for the city, which would obtain direct power over the Cleveland budget. "We're looking at the New York City example," one aide to the Ohio governor told the press.[54] Cleveland also mirrored New York's aggressive effort to win outside investment. Dennis Kucinich, Cleveland's young, populist mayor, who had refused to privatize a city-owned electrical plant in order to repay debts owned by a few local banks, was unseated in the next election by George Voinovich, a Republican backed by business leaders. "I like fat cats," Voinovich told the *New York Times*. "I want as many in Cleveland as I can get."[55]

New York even seemed to become a model for the private sector. When the Chrysler Corporation seemed on the edge of bankruptcy in 1979 and appealed to the federal government for aid, the response of the Carter administration evoked what had happened in New York. Carter proposed to extend loan guarantees to Chrysler—but only if the auto giant agreed to "substantive concessions from all those who have an interest in Chrysler's future," as Treasury Secretary G. William Miller said.[56] In the congressional debate over aiding Chrysler, legislators repeatedly referenced New York City's loan guarantees. Reporters and politicians alike compared New York's severe treatment of public employees with the concessions that the United Auto Workers might be persuaded to adopt in return for federal aid.[57] Thirty-five thousand Chrysler workers (out of 140,000) were laid off, while another 40,000 were put on part-time schedules.[58] The federal government eventually created a "Chrysler Loan Guarantee Review Board" to oversee the company's budgets, echoing the title of the EFCB in New York.[59]

But while New York appeared to be heading back to fiscal health, the social chaos left behind by the crisis and the cuts endured. The poverty rate in the Bronx rose from 19.5 percent in 1970 to 27.6 percent in 1980; in Brooklyn, it climbed from 17.6 to 24 percent. The city was becoming poorer at the same time as services for the poor were withdrawn.[60] For the first time since the Great Depression, the number of people living on the streets of the city—driven there by the closure of mental hospitals and the shortage of affordable housing—was starting to climb. The sight of beggars on the subways and street corners, once rare, became familiar.[61]

The streets of New York were dirtier than ever, too, perhaps because the number of people employed in the city's street-sweeping teams had fallen to a hundred-year low, dropping from 2,700 people in 1975 to just 500 in 1980. Crime on the subways was climbing rapidly: the number of felonies jumped by 70 percent between 1979 and 1980, even as the number of transit police fell dramatically. (In one case, six patrolmen were left to cover 61 stations.) The cutbacks in the police department were so severe that people started to organize their own quasi-vigilante anticrime groups, such as the red-capped, red-jacketed Guardian Angels. They rode the subways to make up for the missing transit cops, promising protection where the police had fallen down on the most basic of jobs.[62]

The city was growing more dangerous in other ways as well. Doctors had believed tuberculosis to be on the way to complete eradication in New York, but in the 1980s it began to flourish in central Harlem and other poor neighborhoods, the very neighborhoods that had lost the kinds of public health clinics that might have stopped the illness from spreading so fast. The early 1980s also saw a strange new illness—AIDS—sweep through the city, characterized by unexpected diseases that suddenly struck the young and strong: Kaposi's sarcoma, fungal infections, pneumocystis pneumonia.[63] It was particularly prevalent in the gay scene and in the city's poorest neighborhoods. The health commissioner warned that there might not be enough hospital beds to house the growing numbers of the sick.

In 1979, the Community Service Society surveyed residents of Harlem and the South Bronx, asking how their neighborhoods had been affected by service cuts. Half of those polled said they wanted to send their children to day care but could not find a space; almost a quarter of those with children of college age said the cost of higher education would keep them from attending college; 60 percent reported that it was difficult to find a doctor or nurse, and almost as many said fewer police patrolled their neighborhoods than before. About half said it was more difficult to get welfare than it had been a few years earlier, and almost 80 percent said the streets in their neighborhoods were dirty and in disrepair. The poorest people in the survey were also those most likely to feel that the government was not set up to represent "people like me."[64]

This was the frame of mind summed up by the opening lines of "The Message" by Grandmaster Flash and the Furious Five, one of the best-selling rap singles of 1982: "It's like a jungle sometimes / It makes me wonder how I keep from going under." In tense, jagged lyrics, the narrator paints a picture of a post-crisis New York populated by drug dealers, bill collectors, subway pushers, striking transit workers, junkies, roaches, rats, numbers runners, panhandlers, and washed-up party girls turned homeless bag ladies. It is a city in which the illegal economy is far more appealing than staying in school. The local government's only presence is oppressive: the song concludes with police officers arresting the narrator and his friends for no reason as they stand on a street corner (anticipating the "stop-and-frisk" policies of a later generation). It is a New York whose social compact has entirely dissolved.

Initially, the group's leader, Flash, hadn't wanted to make the song at all, worried that crowds angered by the somber, nihilistic plot line would boo the group off the stage.[65] Instead, it became a breakthrough hit—a song for a city coming undone.

The conflict between the brisk, business-oriented city that Koch promised to create and the deepening poverty and despair of those New Yorkers set adrift came to the fore in one of the last major protests of the era: the fight over the future of Sydenham Hospital.

Sydenham was located in the heart of Harlem, in a handsome ten-story building at 124th Street and Manhattan Avenue. In the 1940s it became the first hospital in New York City to completely desegregate its medical staff, giving black doctors a place to practice. Taken over by the city in 1950, it continued to hire black doctors and nurses when few other hospitals in the city would do so. As a result, it helped sustain a black middle class, and it was a place where black leadership was visible to all.

A small facility with 119 beds, Sydenham was very much part of the Harlem community. The overwhelming majority of the people who visited the hospital's emergency room lived in the neighborhood and came there without using an ambulance. Harlem had intense health needs: the neighborhood had been designated a federal "medical disaster area" in 1977. The rate of death in the neighborhood (14.5 per 1,000 people per year) was almost 50 percent higher than that in the city as a whole. Forty-two out of every thousand babies born in Harlem died, compared to nineteen per thousand for the entire city.[66] Tuberculosis rates were more than twice as high as the city average.[67] The neighborhood had few pharmacies and a paucity of doctors. Whether Sydenham Hospital was the solution to these problems was far from clear; by the late 1970s its facilities were out of date, and it accounted for less than 10 percent of all hospital care in Harlem.[68] Still, it commanded an intense loyalty in the neighborhood.

The city had proposed closing Sydenham in 1976, but Beame ultimately backed off the plan—in part because of fears that Harlem Hospital, another public hospital that was affiliated with Columbia University, would get a massive influx of patients beyond what it could handle.[69] Community leaders in Harlem had organized a Save Sydenham Coalition, drawn both by the hospital's historic legacy and by their awareness of the perennial health crises of the neighborhood. While he was running for office, Koch had pledged to keep the hospital open.[70] Once elected, though, Koch said that it was fiscally necessary to close Sydenham, along with East Harlem's Metropolitan Hospital. Again there was intense protest—the NAACP filed a class-action lawsuit, one black official resigned from the Koch administration, and neighborhood organizations lodged many complaints.[71]

Of the two hospitals, Sydenham was far more vulnerable than the larger Metropolitan. It was small; it was running a deficit; its equipment

was outmoded; the city could save more than $9 million per year by
shuttering it. As a *New York Times* editorial put it, "The decrepit facility
should be closed down, beyond doubt."[72] What's more, closing Sydenham
would have symbolic value for Koch, demonstrating that no one—
not protesters, community leaders, or public campaigns—could inter-
fere with the mayor in his pursuit of fiscal rectitude.

Koch's willingness to take up the fight was informed by his success
in the April 1980 transit strike. That month, the transit workers walked
out for the first time since 1966, hoping to win back some of the economic losses they had suffered during the fiscal crisis. It had been years
since they had seen a wage increase, and their salaries had been severely
eroded by inflation. Koch seemed to relish the confrontation. On the
first morning of the strike, when he saw a great line of commuters coming across the Brooklyn Bridge on foot or by bicycle, he could hardly
restrain himself, running down to the bridge to greet them: "Just wanted
to say hello. Just wanted to thank you for helping."[73] Supporting striking workers was no longer a litmus test for liberalism. The fiscal crisis
had made the difference. "The public has become attuned to the belief
that the government doesn't have any money," said Stanley Friedman,
the Bronx borough president. "People know Washington won't give the
Mayor any help if they think he's giving away the store. People are
attuned to cut, cut, cut."[74] After eleven days the strikers returned to
work with a much smaller wage increase than they had sought, their
monetary gains eroded still further since Koch insisted on collecting the
fines levied on public workers for striking.[75]

Perhaps emboldened by these events, in the summer of 1980 Koch
announced that it was time for Sydenham to go. It would no longer be a
hospital. It might—with support from the federal and state governments—
become a drug and alcohol treatment center, but even this was unclear.
On September 16, the hospital stopped admitting new patients, and
police officers locked the door to the emergency room. Surgeries were
continuing and the hospital still had sixty-nine patients in its wards, but
once they recovered or were transferred the hospital would close.

As soon as the news arrived that closure was imminent, protests
formed outside the hospital doors. As the lockdown began, demon-

strators burst into the main corridor and broke open a side door to the emergency room. "We'll stay here forever if that's what it takes," one demonstrator yelled. A small group of protesters took over the offices of the hospital administration, saying they would not leave until there was a commitment to reopen the hospital.[76] Police promptly barricaded the building.[77] Koch said he would not order cops to drag out the protesters, but nor would he allow the rabble-rousers to change his mind. "There are people who believe they can get their way with battering rams," he told the newspapers. "That may have been the case before this administration, but it is no longer the case."[78] Of the street protests, he dismissively said, "Am I supposed to give in to mob rule just because it's a black mob? I'll never give in to unreasonable demands or threats by any group."[79]

Why was there such support for keeping Sydenham open? On one level, there were practical concerns. There was a well-known shortage of doctors in Harlem, and many people in the neighborhood felt they could not get sufficient, respectful attention at other hospitals in the city—places that demanded insurance cards before being willing to offer care. "Harlem Hospital is always crowded, and our only alternative is to go downtown for treatment. But they don't want poor or black people down there in their hospitals," one patient told the *Daily News*. Another one sobbed: "What am I going to do when I get sick, or my little girl, Sherry Ann, where can I take her in the middle of the night when she gets sick?"[80] "My leg is about to come off and I can't get no care," another neighborhood resident told the *Amsterdam News*. A man whose four children had been born at Sydenham said, "We need that hospital. It's right here in the neighborhood."[81] Closing a hospital in the middle of one of the most medically needy neighborhoods in the city seemed to defy logic, aggressively denying the real needs of the community.

At the same time, as with the protests a few years earlier about shuttering Engine 212 in Northside, there was another aspect to the anxiety about the hospital shutdown. For Sydenham to be closed, abandoned, or transformed into a treatment facility for drug addicts suggested a collapse and abandonment of the neighborhood in general. Losing this bastion of black professionalism and responsibility would represent a permanent decline. A columnist for the *Daily News* said the hospital was one of the forces that "keeps the junkies from taking over this neighborhood."[82] On a block filled with empty buildings, Sydenham was the last anchor of a more secure future.[83] As one resident put it, "It seems to me they're closing down Harlem."[84]

The Saturday after the occupation began, police clashed with a group of demonstrators, rushing at them with clubs while some in the crowd threw rocks.[85] The next day, three thousand people came to protest in front of the hospital—many arriving straight from church, marching in their Sunday suits and dresses past police in riot gear.[86] Inside Sydenham, the occupiers remained holed up in the administration offices. The police had cut the phone lines, so they were isolated from the outside world, and they had no food except for what was already in the hospital storerooms. But they peered out periodically to rally the crowds below, and dangled an effigy of Koch from a third-floor window.[87]

A few days later, police officers burst into the hospital offices at 1:30 in the morning, waking up the occupiers and ordering them to vacate the premises immediately. The police commissioner alleged that he had heard rumors about guns, and that some "agitators from the Communist Workers Party" had been seen in the neighborhood, so the eviction was necessary due to fears of violence. The protesters went limp and were carried out of the hospital.[88] They were not arrested, and the next morning they were back to demonstrating outside Sydenham.[89]

Daily rallies continued outside the hospital building throughout the fall months, but they had no impact.[90] The last patient checked out of Sydenham on October 10. The operating rooms went quiet, the wards were deserted, and only a few guards were left behind to watch the silent hallways. The hospital formally closed in late November, when the city transferred its license to the state.[91] Koch, meanwhile, won federal funding to run a health maintenance organization for poor people at Metropolitan Hospital, now spared from closure—although people proved reluctant to join the H.M.O. and give up the freedom of choice they had had through Medicaid.[92]

Sydenham stood vacant for six years. No one stepped forward with funds to reopen the building as a nonprofit hospital, as was once suggested. Nor was it made into a drug treatment center, even as heroin gave way to crack cocaine. Eventually, a nonprofit developer turned the ten-story structure into apartments for the elderly.

Over the next few years the city proceeded to shutter Greenpoint Hospital and Cumberland Hospital, both in Brooklyn. (Woodhull, a more modern public hospital, would open in North Brooklyn in 1982, after years of delay. Koch argued that it more than compensated for the loss of the neighborhood municipal facilities, but community activists disagreed, pointing out the distance of Woodhull from the neighborhoods previously served by Cumberland and Greenpoint and arguing that the smaller hospitals should have continued to operate even at reduced capacity.)[93] The closings of Greenpoint and Cumberland occasioned a few scattered demonstrations, but there were few serious protests. The effort to save Sydenham was the last such outburst of the fiscal crisis era—the final attempt by a community to insist on the protection and maintenance of its public services.

For all the accomplishments of the local, neighborhood-driven resistance to cuts and retrenchment, activists involved in particular struggles around the city had never been able to unify their protests into a single movement, one that could articulate a different direction for the city as a whole. As a CUNY student who had fought against tuition at the school remembered later, "the tragedy wasn't that it started atomized and fragmented, because that's the only way it could start. They hit us so fast it wasn't funny. The tragedy is we never managed to put it all together."[94]

From City Hall, however, the news was all good. In March 1981, only a few months after Sydenham Hospital shut down for good, the bond rating agency Standard & Poor's gave New York's general obligation bonds a BBB rating, deeming the city able to repay its debts "in a timely manner." This marked the first time since 1975 that S&P judged New York's long-term debt worthy of any consideration by investors. The rating agency officials made special mention of Koch's "candor in recognizing problems and proposing solutions." Koch called the rating a "milestone" in the city's recovery; when one of his deputy mayors heard the news, he raised his arms above his head in triumph.[95]

At the end of the month, New York auctioned off $75 million worth of city bonds in the kind of bankers' gathering last seen at the Municipal

Building six years before. The sale went smoothly: in only four hours, the city sold all the bonds to the brokers and bankers who would then market them to the public. Such a success offered hope that other sales would go similarly well, so that the city could work its way up to borrowing $1 billion a year again to repair its crumbling infrastructure. As Goldin put it, the strength of the market was a sign that the "city has come back as far as anybody would have dreamed by this juncture."[96] Making the situation appear still rosier, the city reported in May 1981 that it anticipated a budget surplus of $243 million for the year—its first budget surplus since the 1960s. (To be sure, the city's finances were helped not just by budget cuts but by the state's assumption of many of the costs of running CUNY and the court system, and the promise that the state would take over more of Medicaid.)[97]

New York's ability to borrow money mattered not just for economic reasons—it was also said to be a judgment on the moral and political direction of the city. Donald Regan, Ronald Reagan's treasury secretary, told the audience at a Waldorf-Astoria breakfast meeting of the Association for a Better New York that he was greatly impressed by Koch's management of the city, and that the bond sale spoke "eloquently of New York's progress to date."[98] Robert Gerard, a managing director of the investment banking company Dillon, Read & Co., and former Assistant Secretary of the Treasury under Simon, wrote an op-ed for the *New York Times* praising the self-control and mastery demonstrated by the city government's willingness to push through a massive round of cuts: "No governmental body of any magnitude has ever come close to matching this remarkable level of fiscal discipline."[99] A few years later, as New York was paying back its last federal debts, Senator William Proxmire would trumpet its progress as a model for Congress and the nation as a whole. In a statement titled "New York City—a Lesson in How to Get the Federal Deficit under Control," he extolled the city he'd once castigated. "If New York City, with its long tradition of permissive, easygoing government and its notorious lack of discipline, can embrace austerity and succeed, why can't this Congress?"[100]

Whatever the condition of the city it had left behind, the fiscal crisis was over.

Epilogue

Early in 1982, President Ronald Reagan arrived in New York City to speak with an audience of business leaders gathered at the Waldorf-Astoria Hotel. A year into Reagan's first term, the country had fallen into a deep recession. In his speech to the enthusiastic crowd, though, the president found reason to hope.

Wearing a scarf decorated with an "I ♥ NY" logo, a gift from Mayor Koch, Reagan praised the way that New York had pulled together when it faced bankruptcy in the 1970s.[1] "When New York was in trouble, groups which had quarreled for years joined together for the greater good of saving the city," he insisted. "Labor, business, voluntary associations all pitched in." What had saved the city was "private initiative"—and this, Reagan was sure, would save the nation as a whole. "I think we've made our choice and turned a historic corner. We're not going back to the glory days of big government."[2]

The notion that fiscal responsibility necessitated opposing organized labor and cutting back on services would resonate throughout the early 1980s, both in the United States and internationally. Only five months before his appearance in New York, Reagan had fired more than 11,000 striking federal employees—the nation's air traffic controllers—breaking their labor union. Seven months after Reagan's Waldorf-Astoria speech, the Mexican government defaulted on its debts and was pressed by the International Monetary Fund into a program of austerity, privatization, and structural reform. A few years later, Margaret Thatcher broke a yearlong strike of coal miners in Great Britain, insisting that she did so in order to demonstrate that labor unions could not dictate the public policy of the nation.[3]

In the United States, as Reagan's speech suggested, New York's story would be held up time and again as a cautionary tale of the dangers of Great Society liberalism and the virtues of the free market and private enterprise. Reflecting on the crisis ten years afterward, Felix Rohatyn observed that it had "redefined the political dialogue" in New York City. The crisis had underlined "in the most brutal way possible the limits of any unit of government to create money itself and to promise all things to all citizens without a very solid private sector base." In the future, he said, there would be an understanding that "business has to be supported and not just tolerated."[4]

Rohatyn was right: the nature of political life changed markedly after the crisis. There was no premeditated plan to seize and transform New York's government, nor were the actors who gained power during the crisis simply acting upon an ideology constructed in the abstract. But the scare of the near-bankruptcy brought together the elite groups within the city, and enabled them to act in concert in ways that otherwise would have proved difficult to attain. The framework of "crisis" and the power that debt grants creditors generated a sense of inevitability, making it seem that there were no alternatives. Across the Atlantic, "there is no alternative" would soon become one of Thatcher's favorite slogans.

Upending common wisdom about the proper role of city government, the crisis marked the beginning of a new age. A corporate and financial elite, along with technocratic politicians responsive to that group, gained increasing control over New York's politics. They could be counted on to prioritize the interests of business and the wealthy; indeed, they often regarded that as the only way to help the city. This new perspective closed off an older vision of New York, shutting down debate over whether city government should seek to guarantee a set of social rights for all. New York City still has not transcended this constriction of its politics. Neither has the nation as a whole.

Forty years after the fiscal crisis, New York appears in many ways radically different from its 1970s self. The crime rate has fallen, as it has throughout the nation. Once-decrepit Bryant Park now hosts corporate-sponsored ice skating in the winter and classic films on the lawn in the summer. The junkies who used to linger in the infamous "Needle Park" at the corner of 72nd Street and Broadway have vanished, the square itself turned into a pleasant plaza. The downtown waterfronts that once ended in rotting wooden piers have become a network of lawns, water parks for kids, smooth paths for joggers and bikers, and plazas for sunbathing that stretch out into the Hudson. The subways have been cleaned of graffiti, gleaming instead with advertisements that stretch the length of entire cars. The scrubby East Village apartments and SoHo lofts that formerly housed artists and no-wave bands now rent to boutique chains. The abandoned piles of brick on the Lower East Side have morphed into charming pieds-à-terre. The neighborhoods that burned forty years ago are filled with hot properties. Luxury condos boasting indoor pools, screening rooms, children's playrooms, and a perfectly packaged Brooklyn experience have sprouted on the Williamsburg waterfront, only blocks from where the People's Firehouse once stood.

But the contemporary wealth of the city exists alongside staggering poverty. Twenty-one percent of New Yorkers—about 1.7 million people— lived below the poverty line in 2013. The average household in the top 5 percent earned eighty-eight times as much as a household in the poorest 20 percent.[5] The fabric of everyday life in the city is shot through with that reality. The schools are more racially segregated now than they have been in a generation; parents in wealthy neighborhoods raise hundreds of thousands of dollars for basic classroom supplies and enrichment classes that the Board of Education no longer provides, but only for their own children in their own schools. The pavement is cracked and the equipment broken at many parks in poor neighborhoods; libraries constantly scramble for the funding they need. The working-class and poor people who most vigorously fought the changes of the fiscal crisis era were right about what these transformations would mean for them.

Meanwhile, as New York has been transformed into the model of postindustrial urban triumph, the 1970s have become the object of acute nostalgia. The recent successes of Patti Smith's memoir *Just Kids*, focusing on her relationship with photographer Robert Mapplethorpe in a broken-down city, and of Garth Risk Hallberg's novel *City on Fire* suggest an idealization of New York at the moment of collapse. They paint an image of 1970s New York as more authentic and free than the contemporary city, a place more accessible to everyone—especially artists—than the wealth-bound metropolis of today. The seventies marked the moment before the rise of neoliberal New York, the emergence of Donald Trump, the stock market's climb—a time when New York (and America) still felt open, when one could dream of a different future in a way that no longer seems possible.

Such evocations of a gritty and exciting New York are often accompanied by embarrassed disavowals, by a sense that the 1970s city was a violent wasteland with nothing worth recovering or going back to, best left behind and remembered only as a vivid curiosity. In law-and-order rhetoric, 1970s New York continues to figure as a bogeyman: "Do we want to go back to the bad old days?"

But recalling what the political stakes of the fiscal crisis era really were can make us reevaluate both the nostalgia and the sense of superiority. The social and political tumult of the city back then was not only a reaction to bankruptcy, disinvestment, chaos, and general disorder. Those passions also grew out of a fierce and intense contest over the future of the city, a mobilization of its poor and working classes that was met by a sharp rebuke from the political and economic elites.

What is more, thinking of the seventies solely in terms of cultural nostalgia or high levels of crime can make us overlook how many of the policies that were dismantled during the fiscal crisis seem highly relevant to the social problems of the city even now. From rent regulation to tuition-free universities, from local health clinics to social services in public schools, from expanded library hours to free museum admissions and inexpensive mass transit, those policies and institutions embody the aspiration for a more egalitarian New York. By supporting a greater level of economic equality, they once helped create a more open city.

The fiscal crisis was not only a moment of transformation for the city. It was also personally transformative for many of those who played a role in responding to it—the activists who protested the cuts, the politicians who tried to lead New York through the turmoil, the people who found themselves suddenly thrust into positions of unexpected prominence at newly created extra-electoral agencies. For many of these participants, the crisis marked a high point of their lives—a time when it seemed as though what they did really mattered, when every action was charged with meaning and where their decisions could turn the city in one direction or another. They recall it with a fondness and enthusiasm that might appear surprising from the outside.

For the most part, the younger generation of behind-the-scenes consultants, advisers, and policy makers who rose during the fiscal crisis prospered in the new New York. Stephen Berger, the uncompromising thirty-five-year-old executive director of the EFCB, headed the Port Authority from 1985 to 1990 before becoming cofounder and principal of a private equity fund. He still participates in public life, recently chairing a New York State commission that recommended—despite great community protest—the closure of Long Island College Hospital and other hospitals in Brooklyn. Steve Clifford, the hippie of the comptroller's office whose memos helped stir awareness of the city's precarious fiscal position, moved to Seattle, where he had an extraordinarily successful business career as president and CEO of a TV and radio broadcasting company. He continues to comment on politics, his wit as sardonic as ever, writing a semiregular column for the *Huffington Post*.

The comptroller himself, Harrison J. Goldin, managed to survive the political fallout of the fiscal crisis. He continued on as comptroller until 1989, when he finally made his play to become mayor but lost to David Dinkins in the primaries. Goldin then retired from public service and opened a consulting firm for companies and public bodies on the brink of bankruptcy, representing creditor interests in Detroit, Puerto Rico, and the fiscally troubled Jefferson County, Alabama, as well as at Enron.

Felix Rohatyn left MAC in late 1978, returning to his work at Lazard Frères. But even though he was no longer brokering the city's financing deals, from his position atop the social order he remained one of the chief interpreters of the crisis. In a series of articles for the *New York Review of Books* in the early 1980s, he celebrated the coalition efforts in New York, the supposed rallying of the city in support of austerity—a course he viewed as best for the nation as a whole.

Rohatyn is often seen as the "fiscal savior" of the city, testament to the energy he put into brokering meetings with bankers and union leaders, persuading them to buy the MAC bonds and city debt that kept New York afloat. He was also instrumental in pressing elected leaders to restructure the budget and cut down on spending. His efforts on behalf of the city—or, at least, on behalf of a certain kind of city—do mark him as different from the financial executives of later decades, who would devote themselves without compunction to their own enrichment, insisting that money-making itself was automatically beneficial for society. Over time, Rohatyn's notion of bringing the unions into city government, finding some shared purpose around austerity—came to seem more and more old-fashioned. A place for labor at the table, no matter how limited, felt like a relic of midcentury politics.

As the years went by, Rohatyn seemed ill at ease with the ideologies of the elite business figures whom his actions had empowered during the crisis. Throughout the 1980s and 1990s he became increasingly anxious about the direction of federal policy, observing with alarm Washington's strident embrace of free-market ideology. He published passionate books and articles pointing out that capitalism ultimately depended on regulation to guarantee social stability, and advocating more public investment in urban infrastructure. Yet he seems never to have felt a tension between advocacy of greater federal government involvement and his embrace of austerity for New York. Such ambivalence may reflect the larger predicament of liberalism in the post–fiscal crisis era.

Victor Gotbaum continued to lead DC 37, the union representing the widest variety of city employees, throughout much of the 1980s. The union never again adopted the militant stance toward city government that it had early in the fiscal crisis. Instead, Gotbaum and Rohatyn became close friends, and he even served as Rohatyn's best man at his wedding. Later, in the 1990s, the union became plagued by corruption scandals, which damaged still further its ability to provide a strong voice for city workers, let alone to articulate a different vision for the city as a whole.

Donna Shalala, the only woman on MAC, became the president of Hunter College in 1980 and chancellor of the University of Wisconsin–Madison in 1987, and then served in the administration of President Bill Clinton as Secretary of Health and Human Services. Today she is president of the Clinton Foundation. Her time at MAC left an "indelible" mark on her, she says—not only because, in her thirties, she was placed in a position of remarkable power and responsibility, but because it was a time when her own politics were transformed. As a result of her experiences at MAC she became far more mindful of the "limitations of government" and the importance of having people with professional training in charge of complex governmental affairs. As she remembered years later, "Even though everyone thought I was a raging liberal coming out of NYC, I was really not, because of the fiscal crisis. It sobered me." She felt pangs, though, during her presidency at Hunter, where she saw the sidewalks of the campus pockmarked with holes because all capital investment had been put on hold during the crisis years—"I had been part of the group that had caused that pain."[6]

Hugh Carey continued to govern New York State until the end of his second term in 1982. He gained national recognition for his opposition to the death penalty, and, along with other Irish American Democratic politicians, for his encouragement of a negotiated settlement that would result in a unified Ireland. But his later years in Albany were fraught, and he never emerged as a candidate for national political office, as Ford's White House advisers had once feared. His own lieutenant governor, Mary Anne Krupsak, challenged him in his race for a second term. Even after he won, he managed to alienate many of his previous allies in the State Legislature.

In 1981, after less than three months' courtship, he married a woman he had met at Ronald Reagan's inaugural festivities—a woman who alleged that her former husband had died, but who actually turned out to have three prior husbands alive and well. Suddenly the sober Catholic governor seemed to be taking on the style of a playboy, going out dancing and dyeing his hair.[7] With news coverage turning against him, he decided against seeking a third term. Still, upon his departure from Albany the *New York Times* praised him as a "governor for hard winters."[8]

Abraham Beame continued to defend his record as mayor during the financial crisis to the end of his days. At a conference in 1989, he recounted with fondness how he had given a speech at the National Press Club one week after Ford's disastrous address there. Beame recalled asking the audience a paraphrase of Ford's question: "If we allow our cities to decay and die who will, when that day of reckoning comes, bail out the United States of America?" The entire crowd of cynical journalists, he said, rose to their feet in applause. "It was a marvelous feeling, after the trepidation I felt when I arrived there. And I knew we had won!"[9]

Ed Koch served for three terms as mayor of New York. During his second and third terms the city's economy improved as the financial sector took off, and municipal spending grew accordingly. By 1989 the city's budget in inflation-adjusted dollars was nearly as large as it had been in 1975—but the rhetoric around it was far different. Koch governed as an openly pro-business mayor, mocking the city's social welfare traditions.[10] In an interview on the tenth anniversary of the crisis, he said that in the past city leaders had not talked about "jobs and growth," but rather "how do you get New York City to be the No. 1 welfare city in America."[11]

This caricature of the city's earlier spending programs was a way of showing that under his mayoralty they would no longer hold the same priority. Indeed, he portrayed the crisis as an event that had pushed the city in a positive direction. "While it would be foolish to say that the fiscal crisis was good for the city, it did have many beneficial consequences," Koch wrote in a 1986 report. Most important, it had helped to bring about a "change in attitude, both in the city government and the city at large." As he put it, "there is a general recognition that government has its limits, and that we must make choices that are not always easy or simple. As a city, we must live within our means, and we must adjust our estimate of those means to allow the city to compete successfully in an ever-more-competitive world economy."[12]

Many of the people who became activists during the crisis continued to take part in city and state politics, pressing for greater economic justice for New Yorkers. Ramón Jiménez, the young professor who had organized the Community Coalition to Save Hostos, was for many years a lawyer representing low-income people, his office across the street from the college he'd helped to keep open. He continued to work with activists, including the community leaders trying to save Sydenham Hospital, and in 2014 ran for attorney general of New York State on the Green Party ticket. Hostos itself continues to thrive as a South Bronx institution, serving more than 7,000 students each year, nearly two-thirds women and 98 percent nonwhite. Today, four decades after protesters set up child care in the Hostos president's office, visitors to the school's main building will find a Children's Center on the first floor, providing day care to young children of Hostos students.

Adam Veneski kept up the struggle for a more equal New York until the end of his life, running the People's Firehouse community assistance program for twenty-five years. He died in 2000, collapsing in the middle of the street from a heart attack after climbing the steps out of the Bedford Avenue subway stop. He was briefly revived by firefighters from Engine Company 212, but died while being driven to Woodhull Hospital, a longer trip than a ride to the now-shuttered Greenpoint Hospital would have been. At the firehouse, the flag was hung at half mast. Firefighters served as his pallbearers, and when the hearse drove Veneski's body to its resting place in upstate New York, it was escorted out of the city by the fire truck that he had saved.[13] Only three years later, the Bloomberg administration moved to close Engine Company 212. Paul Veneski, Adam's son, tried to lead an opposition, but it was unsuccessful. Twenty-six years after it was first slated for closure, the firehouse was shut down.

Meanwhile, some of the institutions created during the crisis have quietly folded up shop. The Municipal Assistance Corporation voted itself out of existence in 2008, closing its offices, disposing of its computers, and settling affairs with its three remaining workers. Although it took a long while, all creditors who had bought the city's bonds and notes in the years leading up to the crisis and even during the crisis itself were made good in the end; the pension funds were repaid. "Our duties have successfully been undertaken and concluded," said the board's chairman at the start of its final meeting. "It's clear that 'Big MAC' saved New York City."[14]

In 1978 the word "emergency" was dropped from the name of the Emergency Financial Control Board, and in 1986 the Financial Control Board ceased to have formal approval of the city's financial plans. By this time, New York had fully adopted generally accepted accounting principles into its budget process. It had grown accustomed to preparing four-year financial plans to chart future expenses. Following the crisis, the budget office adopted a computerized "integrated financial management system," which helped track revenues and expenses. Perhaps most important, in 1986 the city repaid the federal government the last installment on the more than a billion dollars' worth of loans it had taken out.[15]

Still, despite its reduced powers, the FCB continues to exist to this day, hidden down a side street in the financial district. It reviews the city's budgets each year. Most of the time, people pay little attention to it. But should the city ever violate the 1975 New York State Emergency Financial Act, run a deficit of more than $100 million in a fiscal year, or fail to repay its debts, the FCB would automatically once again gain the authority to approve or deny the budgets of the city.[16]

Just as the FCB continues to exert a shadow power over the city's finances, so too the fiscal crisis haunted the mayors who came after the 1980s—David Dinkins, Rudolph Giuliani, and Michael Bloomberg. For all of them, the crisis represented the nadir against which their leadership would be measured. When the poor economy of the early 1990s hurt the city under Dinkins, the real fear was of a return to unbalanced budgets and financial panic. Giuliani's bullying hostility to public sector unions, his antagonism toward controversial artists, his embrace of workfare programs for poor women, his harsh attacks on the Board of Education and the public school system, and his adoption of "broken windows" policing strategies all drew on the punitive rhetoric of the crisis years, as though he wanted to discipline the city both financially and morally. Bloomberg, for his part, seemed the epitome of a postcrisis mayor: a business executive whose vast wealth and lack of overt politics seemed to be precisely what qualified him to lead the city, his independence from any democratic movement coming across as his strongest selling point. He was a man who prospered in the city as its economic divisions grew, the type of person for whom the new New York was meant. Today, in the mayoralty of Bill de Blasio, the most liberal mayor to govern the city since the crisis, the issues that were raised in the 1970s continue to reverberate—especially the question of what, if anything, the city government can do to counter the problem of inequality.

As New York City has gone, so, in many ways, has the country as a whole. Ever since the 1980s, the embrace of private enterprise as the sole way to fuel social development has helped to justify and legitimate the economic inequality that seems to define our day. As the American economy recovered from the blows of the 1970s, it was remade, as many have noted, on completely different terms. The idea of using the state to remedy poverty and improve social conditions has given way to the sense that doing so is simply too expensive—a social cost we cannot take on for fear of deficits and debt. Tax cuts have starved state and local governments, leaving them without the resources they need to provide education and other basic functions. Attempting to save money, local governments have contracted out to private companies essential public goods such as fire protection and ambulance services, leaving homeowners and patients to foot the bills. Throughout the country, at every level of government, public budgets suffer even as private fortunes grow, and the high wages and labor unions of civil servants are blamed for bankrupting the public trust. The inequality that characterizes our society today seems to be accompanied by the constant sense that any hope for a better society, any notion of collective action, must be a pipe dream—irresponsible, impossible to afford.

There were, of course, real limits to what was possible in the 1970s. The issues of economic inequality and urban poverty that the city government sought to confront—in whatever partial way—were problems of national scope, as was noted at the time by Bishop Paul Moore and others. City Hall's dubious accounting practices aside, the plight of New York in the early 1970s was largely not of the city's making. It was the result of the dismantling of the urban manufacturing economy, the flight of companies to poorer parts of the world, the construction of highways that made suburban life more appealing. When it made some attempt to address the economic and social problems that resulted, the city government faced profound and tragic structural limitations—its limited ability to tax incomes, its restricted role under the state constitution, its economic vulnerability.

Perhaps the nature of the underlying crisis was such that it simply could not be effectively combated at the local level. Still, had the federal government not been so relentlessly hostile to the city, New York might have had an easier time finding a way to renegotiate its debts. And had a national government been in place that was willing to accept more responsibility—by assuming a greater proportion of the cost of health care for the very poor, for example—the city might not have had to make the kind of cuts it did. One can even imagine that the fiscal crisis could have prompted some effort to redraw the boundaries between cities and their suburbs in ways that might make more resources available for city governments.

Such broader transformations were never pursued, of course, and the absence of national support made the solutions that the city did adopt—budget cuts and turning to the private sector to rebuild parks, schools, the city as a whole—seem like the only realistic choices. But that has more to do with power than with policy.

During the four decades that have passed since the fiscal crisis, critics on the right and left alike have interpreted it as an object lesson in the fragility of the public sector. From the vantage point of the present day, however, it is remarkable that the city did not lose *more* of its public sector than it did. The New York public school system remains viable despite its flaws, in far better shape than the school systems in cities such as Philadelphia, New Orleans, or Detroit. The subways remain public, a vast network unparalleled elsewhere in the nation. Despite the expanded role

of private philanthropy, no one has privatized the parks or the libraries. CUNY continues to exist and to be fairly affordable. Eleven public
hospitals and a network of community health centers and school-based
clinics continue to provide health care to millions of New Yorkers. The
city's labor unions remain a powerful force; there were no efforts to
break them altogether, as we have seen in states such as Wisconsin and
Illinois in recent years. Even today, some of the most valuable real estate
in the entire country has remained completely off limits to developers:
there are still whole blocks of Chelsea, the Lower East Side, and the
Upper West Side occupied by public housing projects, poor people living in the midst of astounding wealth.[17] All the clout of the city's economic elites—who are by some measures the richest and most powerful
people in the world—has not been able to dislodge these impoverished
tenants. For all the pain of the cutbacks, one can imagine much worse
outcomes.

Once public institutions have been created they possess a curious
resilience and stability. For a few years in the mid-1970s, it seemed possible for a newly energized group of elites to completely sweep aside
the city's history, to create a new set of norms for city government that
would exclusively serve their needs. They did achieve much, gaining a
new level of control over the city's finances and bringing about a program of cuts that under normal circumstances would have been impossible to implement. But there were too many people too committed to
the old public institutions for this to be a frictionless change. The vocal
protests against the cutbacks showed how difficult it would be to entirely
transform New York. As a result, many of the social democratic institutions of the postwar years managed to endure in the city to some
extent—just as at the national level, the gains of the 1930s and 1940s
(Social Security, the minimum wage, the right to organize) have proved
far more difficult to eliminate than insurgent conservative movements
might have hoped.

History rarely moves in one direction only. Amid the prosperity that
now dominates New York, there is also desperate poverty and an acute
sense that a different, older metropolis full of possibility has been lost.
Even those who celebrate without ambivalence the city as it exists today

should not overlook the real suffering that followed the crisis in the 1970s and 1980s. Nor should we forget that the policy choices that brought us to this point were often made without the full participation of the people of the city itself. At the same time, it's worth noting that to this day, few other places in the United States offer as many possibilities for common, public life. No matter how much the wealthy might seek to retreat into high-rises from which the people below look small and insignificant, eventually they too must descend into the city streets, the life that we all share here together.

NOTES

ARCHIVES AND MANUSCRIPTS

Archives of the Archdiocese of New York, Yonkers, New York

Alfred E. Smith Memorial Dinner Collection

Association for a Better New York (ABNY) Archives, New York City

Baruch College, Archive on Municipal Finance and Leadership, City University of New York

Jack Bigel Collection
Municipal Assistance Corporation (MAC) Papers

Centro de Estudios Puertorriqueños / Center for Puerto Rican Studies, Hunter College, City University of New York

Carlos Ortiz Papers

Citibank Archives, New York City

Joan Silverman Papers
Mary S. Turner Memoranda and Drafts

Citizens Committee for New York City Archives, New York City

City College of New York Archives, City University of New York

Board of Higher Education Minutes
City College of New York (CCNY) Papers

City Hall Library, New York City

Columbia University Rare Books and Manuscripts Collection

Community Service Society Records

Downtown Collection, Fales Library, New York University

Terence Sellers Papers

Financial Control Board, New York City

Papers of the Emergency Financial Control Board (EFCB)

Freedom of Information Act Request for the papers of the *Securities and Exchange Commission Staff Report on Transactions in Securities of the City of New York* **(SEC FOIA Request)**

Gerald R. Ford Presidential Library (GFPL), Ann Arbor, Michigan

Council of Economic Advisers, Alan Greenspan Files
Gerald R. Ford Presidential Handwriting File
James M. Cannon Files
John G. Carlson Files
John Marsh Files
L. William Seidman Files
Max Friedersdorf Files
Robert T. Hartmann Files
Robert T. Hartmann Papers
Ron Nessen Papers

Hostos Community College Archives and Special Collections, City University of New York

Gerald J. Meyer Collection

Jimmy Carter Presidential Library (JCPL), Atlanta, Georgia

Office of the Cabinet Secretary
Office of the Congressional Liaison
Office of the Staff Secretary

Lafayette College, Easton, Pennsylvania

William E. Simon Papers

LaGuardia and Wagner Archives at LaGuardia Community College, City University of New York, New York City

Abraham Beame Mayoral Papers
Abraham Beame Pre-Mayoral and Post-Mayoral Papers

Municipal Archives, New York City

Assistant to the Mayor Francis X. McCardle Subject Files
Deputy Mayor John Burton Subject Files
First Deputy Mayor John Zuccotti Administrative Files
First Deputy Mayor John Zuccotti Subject Files

First Deputy Mayor John Zuccotti General Correspondence
Deputy Mayor Kenneth Axelson Subject Files
Records of the New York City Board of Education
    Bernard Gifford Papers
    Irving Anker Papers

New York Public Library Manuscripts and Archives Division

New York Public Library Records (NYPL)
    John Cory Papers
    Hunts Point Branch Library Papers
    James W. Henderson Papers
    New Dorp Branch Library Papers

New York Stock Exchange Archives, New York City

G. Keith Funston Papers

Rockefeller Archive Center, Sleepy Hollow, New York

Nelson Aldrich Rockefeller Vice-Presidential Papers

St. John's University, New York City

Hugh Carey Papers

Stony Brook University, Long Island

Jacob Javits Papers

Tamiment Library, New York University

Bernard Bellush Papers
Professional Staff Congress Archives

Tufts University, Boston, Massachusetts

Walter B. Wriston Archives

I have also made use of private archives shared by Ann Ambia, Steve Clifford, Peter Goldmark, Ira Millstein, Ida Susser, Jonathan Weiner, and District Council 37. I have noted the memos that people shared with me of which I have copies. In cases where I looked at the material in someone's home or office, I have noted those as privately held collections.

PERIODICALS

New York Times
New York Daily News
New York Post
New York Amsterdam News
Chelsea Clinton News
Village Voice

Soho Weekly News

Daily Bond Buyer

Catholic News

The Westsider

The Link

AUTHOR INTERVIEWS

Stephen Berger

Steve Clifford

Herbert Elish

Tom Gogan

Harrison J. Goldin

Peter Goldmark

Marvin Jacob

Ramón Jiménez

Ira Millstein

Gerry Owens

William Quirk

Richard Ravitch

Felix Rohatyn

Bob Roher

Howard Rubenstein

Charles Sanford

Tim Schermerhorn

Donna Shalala

Stanley Sporkin

Al Viani

Paul and Brigitte Veneski

Jonathan Weiner

I am also grateful to the following people for meeting with me and sharing their reflections on the fiscal crisis. Although I did not cite their interviews directly, their insights and memories informed mine: Brian Balogh, Charles Brecher, Maurice Carroll, John Darnton, Janie Eisenberg, Fred Feretti, Dall Forsythe, Mel Gritzer, Michael Guglielmo, Eugene Keilin, Don Kummerfeld, Carl Lobell, Ronnie Lowenstein, Gerald Meyer, Harvey Miller, Frank Possilico, Bernard Rosen, Nilsa Saniel, George Sweeting, Jim Tallon, and Steven Weisman.

INTRODUCTION

1. Transcript of President's Talk on City Crisis, Questions Asked and His Responses, *New York Times*, 10/30/75.
2. Lyn Smith to Jacob Javits, 4/16/75, Roll 5, Series: General Correspondence, Federal and State, Abraham Beame Papers, New York City Municipal Archives.
3. See Stanley Corkin, *Starring New York: Filming the Grime and the Glamour of the Long 1970s* (New York: Oxford University Press, 2011). There are many wonderful works on the cultural life of New York City in the 1970s more generally; among them, see Tim Lawrence, *Love Saves the Day: A History of American Dance Music Culture, 1970–1979* (Durham, N.C.: Duke University Press, 2003); Will Hermes, *Love Goes to Buildings on Fire: Five Years in New York That Changed Music Forever* (New York: Farrar, Straus and Giroux, 2011); Jay Sanders, ed., *Rituals of Rented Island: Object Theater, Loft Performance and the New Psychodrama: Manhattan, 1970–1980* (New York: Whitney Museum, 2013); Brian Tochterman, "Welcome to Fear City: The Cultural Narrative of New York City, 1945–1980"), Ph.D. Diss., University of Minnesota, 2011; Jim Fricke and Charlie Ahearn, *Yes Yes Y'all: The Experience Music Project's Oral History of Hip-Hop's First Decade* (New York: Da Capo Press, 2002); Jeff Chang, *Can't Stop Won't Stop: A History of the Hip-Hop Generation* (New York: Picador, 2006); and most of all, Jonathan Mahler, *Ladies and Gentlemen, the Bronx Is Burning: 1977, Baseball, Politics and the Battle for the Soul of the City* (New York: Macmillan, 2005).
4. Christopher Lasch, *The Culture of Narcissism: American Life in an Age of Diminishing Expectations* (New York: W. W. Norton, 1979), xiii.
5. See, for example, Fred Siegel and E. J. McMahon, "Gotham's Fiscal Crisis: Lessons Unlearned," *Public Interest*, Winter 2005; also Peter D. McClelland and Alan L. Magdovitz, *Crisis in the Making: The Political Economy of New York State Since 1945* (New York: Cambridge University Press, 1981), and Charles Morris, *The Cost of Good Intentions: New York City and the Liberal Experiment, 1960–1975* (New York: W. W. Norton, 1980). Some of the other journalistic treatments of the crisis in its immediate aftermath also reflect these arguments although without making them so polemically: Ken Auletta, *The Streets Were Paved with Gold* (New York: Vintage Books, 1980); and Fred Ferretti, *The Year the Big Apple Went Bust* (New York: Putnam, 1976).
6. Felix Rohatyn, "The Coming Emergency and What Can Be Done About It," *New York Review of Books*, 12/4/80.
7. Here I echo arguments made by Greta Krippner, *Capitalizing on Crisis: The Political Origins of the Rise of Finance* (Cambridge: Harvard University Press, 2011), about the rise of the financial sector and the adoption of policies that favored it on the national level.
8. On the idea of crisis more generally, see Janet Roitman, "Crisis," *Political Concepts*, Issue 1, http://www.politicalconcepts.org/issue1/crisis/.

9. A rich literature addresses civil rights politics and the political movements of poor and working-class people in postwar New York City: Martha Biondi, *To Stand and Fight: The Struggle for Civil Rights in Postwar New York City* (Cambridge, Mass.: Harvard University Press, 2003); Clarence Taylor, ed., *Civil Rights in New York City: From World War II to the Giuliani Era* (New York: Fordham University Press, 2011); Tamar Carroll, *Mobilizing New York: AIDS, Antipoverty and Feminist Activism* (Chapel Hill: University of North Carolina Press, 2015); Walter Thabitt, *How East New York Became a Ghetto* (New York: New York University Press, 2003); Jeanne Theoharis and Komozi Woodard, eds., *Freedom North: Black Freedom Struggles Outside the South, 1940–1980* (New York: Palgrave Macmillan, 2003); Roberta Gold, *When Tenants Claimed the City: The Struggle for Citizenship in New York City Housing* (Urbana-Champaign: University of Illinois Press, 2014); and Craig Wilder, *A Covenant with Color: Race and Social Power in Brooklyn* (New York: Columbia University Press, 1994).

10. Social scientists have looked at the crisis in terms of what it reveals about urban political dynamics, and in doing so have produced extremely important accounts of the city's fiscal structure. See, for example, Martin Shefter, *Political Crisis/Fiscal Crisis: The Collapse and Revival of New York City* (New York: Basic Books, 1985); Ester Fuchs, *Mayors and Money: Fiscal Policy in New York and Chicago* (Chicago: University of Chicago Press, 1992); Raymond Horton and Charles Brecher with Robert A. Cropf and Dean Michael Mead, *Power Failure: New York City Power and Politics Since 1960* (New York: Oxford University Press, 1993); and John Mollenkopf, *A Phoenix in the Ashes: The Rise and Fall of the Koch Coalition in New York City Politics* (Princeton, N.J.: Princeton University Press, 1994). There are also a number of historical accounts that deal with city politics in the postwar years, although less focused on the fiscal crisis. Among the most important for this study are Joel Schwartz, *The New York Approach: Robert Moses, Urban Liberals and Redevelopment of the Inner City* (Columbus: Ohio State University Press, 1993); Samuel Zipp, *Manhattan Projects: The Rise and Fall of Urban Renewal in Cold War New York* (New York: Oxford University Press, 2010); Suleiman Osman, *The Invention of Brownstone Brooklyn: Gentrification and the Search for Authenticity in Postwar New York* (New York: Oxford University Press, 2011); Vincent Cannato, *The Ungovernable City: John V. Lindsay and His Struggle to Save New York* (New York: Basic Books, 2001); and Joseph P. Viteritti, ed., *Summer in the City: John Lindsay, New York and the American Dream* (Baltimore: Johns Hopkins University Press, 2014).

11. For interpretations of the fiscal crisis that reflect a left political perspective, see Roger E. Alcaly and David Mermelstein, eds., *The Fiscal Crisis of American Cities: Essays on the Political Economy of Urban America with Special Reference to New York* (New York: Vintage, 1977); Jack Newfield and Paul DuBrul, *The Abuse of Power: The Permanent Government and the Fall of New York* (New York: Penguin Books, 1978); William Tabb, *The Long Default: New York City and the Urban Fiscal Crisis* (New York: Monthly Review Press, 1982); Robert Bailey, *The Crisis Regime: The MAC, the EFCB and the Political Impact of the New York City Financial Crisis* (Albany: State University of New York Press, 1985); Eric Lichten,

Class, Power & Austerity: The New York City Fiscal Crisis (South Hadley, Mass.: Bergin & Garvey Publishers, 1986); Doug Henwood, *Wall Street: How It Works and for Whom* (New York: Verso, 1997); Joshua Freeman, *Working-Class New York: Life and Labor Since World War II* (New York: The New Press, 2000); Kim Moody, *From Welfare State to Real Estate: Regime Change in New York City, 1974 to the Present* (New York: The New Press, 2007); Miriam Greenberg, *Branding New York: How a City in Crisis Was Sold to the World* (New York and London: Routledge, 2008); Lynne Weikart, *Follow the Money: Who Controls New York City Mayors?* (Albany: State University of New York Press, 2009); Jonathan Soffer, *Ed Koch and the Rebuilding of New York City* (New York: Columbia University Press, 2010); Julian Brash, "Invoking Fiscal Crisis: Moral Discourse and Politics in New York City," *Social Text* 76, Vol. 21, No. 3, Fall 2003; Alice O'Connor, "The Privatized City: The Manhattan Institute, the Urban Crisis and the Conservative Counterrevolution in New York," *Journal of Urban History*, Vol. 34, No. 2, January 2008, 333–53; Jamie Peck, "Pushing Austerity: State Failure, Municipal Bankruptcy and the Crises of Fiscal Federalism in the USA," *Cambridge Journal of Regions, Economy and Society*, June 2013; and John Krinsky, "Neoliberal Times: Intersecting Temporalities and the Neoliberalization of New York City's Public Sector Labor Relations," *Social Science History Review*, Fall 2011, 381–422. Also see two dissertations, as yet unpublished: Michael Spear, "A Crisis in Urban Liberalism: The New York City Municipal Unions and the 1970s Fiscal Crisis" (CUNY, 2005), and Benjamin Holtzman, "Crisis and Confidence: Reimagining New York in the Late Twentieth Century" (Brown University, 2016).

12. For works on the politics of the 1970s, see Daniel Rodgers, *Age of Fracture* (Cambridge, Mass.: Harvard University Press, 2011); Laura Kalman, *Right Star Rising: A New Politics, 1974–1980* (New York: W. W. Norton, 2010): Jefferson Cowie, *Stayin' Alive: The 1970s and the Last Days of the Working Class* (New York: The New Press, 2010); Judith Stein, *Pivotal Decade: How the United States Traded Factories for Finance in the 1970s* (New Haven, Conn.: Yale University Press, 2010); Rick Perlstein, *Nixonland: The Rise of a President and the Fracturing of America* (New York: Scribner, 2000); Rick Perlstein, *The Invisible Bridge: The Fall of Nixon and the Rise of Reagan* (New York: Simon & Schuster, 2014); Lily Geismer, *Don't Blame Us: Suburban Liberals and the Transformation of the Democratic Party* (Princeton, N.J.: Princeton University Press, 2014).

1. WARNINGS

1. Robert Lindsey, "West Side Highway: 43 Years, All Downhill," *New York Times*, 6/23/74.

2. Murray Schumach, "Highway Repairs to Start in Fall," *New York Times*, 8/19/73.

3. "Truck and Car Fall as West Side Highway Collapses," *New York Times*, 12/16/73.

4. Emanuel Perlmutter, "Section of West Side Highway Closed to Traffic Indefinitely," *New York Times*, 12/17/73.

5. Robert McG. Thomas Jr., "Children Supplant Cars on West Side Highway," *New York Times*, 1/27/74.

6. Frederic Morton, "Walking the West Side Highway," *New York Times*, 3/7/74.

7. Terence Sellers Papers, Journal, February–November 1975, Series 2, Box 2, Folder 57, August 9, 3 a.m, Fales Library Downtown Collection, Elmer Bobst Library, New York University.

8. Alfred E. Clark, "Boy on West Side Highway Dies in Fall Through Hole," *New York Times*, 8/17/74.

9. Mason Williams, *City of Ambition: FDR, La Guardia and the Making of Modern New York* (New York: W. W. Norton, 2013). As Williams puts it, "For several decades after the end of the Second World War, New Yorkers would reach instinctively for state-driven solutions to social problems" (xv).

10. Freeman, *Working-Class New York*, 55.

11. Ibid., 66–67. Also see Williams, *City of Ambition*, 392–3.

12. Ida Susser, *Norman Street: Poverty and Politics in an Urban Neighborhood, Updated Edition* (New York: Oxford University Press, 2012), 83–104.

13. Emanuel Perlmutter, "Our Changing City: Northern Brooklyn," *New York Times*, 7/22/55; Meyer Berger, "About New York," *New York Times*, 3/31/54.

14. "Children's Choral Group Holds Music Festival," *New York Times*, 8/29/52.

15. "Marionette Circus Plans 88 Programs," *New York Times*, 6/14/53; "City to Be Aglow for Yule Season," *New York Times*, 12/11/56.

16. Evelyn Gonzalez, *The Bronx* (New York: Columbia University Press, 2004), 115–16.

17. "2D Salk Shots Set for 171,500 Pupils," *New York Times*, 8/8/55. The city had floated $150 million on bonds to improve public health programs and facilities in 1949. Freeman, *Working-Class New York*, 67.

18. "Orthodontic Clinic Opened," *New York Times*, 4/29/50.

19. "Home Aid to Extend City Hospital Care," *New York Times*, 5/3/48.

20. "Integration Gain Seen," *New York Times*, 12/23/56.

21. "Rebirth of School Is Hailed in Bronx," *New York Times*, 5/11/52; Charles G. Bennett, "$50,000 Allocated to Fight Teen-Age Gangs in Bronx," *New York Times*, 5/13/55; Mark Naison, "Morrisania Roots of Hip-Hop Culture," viewed online at http://www.hiphoparea.com/rap/morrisania-roots-of-hip-hop-culture.html, 7/7/16; Manny Fernandez, "Morrisania Melody," *New York Times*, 4/30/06.

22. Little has been written about the city's continuing education programs, but see "Ex-GI's Attending Night High School Classes Surpass Non-Veterans in Regents Tests," *New York Times*, 7/24/47; "400 Welfare Recipients Graduate," *New York Amsterdam News*, 8/14/71; "New Kind of Success Story . . . They're Filling Up Adult Education Classes," *New York Amsterdam News*, 5/7/75.

23. Freeman, *Working-Class New York*, 7.

24. Ibid., 42.

25. Taylor, *Civil Rights in New York City*; Walter Thabit, *How East New York Became a Ghetto* (New York: New York University Press, 2003); Martha Biondi, *To Stand and Fight: The Struggle for Civil Rights in Postwar New York City* (Cambridge: Harvard University Press, 2003); Theoharis and Woodard, *Freedom North*.

26. Robert Fitch, "Planning New York," in Alcaly and Mermelstein, *The Fiscal Crisis*

of American Cities, 246–84; also see Robert Fitch, *The Assassination of New York* (New York: Verso, 1993), 60, 122.

27. The idea of a "right to the city" is drawn from Henri Lefebvre, Eleonore Kofman, and Elizabeth Lebas, *Writings on Cities* (Oxford, UK: Blackwell Publishers, 1996), and David Harvey, "The Right to the City," *New Left Review* 53, September–October 2008.

28. Merrill Folsom, "Companies Tell Why They Leave," *New York Times*, 2/16/67; also see Robert Alden, "Land for Industry," *New York Times*, 10/15/66.

29. New York City Department of Social Services, *Monthly Statistical Report*, City Hall Library. This is a total for all the different forms of public assistance: home relief, old age assistance, aid to the blind, and aid to disabled people, in addition to Aid to Dependent Children—what people usually think of when they think of welfare. The growth in the number of people receiving Aid to Dependent Children, though, is primarily responsible for the rise. Also see Charles Brecher, *Where Have All the Dollars Gone? Public Expenditures for Human Resource Development in New York City, 1961–1971* (New York: Praeger, 1974), 7.

30. Freeman, *Working-Class New York*, 197. Also see Jonathan Rieder, *Canarsie: The Jews and Italians of Brooklyn Against Liberalism* (Cambridge: Harvard University Press, 1985).

31. McClelland and Magdovitz, *Crisis in the Making*, 312.

32. Quoted in Rieder, *Canarsie*, 101–102.

33. Eli Ginzburg, "Foreword," in Brecher, *Where Have All the Dollars Gone?*, viii.

34. Ibid., 93.

35. Shefter, *Political Crisis/Fiscal Crisis*, 118–19; also see Fuchs, *Mayors and Money*, 124–28, 144, and Morris, *The Cost of Good Intentions*, 172–85.

36. Metropolitan and Regional Research Center, *New York City: Economic Base and Fiscal Capacity* (Maxwell School of Citizenship and Public Affairs, Syracuse University, 1973), 6–7.

37. Brecher, *Where Have All the Dollars Gone?*, vii–viii.

38. Comptroller's Reports, 1964–65 and 1970–71, City Hall Library.

39. Fuchs, *Mayors and Money*, 160.

40. Although use of welfare in New York City increased about five years earlier than it did in the rest of the country, the rate of increase from 1960 to 1975 was similar. Charles Morris, "Of Budgets, Taxes and the Rise of a New Plutocracy," in Viteritti, *Summer in the City*, 95; also see Morris, *The Cost of Good Intentions*, 193. New York City had to bear a larger proportion of the cost of welfare than did other cities, but this reflected state politics, not the spending priorities of the city.

41. "President Pledges an End to 'Era of Permissiveness,'" *New York Times*, 11/10/72.

42. Fuchs, *Mayors and Money*, 160. The money the city got from the state and federal governments had risen by 172 percent between 1965 and 1969; between 1969 and 1973 it continued to climb, but only by 35 percent.

43. Ibid., 191; Michael S. Sparer, *Medicaid and the Limits of State Health Reform*

(Philadelphia: Temple University Press, 1996), 79; Morris, *The Cost of Good Intentions*, 188–89.

44. The city had to subtract the value of its short-term debt service from this limit, meaning that it was even lower than it would have been otherwise. Long-term debt service was not included in operating expenses. Roy W. Bahl, Alan K. Campbell, and David Greytak, *Taxes, Expenditures, and the Economic Base: Case Study of New York City*, Maxwell School of Citizenship and Public Affairs, Syracuse University (New York: Praeger, 1974), 81.

45. Ibid.

46. Joe Flood, *The Fires: How a Computer Formula, Big Ideas, and the Best of Intentions Burned Down New York City—and Determined the Future of Cities* (New York: Riverhead Books, 2011); Newfield and du Brul, *The Abuse of Power*, 132–34, 297–99; also see Fuchs, *Mayors and Money*, 185.

2. THE GAP

1. Brecher, *Where Have All the Dollars Gone?*, 13–14.

2. James F. Clarity, "Robert Wagner, 80, Pivotal New York Mayor, Dies," *New York Times*, 2/3/91.

3. Adina Back, "Exposing the 'Whole Segregation Myth': The Harlem Nine and New York City's School Desegregation Battles," in Theoharis and Woodard, *Freedom North*; Clarence Taylor, "Conservative and Liberal Opposition to the New York City School-Integration Campaign," in Taylor, *Civil Rights in New York City*; Carroll, *Mobilizing New York*.

4. Michael W. Flamm, *In the Heat of the Summer: The New York Riots of 1964 and the War on Crime* (Philadelphia: University of Pennsylvania Press, 2016).

5. Federal Bureau of Investigation, Uniform Crime Reports for the United States. While these reports have often been described as problematic (for example, they report a large increase in crime between the Wagner and Lindsay administrations, which is primarily a result of changes in reporting), the homicide numbers are the most reliable.

6. "New York, Greatest City in the World—and Everything Is Wrong with It," *New York Herald Tribune*, 1/25/65.

7. Morris, "Of Budgets, Taxes, and the Rise of a New Plutocracy," 87; also see New York City Department of Social Services, *Monthly Statistical Report*, January 1964 and January 1965.

8. Robert F. Wagner, "Message of the Mayor," *Journal of Proceedings of Special Meeting of the Board of Estimate*, 5/13/65.

9. Ibid.

10. Ibid. Also quoted in Nicholas P. Giuliano, Timothy J. Heine, and Tammy Elaine Tuller, "The Constitutional Debt Limit and New York City," *Fordham Urban Law Journal*, Vol. 8, Issue 1, 1979, 185.

11. Citizens Budget Commission, "Borrowing Trouble," May 25, 1965.

12. Clayton Knowles, "Foes of Realty Tax to Spend $400,000," *New York Times*, 12/24/65.

13. "A Reckless City Budget," *New York Times*, 6/9/65; "Helping the City Go Broke," *New York Times*, 6/17/65.

14. Robert D. McFadden, "John V. Lindsay, Mayor and Maverick, Dies at 79," *New York Times*, 12/21/00.

15. "Mr. Lindsay for Mayor," *New York Times*, 10/14/65; Geoffrey Kabaservice, "On Principle: A Progressive Republican," in Viteritti, *Summer in the City*, 48.

16. Charles G. Bennett, "Funds Available to Paint Mansion," *New York Times*, 11/16/65; "Lindsay Will Cut Mayor Pay $5,000," *New York Times*, 11/22/65.

17. Bahl, Campbell, and Greytak, *Taxes, Expenditures, and the Economic Base*, 132; also see Benjamin Holtzman, "Crisis and Confidence," Ph.D. dissertation, Brown University, 2016, 17. The Syracuse researchers noted that the areas in which employment was growing in the 1960s—services and government, the latter accounting for three out of every four jobs added to the city during the decade—were also those that generated the least tax revenues for the city. Although property taxes accounted for a majority of local taxes in the city, New York by the end of the 1960s was more reliant on other forms of revenue (income, sales, and business taxes) than other cities in the nation, so changes that affected its income tax base were especially important. Bahl, Campbell, and Greytak, *Taxes, Expenditures, and the Economic Base*, 76.

18. Damon Stetson, "Jobless in State Reach July Peak," *New York Times*, 8/24/72.

19. Judith Glazer, "A Case Study of the Decision in 1976 to Initiate Tuition for Matriculated Undergraduate Students of the City University of New York," Ph.D. diss., New York University, 1981, 306.

20. "Report of the Ad Hoc Committee on Lincoln Hospital," quoted in Merlin Chowkwanyun, "The New Left and Public Health: The Health Policy Advisory Center, Community Organizing and the Big Business of Health, 1967–1975," *American Journal of Public Health*, Vol. 101, No. 2, February 2011.

21. Cannato, *The Ungovernable City*; Johanna Fernandez, "Between Social Service Reform and Revolutionary Politics: The Young Lords, Late Sixties Radicalism and Community Organizing in New York City," in Theoharis and Woodard, *Freedom North*; Premilla Nasaden, *Welfare Warriors: The Welfare Rights Movement in the United States* (New York: Routledge, 2004); Bryan Burrough, *Days of Rage: America's Radical Underground, the FBI, and the Forgotten Age of Revolutionary Violence* (New York: Penguin Press, 2015); "Prisoners in Tombs Riot for Second Day: 800 Hold 3 Guards Hostage," *New York Times*, 8/12/70.

22. Kabaservice, "On Principle," 48.

23. Morris, "Of Budgets, Taxes and the Rise of a New Plutocracy," 89; Morris, *The Cost of Good Intentions*, 158–59. Most of the increase in day care spending occurred in Lindsay's second term when expanding day care became a national political issue.

24. Seth S. King, "Business Leaders Joining Officials on City Problems," *New York Times*, 4/17/67.

25. G. Keith Funston to Clarence Francis, 5/23/66. G. Keith Funston Papers, Box 4, Folder 3, NYSE Archives.

26. Press release, 6/2/71, Folder "The Very Beginning," ABNY Archives.

27. For descriptions of the deepening role of the private sector in city politics in the 1960s, see Benjamin Holtzman, "Crisis and Confidence: Reimagining New York City in the Late Twentieth Century," 2016; Merlin Chowkwanyun, "Dilemmas of Community Health: Medical Care and Environmental Health in Postwar America," Ph.D. diss., University of Pennsylvania, 2013; Flood, *The Fires*; Jack Newfield and Paul du Brul, *The Abuse of Power* (New York: Penguin Books, 1978).

28. Will Lissner, "City Seeks to Tax Exempt Property to Aid Hospitals," *New York Times*, 3/18/68; "Facing Up to Tax Exemption," *New York Times*, 4/14/66; Richard Phalon, "City's Finance Chief Orders a Realty Tax Study," *New York Times*, 8/21/68.

29. "Digest of Lindsay's Budget Message to Board of Estimate and City Council," *New York Times*, 4/16/66; John Sibley, "Welfare Budget Is Up $129 Million," *New York Times*, 4/16/66.

30. Robert Alden, "26 Top Executives Reject Tax Plan Sought by Mayor," *New York Times*, 4/5/66.

31. "Morgan Bank Calls Lindsay Tax Plans Unfair to Business," *New York Times*, 3/17/66.

32. G. Keith Funston to "Punch," 3/21/66, G. Keith Funston Papers, Box 3, Folder 7, NYSE Archives. For letters to politicians, see G. Keith Funston to Earl W. Brydges, 7/8/66, G. Keith Funston Papers, Box 3, Folder 1; G. Keith Funston to Warren Anderson, 5/11/66, G. Keith Funston papers, Box 3, Folder 1, among others.

33. Henry Harris, George Leness, and Henry Watts to Board of Governors, Subject: Final Report on the Mayor's Committee to Keep the New York Stock Exchange in New York City, 3/8/67, G. Keith Funston Papers, Box 6, Folder 6, NYSE Archives.

34. Morris, "Of Budgets, Taxes and the Rise of a New Plutocracy," 89–90.

35. Ibid.

36. Clayton Knowles, "More Home Rule Is Urged for City," *New York Times*, 5/10/67.

37. Emanuel Perlmutter, "Lindsay to Ask Albany for More of State Income Tax," *New York Times*, 3/3/69.

38. Executive Budgets, City Hall Library.

39. Comptroller's Report, FY 1972–73 and FY 1973–74, City Hall Library.

40. Morris, "Of Budgets, Taxes and the Rise of a New Plutocracy," 93–94.

41. Money was being used to pay for goods for middle-class people as well as the poor. For example, the city floated bond-anticipation notes to build middle-income housing at a lower interest rate than it would have faced for long-term bonds. The assumption was that later on it would float bonds to cover the anticipation notes. This never happened. As a result, the city kept borrowing in the short-term market to cover the bond-anticipation notes. Donna E. Shalala and Carol Bellamy, "A State Saves a City: The New York Case, 1976," *Duke Law Journal*, 1977, 1119–32.

42. Executive Budget 1973–74, City Hall Library; also see Max H. Seigel, "City Cautioned on Use of Debt," *New York Times*, 7/8/73; Peter Kihss, "Citizens Unit Assails City Borrowing," *New York Times*, 4/17/72. The city had lobbied Albany for the right to be able to shift spending to the capital budget; see David K. Shipler, "City Seeks Right to Shift Money," *New York Times*, 4/28/72.

43. Executive Budget 1973–1974, City Hall Library.

44. "Measuring City 'Gaps,'" *New York Times*, 5/16/72; McClelland and Magdovitz, *Crisis in the Making*, 327–28.

45. "The 'A' Rating," *New York Times*, 12/20/73; "N.Y.C.: Good Risk," *New York Times*, 12/7/72.

46. John H. Allan, "City Bond Rating Upgraded Again," *New York Times*, 12/15/73.

47. See Coopers & Lybrand and the University of Michigan, *Financial Disclosure Practices of the American Cities: A Public Report* (Ann Arbor: University of Michigan, Graduate School of Business Administration, 1976).

48. McClelland and Magdovitz, *Crisis in the Making*, 301.

49. Murray Schumach, "Beame Inaugurated, Vows Integrity and Efficiency," *New York Times*, 1/2/74.

3. THE NEIGHBORHOOD BOOKKEEPER

1. Maurice Carroll, "Quiet Ceremony Held at Home," *New York Times*, 1/1/74.

2. Schumach, "Beame Inaugurated, Vows Integrity and Efficiency."

3. Abraham Beame interview, 5/17/93, Ellis Island Oral History Project, LaGuardia and Wagner Archives.

4. New York State Census, 1915; New York City Directory, 1916. Accessed at Ancestry.com.

5. Robert Daley, "The Realism of Abe Beame," *New York Times Magazine*, 11/18/73; also see Abraham Beame interview, Ellis Island Oral History Project, 5/17/93.

6. For the Beame family's address in 1916, see U.S. City Directories, 1822–1995; also New York State Census, 1915. Accessed via Ancestry.com, 6/24/16. For the Triangle Shirtwaist fire, see The Bowery Boys: New York City History, "Where They Lived: Remembering the Victims of the Triangle Shirtwaist Fire," http://www.boweryboyshistory.com/2016/03/lived-triangle-factory-fire-105-years-later.html, accessed 6/24/16; also see "The Triangle Shirtwaist Fire 1911," Authentic History, http://www.authentichistory.com/1898-1913/2-progressivism/3-laborreform/3-trianglefire/victim_list.html, accessed 6/24/16.

7. Irving Howe, *World of Our Fathers: The Journey of the East European Jews to America and the Life They Found and Made* (New York: Galahad Books, 2001), 307.

8. Ibid., 625.

9. Daley, "The Realism of Abe Beame."

10. Jerome Krase and Charles Lacerra, *Ethnicity and Machine Politics* (Lanham, MD: UPA, 1991), 31, 41.

11. Ibid., 88.

12. "We Back a Split Ticket," *New York Times*, 10/20/61.

13. Cannato, *The Ungovernable City*, 51.

14. Ibid., 73, 67, 51.
15. "Beame vs. Badillo," 6/5/73, *New York Times*, 40.
16. Tom Buckley, "Beame Relies on Experience to Win Race," *New York Times*, 4/23/73.
17. Address by Comptroller Abraham D. Beame to Deadline Club, October 23, 1973, Box O, Campaign Materials, Subject: SEC, Abraham Beame Papers, Municipal Archives.
18. Howard Rubenstein interview, 5/19/11.
19. "Beame Calls on Medical Profession to Cooperate with Government in Providing Medical Care to Public," 10/16/73, Box O, Campaign Materials, Subject: SEC, Beame Papers, Municipal Archives.
20. Maurice Carroll, "New Mayor a Courtly Man of Caution," *New York Times*, 11/8/73.
21. Abraham Beame to Henry Jackson, 1/8/74, Abraham Beame Papers, Reel 5, Municipal Archives.
22. Mary Breasted, "Violence at New Year's Leaves 13 Dead," *New York Times*, 1/2/74.
23. Warren Smith, ed., *Predictions for 1974* (New York: Award Books, 1973), 74; also see Perlstein, *The Invisible Bridge*, 177.
24. Isadore Barmash, "City Businessmen More Pessimistic," *New York Times*, 1/5/74.
25. David Burnham, "Most Call Crime Worst City Ill," *New York Times*, 1/16/74.
26. Hermes, *Love Goes to Buildings on Fire*, 97.
27. "Mayor Beame Asserts Crises Make Days Longer," *New York Times*, 3/4/74.
28. Patti Smith, *Just Kids* (New York: Ecco, 2010), 239–46.
29. Fricke and Ahearn, *Yes Yes Y'all*, 22–45. Also see Chang, *Can't Stop Won't Stop*.
30. Hermes, *Love Goes to Buildings on Fire*, 37.
31. J. Hoberman, "'Like Canyons and Rivers': Performance for Its Own Sake," Sanders, *Rituals of Rented Island*, 12.
32. Christopher Mele, *Selling the Lower East Side: Culture, Real Estate and Resistance in New York City* (Minneapolis: University of Minnesota Press, 2000), 199; Hermes, *Love Goes to Buildings on Fire*, 133.
33. Roslyn Kramer, "SoHo Artists Meet," *SoHo Weekly News*, 10/17/74; Janel Bladow, ". . . and March," *SoHo Weekly News*, 10/17/74.
34. Chang, *Can't Stop Won't Stop*, 67–70; Grace Lichtenstein, "Fox Street: Trash-Littered War Zone," *New York Times*, 5/10/74.
35. "Governor of Puerto Rico Says the Ills of South Bronx 'Wasteland' Spread to His Island," *New York Times*, 5/13/74.
36. Uniform Crime Reports for the United States, "Number of Offenses Known to the Police," New York, N.Y.
37. Michael Stern, "Continued Job Declines Threaten City Economy," *New York Times*, 7/21/74.
38. Lee Dembart, "Unemployment 7% Here but Skilled Jobs Are Open," *New York Times*, 12/7/74.

39. Howard Rubenstein interview, 5/19/11.
40. Thomas J. Lueck, "James A. Cavanagh, 86, Adviser to Beame in Fiscal Crisis," *New York Times*, 9/2/00; Ferretti, *The Year the Big Apple Went Bust*, 384.
41. Maurice Carroll, "Grading the Mayor: 'A' for Effort," *New York Times*, 4/7/74.
42. Maurice Carroll, "Beame Strolls City Streets to Show They're Safe," *New York Times*, 4/26/74.
43. Maurice Carroll, "Beame Tells News Executives City Faces 'Insuperable' Deficit," *New York Times*, 3/23/74.
44. Maurice Carroll, "8-Cent Sales Tax Proposed by City to Cut Fiscal Gap," *New York Times*, 4/10/74; also see Edward Ranzal, "Beame Is Victor in Budget Fight," *New York Times*, 6/21/74.
45. McClelland and Magdovitz, *Crisis in the Making*, 325.
46. Maurice Carroll, "Council Briefed on Budget Plight," *New York Times*, 4/20/74.
47. McClelland and Magdovitz, *Crisis in the Making*, 301.
48. Ibid., 308.
49. Michael Stern, "Goldin Sees Peril in City Borrowing," *New York Times*, 11/1/74.
50. "Ten Good Reasons for Investing in the Tax-Exempt Bonds of the City of New York," Litigation Series, Box 3, Flushing National Bank vs. City of New York, 1975–77, MAC Archives, Baruch College.
51. Harrison J. Goldin to Herbert Stein, 7/22/74, Jonathan Weiner Collection, copy of letter in the possession of the author. Goldin, then the city's comptroller, was actually asking Stein to advance the city federal aid more rapidly, so the city could avoid the market for short-term debt, and, if this was not possible, to see if the government might be able to lend the city amounts equivalent to anticipated federal aid at low interest.
52. Maurice Carroll, "Dutiful Beame Enters Limelight," *New York Times*, 6/24/74.
53. James Cavanagh to Abraham Beame, 10/26/74, cited in *Securities and Exchange Commission Staff Report on Transactions in Securities of the City of New York*, August 1977, 15.
54. Fitch Investors Service, "New York City—Its Debt Financial Structure (Financial Future?)—An Analysis," An Update of 7/24/74 Report, 10/10/74, SEC FOIA Request, Box 1, 46.

4. SOUNDING THE ALARM

1. John Darnton, "Audit Discovers $5.4 Million Gone from City Vault," 7/15/74, *New York Times*; John Darnton, "Audit May Show That City Had $40 Million Unrecorded in Bank," *New York Times*, 7/18/74; John Darnton, "Beame Tells of Vain Effort to Reconcile City's Books," *New York Times*, 7/19/74; David A. Andelman, "Controller Finds Records of City in 'Chaotic' State," *New York Times*, 7/22/74; "The Mess in City Hall," *New York Times*, 7/22/74; Maurice Carroll, "Beame Responds to Goldin Reports as 3d Is Released," *New York Times*, 7/23/74; John Darnton, "Millions 'Missing' from City Vault Were Never Lost," *New York Times*, 8/1/74; John Darnton, "City Securities Shifted to Bank," *New York Times*, 8/9/74.

2. John Darnton, "Beame Denounces Goldin's Tactics as 'Distortions,'" *New York Times*, 7/29/74.

3. Steve Clifford interview, 4/30/12.

4. "Office of the Comptroller of the City of New York," prepared for the Charter Revision Commission under the direction of Steven Clifford, November 1973, Jack Bigel Papers, Box 9, Baruch College Archives.

5. Harrison J. Goldin interview, 1/24/12.

6. Memo from Weiner to Goldin, 5/6/74, cited in *Securities and Exchange Commission Staff Report on Transactions in Securities of the City of New York*, August 1977, 2. Also see Jonathan Weiner Collection, copy of memo in possession of the author.

7. Jon Weiner to Seymour Scher, 10/4/74. Jonathan Weiner Collection, copy in possession of the author.

8. Later audits revealed that Clifford and Weiner were right about this: for example, in June 1975 the city's books reflected that it expected to collect $502 million in unpaid property taxes, $380 million of which was pledged to redeem tax anticipation notes. However, the amount was overstated: $126.6 million was actually on publicly owned properties, $4.7 million on diplomatic property, $53 million on buildings in the Mitchell-Lama subsidized housing program, $54.4 million on properties pending foreclosure, and $43.9 million on properties owned by the bankrupt Penn Central Corporation. See New York State Division of Audits and Accounts, *Summary of Audit Reports Relative to Central Budgetary, Accounting and Finance Systems and Reporting Practices of New York City* (1978), 8–9.

9. Correspondence with Steve Clifford, 2/8/16.

10. Steve Clifford to Harrison J. Goldin, 10/1/74. Steve Clifford Collection, copy of the memo in author's possession. Clifford had also written a lengthy memo to the commissioners of the Charter Review process in May 1974 describing some of the problems he felt the city faced, which included an appendix titled "Heading Off Reality at the Budget Gap": "In the land of Budget Gap, anything and everything can become revenue. There may be no cash in the XYZ fund, but if it has a positive book balance, call it revenue." Steve Clifford Collection, copy of memo in author's possession.

11. Jonathan Weiner to Harrison J. Goldin, Subject: "Bankers Agreement of 1933," undated memo, Jonathan Weiner Collection, copy in author's possession.

12. Steve Clifford interview, 4/30/12; also see *Deposition Upon Oral Examination of Steven Clifford, in re: New York City Municipal Securities Litigation*, 12/4/79, 243–50. Clifford was vague about when exactly he had spoken with bankers, suggesting that it might have been in late fall 1974, or maybe only in the winter and spring of 1975.

13. Steve Clifford to Roy Goodman, 11/21/74, "The Fiscal Crisis," in SEC FOIA Request Box 1, 215.

14. "Near-Bankrupt City," *New York Times*, 11/4/74.

15. "News Release for State Senator Roy M. Goodman," 11/26/74, SEC FOIA Request, Box 1, 340. Goodman used the attachments from Clifford's memo almost verbatim in his press release.

16. Abraham Beame to Harrison J. Goldin, 12/12/74, Letter in possession of the

author. Also see Abraham Beame to Victor Gotbaum, 12/12/74, WAG 030, Bernard Bellush Papers, Box 4, "Fiscal Crisis," Tamiment Library.

17. Maurice Carroll, "Beame Cuts 1,510 Workers and Imposes a Job Freeze to Save the City $100 Million," *New York Times*, 11/23/74.

18. Fred Ferretti, "City, in Dismissing 3,725, Includes 1,100 in Schools, 900 in Uniform," *New York Times*, 12/12/74.

19. "Hundreds Protest Closings of Fire Companies," *New York Times*, 12/10/74.

20. Nilda Ortiz to Senator Israel Ruiz, 1/31/75, Roll 12, Subject Files, Abraham Beame Papers.

21. Gene I. Maeroff, "City U. Adopts Budget-Cut Measures," *New York Times*, 12/13/74.

22. R. M. Campbell, vice president of Roan Industries, to Abraham Beame, 1/20/75, Roll 12, Subject Files, Abraham Beame Papers.

23. Chana Klajman to Abraham Beame, 5/9/75, Roll 12, Subject Files, Abraham Beame Papers.

24. For example, see Neal Moylan to Robert R. Douglass, 3/24/71, and Statement by Governor Nelson A. Rockefeller, 3/15/71, Nelson Aldrich Rockefeller Gubernatorial Series, RG 15, Series 10.3, Box 13, Folder 146, Rockefeller Archives Center.

25. John Corry, "Hugh Carey: Portrait of One Politician as a Private Man," *New York Times Magazine*, 6/11/78. Also see Seymour P. Lachman and Robert Polner, *The Man Who Saved New York: Hugh Carey and the Great Fiscal Crisis of 1975* (Albany: State University of New York Press, 2010).

26. Frank Lynn, "Shake-Up by Carey," *New York Times*, 11/6/74.

27. "Rats Find Home in Central Park," *New York Times*, 1/4/75. Also see Carter B. Horsley, "Rise of Vermin in Apartments Is Tied to Garbage Compaction," *New York Times*, 3/27/75; Leslie Maitland, "Things That Bring Dirt and Disease," *New York Times*, 2/20/75. Complaints of rats and vermin in apartment buildings were rising too.

28. Hermes, *Love Goes to Buildings on Fire*, 106–107.

29. Hugh Carey, "Text of Carey's State of the State Message as He Delivered It to the Legislature," *New York Times*, 1/9/75.

5. THINGS FALL APART

1. *Securities and Exchange Commission Staff Report on Transactions in Securities of the City of New York* (Washington, D.C.: Government Printing Office, 1977), Chapter 4, "Report on the Role of the Underwriters," 1–5.

2. Examination of Richard V. Adams before the Securities and Exchange Commission, 6/2/76, 169.

3. Little precise information was gathered about who exactly bought the city's obligations. Indeed, the SEC would later complain that there was a "lack of records which one could reasonably have been expected to be kept by the banks, but which were not," noting the "lack of organization existing in the record-keeping systems of the banks" (*SEC Staff Report*, Chapter 4, 66). But in terms of the market

as a whole—not just New York—$145 billion of the total $207 billion in state and local debt was owned by banks and institutions as of 1975. See *SEC Staff Report*, Chapter 7, Appendix D, Statement of James A. Lebenthal, "Consequences of New York City Default on Individual Bond Owner."

4. The city made available a lower denomination of its short-term debt in the winter of 1974–75 in an effort to lure more small investors, a sign that the bulk of this debt had previously been held by larger institutions and big individual investors. The SEC report also surveyed 500 investors, many of whom characterized themselves as not especially affluent.

5. *SEC Staff Report*, Chapter 7, 3.

6. Krippner, *Capitalizing on Crisis*, esp. 75 for discussion of Citibank.

7. Charles N. Stabler, "Developing Debt," *Wall Street Journal*, 9/28/76; also see Weikart, *Follow the Money*, 30.

8. Financial Accounts of the United States, March 10, 2016, 112, accessed at http://www.federalreserve.gov/releases/z1/current/data.htm.

9. Memo to Mr. Thomas Huerta from Mary Saunders Turner, "Reduction in Citibank Income Tax Burden, 1956–1970," Citibank Book, Mary S. Turner, Memoranda and Drafts, 1978, RG 12, Citibank Archives. For a description of a similar approach at Chase Manhattan Bank, see "Examination of David Rockefeller conducted before the Securities and Exchange Commission," 7/29/76, 29–30, Box 123, "Testimony of People Appearing Before the Securities and Exchange Commission," Abraham Beame Papers, Municipal Archives.

10. Jonathan Weiner to Harrison J. Goldin, Seymour Scher, William T. Scott, 10/11/74. Jonathan Weiner Collection, copy of memo in author's possession.

11. On the history of REITS, see Elizabeth Blackmar, "Of REITs and Rights: Absentee Ownership at the Periphery," in Jeffry M. Diefendorf, ed., *City, Country, Empire: Landscapes in Environmental History* (Pittsburgh: University of Pittsburgh Press, 2005).

12. William Ryan, "Municipal Market," *Daily Bond Buyer*, 3/21/75; Leila Zogby, "NYC Banks Cut Tax-Exempt Holdings 7.28%," *Daily Bond Buyer*, 3/4/75.

13. Shalala and Bellamy, "A State Saves a City," 1126–7.

14. David Rockefeller, *Memoirs* (New York: Random House, 2002), 388.

15. Quoted in Records of the DLMA Finding Aid, 3, Rockefeller Archives Center.

16. David Rockefeller, "Business Must Perform Better," *Wall Street Journal*, 12/21/71. Also see David Rockefeller, "Banks Must Respond to Social Concerns," *New York Times*, 7/18/71; David Rockefeller, "The Essential Quest for the Middle Way: Capitalism, for Better or Worse," *New York Times*, 3/23/73.

17. Richard Reeves, "$10 Billion Asked for 110 New Cities," *New York Times*, 2/17/71.

18. "Our Way of Life, Our Future, and Our Free Enterprise System," speech given to the Society of American Business Writers, Spring 1975. Senator Bill Brock read the speech into the *Congressional Record* on June 24, 1975, after which Wriston wrote Brock a letter thanking him and saying that he hoped the senator concurred about the "dangers and shortcomings of such central economic planning" and the problems that the Javits-Humphrey bill posed: "I think this planning bill is a threat to individual liberty as well as a poor way to deal with economic prob-

lems," Walter Wriston to Bill Brock, 6/30/75, "Political Correspondence," Walter Wriston Papers, Tufts University.

19. Walter Wriston to Richard Nixon, 6/26/73, "Political Correspondence," Walter Wriston Papers, Tufts University.

20. Richard Adams to D. C. Platten, 1/8/75, Box 123, "Testimony of People Appearing Before the S.E.C.," Abraham Beame Papers, Municipal Archives.

21. Amos T. Beason to Frank Smeal, "New York City," 12/13/74, SEC FOIA Request, Box 1, 6.

22. For "Jersey Mafia," see Michael C. Jensen, "Bankers, in Key Role, Shun Spotlight," *New York Times*, 9/8/75.

23. McClelland and Magdovitz, *Crisis in the Making*, 301. These numbers were known at the time: see Capital Markets Section (Mr. Puckett) to Mr. J. Charles Partee, 12/16/74, Arthur Burns Papers, Box B84, Folder: "NYC Financial Difficulties—Dec. 1974–Sept. 1975," Gerald Ford Presidential Library (GFPL).

24. Minutes of the Special Meeting of the Comptroller's Advisory Technical Debt Management Committee, 12/17/74, in *SEC Staff Report*, Chapter 4, "Report on the Role of the Underwriters," Appendix A.

25. *SEC Staff Report*, Chapter 1, "Chronology of Events, October 1, 1974–April 8, 1975," 56.

26. Ibid., 84.

27. Steve Clifford to Harrison J. Goldin, Re: Presentation on Fiscal Crisis to "Influentials," 1/21/75, Steve Clifford Collection, copy of memo in possession of author.

28. Nelson Rockefeller, "The Making of a Just America," meeting of the American Society of Newspaper Editors Luncheon, Shoreham Hotel, Washington, D.C., 4/18/68, quoted in Eric Peterson, "Planning for Capital: The Urban Development Corporation and Urban Crisis in New York," M.A. thesis, School of Architecture, Yale University, 2015, 68.

29. Ibid., 71.

30. Ibid., 59, 68. Also see Eleanor Brilliant, *The Urban Development Corporation: Private Interests and Public Authority* (Lexington, Mass.: D. C. Heath, 1975), 23; Louis K. Loewenstein, "The New York State Urban Development Corporation: Private Benefits and Public Costs, An Evaluation of a Noble Experiment," Working Paper; "The New York State Urban Development Corporation—a Forgotten Failure or a Precursor of the Future?" *Journal of the American Institute of Planners*, 1978, Vol. 44, No. 3, 261–73.

31. Joseph P. Fried, "Banks Assailed by Head of UDC," *New York Times*, 1/17/75; James Ring Adams, "The Collapse of the UDC," *Wall Street Journal*, 4/7/75.

32. Paul Hoffman, "The Man Who Keeps Suing New York," *New York*, 5/9/77.

33. William Quirk interview, 12/10/12.

34. "Suit Delays City's Sale of $260 Million Notes," *New York Times*, 2/11/75.

35. Fred Ferretti, "City Sells $375 Million in Notes at 8%," *New York Times*, 3/14/75; Hoffman, "The Man Who Keeps Suing New York."

36. Fred Ferretti, "City's Dismissals Total 1,724 So Far," *New York Times*, 2/8/75.

37. *SEC Staff Report*, Chapter 1, 104.

38. *SEC Staff Report*, Chapter 4, 46.
39. Memorandum to H. van B. Cleveland, VP, and Thomas F. Huertas, VP, from Joan L. Silverman, "Re: New York City's Financial Crisis—IV," 9/25/80, RG 12, Citibank Book, Memos from Joan Silverman to H. van B. Cleveland and Thomas F. Huertas, 7/12/80, Citibank Archives.
40. *SEC Staff Report*, Chapter 4, 30–35.
41. Charles Sanford interview, 7/31/13.
42. *SEC Staff Report*, Chapter 1, 111.
43. Ibid., 118; Charles Sanford interview, 7/31/13.
44. Edward Ranzal, "City Is Negotiating for Loan to Meet March 14 Payroll," *New York Times*, 3/7/75.
45. Fred Ferretti, "The City Credit Bind," *New York Times*, 3/20/75.
46. Examination of Richard V. Adams, 6/2/76, before the Securities and Exchange Commission, 6/2/76, 170–71.
47. Edward Ranzal, "City Negotiates Its Crucial Loan," *New York Times*, 3/8/75.
48. *SEC Staff Report*, Chapter 1, 188.
49. Ibid., 223.
50. Ibid., 254.

6. WASHINGTON POLITICS

1. *SEC Staff Report*, Chapter 1, 257.
2. Text of Mayor Beame's Fiscal Statement, *New York Times*, 3/24/75.
3. "Beame Purchase Backs His Confidence in City," *New York Times*, 3/24/75.
4. Harrison J. Goldin interview, 10/17/11.
5. Fred Ferretti, "State to Advance Funds to the City to Pay April Bills," *New York Times*, 4/4/75.
6. John Darnton, "City Hall Drafting U.S. Measure to Get Federal Aid," *New York Times*, 4/9/75.
7. Steven Weisman, "Beame and Financiers Trade Accusations About City's Tarnished Fiscal Image," *New York Times*, 4/10/75; "Beame Lays Loss of Confidence in City's Securities to Negativism," *Daily Bond Buyer*, 4/10/75.
8. Weisman, "Beame and Financiers Trade Accusations About City's Tarnished Fiscal Image."
9. David Bird, "Hospitals Agency to Shut Delafield," *New York Times*, 5/9/75.
10. "Research Libraries to Close Saturdays as a Money-Saver," *New York Times*, 5/9/75.
11. Fred Ferretti, "City Plans to Cut 3,975 Off Payroll, for '75–'76 Budget," *New York Times*, 4/23/75.
12. Ronald Smothers, "City Hall Protest Staged by Goldwater's Patients," *New York Times*, 4/30/75.
13. Iver Peterson, "Hunter Students Occupy Dean's Office," *New York Times*, 5/1/75; "More Protest Plan to Cut City U Funds," *New York Times*, 5/9/75.
14. Geoffrey Kabaservice, *Rule and Ruin: The Downfall of Moderation and the Destruction of the Republican Party, from Eisenhower to the Tea Party* (Studies in

Postwar American Political Development) (New York: Oxford University Press, 2012), 346.

15. Yanek Mieczkowski, *Gerald Ford and the Challenges of the 1970s* (Lexington: University Press of Kentucky, 2005), 75.

16. Quoted in Don Oberdorfer, "He Wants to Be Speaker of the House," *New York Times Magazine*, 4/30/67.

17. Mieczkowski, *Gerald Ford and the Challenges of the 1970s*, 73.

18. Ibid., 10.

19. Ibid., 121.

20. Quoted in ibid., 153.

21. Ibid., 150–53.

22. Ibid., 163–64.

23. Ibid., 164.

24. Kabaservice, *Rule and Ruin*, 264, 284, 322.

25. Ibid., 352.

26. "William E. Simon: A Candid Conversation About Money, Energy and Hard Times in the Seventies with the Outgoing, Opinionated U.S. Secretary of the Treasury," *Playboy*, May 1975.

27. Jefferson A. Decker, "How We Got Here: William E. Simon and the Origins of the Financial 1980s," paper presented at "Protest, Politics and Ideas in the American Century: A Conference in Honor of Alan Brinkley," April 15, 2016, Columbia University.

28. "William E. Simon: A Candid Conversation."

29. Steven R. Weisman, "Beame and Carey and Bankers See Simon and Burns," *New York Times*, 5/7/75.

30. Edwin L. Dale Jr., "Simon Says U.S. Won't Aid in Financial Rescue of City," *New York Times*, 5/11/75.

31. Jack Marsh to Gerald Ford, 5/9/75, Box 28, Folder: Local Government N.Y.C. (1), Gerald R. Ford Presidential Handwriting File (subsequently Presidential Handwriting File), GFPL.

32. Capital Markets Section (Mr. Puckett) to Mr. J. Charles Partee, 12/16/74, Arthur Burns Papers, Box B84, Folder: "NYC Financial Difficulties—Dec. 1974–Sept. 1975," GFPL.

33. *SEC Staff Report*, Chapter 1, 221.

34. I. D. Sandberg to Mr. Holmes, 3/14/75, "New York City Budget Problems—Comments by David Grossman of Chase Manhattan Bank," Drawer 24, Folder: New York City 2/75–6/75, Fiche 1, William Simon Papers, Lafayette College.

35. "New York City's Financial Situation," a presentation to the New York City Congressional Delegation, by Jac Friedgut, 3/18/75, in Washington, D.C., Citibank Archives, RG 12, Joan Silverman Papers, "NYC Fiscal Crisis 1975–79," Folder 3 of 5. Also see *SEC Staff Report*, Chapter 1, 192–94.

36. Edward P. Snyder to William Simon, 3/11/75, Drawer 24, "NYC 2/75–6/75," Fiche 1, William Simon Papers.

37. "Memorandum for the President," from William Simon, 3/26/75, Presidential Handwriting File, Box 8, Folder: Federal Aid: Revenue Sharing, GFPL.

38. L. William Seidman to Jerry Jones, 4/1/75, Gerald R. Ford Presidential Handwriting File, Box 8, Folder: Federal Aid: Revenue Sharing, GFPL.

39. "Memorandum for the Vice President," from R. L. Dunham, 3/27/75, Gerald R. Ford Presidential Handwriting File, Box 8, Folder: Federal Aid, Revenue Sharing, GFPL; Nelson Rockefeller to Gerald Ford, 3/28/75, Gerald R. Ford Presidential Handwriting File, Box 8, Folder: Federal Aid, Revenue Sharing, GFPL. Dunham had been a Rockefeller adviser in Albany, and they had both been skeptical about the city's repeated borrowing at that time.

40. Memo to the President from Donald Rumsfeld, 4/12/75. Rumsfeld's note is hand-scrawled on the bottom of a catalogue of the positions of different advisers responding to Simon's suggestion to offer an early payment. Box 8, Folder: Federal Aid—Revenue Sharing, Gerald R. Ford Presidential Handwriting File, GFPL.

41. "Memo Concerning the New York City Financial Crisis," Jim Cannon, 5/12/75, Box 28, Folder: Local Government N.Y.C. (1), Gerald R. Ford Presidential Handwriting File, GFPL.

42. Dick Dunham to James Cannon, 5/9/75, Box 28, Folder: Local Government N.Y.C. (1), Gerald R. Ford Presidential Handwriting File, GFPL.

43. "Proposed Comments on the Consequences of a Default by New York," James M. Cannon Files, Box 23, Folder: "NYC Finances: Meeting with the President, Vice-President, Beame and Carey, 5/13/75," GFPL.

44. Presidential Handwriting File, Box 28, Local Government New York City (1), GFPL.

45. Peter Goldmark interview, 2/25/13.

46. "Meeting with Governor Hugh Carey and Mayor Abe Beame," 5/13/75, from Jim Cannon, James M. Cannon Files, Box 23, Folder "NYC Finances—Meeting with the President, Vice President, Beame and Carey, 5/13/75," GFPL.

47. Ford Daily Diary, 5/13/75, List of Attendees, Appendix D.

48. Ron Nessen Handwritten Notes, May 13, 1975—Meeting with New York City Officials, Ron Nessen Papers, Box 294, GFPL. Both Ron Nessen and (probably) James Lynn took notes on this meeting, transcribing much of what was said. The two accounts are similar but contain slightly different quotations; this account draws on both.

49. Ibid.

50. Ibid.

51. Ibid.

52. "N.Y.C. Meeting, 5/13/75," likely author James Lynn, James M. Cannon Files, Box 23, Folder: "New York City Finances—Meeting with President, Vice President, Beame and Carey, 5/13/75," GFPL.

53. Ron Nessen Handwritten Notes, May 13, 1975—Meeting with New York City Officials, Ron Nessen Papers, Box 294, GFPL.

54. "N.Y.C. Meeting, 5/13/75."

55. Memo for James Cannon from Max Friedersdorf, 5/15/75, James M. Cannon

Files, Box 23, Folder: "NYC Finances—Meeting with the President, 11/18/75," GFPL.

56. UPI, 5/14/75, James M. Cannon Files, Box 23, Folder: "NYC Finances—Meeting with the President, 11/18/75," GFPL.

57. Press Conference of James T. Lynn, Director of the Office of Management and Budget, Hugh Carey, and Abraham Beame, 5/13/75, James M. Cannon Files, Box 23, Folder: "NYC Finances—Meeting with the President, 11/18/75," GFPL.

58. "Memorandum for the President: Subject: Response to New York City's Request for Credit Assistance," from Jim Cannon, 5/14/75, James M. Cannon Files, Box 23, Folder: "NYC Finances—Meeting with the President, Vice President, Beame and Carey, 5/13/75," GFPL.

59. Gerald Ford to Abe Beame, 5/14/75, James M. Cannon Files, Box 23, Folder: "NYC Finances—Meeting with the President, Vice President, Beame and Carey, 5/13/75," GFPL. The original draft (which also included some suggestions for specific cuts the city might make, edited out of the version that went to Beame) was circulated through the White House staff. Alan Greenspan pronounced the letter "excellent," although he felt that Ford should emphasize even more emphatically that a "one-shot bailout" would only worsen the city's problems. Cannon's language quoted here all went into the final version that appeared in the newspapers: "Text of President's Letter," New York Times, 5/15/75.

60. Douglas Martin, "James M. Cannon, an Adviser to Ford, Dies at 93," New York Times, 9/20/11.

61. "Beame's Response," May 1975, James M. Cannon Files, Box 23, Folder: "Meeting with the President—11/18/75," GFPL.

62. Frank Lynn, "Carey and Mayor Express Anger," New York Times, 5/15/75.

63. Ibid.

7. BIG MAC

1. Maurice Carroll, "State to Control Panel to Oversee Budget for the City," New York Times, 6/3/75.

2. "Plan Would Let City 'Sell' Brooklyn Bridge," New York Times, 5/22/75.

3. Ronald Smothers, "$200-Million Suffolk Loan to Tide Over City Studied," New York Times, 5/29/75.

4. "G.O.P. in Albany Rejects Beame's $640-Million Plea," New York Times, 5/16/75.

5. Ellmore Patterson, Chairman, FCLG, to Harrison J. Goldin, 5/22/75, "New York City Financial Crisis," Folder 1 of 5, Joan Silverman Papers (RG 12), Citibank Archives.

6. Martin Mayer, "Plunging into Bankruptcy; or, How to Get New York Back into the Swim," New York Times, 5/19/75. A few days later one of the city's finance writers asked, "Should the City Scale Down Debt Through the Bankruptcy Act?" Michael Stern, New York Times, 5/21/75.

7. Edward Ranzal, "Residents Donate Funds to Aid City," New York Times, 5/26/75; Fred Ferretti, "Reporter's Notebook: The Mayor, in Time of Stress," New York Times, 5/28/75.

8. Fred Ferretti, "The Buck Stops with Gotbaum," *New York Times Sunday Magazine*, June 4, 1978.

9. Ibid. Also Bernard and Jewel Bellush, *Union Power and New York: Victor Gotbaum and District Council 37* (Westport, Conn.: Praeger, 1984), 87.

10. Joseph McCartin, "'A Wagner Act for Public Employees': Labor's Deferred Dream and the Rise of Conservatism, 1970–1976," *Journal of American History*, June 2008, 123–48.

11. Sam Zagoria, ed., *Public Workers and Public Unions* (Englewood Cliffs, N.J.: Prentice-Hall, 1972), quoted in Bellush and Bellush, *Union Power and New York*, 161.

12. Ibid., 189.

13. William D. Cohen, *The Last Tycoons: The Secret History of Lazard Frères & Co.* (New York: Doubleday, 2007), 1–10; Peter Hellman, "The Wizard of Lazard," *New York Times*, 3/21/76; Doug Henwood, "Felix the Fox," *Village Voice*, 7/31/90, 29–32; also see Felix G. Rohatyn, *Dealings: A Political and Financial Life* (New York: Simon & Schuster, 2010), 77–78.

14. Terry Robards, "Healer: Stanching a Wall Street Crisis," *New York Times*, 1/24/71.

15. Rohatyn, *Dealings*, 84–99.

16. Ibid., 102–3.

17. Rohatyn, "A New RFC Is Proposed for Business," *New York Times*, 12/1/74. Rohatyn had also been called in when several major brokerage houses seemed about to go bankrupt in the summer of 1970, as the go-go market of the 1960s was ending—he headed up a "Crisis Committee," persuading investors not to withdraw their funds from the brokers.

18. Felix Rohatyn interview, 3/19/13.

19. Henwood, "Felix the Fox"; also see Cohen, *The Last Tycoons*.

20. Nicholas von Hoffman, "The Biggest Loser in the ITT Case," *Washington Post*, 3/10/72.

21. Rohatyn, *Dealings*, 124.

22. Robert Polner interview with Hugh Carey and David Burke, 2/25/09.

23. Rohatyn, *Dealings*, 117–19.

24. "Petition to Commissioner Hon. Benjamin J. Malcolm," from "We, the undersigned, trial detainees and time-serving inmates presently incarcerated at Ricker's Island Hospital Correctional Facility," 11/29/74, "NYC Fiscal Crisis 1974–5, Layoffs—Contracting Out," DC 37 Archives.

25. Henry Alteras, 1974, "NYC Fiscal Crisis 1974–5, Layoffs—Contracting Out," DC 37 Archives.

26. Telegram to Benjamin Malcolm from Victor Gotbaum and Lillian Roberts, 11/25/74, "NYC Fiscal Crisis 1974–5, Layoffs—Contracting Out," DC 37 Archives.

27. Victor Gotbaum to Abraham Beame, 12/5/74, WAG 030, Bernard Bellush Papers, Box 4, "Fiscal Crisis—1975–1978," Tamiment Library, NYU.

28. MLC Steering Committee Meeting Minutes, 2/24/75, Jack Bigel Papers, Baruch College.

29. Freeman, *Working-Class New York*, 215–27.

30. "Rally and Boycott of First National City Bank—Facts and Background," 5/20/75,

"Layoffs 1975," DC 37 Archives; Sample Letter to Walter Wriston, 5/20/75, "Layoffs 1975," DC 37 Archives; advertisement in *New York Times*, 5/28/75.

31. Stephen J. Crowley to Victor Gotbaum, 5/23/75, "Layoffs 1975," DC 37 Archives.
32. Weikart, *Follow the Money*, 23–25.
33. Memorandum to Citibank Managers at 111 Wall Street, Re: June 4th Demonstration by Municipal Employees; Meet Next Thursday 5/29, re: Demonstration June 4th, Citibank Archives, RG 12, Joan Silverman Papers, New York City Financial Crisis 1975 (Folder 1 of 5, 1975).
34. To LBS, Re: Proposed News Conference, Citibank Archives, RG 12, Joan Silverman Papers, New York City Financial Crisis 1975 (Folder 1 of 5, 1975).
35. BBDO Research Report, "Hotline IV on New York City Finance Difficulties Related to FCNB," 6/6/75, Citibank Archives, RG 12, Joan Silverman Papers, New York City Financial Crisis 1975 (Folder 1 of 5, 1975).
36. Memorandum to All Citibankers, from William I. Spencer, Re: Citibank and the City of New York; also includes Spencer to Victor Gotbaum, 5/20/75, Citibank Archives, RG 12, Joan Silverman Papers, New York City Financial Crisis 1975 (Folder 1 of 5, 1975).
37. Fred Ferretti, "Beame to Present Two Budgets Today, One a 'Crisis' Plan," *New York Times*, 5/29/75; Fred Ferretti, "Mayor Emotional," *New York Times*, 5/30/75.
38. Ferretti, "Mayor Emotional."
39. "Transcript of Mayor Beame's Speech Describing an Austerity Budget for City," *New York Times*, 5/30/75.
40. "Beame Cuts Awe Tourists," *New York Times*, 5/31/75.
41. John Darnton, "Civil Service Rally Assails Bank's Role in Budget Cuts," *New York Times*, 6/5/75.
42. "Unions Withdrawn $15 Million at Banks," *New York Times*, 6/1/75.
43. Leslie Maitland, "Budget Crisis Affects Beames as Well," *New York Times*, 6/8/75.
44. Fred Ferretti, "Reporter's Notebook: The Mayor, in Time of Stress," *New York Times*, 5/28/75.
45. Fred Ferretti, "State Aid Agency City's Only Option, Panel Maintains," *New York Times*, 6/5/75.
46. Alfred Miele, "City Yielding on State Plan for Rescue Agency," *Daily News*, 6/5/75.
47. Ferretti, "State Aid Agency City's Only Option, Panel Maintains."
48. Prepayment of Real Estate Taxes, Letters of Intent Received as of 6/5/75, "Fiscal Crisis 1970s," ABNY Archives; Press Release, 6/5/75, "Fiscal Crisis 1970s," ABNY Archives.
49. William Spencer to Lew Rudin, 6/12/75, "Fiscal Crisis 1970s," ABNY Archives.
50. Press Release, 6/5/75, "Fiscal Crisis 1970s," ABNY Archives.
51. Edward Ranzal, "City Stages Brief Drama and Gains $115 Million," *New York Times*, 6/7/75.
52. Francis X. Clines, "Legislators Act on Plan to Block Default by City," *New York Times*, 6/10/75.

53. Donna Shalala interview, 5/22/13.
54. "S&P's President Says MAC Bonds Should Not Be Confused with NYC Issues," *Daily Bond Buyer*, 6/27/75.
55. Memorandum to the Economic Policy Board from Gerald Parsky, "New York City Financial Situation," 6/11/75, Box 78, New York City, May–October 1975 (1), L. William Seidman Files, GFPL.

8. FEAR CITY

1. "Welcome to Fear City," "Layoffs 1975," DC 37 Archives.
2. Advertisement in *New York Times*, 6/10/75.
3. Glenn Fowler, "Union 'Guide' to 'Fear City' Is Banned by a Court Order," *New York Times*, 6/13/75.
4. Glenn Fowler, "Police and Firemen Take Job Campaign to Street," *New York Times*, 6/20/75.
5. Bert Shanas, "Budget Cuts Mean the End of Education: Anker," *Daily News*, 6/10/75.
6. "They Marched, Met and Won," *Daily News*, 6/25/75.
7. Emanuel Perlmutter, "City Rescinds Suspensions and Sanitationmen Return," *New York Times*, 6/29/75; Murray Schumach, "City Budget Slashes Fail to Shock Public," *New York Times*, 6/30/75.
8. Lawrence van Gelder, "Layoffs of 40,000 Ordered as City Ends Fiscal Year," *New York Times*, 7/1/75.
9. Lee Dembart, "DeLury, After Court Loss, Says Strike Is 'Inevitable,'" *New York Times*, 7/1/75.
10. Neal Hirschfeld and William McFadden, "Cop Teletypes Utter Chilling Word: Layoff," *Daily News*, 7/1/75.
11. George F. Will, "Bailing Out New York," *Washington Post*, 6/18/75.
12. Joseph B. Treaster, "26 Fire Department Companies Closed," *New York Times*, 7/3/75.
13. Robert Crane, Vincent Lee, and Donald Singleton, "Strike Has Garbage Piling Up," *Daily News*, 7/2/75.
14. Beth Fallon and Michael Patterson, "Cuts & Bruises: Layoffs Hurt Services," *Daily News*, 7/2/75.
15. Van Gelder, "Layoffs of 40,000 Ordered as City Ends Fiscal Year."
16. Fred Ferretti, "City's 10,000 Sanitationmen Strike; Police and Firemen Also Discuss Job Actions to Protest Layoffs," *New York Times*, 7/2/75; John Corry, "'What Can You Do?' People Ask," *New York Times*, 7/2/75.
17. Tom Buckley, "About New York," *New York Times*, 7/2/75.
18. Ferretti, "City's 10,000 Sanitationmen Strike"; Selwyn Raab, "Ex-Policemen Block Brooklyn Bridge," *New York Times*, 7/2/75.
19. Patrick Doyle and Steven Matthews, "Fired Cops Wage Battle with Ins," *Daily News*, 7/2/75; also see Deidre Carmody, "Laid-Off Women Police Officers Embittered," *New York Times*, 7/3/75.
20. Crane, Lee, and Singleton, "Strike Has Garbage Piling Up."

21. Vincent Lee and Robert Patterson, "'Sick' Firemen Join in Protest," *Daily News*, 7/3/75.

22. Robert McG. Thomas Jr., "Firecrackers, Not Fires, Explode in East Harlem," *New York Times*, 7/4/75.

23. "Numerous Garbage Blazes Give Firemen One of 'Busiest Nights,'" *New York Times*, 7/3/75.

24. Peter Kriss, "Fiscal Cuts Hit Home in Streets of Bayside," *New York Times*, 7/3/75.

25. Raab, "Ex-Policemen Block Brooklyn Bridge."

26. Peter Coutros, "Fired-Up Brooklyn Parents Fight Firehouse Closings," *Daily News*, 7/3/75.

27. Lee and Patterson, "'Sick' Firemen Join in Protest."

28. Joseph McCartin, "A Wagner Act for Public Employees,'" *Journal of American History*, June 2008, 138–39.

29. Andrew H. Malcolm, "Police Out, San Francisco Faces Fire and Transit Strikes," *New York Times*, 8/20/75.

30. Andrew H. Malcolm, "Alioto Imposes Pact in the Face of Dissent," *New York Times*, 8/22/75.

31. Brent Appel, "Emergency Mayoral Power: An Exercise in Charter Interpretation," 65 *Cal. Law Review*, 686, 1977, 688–91; Winston Crouch, *Organized Civil Servants: Public Employer-Employee Relations in California* (Berkeley: University of California Press, 1978), 227–31.

32. Ibid., 139.

33. Ibid., 142.

34. Minutes of the Meeting of the Board of Directors, 7/1/75, MAC Archive, Baruch College. Many—although not all—of the minutes of MAC meetings are available online at http://www.baruch.cuny.edu/library/alumni/online_exhibits/amfl/mac /S2_BODMTGMIN.html.

35. Memorandum for the Economic Policy Board, from William E. Simon and James M. Cannon, Subject: New York City Financial Problem, Box 78, Folder: NYC May–October 1975 (2), L. William Seidman Files, GFPL.

36. Steven Weisman, "2,000 Policemen and 750 Firemen Are Rehired Here," *New York Times*, 7/5/75.

37. Herbert Elish interview, 4/4/13.

38. John Darnton, "Need for Quick Action Unites MAC Board," 7/29/75.

39. Ferretti, *The Year the Big Apple Went Bust*, 243.

40. "July 17, 1975," MAC Minutes, in Abraham Beame Papers, Box 070013, Folder 11, LaGuardia and Wagner Archives, LaGuardia Community College.

41. Ibid.

42. Ibid. Also see Maurice Carroll, "Mayor Is a Little Brusque but He Is Bearing Up," *New York Times*, 7/19/75; John Darnton, "M.A.C. Urges Dramatic Cuts on City to Reopen Bond Market," *New York Times*, 7/18/75.

43. David Bird, "Garbage Pickups to Be Cut in Half," *New York Times*, 7/19/75; Ronald Smothers, "City Will Dismiss 1,434 in Sanitation Force Today," *New York Times*, 7/18/75.

44. Bird, "Garbage Pickups to Be Cut in Half."
45. David Bird, "Sanitation Chief Says Tons of Garbage Are Uncollected as a Result of Cutbacks," *New York Times*, 7/22/75; David Vidal, "Rapid Garbage Pileup Is Laid to Layoffs, Confusion and Slowdowns," *New York Times*, 7/26/75; David Vidal, "City Removes Garbage Tossed in Street Protest," *New York Times*, 7/25/75; Charles Kaiser, "Garbage Pile-Ups Anger Residents," *New York Times*, 7/30/75.
46. Charles Kaiser, "292 Garbage Fires Set in City in Day," *New York Times*, 7/31/75.
47. MAC Minutes, 7/18/75, MAC Archive, Baruch College.
48. Fred Ferretti, "Beame and M.A.C. Agree on 3 Moves to Avert a Crisis," *New York Times*, 7/21/75.
49. Al Viani interview, 2/9/13.
50. DC 37 Special Executive Board Meeting Minutes, 7/31/75, 5:30 p.m, Jack Bigel Papers, Baruch College.
51. MLC Steering Committee Minutes, 6/12/75, Jack Bigel Papers, Baruch College.
52. My interpretation of Gotbaum's focus on collective bargaining is indebted to Michael Spear's dissertation, "A Crisis in Urban Liberalism" (see Introduction, n. 10).
53. Lee Dembart, "City's Fiscal Ills Create Municipal-Union Split," *New York Times*, 7/21/75.
54. MAC Minutes, 7/21/75, MAC Archive, Baruch College.
55. Ibid.
56. Fred Ferretti, "Beame and MAC Ask a Quick Rise in Transit Fares," *New York Times*, 7/25/75.
57. MAC Minutes, 7/29/75, MAC Archive, Baruch College.
58. John Darnton, "Beame Censures His Subordinates," *New York Times*, 7/26/75.
59. Lee Dembart, "Jack Bigel Holds Many Keys to City's Mansions," *New York Times*, 12/11/76.
60. Herbert Elish interview, 4/4/13; Frank Prial, "Union Leaders Display Dual Personalities," *New York Times*, 7/31/75.
61. DC 37 Special Delegate Meeting Minutes, 7/31/75, Jack Bigel Papers, Baruch College Archives.
62. Fred Ferretti, "Beame Asks Pay Freeze in Austerity Plan," *New York Times*, 8/1/75.
63. "Program of Fiscal and Management Reforms Proposed for the City by Municipal Assistance Corporation," *New York Times*, 8/1/75. MAC's proposals differed from the mayor's in several key respects: MAC wanted to see a three-year ceiling on the expense budget, a 10 percent cut for all management employees and elected officials, the creation of more rationalized management practices and strategies for greater productivity, the adoption of standard accounting procedures, and an end to all "budget gimmicks." Beame had felt that the across-the-board salary cut would create "inequities," he rejected the idea of a budget ceiling (initially, MAC had also specified a ban on tax increases), and he was offended by the idea of mandating management reforms. See MAC Minutes, 7/29/75 and 7/30/75, MAC Archive, Baruch College.

64. Ibid.

65. John Darnton, "Beame Seeks a Tight-Belt Image," *New York Times*, 7/21/75.

9. THE FACTS OF LIFE

1. Editorial, *St. Louis Post-Dispatch*, 5/29/75.

2. Editorial, *Washington Post*, 6/2/75.

3. "NY's Big Mac Is 'Cold Turkey,'" *Miami Herald*, 6/11/75.

4. "Contagious New Yorkitis," *Chicago Tribune*, 8/21/75.

5. Editorial, *Baltimore Sun*, 7/24/75.

6. "Mr. Ford on New York," *Boston Globe*, 8/6/75.

7. "A Safety Net for New York," *Washington Post*, 9/15/75.

8. Editorial, *Baltimore Sun*, 7/24/75.

9. Percy Sutton, Paul O'Dwyer, and Robert Abrams to Hugh Carey, Stanley Steingut, and Warren Anderson, 8/19/75, In "Binder on Default and Bankruptcy," Jack Bigel Collection, Baruch College.

10. "Or Usher In a Renaissance," *New York Times*, 8/16/75.

11. Robert D. McFadden, "4th Day in the 90s Here, and No Relief Is in Sight," *New York Times*, 8/4/75.

12. Arthur Browne, "Checks Await 3,000 Kids," *Daily News*, 9/15/75.

13. Alfonso A. Navarez, "2000 Seeking Young Pay Tie Up Traffic in Harlem," *New York Times*, 8/14/75.

14. Robert D. McFadden, "City and Suburban Riders Angered by Fare Increase," *New York Times*, 8/2/75.

15. Fred Ferretti, "Reporter's Notebook: Beame Uses Phone as Weapon," *New York Times*, 8/3/75.

16. Clifford Wolfe, "The City: A Time to Depopulate," *New York Times*, 8/16/75.

17. Steven Weisman, "City Fiscal Needs Grow Next Month," *New York Times*, 8/7/75.

18. Steven Weisman, "Bankers Around US Cool to MAC," *New York Times*, 8/9/75; Steven Weisman, "Issue of $275-Million in MAC Bonds Is Reported Selling 'Kind of Slowly,'" *New York Times*, 8/13/75; Steven Weisman, "MAC Defers End of Its Bond Sale to Win Customers," *New York Times*, 8/14/75; Vartanig G. Vartan, "Municipals Pale in MAC Plunge," *New York Times*, 8/14/75.

19. From Butcher & Singer Municipal Bond Department, Re: New York City, 10/8/75, William E. Simon Papers, Drawer 24, Folder 33, "NYC 1975 (Oct.)," Lafayette College.

20. Pool Report #8, 8/4/75, "The President at City Hall," James M. Cannon Files, Box 23, "NYC Finances—May–August 1975," GFPL.

21. Lee Dembart, "Ford Nettles Beame in Telling Yugoslavs City Is Fiscally Inept," *New York Times*, 8/5/75.

22. 8/1/75, Memorandum to the President from Jim Cannon, Subject: New York City Financial Situation. "Here is a status report by Dick Dunham on the financial situation of New York as it stands today. This was prepared by Dick

in consultation with Treasury officials and Bill Seidman." James M. Cannon Files, Box 23, "NYC Finances—May–August 1975," GFPL.

23. MAC Minutes, 7/25/75; MAC Minutes, 7/29/75, MAC Archive, Baruch College.

24. Steven Weisman, "MAC Calls on US to Pay for Relief," *New York Times*, 8/10/75.

25. Report on New York City: Memorandum for the President, Edwin H. Yeo III, Presidential Handwriting Files, Box 28, Folder: "Local Government, NYC," GFPL.

26. Memorandum for the President, from L. William Seidman, 9/2/75, Subject: New York City, Tab C: Actions: Promises and Deliveries, Presidential Handwriting File, Box 28, Folder: "Local Government, NYC," GFPL.

27. Memorandum for the President, New York City Situation, Presidential Handwriting Files, Box 28, Folder: "Local Government, NYC," GFPL.

28. Donald Rumsfeld to William Simon, 9/2/75, William Simon Papers, Series IIIB Subject Files, Drawer 24, Folder 24:32, "NYC: 1975 (September)," Lafayette College.

29. "Possible Actions with Respect to Default by New York City," Presidential Handwriting File, Box 28, Folder: "Local Government," GFPL.

30. "Banks with NYC Holdings Totaling 125% or More of Capital," "Banks with NYC Holdings Totaling 75%–124% of Capital," "Banks with NYC Holdings Totaling 50–75% of Capital," Presidential Handwriting File, Box 28, Folder: "Local Government," GFPL.

31. "Possible Actions with Respect to Default by New York City."

32. MAC Minutes, 8/27/75, MAC Archive; Bailey, *The Crisis Regime*, 37; also see 8/27/75 memo, Citibank Archive, RG 12, Joan Silverman Papers, "New York City Fiscal Crisis, 1974–75," Folder 5 of 5.

33. Peter Goldmark to Hugh Carey, 8/4/75. Copies of the memo also went to Judah Gribetz and David Burke. Peter Goldmark Collection, copy in possession of the author.

34. Quoted in Bailey, *The Crisis Regime*, 39.

35. William Sherman and Thomas Poster, "Big Max-imum Effort on Vote," *Daily News*, 9/6/75.

36. Special MLC Steering Committee Meeting, 9/3/75, MLC Minutes, Jack Bigel Papers, Baruch College.

37. Michael C. Jensen, "For the City's Fiscal Crisis, Executive Troubleshooters," *New York Times*, 9/24/75.

38. Harold Menefee Jr., executive director, Fort Greene Community Corporation, to Hugh Carey, undated, Reel 64, Hugh Carey Papers, St. John's University. For another letter making a similar case, see Fred Wallace, executive director, Harlem Teams for Self Help, Reel 64, Hugh Carey Papers.

39. Steven Weisman, "Governor Is Considering a Session on Fiscal Panel," *New York Times*, 8/30/75.

40. See Lachman and Polner, *The Man Who Saved New York*, 113–14. This anecdote features Cavanagh blithely telling Simon Rifkind that the city really had no books.

41. Fred Ferretti, "Banks Amenable to MAC's Plan; Mayor Resistant," *New York Times,* 9/4/75.

42. Sam Roberts, "MAC Group Tried to Ax Abe Power," *Daily News,* 9/2/75; also see Maurice Carroll, "Mayor Refused to Oust Cavanagh and Lechner," *New York Times,* 8/29/75.

43. Fred Ferretti, "Beame and Fiscal Crisis: A Mayor Loses Stature," *New York Times,* 9/7/75.

44. Mary Perot Nichols, "Meet Your Junta: 'No More Mr. Nice Guy' Takes Over City Hall," *Village Voice,* 9/29/75.

45. Fred Ferretti, "Axelson Sworn In as Aide to Mayor on Fiscal Affairs," *New York Times,* 9/17/75.

46. "A New New York City?" in Citibank's New York City Money Market Letter, 9/16/75, Kenneth Axelson Subject Files, Box 3, Folder #52, Correspondence—General, Municipal Archives.

47. James Cavanagh to Abraham Beame, 9/3/75, "Default," Binder on Default and Bankruptcy, Jack Bigel Collection, Baruch College.

48. Agenda for Discussion, Contingency Committee, 10/23/75, Kenneth Axelson Subject Files, Box 3, Folder 50, Municipal Archives.

49. Mayor's Contingency Committee, Minutes of Meeting 10/9/75, Axelson Subject Files, Box 2, Folder 28, Bankruptcy, Municipal Archives.

50. Charlayne Hunter, "Beame Turns On the Charm for Bankers," *New York Times,* 10/4/75.

51. Michael C. Jensen, "Poll of Bankers Predicts Default," *New York Times,* 10/8/75.

52. "A Communication: Theodore H. White, Yeoman of the Guard, Common Warden of that Stretch of the Southern Walk of the Sixty-Fourth Street Which Runneth Between the Third Avenue and the Avenue Lexington, Salutes: Sir Osborn Elliott, Lord Seneshal, Marshall of the Great Keep of Gracie Square where Our Reverend and Honorable Lord Mayor Lies Beleaguered by the Many Enemies Who Seek to Do Ill to This Our Beloved City," 10/10/75, Jacob Javits Papers, Coll. 285, Subseries 1, Series 10, Box 28, "Citizens Committee for New York City," 1975, Stony Brook University.

53. Another potential name was the "Citizens Committee to Save New York," but this was rejected because it sounded too desperate—as though New York were terminally ill.

54. Memo from Jack Marsh and Dick Cheney to Ford through Donald Rumsfeld, 9/4/75, Box 22, Folder: NYC (1), John Marsh Files, GFPL.

55. Meeting of the Citizens Committee to Save NYC, 9/5/75, Jacob Javits Papers, Coll. 285, Subseries 1, Series 10, Box 28, "Citizens Committee for New York City," 1975, Stony Brook University.

56. Arthur Mulligan, "Resentful but Resigned, Riders Shell Out," *Daily News,* 9/3/75.

57. Hugh Wyatt, "City Hospital Docs Threaten to Walk Over Budget Cuts," *Daily News,* 9/16/75; Hugh Wyatt, "Seize Health Offices to Protest Firings," *Daily News,* 9/25/75.

58. Leonard Buder, "Teachers Vote to Strike Today," *New York Times,* 9/9/75; "Budget Cuts Will Mean Bigger Classes and Less Personal Aid for City Pupils," *New*

York Times, 9/8/75; Lynne A. Weikart, "Decision Making and the Impact of Those Decisions During New York City's Fiscal Crisis in the Public Schools, 1975–77," Ph.D. dissertation, Columbia University, 1984, 77. Others were less certain than Gifford that Cavanagh and other city officials were behind the decision not to release the money, even wondering if it were real.

59. Buder, "Teachers Vote to Strike Today"; "Budget Cuts Will Mean Bigger Classes and Less Personal Aid for City Pupils."

60. John Corry, "On the Picket Lines, a Mournful Militance," *New York Times*, 9/10/75.

61. "Court Orders Teachers Back," *Daily News*, 9/10/75.

62. Bert Shanas, "Nonstop Talks Slated in Teachers' Strike," *Daily News*, 9/14/75.

63. Corry, "On the Picket Lines, a Mournful Militance."

64. Spear, "A Crisis in Urban Liberalism," 148.

65. Minutes of the Meeting of the EFCB, 9/29/75, in Kenneth Axelson Subject Files, Box 5, Folder #78, EFCB, Municipal Archives. Also see Keith Moore and Bert Shanas, "Watchdogs Nix Teacher Pact," *Daily News*, 10/8/75.

66. Leonard Buder, "Students Protest Oversized Classes," *New York Times*, 10/6/75.

10. ON THE BRINK

1. Gerald Ford, "Address Before a Joint Session of the California State Legislature," 9/5/75, Public Papers of the Presidents of the United States, Gerald R. Ford, 1975, 532.

2. James M. Naughton, "Ford Safe as Guard Seizes a Gun," *New York Times*, 9/6/75; Perlstein, *The Invisible Bridge*, 498.

3. Andrew H. Malcolm, "Accused Ford Assailant Has Led a Tangled Life," *New York Times*, 9/24/75; Perlstein, *The Invisible Bridge*, 510.

4. Alan Greenspan to Donald Rumsfeld, Dick Cheney, and Bob Goldwin, 9/25/75, Council of Economic Advisers Papers, Alan Greenspan Files, Box 19: Folder: Alan Greenspan (1), GFPL.

5. Alan Greenspan, Memorandum for Donald Rumsfeld, "The Financial Crisis of New York City," 9/12/75, Council of Economic Advisers, Alan Greenspan Files, Box 19, Folder: Alan Greenspan (1), GFPL.

6. Ibid.

7. James M. Naughton, "Ford Will Veto a Tax Reduction Without Fund Cut," *New York Times*, 10/10/75.

8. Memorandum to the President from William Simon, 9/8/75, William Simon Papers, Series IIIB, Subject Files, Drawer 24, Folder 24:32, NYC: 1975 (Sept.). Also see Presidential Handwriting File, Box 28, Folder: "Local Government— NYC (4)," GFPL.

9. Statement of the Honorable William E. Simon, Treasury of the Secretary, Before the Joint Economic Committee, 9/24/75, James M. Cannon Papers, Box 23, Folder: NYC Finances, September 1975, GFPL.

10. Warren Anderson Memo, forwarded as attachment to the president along with

Confidential Memorandum of 9/23/75, "New York City, For Your Information," James M. Cannon Papers, Box 23, NYC Finances (September 1975), GFPL.

11. "Decision Memorandum: Subject: Financial Assistance for New York City," 9/8/75, William Simon Papers, Series IIIB, Subject Files, Drawer 24, Folder 24:32, NYC: 1975 (Sept.).

12. Memorandum to the President from William Simon, 9/8/75, William Simon Papers, Series IIIB, Subject Files, Drawer 24, Folder 24:32, NYC: 1975 (Sept.). Also see Presidential Handwriting File, Box 28, Folder: "Local Government— NYC (4)," GFPL.

13. Charls Walker to President Ford, 10/7/75, "Some Thoughts on the NYC Problem," Presidential Handwriting File, Box 28, Local Government, NYC, Folder 5, GFPL; Charls Walker Newsletter, Presidential Handwriting File, Box 28, Local Government, NYC, Folder 5, GFPL.

14. Statement of A. W. Clausen, President BankAmerica Corporation, San Francisco, California, before the Senate Committee on Banking, Housing and Urban Affairs, October 18, 1975, Hearings Before the Committee on Banking, Housing and Urban Affairs, United States Senate, 94th Congress, First Session on S. 1833, S. 1862, S. 2372, S. 2514, and S. 2523 (Washington, D.C.,: Government Printing Office, 1975), 666.

15. "Standard & Poor's Sees Default by City," New York Times, 10/8/75.

16. Charles Luce to Gerald Ford, 11/4/75, telegram, Binder Title: Default & Bankruptcy (articles, notes and correspondence) May 1975–Dec 1976, Jack Bigel Papers, Baruch College. Luce was, of course, also concerned about whether a bankrupt New York would still pay its electric bills.

17. John Connor, "NACO Officials Reluctant to Aid NYC but Worried about Tax-Exempt Market," Daily Bond Buyer, 10/17/75.

18. New York Times Advertisement, 10/15/75. The New York Law Journal, while a specialized publication, had a special power in the city's legal community because its publication of court decisions and analysis of laws shaped the basic information possessed by judges and lawyers.

19. Memorandum of Conversation, 10/3/75, National Security Adviser Memoranda of Conversation Collection, Box 15, Folder: "October 3, 1975—Ford, Kissinger, FRG Chancellor Helmut Schmidt," GFPL. Also see David Binder, "Schmidt Fears Effects of City Crisis," New York Times, 10/5/75.

20. In an October 24 press conference in Milwaukee, where Rockefeller was attending a dinner organized by the United Negro College Fund, Rockefeller cited Schmidt's concerns as helping drive his own: "When you have men like Helmut Schmidt of Germany, who is a very able economist and now Prime Minister, saying publicly that he is concerned about this situation, a man who is that well informed isn't doing this just out of idle conversation. He is saying it because he is worried." "Office of the Vice President: Press Conference at the Pfister Hotel, Milwaukee, Wisconsin, 10/24/75," accessed online at https://www.fordlibrarymuseum .gov/library/document/0248/whpr19751024-003.pdf, 9/21/16.

21. Nelson Rockefeller to Gerald Ford, 6/3/75, Nelson Aldrich Rockefeller Vice Presidential Papers, Working Papers of the Vice President, RG 26, Vol. 32, Rockefeller

Archive Center. Rockefeller proposed that Ford endorse the idea of federal guarantees for city debt, but only if the debt had received a prior guarantee from the state government. Rockefeller was also bolstered by his correspondence with Jerry Finkelstein, the wealthy publisher of the *New York Law Journal*, who pushed for federal aid or a guarantee for the city's debt. See Jerry Finkelstein to Nelson Rockefeller, 5/28/75, NAR Vice Presidential Papers, Working Papers of the Vice President, RG 26, Vol. 32, Rockefeller Archive Center. The correspondence continued throughout July, as Finkelstein urged Rockefeller to come up with some plan for aid (he proposed creating a federal agency to insure municipal bonds): see Jerry Finkelstein to Nelson Rockefeller, 7/9/75; Nelson Rockefeller to Jerry Finkelstein, 7/30/75, NAR Vice Presidential Papers, Working Papers of the Vice President, RG 26, Vol. 32, Rockefeller Archive Center.

22. Remarks of the Vice President at the Annual Columbus Day Dinner, Waldorf-Astoria Hotel, 10/11/75, James M. Cannon Files, Box 23, Folder "NYC Finances—10/1—10/27/75," GFPL. Also see Steven Weisman, "Rockefeller Calls Help in Congress for City 'Crucial,'" *New York Times*, 10/12/75.

23. Ibid.

24. Rowland Evans and Robert Novak, "Rockefeller's New York Strategy," *Washington Post*, 10/16/75.

25. Memorandum for the President from William T. Coleman, 10/14/75, Simon Papers, Drawer 24, Folder 33, NYC 1975 (October), Lafayette College.

26. Jesse Werner to William Simon (Bill), 10/13/75, Simon Papers, Drawer 24, Folder 33, NYC 1975 (October), Lafayette College.

27. Senior Staff Meeting Handwritten Notes, 10/13/75, Box 295, Ron Nessen Papers, GFPL.

28. Martin Tolchin, "Ford Again Denies Fiscal Aid to City," *New York Times*, 10/18/75; also see Jeff Nussbaum, "The Night New York Saved Itself from Bankruptcy," *New Yorker*, 10/16/75.

29. Linda Greenhouse, "A Night of Anxiety on the Brink of Default," *New York Times*, 10/18/75; John H. Allen, "Dow Is Off 5.67 Despite a Rally," *New York Times*, 10/18/75; Michael C. Jensen, "A Rally Follows," *New York Times*, 10/18/75.

30. Financial Plan, October 1975, in Binder of EFCB Minutes, 9/75–10/75, EFCB. Also see Francis X. Clines, "Beame Submits New Cuts Requiring Added Layoffs Running into the 'Thousands,'" *New York Times*, 10/16/75.

31. Abraham Beame to Hugh Carey, 10/15/75, in Binder of EFCB Minutes, 9/75–10/75, EFCB.

32. 10/14/75 Statement by the Municipal Labor Committee, MLC Steering Committee Minutes, Jack Bigel Collection, Baruch College.

33. Minutes of the Meeting of the EFCB, 10/16/75, Kenneth Axelson Subject Files, Box 5, Folder #78, EFCB, Municipal Archives.

34. Greenhouse, "A Night of Anxiety on the Brink of Default."

35. The Annual Alfred Emanuel Smith Memorial Foundation Dinner, 10/16/75, F-79, ST-G-2, Folder 18, St. Joseph's Seminary.

36. Harrison J. Goldin interview, 1/24/12.

37. Nussbaum, "The Night New York Saved Itself from Bankruptcy."

38. Ibid.

39. Petition, photo in possession of author. Original is in the conference room of Weil, Gotshal & Manges.

40. Statement by Mayor Abraham D. Beame, 10/17/75. Copy in possession of the author courtesy of Ira Millstein.

41. Richard Ravitch interview, 10/11/11. Also see Richard Ravitch, *So Much to Do: A Full Life of Business, Politics and Confronting Fiscal Crises* (New York: PublicAffairs, 2014), 90–94.

42. Ibid.

43. Handwritten Notes—October 1975, n. d. Ron Nessen Papers, Box 295, GFPL.

44. Tolchin, "Ford Again Denies Fiscal Aid to City." Peter Goldmark was one of the point people, calling Washington repeatedly throughout the morning. See Notes on Phone Call with Peter Goldmark, 10/17/75, James M. Cannon Files, Box 23, Folder: "NYC Finances, October 1–27, 1975, GFPL. Also see notes from Ron Nessen Press Conference, James M. Cannon Files, Box 23, Folder: NYC Finances, October 1–27, 1975," GFPL.

45. Jeffery Antevil and James Wieghart, "Ford Refuses to Play Hero in Cliff-Hanger," *Daily News*, 10/18/75.

46. "No Time for Optimists," *Daily News*, 10/18/75.

47. Bert Shanas, Thomas Poster, and Mark Lieberman, "City May Default This Morning," *Daily News*, 10/17/75.

48. Richard Ravitch interview, 10/11/11; also see Ravitch, *So Much to Do*, 92–93.

49. Steven R. Weisman, "$150-Million Pact," *New York Times*, 10/18/75.

50. Bryant Mason and Donald Singleton, "Ending on a High Note, City Gives Creditors Their Due," *Daily News*, 10/18/75.

51. Richard Ravitch interview, 10/11/11.

11. DROP DEAD

1. "Phillips Warns NYC Default Could Spread," *Daily Bond Buyer*, 10/23/75.

2. John Connor, "Federal Aid for NYC Is Still Unsure: Filibuster Feared," *Daily Bond Buyer*, 10/21/75. The Spokane mayor was not the only city politician to condemn New York in order to buff up his own city's image. The civic leaders of Wichita, Kansas, sought to appeal to jittery investors by creating an Association of Fiscally Responsible Cities, saying they did not wish to have their "credit damaged" by a "few cities which have not adhered to some of the basic rules of good fiscal management." "Wichita, Kan. Clears Resolution to Begin Association of Fiscally Responsible Cities," *Daily Bond Buyer*, 10/29/75.

3. Connor, "Federal Aid for NYC Is Still Unsure: Filibuster Feared."

4. Handwritten Notes, NY City Meeting, 10/24/75, Ron Nessen Papers, Box 295. GFPL.

5. Undated, unsigned memo, "Thoughts on the New York City Situation," Robert T. Hartmann Files, Box 13, Folder NYC (1), GFPL.

6. Max Friedersdorf to the President, 10/27/75, Subject: "Joint Session on New York

City." Also see Max Friedersdorf to the President, 10/28/75, Subject: "Joint Session of Congress Address on New York City," Presidential Handwriting File, Box 28, Folder: "Local Govt., NYC," Folder 5, GFPL.

7. Jerry Jones to Donald Rumsfeld, Subject: Forums for Presidential Message on New York City, 10/23/75, James M. Cannon Files, Box 23, "New York City Finances 10/1/75–10/27/75," GFPL.

8. "New York City," 10/20/75, Robert T. Hartmann Papers, Box 178, Folder "10/29/75 NYC Speech (1)," GFPL.

9. Second Draft, 10/24/75, Robert T. Hartmann Papers, Box 178, Folder "10/29/75 NYC Speech (1)," GFPL.

10. Fourth Draft, 10/25/75, Robert T. Hartmann Papers, Box 178, Folder "10/29/75 NYC Speech (2)," GFPL.

11. Fifth Draft, 10/26/75, Robert T. Hartmann Papers, Box 178, Folder "10/29/75 NYC Speech (3)," GFPL. The word *public* is handwritten into the draft.

12. Fifth Draft, 10/26/75, Robert T. Hartmann Papers, Box 178, Folder "10/29/75 NYC Speech (3)," GFPL. The famous lines are added in handwriting, probably Hartmann's. Speechwriter David Gergen, who was at the time a special assistant to William Simon, has said that after Hartmann's speechwriting team wrote the initial draft, he was asked by Rumsfeld to write an alternative version. He did so, assuming that his hard-edged prose would be smoothed out in revisions. Instead, his rough passages went directly into the final text. Robert Hartmann, in his memoirs, also presents the writing of the speech as a battle between his gentler approach and the strident efforts of Simon, Greenspan, and others. However, the changes in the speech also were subtle—from the outset it was more critical of New York than Gergen or Hartmann recollect. For Gergen's claims, see Sam Roberts, "Infamous 'Drop Dead' Was Never Said by Ford," *New York Times*, 12/28/06. See also Robert Hartmann, *Palace Politics: An Inside Account of the Ford Years* (New York: McGraw-Hill, 1980), 358–59, for recollections of writing the speech.

13. James Feron, "Nine Banks Tell Yonkers It Might Default in a Month," *New York Times*, 10/28/75.

14. Thomas P. Ronan, "Ball Says Default by City Would Help Communism," *New York Times*, 10/28/75.

15. Dena Kleiman, "Closing of a Police Station Is Protested in Chinatown," *New York Times*, 10/29/75.

16. Russ Rourke to Max Friedersdorf, 10/23/75, John Marsh Files, Box 22, Folder: "NYC (1)," GFPL. Also see William T. Kendall through Max Friedersdorf, "Meeting with Senator James L. Buckley," 10/28/75, Max Friedersdorf Files, Box 7, Folder: "Presidential Meetings with Senate Members," GFPL.

17. "Mtg. Policemen and Firemen," 10/28/75, John G. Carlson Files, Box 4, Folder: "New York City Financial Crisis (2)," GFPL.

18. In an early draft of the speech, Ford raised his final query by saying that he had no time for questions but would leave the audience with one of his own.

19. "Transcript of President's Talk on City Crisis, Questions Asked and His Responses," *New York Times*, 10/30/75.

20. Remarks of the President at a GOP Dinner at the Century Plaza Hotel, 10/29/75, Office of Editorial Staff, Paul Theis and Robert Orben Files, Box 26, Folder: "10/29/75—CA GOP Fundraising Dinner," GFPL.

21. Remarks of the President at the GOP Fundraising Luncheon, St. Francis Hotel, San Francisco, 10/30/75, Office of Editorial Staff, Paul Theis and Robert Orben Files, Box 26, Folder: "10/30/75—San Francisco GOP Fundraising Luncheon," GFPL.

22. Remarks of the President at Uihlein Hall Performing Arts Center, Milwaukee, WI, 10/30/75, Office of Editorial Staff, Paul Theis and Robert Orben Files, Box 26, Folder: "10/30/75—Milwaukee, Wisconsin GOP Fundraising Dinner," GFPL.

23. "Headline," New Yorker, 11/17/75; Josh Getlin, "The Birth of the Headline Heard Round the World," Los Angeles Times, 7/28/75.

24. Memorandum for James Cannon from Jim Cavanaugh, Subject: New York City Stories, 10/29/75, James Cannon Papers, Box 23, Folder: NYC October 1975 (3), GFA.

25. Frank Van Riper, "Ford to City: Drop Dead," Daily News, 10/30/75.

26. "Gotbaum Predicts Controlled Chaos," Daily News, 10/30/75.

27. Alan Bautzer, "State, City Leaders Assail President for Bid to Bankruptcy," Daily Bond Buyer, 10/30/75.

28. "Moody's Downgrades City's Rating to Caa from Ba," Daily Bond Buyer, 10/30/75.

29. "Presidential Default," New York Times, 10/30/75.

30. James P. Sweeney to Gerald Ford, 10/31/75, Reel 62, Hugh Carey Papers.

31. Rabbi Dov Rapaport, 10/29/75, Reel 62, Hugh Carey Papers. In a separate letter to Carey, Rabbi Rapaport wrote that he was one of the 160,000 individuals holding city bonds, which he had bought using money obtained when his wife became brain damaged and paralyzed.

32. Billie Biederman to Ed Koch, 10/30/75, Reel 62, Hugh Carey Papers.

33. Howard S. Rogers to Gerald Ford, 10/31/75, Reel 62, Hugh Carey Papers.

34. Barbara Wiplush to Gerald Ford, 10/31/75, Reel 62, Hugh Carey Papers.

35. Wolcott Street to Governor Carey and the Editors of the New York Times, 10/31/75, Reel 62, Hugh Carey Papers.

36. Abe Siegel, Manhasset Hills, Long Island, "No Town Is an Island," New York Times, 11/3/75.

37. "Gotham Roundelay," New York Times, 11/6/75.

38. Memorandum for Max Friedersdorf from William T. Kendall, 10/29/75, Box 22, Folder: "NYC" (1), John Marsh Files, GFPL.

39. Vern Loen to Max Friedersdorf, 10/29/75, "Congressional Reaction to the President's New York City Speech," Box 22, Folder: "NYC" (1), John Marsh Files, GFPL.

40. Handwritten Notes, Senior Staff Meeting, 11/3/75, Box 296, Ron Nessen Papers, GFPL.

41. Perlstein, The Invisible Bridge, 526–35.

42. "Ford to Interviewer: No, Not 'Drop Dead,'" Daily News, 10/31/75.

43. For example, see Sam Roberts, "Infamous 'Drop Dead' Was Never Said by Ford," *New York Times*, 12/28/06.

44. Owen Moritz, "A History Lesson for Ford: U.S. Did Aid Frisco in Quake," *Daily News*, 10/31/75. See "The President Asks for $1,500,000 More; Army's Relief Work Has Already Cost That Much," *New York Times*, 4/22/1906.

12. PASTRAMI AND RAMBOUILLET

1. Francis X. Clines, "Buckley Urges Voluntary Bankruptcy as Best Course of Action for the City," *New York Times*, 11/1/75.

2. Maurice Carroll, "Poll Finds Nation Closely Split on City Aid," *New York Times*, 11/2/75.

3. "$1 Drive for City Started," *New York Times*, 11/1/75.

4. Irving Spiegel, "Jewish Leader Asserts Default Would Add to Ethnic Tensions," *New York Times*, 11/1/75.

5. Charles Pendergast, "Cardinal Cooke, Bishop Mugavero Ask Federal Guarantees to Save City," *Catholic News*, 11/13/75. Their call was affirmed a few days later by the United States Catholic Conference, representing Catholic bishops around the country.

6. Wilbur Monroe to J. M. Dunn, through Samuel Rosenblatt, 11/12/75, Subject: International Considerations of the New York City Financial Crisis. The note at the top directing Seidman's attention to the memo reads, "This tracks with my own conversations with similar types." L. William Seidman Files, Box 79, NYC 11/75–7/76 and undated (2), GFPL.

7. Peter T. Kilborn, "Cities Abroad Hurt by the Crisis Here," *New York Times*, 11/21/75.

8. Deidre Carmody, "British Speak Out for City Help," *New York Times*, 11/1/75.

9. David K. Shipler, "Moscow's Mayor Thinks Default Is for Capitalists," *New York Times*, 11/19/75.

10. Memorandum for the President from William Simon, Subject, "New York City," 11/3/75, Box 29, Folder: Local Government—New York City (6), Presidential Handwriting File, GFPL.

11. Bernard Gifford to Kenneth Axelson, 11/6/75, Kenneth Axelson Subject Files, Box 5, Folder #70, "Board of Education," Municipal Archives. Gifford was hoping that a Board of Education representative could sit on the EFCB; Axelson referred him to the Contingency Committee instead of agreeing to put this idea forward.

12. Sanford Solender, Chairman, Task Force on the New York City Crisis, Community Council of Greater New York, to Robert Rivel, 11/21/75, Kenneth Axelson Subject Files, Box 3, Folder #49, "Contingency Committee," Municipal Archives.

13. "Water Supply Jobs Termed Important in the City's Crisis," *New York Times*, 11/1/75.

14. Charles Luce to Gerald Ford, 11/4/75, L. William Seidman Files, Box 78, Folder "NYC—May–October 1975" (7), GFPL.

15. "Default, Some Problems and Litigation—A Discussion Memorandum Prepared

for the City of New York," 11/11/75, Kenneth Axelson Subject Files, Box 3, Folder #49, "Contingency Committee," Municipal Archives.

16. Robert B. Rivel to Abraham Beame, 11/24/75, Kenneth Axelson Subject Files, Box 3, Folder #49, "Contingency Committee," Municipal Archives.

17. Perlstein, *The Invisible Bridge*, 526.

18. Maurice Carroll, "Cavanagh Forced Out by Elusive Rumors," *New York Times*, 11/17/75. Also see Martin Gottlieb, "New York's Rescue: The Offstage Dramas," *New York Times*, 7/2/85, for Cavanagh's recollections.

19. Carroll, "Cavanaugh Forced out by Elusive Rumors," *New York Times*, 11/17/75.

20. Gottlieb, "New York's Rescue."

21. Carroll, "Cavanagh Forced Out by Elusive Rumors."

22. Fred Ferretti, "Cavanagh Tendered Last Hurrahs by 1000 at Dinner," *New York Times*, 12/17/75.

23. Carroll, "Cavanagh Forced Out by Elusive Rumors."

24. Beth Fallon, "Had to Rub It In, Says Cavanagh of Executioners," *Daily News*, 11/17/75.

25. Ronald M. Joseph, "The 1976 New York State Fiscal Crisis," draft of paper written for Boston University School of Management Public Management Program, August 1981; also see Peter Goldmark to Hugh Carey, 11/28/75. Peter Goldmark Collection, copy of both in possession of author.

26. Hugh Carey to Gerald Ford, 11/4/75, L. William Seidman Files, Box 78, Folder: "NYC May–October 1975 (7)," GFPL.

27. Hugh Carey to Paul Volcker, 11/4/75, L. William Seidman Files, Box 78, Folder: "NYC May–October 1975 (7)," GFPL.

28. L. William Seidman to Hugh Carey, 11/7/75, L. William Seidman Files, Box 79, Folder: "NYC May–October 1975 (7)," GFPL.

29. Interview by Seymour P. Lachman and Robert Polner with Hugh Carey and Tom Regan, 12/18/09. In possession of the author. Also see account in Lachman and Polner, *The Man Who Saved New York*.

30. David L. Rosenbaum, "New York's Delegation Lobbying for Aid to City," *New York Times*, 11/12/75; Memorandum for the President from L. William Seidman, 11/11/75, L. William Seidman Files, Box 79, Folder: "NYC November 1975–July 1976 and undated (2)," GFPL.

31. Lachman and Polner, *The Man Who Saved New York*, 161–62.

32. David L. Rosenbaum, "New York's Delegation Lobbying for Aid to City," *New York Times*, 11/12/75.

33. Memorandum for the President from L. William Seidman, 11/11/75, L. William Seidman Files, Box 79, Folder: "NYC November 1975–July 1976 and undated (2)," GFPL.

34. See letters from Victor Gotbaum, Albert Shanker, and John DeLury; Ellmore Patterson of Morgan Guaranty; Gabriel Hause of Manufacturers Hanover; Charles Buek of U.S. Trust Company; Walter E. Van de Waag of National Bank of North America; Joseph Rice of Irving Trust Company; Donald Platten of Chemical Bank; Elliott Averett of the Bank of New York; John Hannon of Bankers Trust; Russell Knisel of Marine Midland Bank; William Spencer of Citibank; and David

Rockefeller of Chase Manhattan. In packet from Felix Rohatyn to William Simon, 11/13/75, L. William Seidman Files, Box 79, Folder: "NYC November 1975–July 1976 and undated (3)," GFPL.

35. Steven R. Weisman, "A Matter of Principle," *New York Times*, 11/28/75.

36. Linda Greenhouse, "Debt Moratorium of Three Years in City Passed in Albany," *New York Times*, 11/15/75.

37. John Darnton, "M.A.C. Faces Snag in Bond Trade-Off," *New York Times*, 11/21/75.

38. The request was not only for the city but at times for the state as well. As the chairman of Chemical Bank wrote, "We cannot overemphasize our sincere belief . . . that it is only realistic to anticipate the need for Federal sponsorship for New York State's seasonal borrowings during 1976." Donald Platten to Felix Rohatyn, 11/13/75, L. William Seidman Files, Box 79, "Folder: NYC November 1975–July 1976 and undated (2)," GFPL.

39. Richard D. Lyons, "Carey Turns Lobbyist in His Former Haunts," *New York Times*, 11/19/75.

40. Max Friedersdorf to John Marsh, 11/7/75, L. William Seidman Files, Box 79, Folder: "NYC November 1975–July 1976 and undated (2)," GFPL.

41. Martin Tolchin, "House Unit Votes Loan Guarantees to Assist the City," *New York Times*, 11/1/75.

42. Thomas Ludlow Ashley to Gerald Ford, 11/6/75, Presidential Handwriting File, Box 29, Folder: "Local Government, NYC (6)," GFPL.

43. Thomas L. Ashley, "The Ohio Way," *New York Times*, 11/19/75.

44. GOP Leadership Meeting Minutes, 11/4/75, Box 29, Presidential Handwriting File, Folder: "Local Government NYC (6)," GFPL.

45. Meeting with Republican Congressional Leaders, 11/3/75, Box 28, Presidential Handwriting File, Folder: "Local Government NYC (5)," GFPL.

46. "NYC Senators Meeting, Handwritten Notes," 11/10/75, John G. Carlson Papers, Box 4, Folder: "NYC Financial Crisis (3)," GFPL. The handwritten notes have been edited for grammar and clarity in the manuscript.

47. Max Friedersdorf, Memorandum for the President, 11/13/75, Box 29, Folder: Local Government—NYC (7), Presidential Handwriting File, GFPL; Martin Tolchin, "Rhodes and Burns Lessen Resistance to City Help," *New York Times*, 11/12/75.

48. All references from Memorandum of Conversation, 11/15/75–11/17/75, Rambouillet, France, "Economic Summit," Box 16, Folder "November 15–17, 1975, Rambouillet Economic Summit," National Security Adviser Memoranda of Conversation Collection, GFPL.

49. Steven R. Weisman, "Lack of Cash to Pay Municipal Employees Next Week," *New York Times*, 11/19/75.

50. Steven R. Weisman, "Tuesday's Crisis Tied to Taxes and Ford," *New York Times*, 11/20/75.

51. Peter Goldmark to Hugh Carey, 11/28/75. Peter Goldmark Collection, copy of memo in possession of author.

52. Handwritten Notes, 11/24/75—Senior Staff Meeting, Ron Nessen Papers, Box 296, GFPL.

53. Hugh Carey to Gerald Ford, 11/26/75, Box 23, "NYC Finances—Nov–Dec 1975," James M. Cannon Files, GFPL.

54. Martin Tolchin, "8% Interest Rate," *New York Times*, 11/27/75.

55. Handwritten Notes, 11/28/75—Senior Staff Meeting, Ron Nessen Papers, Box 296, GFPL.

56. Tolchin, "8% Interest Rate."

57. Martin Tolchin, "Ford Signs Aid Bill," *New York Times*, 12/10/75.

58. "How City Plans to Meet Borrowing Necessities," *New York Times*, 11/27/75.

59. "Dollar Up Abroad on Move by Ford to Aid New York," *New York Times*, 11/28/75.

60. Fred Ferretti, "MAC Head's Prediction: City's 'Pain' Just Starting," *New York Times*, 12/10/75.

61. Frank Prial, "Marchers Here Protest Antipoverty Project Cuts," *New York Times*, 11/19/75.

62. John T. McQuiston, "Rikers Rioters Seize Five and Hold Two Cell Blocks," *New York Times*, 11/24/75; Peter Kihss, "Rikers Island Revolt Ends With Release of Hostages," *New York Times*, 11/25/75.

13. STATE OF EMERGENCY

1. For a brief description of the program, see Leslie Maitland, "City to Bar 5,000 Day-Care Children," *New York Times*, 8/31/74. To be eligible for child care, families had to earn annual salaries under $12,500. Forty-five percent of families enrolled paid nothing at all; the rest paid between $2 and $25 per week. In addition to the four hundred larger centers, the day care network also included more than a thousand smaller family day cares run out of providers' homes.

2. Robert Abrams to Abraham Beame, 5/27/76, Abraham Beame Papers, Roll 10, Municipal Archives.

3. A 1982 study by the Community Service Society showed that at least 19 percent of women surveyed admitted to leaving their children at home alone occasionally while they went to work when other child care arrangements fell through at the last minute. Community Service Society, *Day Care and the Working Poor: The Struggle for Self-Sufficiency*, 4. Also see press release, "CSS Completes Major Study on Day Care in New York City," 5/25/82, Box 594B, Folder: "Day Care," Community Service Society Papers, Columbia University Rare Book and Manuscript Library.

4. David Vidal, "Many Day Care Facilities Open Despite Aid Cutoff," *New York Times*, 7/22/76. The city trumpeted that it had defunded 77 day care centers. In reality, many of those soldiered on, patching together piecemeal funding from other sources. Nadine Brozan, "The City's Day-Care System: Resilient in Difficult Times," *New York Times*, 3/13/79.

5. See "Day Care Is About More Than Children," *The Link*, April 1976; Tom Rosenthal, "New Daycare Rules Called Disastrous," *The Westsider*, 6/8/73.

6. Peter Kihss, "New York City Cracks Down on Direct-Lease Day Care Centers,"

New York Times, 6/9/76; John Raymond, "ACD Is 'Silent' at Day Care Hearings," *Chelsea Clinton News*, 10/7/76.

7. John Raymond, "Kids Lose in Day Care Rip-Off," *Chelsea Clinton News*, 6/10/76; "Suit Filed Against Day Care Closings," *Chelsea Clinton News*, 6/24/76; Raymond, "ACD Is 'Silent' at Day Care Hearings."

8. Kihss, "New York City Cracks Down on Direct-Lease Day Care Centers"; Peter Kihss, "$37 Million Waste Found in Day Care," *New York Times*, 10/7/76. Later studies found that the rents charged by the direct-lease centers were not as high as had originally been thought, although the centers themselves were badly built and in some cases unsafe. Peter Kihss, "Day Care 'Hazards' Are Reported by U.S.," *New York Times*, 1/18/77.

9. James M. Hartman, "Expenditures and Services," in Raymond D. Horton and Charles Brecher, *Setting Municipal Priorities: 1980* (Montclair, N.J., and New York: Landmark Studies, Allanheld/Universe, 1979), 62. The number of city employees went from 294,575 in FY 1975 to 224,903 in FY 1978.

10. See Hartman, "Expenditures and Services," 65. For lead paint inspections, see Mayor's Management Report, August 1977.

11. Roger Sanjek, *The Future of Us All: Race and Neighborhood Politics in New York City* (Ithaca, NY: Cornell University Press, 2000), 93.

12. Ibid.

13. Francis X. Clines, "City Layoffs Hurt Minorities Most," *New York Times*, 2/20/76. One study done by the Commission on Human Rights found that by February 1976, the city had already laid off half of its Spanish-speaking workers, 40 percent of the black males it employed, and one-third of its female employees.

14. Joseph P. Fried, "City's Housing Administrator Proposes 'Planned Shrinkage' of Some Slums," *New York Times*, 2/3/76.

15. Roger Starr, "Making New York Smaller," *New York Times Magazine*, 11/14/76.

16. "Minorities Accuse Roger Starr of "Benign Neglect," *New York Amsterdam News*, 3/6/76.

17. Fried, "City's Housing Administrator Proposes 'Planned Shrinkage' of Some Slums"; Glenn Fowler, "Starr's 'Shrinkage' Plan for City Slums Is Denounced," *New York Times*, 2/11/76; "Minority Caucus Bids Starr Quit," *New York Times*, 3/5/76; Joseph P. Fried, "Starr Resigning as Chief of New York City Housing," *New York Times*, 7/9/76.

18. Francis X. Clines, " 'Blighted Areas' Use Is Urged by Rohatyn," *New York Times*, 3/16/76.

19. Thomas A. Johnson, "Rohatyn Scored by Congressmen," *New York Times*, 3/17/76; Doris Duhl, "Agri-Bronx?," *New York Times*, 12/12/76.

20. Charles Brecher and Raymond D. Horton, *Setting Municipal Priorities 1981* (South Fullerton, N.J. : Landmark Studies, Allanheld, Osmun, 1980), 2.

21. Brozan, "The City's Day-Care System: Resilient in Difficult Times."

22. *Mayor's Management Report*, 1977, City Hall Library.

23. L. D. Solomon, "For New York, A Time of Testing as the Nation Looks On," *New York Times*, 2/21/76. Quoted in Henwood, *Wall Street*, 297.

24. John Darnton, "The Control Board and How It Works," *New York Times*, 10/14/75.
25. Members of EFCB, 9/75. Binder of Minutes beginning 9/75, FCB Archives.
26. EFCB Minutes, 10/7/75. All EFCB Minutes are at the FCB Archives.
27. Ibid., 10/19/75 and 10/20/75.
28. Ibid., 11/7/75.
29. Ibid., 11/19/75.
30. Herbert Elish interview, 4/4/13.
31. Stephen Berger interview, 1/12/12.
32. Berger in fact did both of these. He led the EFCB in turning back a contract between the Transit Authority and the Transit Workers Union because of cost-of-living increases that threatened to violate the financial plan, he pressed the EFCB to set out clear provisions the city could use to guide collective bargaining (something others viewed as overstepping the powers of the board, which were supposed to be to simply look over contracts once completed), and he also urged the city to take a stringent line with the teachers' union.
33. Stephen Berger interview, 1/12/12.
34. Stephen Berger and EFCB to Governor Carey and members of the EFCB, 6/3/76, Binder beginning 1/9/76, EFCB Archives; Report of the Executive Director of the EFCB, "The New York City Expense Budget for FY 1977 as It Relates to the Financial Plan," Binder beginning with meeting minutes for 1/9/76, EFCB Archives.
35. Francis X. Clines, "City Union 'Observer' Admitted by State Fiscal Control Board," *New York Times*, 1/8/76.
36. EFCB Minutes, 12/8/75.
37. Ibid., 1/30/76.
38. Ibid., 1/23/76.
39. Chowkwanyun, "Dilemmas of Community Health," 96.
40. Ibid., 32–35.
41. Sandra Opdycke, *No One Was Turned Away: The Role of Public Hospitals in New York City Since 1900* (New York: Oxford University Press, 1999), 156–58.
42. James Colgrove, *Epidemic City: The Politics of Public Health in New York* (New York: Russell Sage Foundation, 2011), 96.
43. Howard Blum, "A Hospital Is Dying," *New York Times*, 6/19/75; "Columbia Sues City Hospital Corporation," *New York Times*, 2/15/76.
44. Leslie Maitland, "City Hospitals to Get Delafield's Equipment," *New York Times*, 8/5/75.
45. David Bird, "City Decision to Shut Four Hospitals Approved by State Health Chief," *New York Times*, 3/13/76.
46. Chowkwanyun, "Dilemmas of Community Health," 98–99.
47. David Bird, "Why the Fight for 'Deplorable' Fordham Hospital," *New York Times*, 4/23/76.
48. "Defender of Health Care for Poor," *New York Times*, 10/21/76.
49. George Todd, "Declares Hospital System Must Change to Survive," *New York Amsterdam News*, 5/8/76.

50. EFCB Minutes, 10/15/76.

51. "Hospital Coup," *New York Times*, 11/8/76; "Holloman Calls Koch a Racist, Leaves Hearing," *New York Amsterdam News*, 1/27/76.

52. Lowell Bellin to Abraham Beame, 9/24/75, Beame Papers, Roll 13, Municipal Archives.

53. Ronald Sullivan, "Hospitals Corporation Votes 9–7 to Remove Holloman as President," *New York Times*, 1/27/77.

54. "Beame's Fiscal Aide Gets Hospital Post," *New York Times*, 4/27/77.

55. Zamir Nestelbaum, "The Fall and Fall of the NYCDOH," *Health/PAC Bulletin*, June 1978.

56. "Brooklyn Nurse School Holds Final Graduation," *New York Times*, 1/30/77.

57. Cosgrove, *Epidemic City*, 92.

58. Pascal J. Imperato, "The Effect of New York City's Fiscal Crisis on the Department of Health," *Bulletin of the New York Academy of Medicine*, March 1978, 54 (3), 282. Imperato was the Commissioner of Health during the crisis years.

59. Nestelbaum, "The Fall and Fall of the NYCDOH."

60. Leslie Maitland, "50 City Hospital Clinics Will Close," *New York Times*, 11/6/75; "Unaborted Clinics," *New York Times*, 12/27/75; Peter Kihss, "Citing 'a Wounded City,' Group Assails Cut in Budget," *New York Times*, 2/15/76.

61. Laurie Johnson, "Budget Cuts Cool Some 'Hot Lines,'" *New York Times*, 1/29/77.

62. Mayor's Management Report August 1977, City Hall Library; Nicholas Freudenberg, Marianne Fahs, and Andrew Greenberg, "The Impact of New York City's 1975 Fiscal Crisis on the Tuberculosis, HIV and Homicide Syndemic," *American Journal of Public Health*, March 2006, 96(3), 424–34.

63. Johnson, "Budget Cuts Cool Some 'Hot Lines.'"

64. Selwyn Raab, "Illegal Narcotics Traffic Is Worst Here in Five Years," *New York Times*, 12/8/75.

65. Julilly Kohler-Hausmann, "'The Attila the Hun Law': New York's Rockefeller Drug Laws and the Making of a Punitive State," *Journal of Social History*, 2010; Vol. 44, Issue 1, 71–95.

66. Gladys Schweiger to Abraham Beame, 4/6/76, John Zuccotti Subject Files, Box 1, Folder 2, ASA Letters 1975–6. For problems of the ASA, see, for example, Howard Blum, "Bronx Drug Project Loses Its State Funds," *New York Times*, 4/7/77.

67. "300 in Drug Programs Keep Vigil at Gracie Mansion," *New York Times*, 4/10/76.

68. Stephen Berger and EFCB to Governor Carey and members of the EFCB, 6/3/76, EFCB Archives; Report of the Executive Director of the EFCB, "The New York City Expense Budget for FY 1977 as It Relates to the Financial Plan," EFCB Archives.

69. Memorandum from Abraham Beame to all Administrators, Commissioners and City Heads, 2/12/76, "Citizen Involvement to Fill Service Gaps"; "Mobilizing New Yorkers to Fill Service Gaps in City Departments During the Fiscal Crisis," Citizens Committee for New York City Archives.

70. "Volunteers," WCBS Newsradio Editorial, 2/26/76, Citizens Committee for New York City Archives.

71. Citizens Committee Press Release, "The Biggest, Boldest, Most Imaginative Volunteer Attack in American History," undated, Citizens Committee for New York City Archives.

72. Lt. Kane to Dennis Allee, 5/12/76; Marcia Shalen to Dennis Allee, 4/12/76, Citizens Committee for New York City Archives.

73. Mary Heller to Irving Anker, 8/6/76, Bernard Gifford Papers, Series 1202, Box 41, "Budget 1976–77, CUTS," Records of the New York City Board of Education, Municipal Archives.

74. The exact date when the "call to arms" advertisement ran in the *New York Times* is not clear, but it was probably in February 1976.

75. "Starting a Merchants' Association," Citizens Committee for New York City Archives.

76. "New York Self Help Hand Book," Citizens Committee for New York City Archives.

77. Mae Miller to Dennis Allee, 2/25/76, Citizens Committee for New York City Archives.

78. "From Teaching to Sweeping Streets: It's Citizens to the Rescue," *U.S. News and World Report*, 6/21/76.

79. "Promoting New York," Citizens Committee for New York City Archives.

80. "Self-Help and Survival," *New York Times*, 2/23/76.

81. Hartman, "Expenditures and Services," 68; Marshall Goldman to Bernard Gifford, 9/7/76, Bernard Gifford Files, Box 39, Series 1202, "Pedagogical Personnel, 1975–6," Records of the New York City Board of Education, Municipal Archives. Also see Weikart, "Decision Making," 164.

82. Some organizations—such as the Educational Priorities Panel, a newly formed group that included several of the child advocacy organizations in the city as well as the United Parents Association—argued that the Board of Education allowed cuts to fall disproportionately on teachers, rather than cutting administrative staff. See Weikart, "Decision Making," 132–37. The UFT was also criticized for protecting teacher salaries while 12,000 jobs were cut. Weikert, 211.

83. Bernard Gifford to Jean Stevenson, 10/22/75, Bernard Gifford Files, Series 1202, Box 46, "United Parents Association."

84. Luis Olmedo to Chancellor Irving Anker, 3/5/76, Bernard Gifford Papers, Series 1202, Box 21, Folder: City Council 1/74–6/75.

85. Hugh McClaren to Leonard Lurie, 7/26/76, Bernard Gifford Files, Series 1202, Box 41, "Budget 1976–77, CUTS"; "Draft," 4/26/76, Bernard Gifford Files, Box 41, Series 1202, Budget 1976–77 Hearings. Also see John J. Marchi to Irving Anker, 7/19/76; Bernard Gifford to John J. Marchi, 8/19/76.

86. Albert Shanker to Irving Anker, 3/1/76, Bernard Gifford Files, Series 1202, Box 45, Unions—UFT; Carleton Irish to Irving Anker, 11/17/76, "Incident Statistics," Chancellor Irving Anker, Central Files, Series 1105, Box 4, Records of the New York City Board of Education, Municipal Archives.

87. Arthur Auerbach to Samuel Polatnick, 10/29/76, "Effects of 1976–1977 Budget Cuts," Bernard Gifford Files, Series 1202, Box 41, "Budget 1976-77, CUTS."

88. Louis Ward, "School for Pregnant Girls Closing in Jan.," *New York Amsterdam News*, 10/30/76.

89. Leigh Marriner to Bernard Esrig, 9/23/76, Re: Elimination of Itinerant Speech Services, Bernard Gifford Files, Files 1202, Box 41, "Budget 1976–77, CUTS"; Mary Breasted, "Council and Students Fight to Save Life of Adult Classes," *New York Times*, 7/21/76; Anna Quindlen, "The Adult Center That Refused to Die," *New York Times*, 11/13/77.

90. Betsy Haggerty, "Strike Closes Already Crippled Schools," *Chelsea Clinton News*, 9/11/75.

91. Adam Haridopolos, "Bumping System Upsets Teachers," *Chelsea Clinton News*, 9/16/76.

92. Sanjek, *The Future of Us All*, 94.

93. Ibid.

94. Adam Haridopolos, "Board 2 Suspended; Strike Still On," *Chelsea Clinton News*, 10/14/76.

95. Palmer Poroner, "Parents Help Out," *The Villager*, 9/11/75.

96. Michael Waldholz, "School Shutdown Ordered to Protest Budget Cuts," *The Villager*, 9/23/76.

97. Dennis Mack, "Boycott Succeeds Only at PS 3," *The Villager*, 10/21/76; Dennis Mack, "PS 3 on Chopping Block," *The Villager*, 11/11/76.

98. Robert Collazo, "P.S. 113, Vow to Keep School Open," *New York Amsterdam News*, 2/14/76; Carlos V. Ortiz, "School Protestors Block Harlem Traffic," *New York Amsterdam News*, 4/3/76; Simon Anweke, "District 3 School Board Defies Anker," *New York Amsterdam News*, 4/17/76; "Harlem School Fight," *New York Amsterdam News*, 9/25/76; Simon Anweke, "Threaten School Boycott at IS 10," *New York Amsterdam News*, 10/16/76. Some Harlem school buildings—like that which had housed J.H.S. 120, the James Fenimore Cooper Junior High School—would stand empty for decades until developers turned them into condominiums. Josh Barbanel, "Harlem's Newest Beacon," *New York Times*, 3/11/07.

99. Jean Krampner, "1975 School Cuts May Be 'For Real,'" *The Villager*, 6/12/75.

100. Betsy Haggerty, "Kate Isn't in P.S. 87. Here's Why," *New York Times*, 10/19/76. Haggerty was actually a journalist who wrote extensively about the schools for *The Villager*; in the op-ed, she said she had to leave journalism for a better-paying job in order to pay for the private school.

101. "Public Library Reduces Branch Hours Even Further," *Chelsea Clinton News*, 7/24/75.

102. John Cory to Richard Couper, 3/29/71, "Re: The Future of the Research Libraries," Folder: Internal Case Statement 1, John Mackenzie Cory records. Central Administration. New York Public Library Archives, The New York Public Library, Astor, Lenox and Tilden Foundations.

103. Ada Louise Huxtable, "Library as Friend," *New York Times*, 1/24/71.

104. From Mr. Cory to Mr. Couper, 3/29/71, Re: Future of the Research Libraries,

NYPL. Folder: Internal Case Statement, May 1975, Box 2, RG 6—Central Administration—John Cory Records, New York Public Library Archives.

105. NYPL Handshake 1973. Folder: New York Public Library Handbook. John Cory Records, New York Public Library Archives.

106. James W. Henderson, "Whither the Research Libraries?" Memo to Committee on the Research Libraries, 3/24/76, James W. Henderson Records, New York Public Library Archives.

107. Memo, "Vacancies in Manuscripts and Archives Division—Annex," 11/8/76, James W. Henderson Records, New York Public Library Archives.

108. The Elmhurst, Queens, branch library was one of those to so curtail its hours; see Sanjek, *The Future of Us All*, 94.

109. See Press Release, "Readers Set Inter-Branch Assembly on Library Crisis; Sit-In to End," 2/21/76; Box 2, Folder: "Fiscal Crisis," Hunts Point Branch records, New York Public Library Archives, The New York Public Library, Astor, Lenox and Tilden Foundations.

110. "The Saving of the Columbia Branch Public Library: A Chronology," Hunts Point Branch Library Papers, New York Public Library Archives and Manuscripts.

111. "Branch Libraries: An 'Endangered Species'?" *Library Crisis Bulletin*, Vol. 1, No. 2, October 1976, Box 1, Folder: "Ad Hoc Committee to Save Our Libraries," New Dorp Branch Records, New York Public Library Archives, The New York Public Library, Astor, Lenox and Tilden Foundations.

112. Keven J. Kelley, "New York City's Budget/Human Services Crisis: What Has Been Lost So Far," 2/4/76, Task Force on the New York City Crisis, Box 10, Folder 174, John Zuccotti Papers, Municipal Archives.

113. Betsy Haggerty, "1975: Year the Money Ran Out," *Chelsea Clinton News*, 1/1/76.

14. THE PEOPLE'S FIREHOUSE

1. Author interview with Gerry Owens, 7/7/11.

2. "Sen. Bartosiewicz Testifies at Firehouse Hearings," *Greenpoint Gazette*, 11/2/76.

3. The city contended that these large fires—such as one at the Puerto Rican Social Club in the Bronx, which killed 25—would not have been prevented by more fire service.

4. FDNY Annual Reports. Thanks to Daniel Maye at the George F. Mand Library at the FDNY Fire Academy for sharing these numbers.

5. Flood, *The Fires*; Rodrick Wallace and Deborah Wallace, *Studies on the Collapse of Fire Service in New York City 1972-1976: The Impact of Pseudoscience in Public Policy* (Washington, D.C.: University Press of America, 1977), 48.

6. "Disbanded Companies," George F. Mand, FDNY Fire Academy. List provided by Daniel Maye in possession of author.

7. Rodrick Wallace and Deborah Wallace, *A Plague on Your Houses: How New York Was Burned Down and National Public Health Crumbled* (New York: Verso, 1998), 30.

8. Wallace and Wallace, *A Plague on Your Houses*, 66.

9. Stephen Malanga, "The Death and Life of Bushwick," *City Journal*, Spring 2008.

10. Arthur Browne, "Arson a Devastating Force in Bushwick," *Daily News*, 5/1/77; Thomas Raftery, Mel Greene, and Paul Meskil, "50 Hurt in Brooklyn 10-Alarm Fire," *Daily News*, 7/19/77; Cheryl Johnson, "Boy Indicted in Giant Fire," *New York Post*, 7/30/77; John L. Mitchell, "Arson for Fun and Profit," *New York Post*, 7/21/77; Thomas Raftery, "Suspicious Fire Kills a Boy in Bushwick," *Daily News*, 11/16/77; Timothy Weiner, "Arson 'Holocaust in Bushwick,'" *New York Amsterdam News*, 2/17/79.

11. "Closed!" *Daily News*, 11/14/72.

12. Ray Shultz, "'This Neighborhood Is a Bomb,'" *SoHo Weekly News*, 12/5/74.

13. Susser, *Norman Street*, 86–87.

14. "6 Children Killed as Sand Caves In at Brooklyn Cut," *New York Times*, 6/13/56.

15. Rudy Johnson, "Brooklyn's 'Unknowns' Fight to Save Homes," *New York Times*, 4/10/73; John Darnton, "Residents in Brooklyn Fight Relocation Plan," *New York Times*, 5/25/73; "10 Families Refuse Brooklyn Evictions at Paper Plant Site," *New York Times*, 8/23/73; Mary Breasted, "Brooklyn Eviction Fight Ends in Dust of Demolition," *New York Times*, 9/13/73; also Tom Gogan interview, 12/2/13.

16. Adam Schwartz, Bushwick History Walking Tour, 10/16/10.

17. Cass Vanzi and Claire Spiegel, "Bushwick Fire Kills Baby, Critically Injures Parents," *Daily News*, 6/27/75.

18. Ron Dickman, "Northside Fights to Save Co. 212," *Greenpoint Gazette and Advertiser*, 11/25/75.

19. "Northside Throws Party for Firemen Returning to 'People's Firehouse' After 16-Month Battle to Keep It," *New York Times*, 3/20/77.

20. Causewell Vaughan, "8 Fire Companies Get Ax; O'Hagan Sees Peril to Life," *Daily News*, 11/21/75.

21. Gerry Owens interview, 7/7/11. Paul and Brigitte Veneski interview, 6/27/11.

22. Paul Veneski interview, 6/27/11; Bob Roher interview, 1/10/14; Dickman, "Northside Fights to Save Co. 212."

23. Joyce Wadler, "Report from Engine Co. 212," *New York Post*, 11/26/75.

24. David Bird, "Neighbors Protest Plan to Shut Firehouse Here," *New York Times*, 11/29/75.

25. The firehouse organizing, as Tamar Carroll notes, was but one example of white working-class activism in Greenpoint-Williamsburg that adopted a populist framework without the racist worldview. Besides the protests around S&S, there were other neighborhood efforts, often involving women deeply. For example, following the S&S struggle Italian women in the neighborhood had organized for the creation of a day care center and a senior center. And at the same time as the firehouse protests, activists in Greenpoint-Williamsburg built a new working-class feminist group called the National Congress for Neighborhood Women to press for better social services as well as political education for women. The firehouse organizing built on these projects. See Carroll, *Mobilizing New York*.

26. First Draft, Script, Ann Ambia Notebooks, privately held collection.

27. Rough Draft, People's Firehouse Skit, Ann Ambia Notebooks.

28. "Women Protesters Learn Fire Fighting at Shut Firehouse," *New York Times*, 1/13/76.

29. Tom Gogan interview, 12/2/13.

30. See, for example, Adam Veneski to Commissioner O'Hagan, 1/8/76, Francis X. McCardle Subject Files, Box 9, Folder 166, Northside Community, Municipal Archives. In one meeting at the end of December 1975, Veneski reported that it had taken twenty-two minutes for an engine to reach an alarm box—contradicting the official claim that response time had increased by only thirty seconds. The city also was pressed to conference with local business leaders about whether the industrial character of the neighborhood meant longer response times because of trucks or equipment blocking the streets. See Commanding Officer 94th Precinct to Commanding Officer, Brooklyn North Area, 1/29/76, Francis X. McCardle Subject Files, Box 9, Folder 164, Northside Community, Municipal Archives.

31. Denis Hamill, "A Brooklyn Neighborhood Battles City Hall," *Village Voice*, 12/6/76; Adam Veneski to Abraham Beame, 7/9/76, Francis X. McCardle Subject Files, Box 9, Folder 164, Northside Community, Municipal Archives; Stephen J. Murphy, First Deputy Fire Commissioner, to Frank McCardle, 9/14/76, Subject: Meeting Relative to Engine Company 212, Francis X. McCardle Subject Files, Box 80, Folder 80, "Fire Department"; Sherrill Covan and Victor Crepeau, "People's Firehouse News," *Greenpoint Gazette*, 10/5/76.

32. Nicholas Polonski, "North 9th Street Fire," *Greenpoint Gazette*, 5/4/76; Claire Spiegel, "Fire Victims Flee to Shut Firehouse," *Daily News*, 4/6/76.

33. Tom Gogan, "Northside Strikes Back After Big Blaze," *Greenpoint Gazette*, 4/20/76; "Fire on Northside Leaves 19 Families Homeless," *Greenpoint Gazette*, 4/20/76; also see Paul Veneski, Bob Roher, Tom Gogan, and Gerry Owens interviews for recollections of the BQE protest.

34. For one telling of the naming of the firehouse, see Denis Hamill, "Firehouse Savior Is Gone," *Daily News*, 8/20/2000.

35. Richard Kane, "A Serious Review," *Greenpoint Gazette*, 7/13/76.

36. Bob Roher interview, 1/10/14.

37. City-Wide Fire Protection Coalition Meeting and Rally Notes, Ida Susser, Ida Susser Collection, privately held.

38. *Onward*, Vol. 1, No. 1, November 1976, in Francis X. McCardle Subject Files, Box 9, Folder #165, Municipal Archives.

39. Tom Gogan, "Northside Strikes Back After Big Blaze," *Greenpoint Gazette*, 4/20/76.

40. Thomas Raferty, "Residents Sound Alarm at Phasing Out of Firehouse," *Daily News*, 11/24/75.

41. "Dear Neighbor" flyer, Ann Ambia Notebooks.

42. Photo accompanying Denis Hamill, "A Brooklyn Neighborhood Battles City Hall," *Village Voice*, 12/6/76. This photograph is different from the one in the photographic insert in this book.

43. Lena Williams, "Brooklyn Drive Pressed to Open Local Firehouse," *New York*

Times, 11/28/76; Carol Bellamy to Robert Roher, undated, Francis McCardle Subject Files, Box 9, Folder 165, Northside Community, Municipal Archives.

44. Albert Davila, "The Pyrrhic Victory Could Burn Winners," *Daily News*, date unclear. The article can be found in the "People's Firehouse" clippings file at the Brooklyn Public Library.

45. Carroll, *Mobilizing New York*, 85–86. Also see Susser, *Norman Street*, 237.

46. As Tamar Carroll notes, the People's Firehouse reached out to Harlem lawyer and civil rights activist Basil Paterson to represent the neighborhood in negotiations with the city, which also helped to link the struggle to those of poor and nonwhite communities. Carroll, *Mobilizing New York*, 95.

47. Frank J. Prial, "Protest Is Planned on an Alleged Shift of Fire Company," *New York Times*, 1/22/77; "Residents of Fort Greene Protest Possible Rescue Company Loss," *New York Times*, 1/23/77.

48. Marcia Chambers, "Protests on Rescue Unit Disrupt Golden's Swearing-In," *New York Times*, 1/24/77.

49. Dena Kleiman, "Reopening of 'People's Firehouse' Is Celebrated," *New York Times*, 6/18/78.

50. Joseph Treaster, "Williamsburg Area Finally Wins Battle for a Fire Company," *New York Times*, 6/1/78.

51. Kleiman, "Reopening of 'People's Firehouse' Is Celebrated."

52. Paul and Brigitte Veneski interview, 6/27/11.

15. THE COLLEGE IN THE TIRE FACTORY

1. C. Gerald Fraser, "College Building on a Base of Hope," *New York Times*, 3/1/71, 18.

2. For a brief period in the early 1970s, Hostos even ran a program whereby current prison inmates who were nearing release could come to the school for the day to take courses and participate in student life before returning to the prison at night. Juanita Diaz-Cotto, *Gender, Ethnicity and the State: Latina and Latino Prison Politics* (Albany: State University of New York Press, 1996), 199–202.

3. Peter Kihss, "A Bilingual College Paced for the Individual," *New York Times*, 11/16/75.

4. Ramón Jiménez interview, 7/30/14.

5. Lesly Jones, "Boycott Hostos College," *New York Amsterdam News*, 2/6/71.

6. Fraser, "College Building on a Base of Hope."

7. Sandra Roff and Anthony M. Cucchiara, *From the Free Academy to CUNY: Illustrating Public Higher Education in NYC, 1947–1997* (New York: Fordham University Press, 2000), 4.

8. Ibid., 112–115.

9. Glazer, "A Case Study of the Decision in 1976," 214; "When Tuition at CUNY Was Free, Sort of," *CUNY Matters*, 10/11/12.

10. Glazer, "A Case Study of the Decision in 1976," 412–14.

11. Adrienne Rich, "On Teaching Language in Open Admissions," in *On Lies, Secrets and Silence: Selected Prose 1966–1978* (New York: W. W. Norton, 1979), 55.

Rebecca Nathanson, "New York City Students Rising: The Life, Death and Potential Rebirth of Free Higher Education," senior paper, Gallatin School of Individualized Study, 2014, explores the contradictory meanings associated with free tuition.

12. "CUNY's Budget Has Grown Rapidly," in Professional Staff Congress/City University of New York Records and Photographs, Box 58, Folder 231, Tamiment Library, New York University.

13. Leonard Buder, "Open-Admissions Policy Taxes City U. Resources," *New York Times*, 10/12/70.

14. Flyer, PSC/CUNY Records, Box 58, Folder 21, Tamiment Library.

15. Letter to Dear Faculty from Ira Sher, Lorraine Cohen, and a third signatory, illegible, 12/9/74, PSC/CUNY Records, Box 48, Folder 21, Tamiment Library.

16. To: The College Community, Subject: Budget Crisis, PSC/CUNY Records, Box 58, Folder 21, Tamiment Library.

17. Hugh Carey to Jay Hershenson, 7/27/74, PSC/CUNY Records, Box 58, Folder 231, Tamiment Library.

18. R. E. Marshak to Members of the Chancellor's Task Force on Structural Options, 10/28/75, Folder Title: "New York—City College—Restructuring CUNY 1975," Box 36, Stack 11.6.3, City College Office of the President, Robert Eugene Marshak, City College of New York (CCNY) Archives.

19. Deputy Chancellor Seymour Hyman to R. E. Marshak, 10/20/75, Folder Title: "New York—City College—Restructuring CUNY 1975," Box 36, Stack 11.6.3, City College Office of the President, Robert Eugene Marshak, CCNY Archives.

20. GK to REM, 7/28/75, "Determining the Future of the Institution," Box 36, Stack 11.6.3, CCNY Archives.

21. "Save Hostos Committee Formed," Box 1, Folder: "Save Hostos Committee," Gerald J. Meyer Collection, Hostos Community College, Archives and Special Collections, City University of New York (CUNY). Also see Gerald Meyer, "Save Hostos: Politics and Community Mobilization to Save a College in the Bronx, 1973–1978," *Centro Journal*, Spring 2003, Vol. 15, Issue 1, 88–97.

22. "Save Hostos Committee Update," 12/5/75, Box 1, Folder: "Save Hostos Committee," Gerald J. Meyer Collection.

23. "Save Hostos Committee Update," 12/22/75; letter from elected officials to Alfred Giardino, 11/3/75; both in Box 1, Folder: "Save Hostos Committee," Gerald J. Meyer Collection.

24. Michael Gill to Robert Kibbee, 12/8/75, Box 1, Folder: "Correspondence," Gerald J. Meyer Collection.

25. Open Letter to Our Community, from the Coalition to Save Hostos, Box 1, Folder: "Community Coalition to Save Hostos (CCSH), Save Hostos Committee," Gerald J. Meyer Collection; also Ramón Jiménez interview, 7/31/14.

26. Mary Breasted, "City U. Chancellor Urges Closing of Three Colleges," *New York Times*, 2/23/76.

27. David Vidal, "Evers Students Upset by Kibbee's Plan," *New York Times*, 3/13/76.

28. George Todd, "See Medgar Evers Cut as Elimination Move," *New York Amsterdam News*, 3/6/76.

29. Robert D. Parmat, *Town and Gown: The Fight for Social Justice, Urban Rebirth and Higher Education* (Lanham, MD: Fairleigh Dickinson University Press, 2010), 106.
30. Thomas F. Heavey 2nd, "Saving John Jay," *New York Times*, 3/8/76.
31. Resolution of New York City Community College, 12/16/75, PSC/CUNY Records, Folder 12, Box 118, Tamiment Library.
32. David Vidal, "3500 Chant Outside 42nd St. Hearing," *New York Times*, 3/9/76.
33. "Planned City U. Cuts Spur Protest," *New York Times*, 3/9/76.
34. Tim Schermerhorn interview, 7/2/13.
35. David Vidal, ". . . While Hostos Resists Its Elimination," *New York Times*, 3/6/76.
36. "Why Close It?," Peter Roman, *New York Amsterdam News*, 3/6/76 (the letter was reprinted in the newspaper).
37. Peter Roman to John Zuccotti, 4/28/76, Gerald Meyer Papers, Save Hostos Committee, Correspondence. Zuccotti had responded to Roman's earlier note with his standard formula: "Unfortunately the City must set priorities for its dwindling resources. Basic protective and health services and elementary education must be the City's first regard." John Zuccotti to Peter Roman, 3/10/76, Box 1, Folder: "Save Hostos Committee, Correspondence," Gerald J. Meyer Collection.
38. S. James of Petition Committee, 3/5/76, Box 1, Folder: Save Hostos, Outreach Committee, Gerald J. Meyer Collection. Also see Gerald Meyer, "Save Hostos," 81. Also see Gerald Meyer, "Save Hostos: Politics and Community Mobilization to Save a College in the Bronx, 1973–1978."
39. "Student Constituents at Hostos," Box 1, Folder: "Voter Registration," Gerald J. Meyer Collection.
40. Gerald Meyer, "The Save Hostos Committee: A History," Box 1, "Folder: Save Hostos, Writings," Gerald J. Meyer Collection.
41. Ramón Jiménez interview, 7/30/14. Also see Gerald Meyer, "Save Hostos." Also see Gerald Meyer, "Save Hostos: Politics and Community Mobilization to Save a College in the Bronx, 1973–1978."
42. Efrain Quintana and Alexis Colon, 4/2/76, Box 1, Folder: "Save Hostos, Student Government Organization," Gerald J. Meyer Collection.
43. Ramón Jiménez interview, 7/30/14.
44. Ibid.
45. Ibid.
46. Ramón Jiménez, "Hostos Community College: Battle of the Seventies," *Centro Journal*, Spring 2003, Vol. 15, Issue 1, 107.
47. Flyer 3/31/76, Box 1, Folder: "Community Coalition to Save Hostos," Gerald J. Meyer Collection.
48. "To Whom It May Concern," 3/27/76, Box 1, Folder: "Community Coalition to Save Hostos," Gerald J. Meyer Collection.
49. Cándido de León to Harrison J. Goldin, 3/31/76, Box 1, Folder: "Save Hostos Committee, Correspondence," Gerald J. Meyer Collection.
50. For resolutions passed on 4/7/75, see "Resolutions Passed at the Hostos Community College Faculty/Staff Meeting," Box 1, Folder: "Save Hostos, Faculty Senate," Gerald J. Meyer Collection.

51. "Community Coalition Informs," Box 1, Folder: "Community Coalition to Save Hostos," Gerald J. Meyer Collection.

52. "Protesters Arrested at Two City Colleges; Police Arrest 64," *New York Times*, 4/13/76. A second occupation protesting budget cuts had started at Lehman College—also in the Bronx—on March 31. Also see "After the Siege: Bilingual Program in Jeopardy," *New York Amsterdam News*, and Ramón Jiménez interview, 7/30/14.

53. "We Accuse the Members of the Emergency Financial Control Board of Crimes Against the Community," in Box 1, Folder: "Community Coalition to Save Hostos," Gerald J. Meyer Collection.

54. Flyer for May 10 rally, produced by Puerto Rican Committee for Democratic Rights. Box 1, "Community Coalition to Save Hostos," Gerald J. Meyer Collection.

55. "Bilingual Program in Jeopardy," *New York Amsterdam News*, 5/1/76.

56. Judith Cummings, "Kibbee Puts Off Paying Suppliers," *New York Times*, 4/16/76.

57. Judith Cummings, "8 on Faculty Sue City U. Over Pay," *New York Times*, 5/15/76.

58. Judith Cummings, "Carey Plan Asks City U. Tuition," *New York Times*, 5/6/76.

59. Board of Higher Education Minutes, 5/24/76, City College of New York Archives.

60. Judith Cummings, "Giardino, 3 Others Quit City U. Board Over Carey's Plan," *New York Times*, 5/26/76.

61. "Showdown at CUNY," *New York Times*, 5/29/76; Richard Severo, "Trumpets Silent, No Gowns Rustle at Lehman's 'Noncommencement,'" *New York Times*, 6/3/76.

62. Edith Evans Asbury, "Action Embitters City U. Students and Staff," *New York Times*, 5/29/76.

63. Lillian Weber to Irving [Irwin] Polishook, 6/8/76, PSC/CUNY, Box 42, Folder 9.

64. Statement by Irwin Polishook, 5/31/76, PSC/CUNY, Box 42, Folder 9. Also see Statement by Irwin Polishook, 5/28/76.

65. Judith Cummings, "Frustrations Mount at the University," *New York Times*, 6/2/76; John L. Hess, "Staff of City U. Enduring Lack of Paychecks," *New York Times*, 6/7/76.

66. Thomas Collins, "Years Down the Drain? Tears & Beers on College Closing," *Daily News*, 5/29/76.

67. Fred M. Hechinger, "Who Killed Free Tuition?" *New York Times*, 5/18/76.

68. Minutes of the Special Meeting of the Board of Higher Education, 6/1/76, City College of New York Archives.

69. Edward B. Fiske, "Tuition Imposed at City U., Ending a 129-Year Policy," *New York Times*, 6/2/76. Quinones was an administrator at the Arthur C. Logan Memorial Hospital, a public hospital in Harlem.

70. Glazer, "A Case Study of the Decision in 1976," 550–51. Tuition rates were higher for New York State residents not from the city. With tuition, students became eligible for the state-run Tuition Assistance Plan, which could defray expenses.

71. Robert E. Tomasson, "City U. Reopening Is Set Tomorrow as Bill Is Signed," *New York Times*, 6/13/76.

72. R. E. Marshak, "Retrenchment and Budget Management Plan," 7/14/76, "New York—City College Committee on the Retrenchment," Box 36, Stack 11.6.3, City College Office of the President, Robert Eugene Marshak, CCNY Archives.

73. Glazer, "A Case Study of the Decision in 1976," 560–61.

74. Leonard Buder, "CUNY Cuts Bring Anger and Despair," *New York Times*, 11/17/76. Also see Peter Kihss, "City U. in Turmoil Over Faculty Cuts," *New York Times*, 7/14/76; Judith Cummings, "Community Colleges Cut to the Basics in City U.," *New York Times*, 7/27/76; "CUNY Crisis: The Sinister Stage," letter to the editor from Eric Foner, Judith Stein, Robert Twombly, and Martin Waldman, *New York Times*, 7/17/76.

75. Howard Becknell, Catherine Cunningham, Herbert Fyler, and Richard Kearney to Irwin Polishook, 10/11/76. These were four tenured faculty members at Brooklyn College who were "retrenched" and then reinstated under pressure from the union. PSC/CUNY Records, Box 44, Folder 42. Also see Samuel Vernoff to Colleagues, 8/1/76, PSC/CUNY Records, BOX 44, Folder 42.

76. Judith Cummings, "2 City U. Colleges Drop Dismissals," *New York Times*, 7/31/76.

77. Claude Campbell to Officers, 6/30/76, PSC/CUNY Records, Box 186, Folder 2; Arnold H. Lubasch, "A Suit Challenges Ouster of 1050 City U. Teachers," *New York Times*, 9/3/76.

78. Glazer, "A Case Study of the Decision in 1976," 564.

79. Edward B. Fiske, "City U. Enrollment Declines 17% as Free-Tuition Policy Is Ended," *New York Times*, 9/9/76; Edward B. Fiske, "Graduate Students at City University Decrease by 25%," *New York Times*, 10/8/76.

80. Robert Kibbee to Dear Colleagues, 11/22/76, PSC/CUNY Records, Box 54, Folder 3.

81. Buder, "CUNY Cuts Bring Anger and Despair."

82. Tomasson, "City U. Reopening Is Set Tomorrow as Bill Is Signed."

83. Gerald Meyer, "Save Hostos: Politics and Community Mobilization to Save a College in the Bronx, 1973–1978," 97.

84. Ramón Jiménez interview, 7/30/14.

85. Meyer, "Save Hostos: Politics and Community Mobilization to Save a College in the Bronx," 97.

86. "The Greater Threat," *New York Times*, 6/2/76.

87. Fred M. Hechinger, "Who Killed Free Tuition?," *New York Times*, 5/18/76.

16. A NEW NEW YORK

1. Judy Klemesrud, "Donald Trump, Real Estate Promoter, Builds Image as He Buys Buildings," *New York Times*, 11/1/76.

2. Howard Blum, "Trump: The Development of a Manhattan Developer," *New York Times*, 8/26/80.

3. Jonathan Mahler and Steve Eder, "'No Vacancies' for Blacks: How Donald Trump Got His Start, and Was First Accused of Bias," *New York Times*, 8/27/16.

4. Rick Perlstein, "Avenging Angels," *Washington Spectator*, April 16, 2016; Will Kaufman, "Woody Guthrie, 'Old Man Trump' and a Real Estate Empire's Racist Foundations," *The Conversation*, 1/21/16, viewed 5/4/16, http://theconversation.com/woody-guthrie-old-man-trump-and-a-real-estate-empires-racist-foundations-53026.

5. Wayne Barrett, "Like Father, Like Son: Anatomy of a Young Power Broker," *Village Voice*, 1/15/79; also see Klemesrud, "Donald Trump, Real Estate Promoter."

6. Charles V. Bagli, "Trump Built His Empire as King of the Tax Break," *New York Times*, 9/18/16. The city originally estimated that the tax abatement was worth $4 million a year, but over time, the forgiven taxes were worth $359.3 million with four years remaining. The hotel's owners have paid the city $202.5 million in rent and fees over those 40 years.

7. Donald J. Trump to John Zuccotti, 4/12/76, Box 10, General Correspondence Series, John Zuccotti Papers, Municipal Archives. Richard Ravitch, then head of the Urban Development Corporation, has claimed that Trump told him that if he didn't approve the exemption, he would have Ravitch fired.

8. WCBS editorial, 4/6/76, Box 10, General Correspondence Series, John Zuccotti Papers, Municipal Archives.

9. Carter B. Horsley, "Commodore Plan Is Key to the City's Tax-Aid Strategy," *New York Times*, 3/28/76.

10. Howard Blum, "Trump: The Development of a Manhattan Developer," *New York Times*, 8/26/80.

11. Felix Rohatyn, Address to a Conference on a National Policy for Urban America, sponsored by CCNY, May 21, 1976, Binder: Felix Rohatyn, Jack Bigel Papers, Baruch College.

12. Carter B. Horsley, "In the Air Over Midtown," *New York Times*, 2/11/79.

13. William G. Blair, "After a Lull, Construction of Co-ops Picks Up in Manhattan," *New York Times*, 6/22/80.

14. Stephen Birmingham, "The Auction Crowd," *New York Times* Magazine, 3/6/77.

15. Robert J. Cole, "The Hardy Wall St. Bonus," *New York Times*, 12/24/79.

16. Edward Schumacher, "1979 Is Reported a Record Year for Tourism in New York City," *New York Times*, 12/27/79.

17. Francis X. Clines, "A 'New' Mayor Beame Has Risen From the Ashes of the New York City Fiscal Crisis," *New York Times*, 7/11/76.

18. "Beame Set to Leave for Israel and Rome," *New York Times*, 11/13/76; "Beame, on Israeli Visit, Quips About a Gold Hunt," *New York Times*, 11/15/76.

19. Abraham Beame interview, 5/17/93, Ellis Island Oral History Project.

20. "Banks with NYC Holdings Totaling over 125 Percent or More of Capital," Local Government—NY (3), Box 28, Presidential Handwriting File, GFPL.

21. Steven Weisman, "Invalidation of Moratorium on New York City's Notes Is Called Dawn of New Reality," *New York Times*, 11/25/76.

22. Ibid.; also see Chris McNickle interview with Abraham Beame, 9/28/88, LaGuardia and Wagner Archives, LaGuardia Community College.

23. The Corporate Council (W. Bernard Richland) to Abraham Beame, 11/24/76, Office of the Mayor: Sally Leonard Subject Files, Roll 21, Abraham Beame Papers, Municipal Archives.

24. "New York City's Debt Moratorium Is Upset by State's High Court, but Payment Now Is Not Ordered," *New York Times*, 11/20/76.

25. Draft Memorandum of Meeting, 12/10/76, Office Chronological Files, 12/76, MAC Archives.

26. Orin Kramer to Governor Carter, 11/21/76, Re: New York City. Folder: Domestic Policy 11/76–1/77, Container 1, Series: Office of the Staff Secretary Handwriting

File, Jimmy Carter Presidential Library and Museum; also see Orin Kramer to Governor Carter, 11/24/76, Re: New York City Update, Folder: Domestic Policy 11/76–1/77, Container 1, Series: Office of the Staff Secretary Handwriting File, Jimmy Carter Presidential Library (JCPL). Kramer still referred to Carter as "governor" at this point, because he was president-elect.

27. Steven Weisman, "A Fiscal Replay of 1975," *New York Times*, 1/13/77; Charles Kaiser, "Beame Meets Unions to Devise Way to Pay $1 Billion Note Debt," *New York Times*, 3/6/77; also see Steven Weisman, "Unions Also Opposed," *New York Times*, 3/5/77.

28. Leonard Silk, "Banks Optimistic on Fiscal Solution; Unions Score Terms," *New York Times*, 3/4/77.

29. Charles Kaiser, "New York Offers Plan to End Its Debt Crisis with No New Bank Aid," *New York Times*, 3/10/77. Beame's plan also included the sale of Mitchell-Lama mortgages. At first it was not clear that investors would accept the trade for MAC bonds, but the exchange went smoothly. Steven R. Weisman, "MAC Bond Exchange Off to Rousing Start," *New York Times*, 3/26/77.

30. Minutes of Meeting of 4/7/77, to Participants in the Municipal Union/Financial Leaders Meetings, from George P. Roniger, Municipal Unions/Financial Leaders Group (MUFLG) Files, Walter B. Wriston Archives, Tufts University; also see Memorandum to Walter B. Wriston, Chairman, Meeting of Financial and Municipal Labor Leaders, 4/26/77, MUFLG Files, Walter B. Wriston Archives, Tufts University.

31. Minutes of the MULFG, 11/25/77, Walter Wriston Papers, MULFG Files, Walter B. Wriston Archives, Tufts University.

32. "City Union, Bank Leaders Urge U.S. Aid for Welfare," *New York Daily News*, 6/1/77; Memorandum to Municipal Union/Financial Leaders Group from George P. Roniger, Meeting of 7/21/77, MULFG Files, Walter B. Wriston Archives, Tufts University.

33. "Ten Policy Initiatives: City and State Levels," Business/Labor Working Group, ABNY Archives.

34. Felix G. Rohatyn, "Public-Private Partnerships to Stave Off Disaster," *Harvard Business Review*, November–December 1979, 10.

35. Press Release, 12/20/76, Abraham Beame Papers, Roll 22, Municipal Archives.

36. Mayor's Talking Points, Economic Recovery Presentation, 12/2/76, Office of the Mayor: Sally Leonard Subject Files, Abraham Beame Papers, Roll 22, Municipal Archives.

37. Mayor's Introduction to Strategies for Economic Recovery, 12/2/76, Office of the Mayor: Sally Leonard Subject Files, Abraham Beame Papers, Roll 22, Municipal Archives.

38. "Economic Recovery: New York City's Program for 1977–1982," December 1976, Office of the Mayor: Sally Leonard Subject Files, Abraham Beame Papers, Roll 22, Municipal Archives. Also see Greenberg, *Branding New York*, 165–67.

39. Donald L. Calvin to Victor Marrero, 12/31/76, Box 3, Folder 48, John Burton Subject Files, Municipal Archives.

40. Donald L. Calvin to Victor Marrero, 3/16/77, Box 3, Folder 49, John Burton Sub-

ject Files; George Roniger and Steven J. Smith, "The Financial Community and New York," 6/15/76, Abraham Beame Papers, Roll 22, Municipal Archives. They cited an internal Citibank report on the growing weight of finance in New York and warned that cutting the stock transfer tax might be necessary.

41. Unsigned letter to Osborn Elliott, Deputy Mayor, Economic Development Administration, received 12/30/76, Box 3, Folder 48, John Burton Subject Files, Municipal Archives.

42. Osborn Elliott to John McMullen, 12/15/76, Box 3, Folder 48, John Burton Subject Files, Municipal Archives.

43. Final Report of the Temporary Commission on City Finances, "The City in Transition: Prospects and Policies for New York" (City of New York: June 1977), 1, 2, 137, 216.

44. Gail Collins, "N.Y. Real Estate Tycoon Satisfied," *Los Angeles Times*, 12/9/79.

45. Quoted in Wayne Barrett, "Donald Trump Cuts the Cards," *Village Voice*, 1/22/79.

17. BLACKOUT POLITICS

1. Pete Hamill, "Black Night of Our Soul," *Daily News*, 7/15/77.

2. Ibid.

3. Ibid.

4. "It's Signal 12-12 for Cops Who Work All Day," *Daily News*, 7/15/77.

5. Hamill, "Black Night of Our Soul."

6. William Sherman and Harry Stathos, "Spunk, Cheer Shine Through," *Daily News*, 7/14/77; "It Was Very Unlucky Wednesday the 13th," *Daily News*, 7/15/77; "Caught in the Dark," *Daily News*, 7/15/77. Also see Mahler, *Ladies and Gentlemen, The Bronx Is Burning*, 197–98.

7. "The Darkest Hours of a Dark Time," *New York Times*, 7/13/97.

8. Frank Lombardi, "Coping with Power Failure a Turn-On for Beame Camp," *Daily News*, 7/15/77.

9. Dick Brass, "Blackout!," *Daily News*, 7/14/77.

10. Interview with "John Davis" in Robert Curvin and Bruce Porter, *Blackout Looting!: New York City, July 13, 1977* (New York: Gardner Press, 1979), 188–205. Other important accounts of the blackout are Mahler, *Ladies and Gentlemen, The Bronx Is Burning*, 175–234, which draws on a variety of sources including interviews with police officers, and James Goodman, *Blackout* (New York: Farrar, Straus and Giroux, 2003). The shopkeepers were predominantly but not overwhelmingly white, as it turned out. Of the people who collected "blackout loans" from the Small Business Administration, 387 were white, 80 were black, and 68 Puerto Rican. Most of the merchants lived in Rockland County, Queens, or Long Island.

11. Enid Nemy, "For Some, A Day to Make Light of the Dark," *New York Times*, 7/15/77.

12. Jonathan Mahler, "The New York That's Visible in the Dark," *New York Times*, 8/17/03.

13. Curvin and Porter, *Blackout Looting!*, 86.

14. Anthony Ramirez, "The Darkest Hours of a Dark Time," *New York Times*, 7/13/97.

15. "Harlemites Tell What They Were Doing When the Lights Went Out," *New York Amsterdam News*, 7/23/77.

16. Ernesto Quiñonez, "The Diaper Caper and the Small-Dog Scam," *New York Times*, 7/8/07.

17. John T. McQuiston, "Medical Center's Parking Lot Like War Zone Field Hospital," *New York Times*, 7/15/77; Lawrence K. Altman, "Bellevue Patients Resuscitated With Hand-Squeezed Air Bags," *New York Times*, 7/14/77; Ramirez, "Darkest Hours of a Dark Time."

18. Michael C. Jensen, "Stores, Banking and Wall Street Badly Disrupted," *New York Times*, 7/15/77.

19. "Blackout II—an Eerie Slowdown," *New York Times*, 7/17/77.

20. Donald Singleton, "Lights Go On, End Nightmare," *Daily News*, 7/15/77.

21. "New Paralysis, New Symptoms: Much Uglier," *New York Times*, 7/17/77.

22. Interview with "John Davis" in Curvin and Porter, *Blackout Looting!*, 188–205.

23. Ibid., 214.

24. Ibid., 58.

25. "The Plunderers," *Newsweek*, 7/25/77; also see Curvin and Porter, *Blackout Looting!*, 69; Mahler, *Ladies and Gentlemen, The Bronx Is Burning*, 196–97. There were 3,428 officers on duty when the blackout began; the peak number of officers was about 11,000. Curvin and Porter, *Blackout Looting!*, 67. An additional issue was that when Police Commissioner Michael Codd called up all off-duty officers to report immediately for service, he ordered them to the nearest police station, which meant that many went to the precincts nearest their homes rather than those where they usually worked.

26. Mahler, *Ladies and Gentlemen, The Bronx Is Burning*, 201–2. Also see Curvin and Porter, *Blackout Looting!*, 58–59.

27. Owen Moritz, "Looters Prey on Blinded City," *Daily News*, 7/15/77.

28. Abraham Beame to David Ross, 7/15/77, Office of the Mayor: Sally Leonard Subject Files, Abraham Beame Papers, Roll 23.

29. Joseph B. Treaster, "Blackout Arrests Swamp City's Criminal-Justice System," *New York Times*, 7/15/77; Leslie Maitland, "New York City Jails Are Crowded With Those Waiting Arraignment," *New York Times*, 7/16/77; Tom Goldstein, "After the Blackout, Justice Goes by the Book," *New York Times*, 7/18/77; Pranay Gupte, "A Trial by Heat in New York Jails," *New York Times*, 7/18/77.

30. Alan H. Levine, "The Law Went Dark, Too," *New York Times*, 8/20/77; Curvin and Porter, *Blackout Looting!*, 98–102.

31. Robert D. McFadden, "100 Policemen Hurt," *New York Times*, 7/15/77.

32. Simon Anekwe, "Looting Suspect Dies in Cell," *New York Amsterdam News*, 7/23/77.

33. Selwyn Raab, "Ravage Continues Far Into Day as Gunfire and Bottles Plague Police," *New York Times*, 7/15/77.

34. Anthony Burton, "Few Enjoy Revival of Blackouts of 1965," *Daily News*, 7/15/77.

35. Lawrence van Gelder, "State Troopers Sent Into City as Crime Rises," *New York Times*, 7/14/77.
36. Charlayne Hunter-Gault, "When Poverty's Part of Life, Looting Is Not Condemned," *New York Times*, 7/15/77.
37. "Official Calls Moscow Almost Blackout Proof," *New York Times*, 7/24/77.
38. Letters: "On the Blackout," from Hendrik Ruittenbeek, *New York Times*, 7/23/77.
39. Ibid.
40. "Voice of the People," *Daily News*, 7/24/77.
41. Ibid.
42. "Black Opinion Mixed on Looting," *New York Amsterdam News*, 7/23/77.
43. Bryant Mason, "Blackout Victims: Be Tough on Looters," *Daily News*, 7/21/77.
44. Editorial, *New York Amsterdam News*, 7/23/77; Robert D. McFadden, "Sutton Says Looting Was Criminal, Not Racial," *New York Times*, 7/30/77.
45. "Ministers Express Their Views on the Looting," *New York Amsterdam News*, 7/23/77.
46. Ibid.
47. John Bryan, "See Blackout Looting as 'Class Uprising of the Masses,'" *New York Amsterdam News*, 7/30/77. Debates over the political status of looting, and over whether the term is used in racially charged ways, continue today; see, for example, Willie Osterweil, "In Defense of Looting," *The New Inquiry*, 8/24/14.
48. Jitu Weusi, "A Brooklyn Community Leader Takes Different Look at Looters," *New York Amsterdam News*, 7/23/77.
49. Raab, "Ravage Continues Far Into the Day."
50. Ibid.
51. "People in the Street Tell Us What They Think About the Looting of July 13, 1977," *New York Amsterdam News*, 7/23/77.
52. Patrick J. Buchanan, "Hungry Folks Rob Food, Andy, Right," *Daily News*, 7/21/77.
53. Midge Decter, "Looting and Liberal Racism," *Commentary*, September 1977, 48–54.
54. Nancy MacLean, "Forget Chicago, It's Coming from Virginia: The 1970s Genesis of Today's Attack on Democracy," paper presented at the Economization of the Social in the 1970s Workshop at the New School, 6/6/15.
55. Thomas Mullaney, "Olin: Staunch Fighter for Free Enterprise," *New York Times*, 4/29/77.
56. "Simon: Preaching the Word for Olin," *New York Times*, 7/16/78.
57. Ibid.
58. Milton Friedman to William Simon, 3/24/76, Box 43, Folder 23, William E. Simon Papers, Lafayette College.
59. Andrew M. Carter, Senior Vice President of Jennison Associates, to William E. Simon, 7/9/76, Box 43, Folder 28, William E. Simon Papers.
60. Jefferson Decker, "The Wall Street Politics of William E. Simon," paper presented at the School of Management and Labor Relations, Rutgers University, New Brunswick, N.J., 2/25/11, 10–11.
61. Milton Friedman to William Simon, 5/12/77, Box 43, Folder 28, William E. Simon Papers, Lafayette College.

62. William Simon, *A Time for Truth* (Pleasantville, N.Y.: Reader's Digest Press, 1978), 127.
63. Ibid., 162.
64. Ibid., 142.
65. Ibid., 173.
66. Ibid., 180.
67. Herbert Mitgang, "Behind the Best Sellers," *New York Times*, 11/19/78.
68. "Primary Drive for Simon Planned," *New York Times*, 8/22/79.
69. Alice O'Connor, "The Privatized City: The Manhattan Institute, the Urban Crisis, and the Conservative Counterrevolution in New York," *Journal of Urban History*, 2008: Vol. 34, 333–53.
70. Irving Kristol, "New York Is a State of Mind," *Wall Street Journal*, 12/10/75.
71. Elizabeth Hinton, *From the War on Poverty to the War on Crime: The Making of Mass Incarceration in America* (Cambridge, Mass.: Harvard University Press, 2016), addresses this shift and the ways that the war on poverty anticipated the turn toward criminal justice as a way to cope with poverty in the 1970s.
72. Mario Merola to President Carter, 4/14/77, Abraham Beame Papers, Roll 23, Municipal Archives.
73. Bill Cable to Frank Moore, Memorandum for the President, 7/20/77, Office of the Staff Secretary, Container 32, 7/20/77 (2), Jimmy Carter Library.
74. Hamilton Jordan to President Carter, 7/30/77, Office of the Staff Secretary, Container 34, 8/1/77 (2), Jimmy Carter Library.
75. Stu Eizenstat and Lynn Daft to the President, 8/2/77, Office of the Staff Secretary, Container 35, 8/3/77, Jimmy Carter Library.
76. Thomas P. Dunne to Hugh Carey, n/d., Office of the Staff Secretary, Container 35, 8/3/77, Jimmy Carter Library.
77. "The Added Danger of a Savage Week," *New York Times*, 8/5/77. The paper was editorializing against calls to restore the death penalty.

18. THE FINAL STORM

1. "We Need a Great Mayor—Beame Should Not Run," *Daily News*, 4/7/77.
2. "Statement by Mayor Abraham D. Beame," 8/4/77, Abraham Beame Papers, Roll 15.
3. Mary Breasted, "100,000 Leave New York Offices as Bomb Threats Disrupt City," *New York Times*, 8/4/77.
4. Douglas Martin, "Joel Harnett, 80, Leader of Watchdog Group, Dies," *New York Times*, 8/15/2006.
5. Joel Harnett, "Dismay over the Way New York Has Been Run," *New York Times*, 9/19/76.
6. Interview with Stanley Sporkin and Marvin Jacob, 5/7/13.
7. "Text of Letter to Beame by S.E.C. Chairman," *New York Times*, 8/24/77.
8. "Excerpts from Mayor's Testimony Last September Before S.E.C. on New York," *New York Times*, 8/18/77.
9. Edward C. Burks, "No Fraud Is Alleged: Inquiry Finds Officials Made Reassuring Statements Before Fiscal Collapse," *New York Times*, 8/27/77.
10. "Mayor's Statement on the Report," *New York Times*, 8/27/77.

11. "Beame's Statement on the S.E.C. Report," *New York Times*, 8/28/77. Goldin, too, reacted strongly, holding his own press conference to rebut the claims of the SEC. As he told the press, "To say that I did not disclose the city's fiscal condition is like saying that Ralph Nader did not warn consumers about unsafe cars because people continued to get killed in auto crashes, or Gen. Billy Mitchell did not warn the Navy about air power." Lee Dembart, "Goldin Rebuts S.E.C., Citing His Warnings on Financial Crisis," *New York Times*, 8/29/77.

12. Glenn Fowler, "Carey Says Beame Lacks 'the Integrity' to Run New York City," *New York Times*, 9/1/77.

13. Frank Lynn, "Beame's Six Opponents in Primary Are Taking Different Stances in Response to S.E.C. Charges," *New York Times*, 8/28/77.

14. Maurice Carroll, "7 Democrats Argue About City Finances and Beame's Budget," *New York Times*, 9/5/77.

15. Henry Salfield, New York, 8/28/77, published in the *New York Times*, 9/5/77.

16. Murray Kempton, "The Bloom Goes Off for Abraham Beame," *New York Post*, 9/8/77.

17. "Transcript of Beame's Concession," *New York Times*, 9/10/77.

18. Frank Lynn, "Beame Finishes Third," *New York Times*, 9/9/77.

19. Howard Rubenstein to MacRae Parker, 10/11/77, Abraham Beame Papers, Roll 15.

20. Robert D. McFadden, "Abraham Beame Is Dead at 94," *New York Times*, 2/11/01.

21. Felix Rohatyn to the Directors and Representatives of the Municipal Assistance Corporation, 1/11/78, MAC Binder, Jack Bigel Papers, Baruch College.

22. Columbia University Oral History Research Office, Interview with Ed Koch, Session 15, 1/8/76, 463; ibid., Session 3, 12/20/75, 81.

23. Mahler, *Ladies and Gentlemen, The Bronx Is Burning*, 187.

24. For "poverty pimps" quote, see Soffer, *Ed Koch and the Rebuilding of New York City*, 8. For "poverticians," see Sydney Schamberg, "Poverticians Make Good Campaign Workers," *New York Times*, 7/13/85.

25. Denis Hamill, "Hi, I'm for Capital Punishment. Are You?" *Village Voice*, 9/5/77; Tom Goldstein, "Beame Calls for Tougher Laws on Death Penalty and on Paroles," *New York Times*, 7/6/77.

26. Lee Dembart, "Koch, in Inaugural, Asks That 'Pioneers' 'Come East' to City," *New York Times*, 1/2/78; Text of Address Delivered by Koch at His Inaugural, *New York Times*, 1/2/78.

27. Perlstein, *The Invisible Bridge*, 316–18.

28. Jimmy Carter, State of the Union Address 1978, Jimmy Carter Presidential Library, accessed http://www.jimmycarterlibrary.gov/documents/speeches/su78jec.phtml.

29. Jack Watson and Bruce Kirschenbaum, "Your Meeting with Congressman Ed Koch," 10/19/77, Office of the Staff Secretary, Container 47, 10/20/77 (4), Jimmy Carter Library.

30. Cardinal Cooke to the President, 1/31/78, Office of the Staff Secretary, Container 63, 2/13/78 (1), Jimmy Carter Library.

31. Jack Watson, "Memorandum for the President," 4/13/78, Jimmy Carter Library, Office of the Staff Secretary, Container 71, 4/14/78; Jack Watson to Ed Koch, 4/8/78, Office of the Staff Secretary, Container 70, 4/10/78 (2), Jimmy Carter Library.

32. Edward Brooke and William Proxmire to the President, 12/23/77, Office of the Staff Secretary, Container 58, 1/17/78, Jimmy Carter Library.

33. "A Report by the Mayor of New York City," 4/27/78, in Business-Labor Working Group, 1977–79, ABNY Archives.

34. Quoted in Soffer, *Ed Koch and the Rebuilding of New York City*, 159–60.

35. Quoted in Opdycke, *No One Was Turned Away*, 162.

36. Robert Reinhold, "For the Present, Cleveland Is Sad but Special Case," *New York Times*, 12/17/78.

37. Jimmy Carter to William Proxmire, 1/17/78, Office of the Staff Secretary, Container 58, 1/17/78, Jimmy Carter Library.

38. Memorandum for the President, Stu Eizenstat and Orin Kramer, "Secretary Blumenthal's Testimony on New York City Finances," 3/1/78, Office of the Staff Secretary, Container 76, 3/2/78 (1), Jimmy Carter Library; Lee Dembart, "Accord Is Reached on Loan Guarantee for New York City," *New York Times*, 7/14/78.

39. Gene Godley to Frank Moore, 6/7/78, Office of Congressional Liaison Moore, Container 166, Folder: NYC Financing, 6/5–6/8/78, Jimmy Carter Library.

40. Stu Eizenstat and Frank Moore to the President, 6/14/78, Office of the Staff Secretary, Container 81, 6/15/78, Jimmy Carter Library.

41. Richard Moe Memorandum, 7/11/78, Office of Congressional Liaison, Container 38, Folder: NYC Financing Legislation, 6/6/78–7/11/78, Jimmy Carter Library.

42. Lee Dembart, "Carter Signs Aid Bill for New York at a Gala Celebration at City Hall," *New York Times*, 8/9/78.

43. Dena Kleiman, "Koch Gets City Hall Polished Up for Visit by Carter," *New York Times*, 8/5/78.

44. "Transcript of Carter's Talk at City Hall," *New York Times*, 8/9/78.

45. Daniel Patrick Moynihan to the President, 10/13/78, Office of the Staff Secretary, Container 96, 10/24/78, Jimmy Carter Library.

46. Edward I. Koch to President Jimmy Carter, 12/21/78, Office of the Staff Secretary, Container 101, 12/23/78–1/1/79 (1), Jimmy Carter Library.

47. Stu Eizenstat, Jack Watson, and Orin Kramer to the President, 12/20/78, "Meeting with Senator Moynihan et al.," Office of the Staff Secretary, Container 101, 12/23/78–1/1/79 (1), Jimmy Carter Library.

48. Steven Weisman, "Carter-Koch Harmony a Summer Memory," *New York Times*, 1/9/79; "Carter Aides Assail Koch on Cuts," *New York Times*, 1/7/79.

49. Orin Kramer to Stu Eizenstat, 1/3/79, Office of the Cabinet Secretary, Container 317, Folder: Correspondence with Ed Koch, Jimmy Carter Library.

50. James P. Sterba, "City Will Try to Show U.S. It's Jes' Folks," *New York Times*, 7/15/78.

51. Anna Quindlen, "City Notes Sell Out with Interest Cut to 8% from 8.25%," *New York Times*, 1/23/79.

52. Maurice Carroll, "Book Finally Closed on City Fiscal Blame," *New York Times*, 8/28/79.

53. Dena Kleiman, "Yonkers Seeking to Ease Cutbacks," *New York Times*, 12/28/75; James Feron, "Yonkers Schools Face Added Trims," *New York Times*, 1/9/76; "Yonkers Says It Can't Rehire Teachers," *New York Times*, 8/26/76.

54. Iver Peterson, "State May Oversee Cleveland Finances," *New York Times*, 1/9/79.

55. Edward Schumacher, "Mayor Kucinich Himself Is Issue in Upcoming Cleveland Primary," *New York Times*, 8/26/79.

56. *New York Times*, 8/10/79; also see Joshua Freeman, "If You Can Make It Here," *Jacobin*, Fall 2014, for the comparison with Chrysler.

57. Judith Miller, "Contrasts in Federal Aid: Chrysler vs. New York," *New York Times*, 12/28/79.

58. Judith Miller, "Detroit's Battle for Survival," *New York Times*, 1/6/80.

59. Judith Miller, "Chrysler's Mr. Bailout," *New York Times*, 7/20/80.

60. U.S. Census.

61. Sam Roberts, "'75 Bankruptcy Scare Alters City Plans into 21st Century," *New York Times*, 7/8/85.

62. Reiko Hillyer, "The Guardian Angels: Law and Order and Citizen Policing in the Neoliberal City," paper delivered at the 2014 Organization of American Historians annual meeting, Atlanta, Georgia. Also see Reiko Hillyer, "The Guardian Angels: Law and Order and Citizen Policing in New York City," forthcoming in *Journal of Urban History*, draft in possession of author.

63. On downtown art, see, for example, Marvin J. Taylor, ed., *The Downtown Book: The New York Art Scene, 1974–1984* (Princeton, N.J.: Princeton University Press, 2007); Alan W. Moore, "Artists' Collectives: Focus on New York, 1975–2000," in Blake Stimson and Gregory Sholette, *Collectivism After Modernism: The Art of Social Imagination After 1945* (Minneapolis: University of Minnesota Press, 2007), 193–223; *Blank City*, directed by Celine Dahnier, 2009. On hardcore, see Kelefa Sanneh, "United Blood: How Hardcore Conquered New York," *New Yorker*, 3/9/15. On art and AIDS, see Cynthia Carr, *Fire in the Belly: The Life and Times of David Wojnarowicz* (New York: Bloomsbury USA, 2012).

64. "Survey of Poor in South Bronx and Harlem Reveals Deep Alienation," 5/17/79, Survey: Poor People's Opinions, South Bronx. Box 510, Community Service Society Papers, Columbia University, Rare Book and Manuscript Library.

65. Chang, *Can't Stop Won't Stop*, 178.

66. Michael Sterne, "Residents of Harlem Suffer Worst Health in New York," *New York Times*, 4/10/78; Michael Sterne, "In Last Decade, Leaders Say, Harlem's Dreams Have Died," *New York Times*, 3/1/78.

67. Ebun Adelona, "Sydenham: Politics vs. Health Care," *City Limits*, February 1983.

68. Chowkwaynun, "Dilemmas of Community Health," 100.

69. Ibid.

70. Michael Spear, "The Struggle to Build a Progressive Urban Politics: Frank Barbaro's 1981 New York City Mayoral Campaign," *New York History*, Vol. 91, No. 1 (Winter 2010), 51.

71. Opdycke, *No One Was Turned Away*, 166.

72. "Cooling Off at Sydenham Hospital," *New York Times*, 9/27/80.

73. Anna Quindlen, "Koch Faces Day Ebulliently," *New York Times*, 4/2/80.

74. Maurice Carroll, "Transit Strike Politics Mirror the Climate of a Changed City," *New York Times*, 4/6/80.

75. Soffer, *Ed Koch and the Rebuilding of New York City*, 212–14.

76. Cynthia R. Fagen and Eric Fettmann, "Rebels at Sydenham Defy Court Order," *New York Post*, 9/17/80.

77. Ron Howell and Ned Steele, "Cops Close Sydenham's Emergency Room," *Daily News*, 9/16/80.

78. Jill Smolowe, "Protesters at Sydenham Say They Won't Leave Hospital," *New York Times*, 9/24/80.

79. Paul L. Montgomery, "1,000 Rally at Sydenham to Back Protesters Inside," *New York Times*, 9/22/80.

80. Hugh Wyatt, "Patients Say They're Lost When Sydenham's Gone," *New York Daily News*, 9/5/80.

81. Wista Johnston, "The Sydenham On-Lookers," *New York Amsterdam News*, 10/4/80.

82. Earl Caldwell, "A Fight for Survival on a Battlefield Called Sydenham," *Daily News*, 9/20/80.

83. Earl Caldwell, "Protesters Battle That Empty Feeling," *Daily News*, 9/22/80.

84. Johnson, "The Sydenham On-Lookers"; also see Cenie Williams Jr., "The Battle for Black Dignity," *New York Amsterdam News*, 10/11/80.

85. Paul Montgomery, "30 Hurt as Police and Protesters Clash Outside Sydenham," *New York Times*, 9/21/80.

86. Paul Meskil, "3,000 Hold Nonviolent Sydenham Demo," *Daily News*, 9/22/80.

87. Jill Smolowe, "Protesters 'Setting Up Housekeeping' in Weeklong Sydenham Occupation," *New York Times*, 9/20/80.

88. David Seifman, "Sydenham Siege Ends as Cops Carry Out Last Sit-Ins," *New York Post*, 9/26/80.

89. Earl Caldwell, "Hospital Injects Harlem with a Will to Fight Again," *Daily News*, 9/27/80.

90. "Update on Sydenham Hospital Struggle," *New York Amsterdam News*, 10/18/80.

91. Ronald Sullivan, "Sydenham Hospital Closing Today, Ending a Protracted Harlem Battle," *New York Times*, 11/21/80.

92. "The Right Medicine for Harlem," *New York Times*, 10/6/80; Ronald Sullivan, "Free Health Aid in Harlem Fails to Attract Poor," *New York Times*, 10/5/81.

93. "People's Firehouse Critical Fact Sheet," Ann Ambia Collection; "Public Hearing: Plan Includes Closing of Greenpoint Hospital," *Greenline*, 6/15/78; Hedda Allbray, "Community Presses Fight for Hospitals," *The Williamsburg News*, 6/16–6/22/78; Tom Robbins, "Woodhull: A Second Chance?," *North Brooklyn News*, 2/1/79. The People's Firehouse activists were skeptical about Woodhull: "If Greenpoint closes do you know how to get to Woodhull Hospital? Do you know where it is? Is there ambulance service that would get you to Woodhull? Will you be able to afford Woodhull? Where would you go for emergency health care? For clinic services? General health care? We have few private doctors. . . . With Greenpoint Hospital closed our senior citizens could face a real crisis situation, since the City and volunteer ambulances will be strained even more and in some emergency cases minutes and even seconds can save a person's life."

94. Tim Schermerhorn interview, 7/2/13.

95. Clyde Haberman, "Rating on Bonds Offered by City Now Favorable," *New York Times*, 3/6/81.

96. Clyde Haberman, "City Acts on Own to Sell Bond Issue of $75 Million," *New York Times*, 3/24/81.

97. Edward A. Gargan, "City Surplus Put at $243 Million for the Fiscal Year," *New York Times*, 5/11/81. The city also delayed a payment to MAC, which helped increase its available funds.

98. "Treasury Secretary Hails Fiscal Effort," *New York Times*, 4/16/81.

99. Robert A. Gerard, "New York's Finances: Grounds for Pride," *New York Times*, 3/14/81.

100. Michael Oreskes, "Proxmire Calls City's Recovery a Fiscal Model," *New York Times*, 11/20/85.

EPILOGUE

1. Howell Raines, "Reagan Appeals to Civic Groups to Aid the Poor," *New York Times*, 1/15/82.

2. "Excerpts from Address by Reagan on Role of Private Groups," *New York Times*, 1/15/82. Also see Greenberg, *Branding New York*, 288.

3. Joshua Freeman, "If You Can Make It Here," *Jacobin*, October 2014, accessed at https://www.jacobinmag.com/2014/10/if-you-can-make-it-here/; also see Donald McIntyre, "How the Miners' Strike of 1984–85 Changed Britain Forever," *New Statesman*, 6/16/14.

4. Martin Gottlieb, "A Decade After the Cutbacks, New York Is a Different City," *New York Times*, 6/30/85.

5. Sam Roberts, "Gap Between Manhattan's Rich and Poor Is Greatest in US, Census Finds," *New York Times*, 9/17/14.

6. Donna Shalala interview, 5/22/13.

7. Richard Pérez-Peña, "Hugh Carey, Who Led Fiscal Rescue of New York City, Is Dead at 92," *New York Times*, 8/7/11.

8. Quoted in Lachman and Polner, *The Man Who Saved New York*, 191.

9. Abraham D. Beame, Discussant, "The New York City Fiscal Crisis," in *Gerald R. Ford and the Politics of Post-Watergate America*, Vol. 2, eds. Bernard J. Firestone and Alexej Ugrinsky (Westport, Conn.: Greenwood Press, 1993), 388–89.

10. Brecher and Horton, *Power Failure*, 41–43; also see Mollenkopf, *A Phoenix in the Ashes*, 133–47.

11. Gottlieb, "A Decade After the Cutbacks, New York Is a Different City."

12. Edward I. Koch, "A Short History of New York City's Financial Crisis," June 30, 1986, http://www.baruch.cuny.edu/library/alumni/online_exhibits/amfl/mac/pdf _files/Office_Chron/JUN1986.pdf, accessed 10/12/15.

13. Denis Hamill, "Firehouse Savior Is Gone," *Daily News*, 8/29/00.

14. "Municipal Assistance Corp., New York's 1975 Savior, Says 'See Ya,'" *Daily News*, 9/27/08.

15. Alan Finder, "Financial Control Board Loses Most of Its Control," *New York Times*, 6/30/86.

16. FCB website, http://www.fcb.state.ny.us/mission_statement.asp, accessed 10/14/15.

17. I am indebted to a conversation with Joshua Freeman for this point.

ACKNOWLEDGMENTS

As befits a book about fiscal crisis, I have incurred more than my share of debts writing this one. I'm sure that there is no way that I can pay them back, but it seems worth at least trying to keep a proper account.

Researching this book took a long time, and it had throughout a feeling of serendipity. I received support and guidance from many archivists and librarians, who pointed me to documents I would otherwise have overlooked. I would like to especially thank Leonora Gidlund, Dwight Johnson, Marcia Kirk, and David Ment at the Municipal Archives of the City of New York; Douglas DiCarlo at the LaGuardia and Wagner Archives, LaGuardia Community College; Elizabeth Druga at the Gerald R. Ford Presidential Library in Ann Arbor, Michigan; Sandra Roff and Alex Gelfand at the Newman Library of Baruch College, CUNY; Saleem Shah at the Citizens Committee for New York City; David Paskin of District Council 37; William Casari of the Hostos Community College Archives; David Henshall at the Freedom of Information Act division of the Securities and Exchange Commission; Pedro Juan Hernandez at the Centro de Estudios Puertorriqueños/Center for Puerto Rican Studies at Hunter College, CUNY; Thomas Lannon and Karen Gisonny at the New York Public Library Archives; Lois Kauffman of the Citibank Archives; James

Folts at the New York State Library; Daniel Maye at the George F. Mand Library of the FDNY Fire Academy; and Chela Scott Weber of the Tamiment Library at NYU.

I also benefited greatly from the generosity of individuals who participated in the events of the fiscal crisis years and who shared with me their private paper collections, their reflections, and their memories of that remarkable and tumultuous time. Many also pointed me to other people to speak with, which I always appreciated deeply. I list many of them in the notes, but I must especially thank Brian Balogh, whom I spoke to very early in the project; Dall Forsythe, who, in addition to being interviewed twice, provided guidance in working with the executive budgets that went above and beyond the call of duty; Ira Millstein; Tom Gogan; Janie Eisenberg; Ann Ambia; Richard Ravitch; Harrison J. Goldin; Steve Clifford; David Paskin; and Ida Susser. Richard Sylla shared with me some of his own unpublished writing about the fiscal crisis and pointed me toward the Citibank Archives, while Daniel Rowe generously shared with me his own research in the Jacob Javits Papers at Stony Brook University, and Tamir Butts his work on tuition at CUNY before the fiscal crisis.

My work on this book was aided greatly by my research assistants, all of whom are themselves talented scholars and writers: Stuart Schrader, Lana Dee Povitz, Zach Caceres, and Rebecca Nathanson. Zach in particular helped work on the book keep moving forward at a time when it would otherwise have slowed to a standstill. I am especially indebted to Rebecca Nathanson, who worked on this book for two years and whose labor has improved almost every page. Danielle Lee Wiggins assisted with the research at the Jimmy Carter Presidential Library, and David Mislin aided with the Walter B. Wriston Archive at Tufts University.

At the Gallatin School for Individualized Study of New York University, Susanne Wofford gave me a tremendous amount of freedom and support, which made it possible for me to write this book and for which I could not be more thankful. The patient assistance provided by Cyd Fulton and Gisela Humphreys was also critical. My colleagues and students at Gallatin have taught me a great deal about writing and talking about politics and the economy, and their questions inform this work at a deep level.

While I was researching and writing, I received financial support from the Stephen Charney Vladeck Fellowship, the Humanities Initiative, and the National Endowment of the Humanities Summer Stipend Program. For my year at the Humanities Initiative, I am especially grateful to Jane Tylus and Asya Berger. Much of the book was written during a wonderful year at the Cullman Center for Scholars and Writers at the New York Public Library. The inspiration provided by the beautiful space that is the 42nd Street Library, and the feedback from my colleagues and friends there, helped me to complete the manuscript. Jean Strouse, Marie d'Origny, Julia Pagnamenta, and Paul Delaverdac have my everlasting gratitude.

At Metropolitan Books, I have been extremely lucky to work with Sara Bershtel and Grigory Tovbis. I can't imagine better editors; their insights, sense of narrative drive, sharp questions, engagement with the prose, and close, thoughtful attentiveness to every page of the book have been invaluable. I am especially grateful to Grigory for the time and care he has devoted to this book. Prudence Crowther did a wonderful copy edit. I'm also appreciative of the work of Olivia Croom and Lisa Kleinholz on proofs and the index. Scott Moyers helped to place the book at Metropolitan, and I remain grateful for his work on the proposal, while my agent Andrew Wylie provided feedback and aid down the stretch.

I have been fortunate to engage with many people about New York in the 1970s and the fiscal crisis. Along the way, I benefited from the questions of audiences at the Russell Sage Foundation, the Cullman Center for Scholars and Writers, the Heilbroner Center for Capitalism Studies at New School University (where I especially appreciated the feedback of Julia Ott and Janet Roitman), the New York University Society of Fellows, the John Jay College for Criminal Justice, the Culture and Politics Working Group of the Urban Democracy Lab at NYU, the Queens Museum, the Cullman Center Institute for Teachers, the Economization of the Social in the 1970s Symposium at New School University, and the NYU History Department, as well as those of conference attendees at the American Historical Association, the Policy History Conference, the Organization of American Historians, and the Urban History Association.

Several people contributed more directly by reading drafts. I am very grateful to Joshua Freeman, whose work helped to inspire me to work on the fiscal crisis (my interest in the topic began when I read his *Working Class New York* in 2000). I was honored to have his extensive comments on a draft of the manuscript; they were incredibly helpful. Dall Forsythe also read several chapters on the origins of the crisis and provided useful thoughts and comments. My wonderful writing group comrades Jessica Blatt, Liza Featherstone, and Caitlin Zaloom read every word of this book more than once, talked about each chapter, and shared the long experience of writing. They know well how much they did to shape it; their insights are evident throughout. Their writings are an inspiration to me and their humor and kindness no less. Finally, my dear friend Beverly Gage took the time from her own work to read a draft and offer her invaluable feedback—as well as her support over the years, just as crucial.

The last debts are the most personal. I am profoundly thankful to Courtney Fenwick, Kristin Jones, Sandra Oree, Shaida Khan, Lornette Lewis, Loyan Beausoleil, and the teachers of Happy Feet Playground, University Plaza Nursery School, and PS 3, whose work made it possible for me to write. My father- and mother-in-law, Albert and Geraldine Vargo; my brothers- and sisters-in-law, Mark and Barbara Vargo and Susan and Bill Howe; and my three nephews Alex, Barry, and John, all provide a network of support for which I'm deeply appreciative. I am grateful for the affection and warmth I always receive from Elinor Tucker and Carolyn Phillips. My friends Margaret Adasko Shore (whose father, H. Hardy Adasko, always asks about my progress), Sevinc Ercan, Wibke Grutjen, Hannah Gurman, Hermine Hayes-Klein, Elsie Pan, Becca Lena Richardson, Wiebke Robrecht, Melissa Ann Schwartzberg, the Strauss sisters (Mariya, Kandra, and Taryn), and Nicky Thierfelder have also been very important to me over these years. My sister Jesse Phillips-Fein, my friend and brother-in-law Benin Ford, and my baby nephew Nalo provided encouragement, engagement, and love.

My parents, Charlotte Phillips and Oliver Fein, to whom this book is dedicated, have lived and worked in New York City for more than forty years. Their work, their hope, their love, and their steady example are the foundation of my life. Without the practical and emotional support of my mother, in particular, this book would never have been written.

My beautiful children—my daughter Clara and my son Jonah—were born over the years I have been working on this book. We have enjoyed together the parks, playgrounds, subways, pools, and libraries of the city; their lives have taken shape within the community that is afforded by these public spaces. My husband, Greg Vargo, has supported the writing of this book in countless ways small and large, from our "film series" of '70s movies to his comments on the manuscript. But his intellectual engagement, as treasured as it is, is the least of the gifts he has given me. He has lived the writing with me. Always and forever, more than I can say.

INDEX

ABOUT THE AUTHOR

KIM PHILLIPS-FEIN is the author of *Invisible Hands: The Business-men's Crusade Against the New Deal*. She teaches history at New York University's Gallatin School of Individualized Study, and has written for *The Nation, Dissent, The Baffler, The Atlantic,* and *The New York Times,* among other publications. She lives in New York City.